Windows® Group Policy Resource Kit: Windows Server® 2008 and Windows Vista®

Derek Melber,
Group Policy MVP,
with the Windows Group Policy Team

PUBLISHED BY
Microsoft Press
A Division of Microsoft Corporation
One Microsoft Way
Redmond, Washington 98052-6399

Library of Congress Control Number: 2008920568

Printed and bound in the United States of America.

2 3 4 5 6 7 8 9   QWT   3 2 1 0 9 8

Distributed in Canada by H.B. Fenn and Company Ltd.

A CIP catalogue record for this book is available from the British Library.

Microsoft Press books are available through booksellers and distributors worldwide. For further information about international editions, contact your local Microsoft Corporation office or contact Microsoft Press International directly at fax (425) 936-7329. Visit our Web site at www.microsoft.com/mspress. Send comments to rkinput@microsoft.com.

Acquisitions Editor: Martin DelRe
Developmental Editor: Karen Szall
Project Editor: Valerie Woolley
Editorial Production: S4Carlisle Publishing Services
Technical Reviewer: Linda Zacker; Technical Review services provided by Content Master, a member of CM Group, Ltd.
Cover: Tom Draper Design

Body Part No. X14-55483

To Alexa and Ashelley, where I find inspiration, free spirit, and love without boundaries.

Contents at a Glance

Part VIII   Appendices

Table of Contents

What do you think of this book? We want to hear from you!

Microsoft is interested in hearing your feedback so we can continually improve our books and learning
resources for you. To participate in a brief online survey, please visit:

www.microsoft.com/learning/booksurvey/

Part IV Implementing Security

Part V Using Registry-Based Policy Settings

Part VII Advanced Topics

What do you think of this book? We want to hear from you!

Microsoft is interested in hearing your feedback so we can continually improve our books and learning resources for you. To participate in a brief online survey, please visit:

www.microsoft.com/learning/booksurvey/

Acknowledgments

To my two beautiful girls, Alexa and Ashelley. They are patient and loving through the most troubling times in life. Thank you for teaching me what is important in life. Know I will always be here for you and will always love you above all others.

To my mom, Mary, and grandma, Opal. Where my strength, perseverance, logic, stubbornness, intelligence, caring, giving, and love for others come from. I love and admire these women for what they have accomplished in their lives and how they give to others so freely.

To my friends, who are more like family than just friends: Videssa, Frank, Michael, Danny, Bobby, Jeff, Morgan, Jim, Gordon, my racquetball buddies, friends at TechMentor, friends at the gym, and friends at the cabin.

To the entire Group Policy team for their insight, inside information, dedication to the book, dedication to Group Policy technology, and friendship. To the other Group Policy MVPs, thanks for helping me and keeping the entire Group Policy technology moving forward. To Darren, Todd, Rick, Don, Greg, Kevin, Mark, Kurt, Dan, Mark, and Jeremy, who provide guidance when things are not clear, direction when things stray, correction when things are wrong, and friendship all the time. To my friends in the industry who are supportive, honest, true, and always there for one another.

To the Microsoft Press team of acquisition editors, copy editors, technical editors, and reviewers. Without your in-depth diligence and attention to detail, the book would not be the top-notch quality document that it is today. Thank you!

To all who read my books, read my articles, come to see me speak, and trust me with your most important questions. It is an honor to be a part of this community with you, and I hope that I can continue to provide the technology insight, clarity, and excitement that I have been able to so far.

A special thanks to Videssa Djucich, Darren Mar-Elia, Chris Terpening, Kevin Sullivan, and Mark Gray, who helped with so much of the research, formatting, and support with the book. Thank you very much!

List of Reviewers from the Group Policy Team

Nafisa Bhojawala, program manager

Bryan Garretson, software design engineer in test

Joe Gettys, software design engineer in test

Mark Gray, program manager

Lilia Gutnik, program manager

Judith Herman, programming writer

Rajive Kumar, senior development lead

Jason Leznek, senior product manager

Kevin Sullivan, senior program manager lead

Sreeram Vaidyanath, software design engineer in test

Introduction

Welcome to this in-depth and comprehensive book on Group Policy. The Microsoft Group Policy team, the Group Policy Most Valuable Professionals (MVPs), and members of many other departments at Microsoft have spent countless hours molding Group Policy and making it what it is today. *Windows Group Policy Resource Kit: Windows Server 2008 and Windows Vista* explores the technology that is Group Policy, as well as some of the most innovative, exciting, and powerful additions to Group Policy that you could ever imagine or hope for.

Group Policy has been upgraded, expanded, and enhanced with features, functionality, and capabilities. Group Policy has more than 5,000 individual settings, nearly 40 client-side extensions (CSEs), and management capabilities that make Group Policy administration simple, so you will have no choice but to start to use Group Policy more in your Windows Server 2008 and Windows Vista environments. This book is meant to be your desktop reference, guide, and inside look into the foundational concepts of Group Policy, as well as its new and innovative features. If you are an IT professional who works in any way with Windows Active Directory, this book will make you more adept, efficient, and competent at designing, implementing, and troubleshooting Group Policy.

This book contains all of the technical detail you have come to expect from a Microsoft Resource Kit. The author, Derek Melber, has been crafting the outline and contents of this book for years. Derek has spoken and written about Group Policy for the past nine years and delivers an authoritative, world-class view and description of Group Policy for your reading pleasure, as well as for your career stability and growth. Derek has more than 15 books on his resume, and this book is at the apex of his career and publication library. With the assistance of the Microsoft Group Policy team and his friends and colleagues, Derek presents to you his "masterpiece."

Overview of the Book

The book has 15 chapters and two appendices, with additional information included on the CD. The book is divided into eight sections.

Part I: Introducing Group Policy

- **Chapter 1, "Introduction to Group Policy"**   This chapter provides an overview of what Group Policy technology is, as well as terminology that you will need to know when reading the book.

- **Chapter 2, "What's New in Windows Vista and Windows Server 2008 with Group Policy"**   This chapter focuses on the new features, technologies, and tools that you will see when you work with Group Policy in Windows Server 2008 and Windows Vista.

- **Chapter 3, "Group Policy Basics"**   This chapter provides the fundamentals that everyone needs to work with Group Policy.

Part II: Group Policy Structure

- **Chapter 4, "Architecture of Group Policy"**   This chapter provides an in-depth discussion of the core architecture of Group Policy, including Group Policy object (GPO) storage and details, as well as CSEs, which do the majority of the work of Group Policy.

- **Chapter 5, "Group Policy Processing"**   Group Policy has a default and stable processing flow. You will see how this default behavior works, and you will learn about all of the toggles and switches available for altering this behavior when you need to.

Part III: Administering Group Policy

- **Chapter 6, "GPMC Basics"**   The Group Policy Management Console (GPMC) is your command center for Group Policy management. This chapter focuses on the basics of the tool that you will need to be proficient.

- **Chapter 7, "Advanced GPMC Management"**   This chapter discusses many of the new features and technologies that have been included in the new version of the GPMC.

- **Chapter 8, "Controlling Group Policy via Scripts and Automation"**   Automation is a highly relevant topic today, and this chapter guides you through the tools and options that you can use to make your Group Policy management an automated process.

Part IV: Implementing Security

- **Chapter 9, "Security Delegation for Administration of GPOs"**   Both the GPMC and Microsoft Advanced Group Policy Management (AGPM) provide mechanisms for securing the management of Group Policy. This chapter provides a description of how the technology works and describes how to implement a security structure that meets your needs.

Part V: Using Registry-Based Policy Settings

- **Chapter 10, "ADM Templates, ADMX Files, and the ADMX Central Store"**   Much of Group Policy relies on the settings that are defined and described in .adm templates and ADMX files. As explained in this chapter, .adm templates are still used today, but the new ADMX file structure is innovative and more powerful than its predecessor.

- **Chapter 11, "Customizing ADM Templates and ADMX Files"**   If the standard capabilities provided by .adm templates and ADMX files are not enough, you can create your own custom environment with both technologies. This chapter explains how to do this.

Part VI: Group Policy Settings

- **Chapter 12, "Group Policy Preferences"**   With over 3,000 individual settings, Group Policy Preferences is a feature that should get your attention. This chapter focuses on this new and innovative addition to Group Policy.

- **Chapter 13, "Settings Breakdown for Windows Server 2008 and Windows Vista"**   This chapter is meant to be a guide to the overall structure and settings capabilities that Group Policy provides. The chapter provides guidelines for grouping related settings, as well as a description of what each major section in a GPO is designed to do.

Part VII: Advanced Topics

- **Chapter 14, "Advanced GPO Management with AGPM"**   Advanced Group Policy Management (AGPM) is a Microsoft tool that allows you to perform offline editing, change management, reporting, and so much more with your Group Policy infrastructure. This chapter explores every facet of AGPM to help you install and use it immediately.

- **Chapter 15, "Troubleshooting GPOs"**   This chapter introduces the new Microsoft tools and capabilities that can help you track, pinpoint, and fix issues related to Group Policy.

Part VIII: Appendices

- **Appendix A, "Third-Party Group Policy Tools"**   Microsoft has been working on updating and improving Group Policy, but so have many companies that provide Group Policy software and solutions. This chapter gives you a quick, yet solid, overview of the tools available, and it explains where to go to get help with Group Policy beyond this book.

- **Appendix B, "Additional Resources"**   Some great resources are available when it comes to Group Policy knowledge and technology. This chapter helps you find the information you need.

Find Additional Content Online   As new or updated material becomes available that complements your book, it will be posted online on the Microsoft Press Online Windows Server and Client Web site. Based on the final build of Windows Server 2008, the type of material you might find includes updates to book content, articles, links to companion content, errata, sample chapters, and more. This Web site will be available soon at *http://ww.microsoft.com/learning/books/online/serverclient*, and it will be updated periodically.

Document Conventions

The following conventions are used in this book to highlight special features or usage.

Reader Aids

The following reader aids are used throughout this book to point out useful details.

Reader Aid	Meaning
Best Practices	
Caution	Warns you that failure to take or avoid a specified action can cause serious problems for users, systems, data integrity, and so on.
Important	Calls attention to essential information that should not be disregarded.
Note	Underscores the importance of a specific concept or highlights a special case that might not apply to every situation.
On the CD	Calls attention to a related script, tool, template, or job aid on the Companion CD that helps you perform a task described in the text.
Tip	
Warning	

Sidebars

The following sidebars are used throughout this book to provide added insight, tips, and advice concerning different Windows Vista features.

Sidebar	Meaning
Direct from the Source	Contributed by experts at Microsoft or MVPs to provide "from-the-source" insight into how Windows Vista works, best practices for managing security, and troubleshooting tips.
How It Works	Provides unique glimpses of Windows Vista features and how they work.

Command-Line Examples

The following style conventions are used in documenting command-line examples throughout this book.

Style	Meaning
Bold font	Used to indicate user input (characters that you type exactly as shown).
Italic font	Used to indicate variables for which you need to supply a specific value (for example, file_name can refer to any valid file name).
`Monospace font`	Used for code samples and command-line output.
%SystemRoot%	Used for environment variables.

Companion CD

In addition to the book itself, you also get a CD that contains some great tools and other resources. System requirements for running the CD are at the back of this book. The CD includes the following resources.

Elevation Tools

Many of the third-party Group Policy vendors have kindly provided evaluation versions of their tools that you can install and use to see how Group Policy can be taken to another level.

Management scripts

On the CD-ROM accompanying this book you will find a collection of scripts that illustrate working with Group Policy from within Windows Powershell. These scripts, while illustrative in nature, actually perform some very useful tasks and can simplify many common scenarios faced by network admins. These tasks include reporting on orphaned Group Policy Objects, creating Group Policy Objects, and auditing application of Group Policy Objects. For complete information on these exciting and powerful scripts please refer to the read me file in the same folder as the Group Policy Scripts.

eBook

If you would rather have a searchable electronic copy of the book, there is one on the CD.

Chapter-Related Materials

Some chapters have additional documentation or electronic tools; these are mentioned in the book text and located on the CD.

> **Digital Content for Digital Book Readers:** If you bought a digital-only edition of this book, you can enjoy select content from the print edition's companion CD.
> Visit *http://go.microsoft.com/fwlink/?LinkId=108261* to get your downloadable content. This content is always up-to-date and available to all readers.

Resource Kit Support Policy

Every effort has been made to ensure the accuracy of this book and the Companion CD content. Microsoft Press provides corrections to this book through the Web at the following location:

http://www.microsoft.com/learning/support/search.asp

If you have comments, questions, or ideas regarding the book or Companion CD content, or if you have questions that are not answered by querying the Knowledge Base, please send them to Microsoft Press by using either of the following methods:

E-mail:

rkinput@microsoft.com

Postal Mail:

Microsoft Press
Attn: Microsoft Group Policy Resource Kit, *Editor*
One Microsoft Way
Redmond, WA 98052-6399

Please note that product support is not offered through the preceding mail addresses. For product support information, please visit the Microsoft Product Support Web site at the following address:

http://support.microsoft.com

Part I
Introducing Group Policy

Chapter 1
Why Group Policy?

Group Policy is the de facto method for administrators to centralize the management of computers and users within an Active Directory directory service domain. Group Policy applies to all areas of configuration, including software, security, Microsoft Internet Explorer, the registry, and much more. If you are new to Group Policy or just want to learn more about how Group Policy can make managing an Active Directory enterprise more efficient and cost effective, you have certainly started in the right place. This chapter will provide a quick yet comprehensive overview of where Group Policy came from, where it is today, and where it is headed in the future. You will also quickly gain an appreciation for what Group Policy can do for you and your company, as well as how easy Group Policy can be to implement and maintain.

The Past, Present, and Future of Group Policy

If you have been using Windows for a long time, you probably remember a time when the concepts of "Policy" first started. There have always been forms of management technology built into the enterprise level of the Microsoft network operating systems. As far back as Windows NT 3x, some form of management technology controlled certain aspects of the network. These management technologies gave you the ability to control user password parameters, desktop settings, registry settings, and more. Over time, the technologies placed in the different network operating systems have matured. If you have not seen the latest versions of the management technologies that Group Policy provides in Microsoft Windows Server 2003 and Windows Server 2008, you are in for a real treat.

Group Policy's Past

Instead of going through the entire past of Group Policy and its ancestors, we will look at the technology and features of Group Policy ancestors. Reviewing the technologies that grew into Group Policy will help us understand where policy management used to be, as well as acknowledge some of the limitations of earlier policy management technologies.

To start the history lesson, you will begin at Microsoft Windows NT with System Policies. System Policies were powerful during their time, but they were not without limitations and issues. However, the best technologies and features of System Policies rose to the top and became the predecessors to what you know today as Group Policy. What were they? If you were asked to define System Policy in a short phrase, you would probably answer "a registry modification." This is exactly what a System Policy was: a sophisticated and centralized mechanism to make registry value changes and settings.

System Policies were based on files called ADM templates, named for their .adm file extension. The ADM template contents had an easy and unique format and coding language. The structure was important because the contents of the ADM template performed the following two distinct functions:

- Create policy settings in the System Policy Editor.
- Establish the registry path, value, and data.

When a GPO was first edited, the ADM templates were used within the System Policy Editor, but no settings were applied automatically. Rather, the System Policy Editor decrypted the coding that was in the ADM template to create the folders and policy settings that showed up in the interface. A simple change to the ADM template would result in an immediate change to the System Policy Editor the next time the GPO was edited.

ADM templates were simple, mobile, and stable. There were, however, issues that came along with such a simple technology. Although the issues were not bad enough to force administrators to use other technologies, they did cause some glitches in the way in which administrators could use and implement registry changes using ADM templates. The major issues regarding ADM templates included:

- Persistence of registry values. This was an issue referred to as "tattooing," which will be discussed shortly.
- Lack of support for controlling multivalue entries in the registry.
- Lack of support for controlling binary value entries in the registry.
- Lack of an easy way to develop custom ADM templates (although this was possible and done often).
- Required manual version control. This created problems when several administrators needed to make modifications to System Policies, as well as problems with any custom or updated ADM templates that needed to be managed and implemented on the network.

Although there were many issues associated with ADM templates in System Policies, they were used very often and relied upon to ensure that registry settings were configured properly.

How It Works: Tattooing

Tattooing is when a setting applied by a System Policy remains permanently in the registry, even after you alter the policy. To get a feel for how tattooing works, you need to examine a real-world case of a System Policy setting from inception to completion. For this example, look at a System Policy that modifies the screen saver for a user account. Initially, the setting would be in a policy that targets a user account, because this setting is configured in the HKEY_CURRENT_USER portion of the registry. (You will read more about policy settings and the registry in Chapter 11, "ADM Templates, ADMX Files, and the ADMX Central Store," Chapter 12, "Group Policy Preferences," Chapter 13, "Settings Breakdown for Windows Server 2008 and Windows Vista.")

When the user logs off and then logs on again, the System Policy sets the new screen saver setting automatically. If the user were to configure the screen saver settings, the new screen saver file would be configured already.

Assume now that the administrator no longer wants the screen saver to be established using System Policy. The administrator removes the setting for the screen saver in the System Policy. When the user logs off and then logs on, the screen saver settings established from the recent System Policy remain, even though the new System Policy did not establish a setting for the screen saver.

This behavior is referred to as *tattooing* because the setting tattoos itself, or makes itself permanent, in the registry. A tattooed setting can be altered from System Policy in only two ways:

- By creating an alternate setting using System Policy that changes the registry entry at next reboot or logoff and logon

- By manually modifying the registry using a tool such as RegEdit.exe or RegEdt32.exe

Group Policy's Present

When talking about Group Policy in the present tense, you should be thinking about Windows 2000 Server and beyond. The majority of the technology and features are built on this foundation; only minor features have been added. Regardless, it is important to understand how Group Policy changed from System Policy to become the powerhouse that it is today.

At first glance, it is easy to see that Group Policy is much more than the ancestor of System Policy. Sure, Group Policy still contains some remnants of ADM templates and registry alterations, but the overall makeup and structure has changed radically. You should be fully aware of what Group Policy does provide, as well as what it does not provide. These topics are discussed in the following sections.

Group Policy Requires Active Directory

It is no secret that Group Policy requires Active Directory to be a full-fledged powerhouse of a management solution. Although you can have local Group Policy objects (GPOs) that control a single computer, this is really not a book for home or small business use. For the enterprise, Group Policy relies on Active Directory's structure to help distribute the settings stored in GPOs to the correct users and groups. This task is accomplished by intertwining Group Policy technology with the Active Directory design structure. In essence, GPOs are linked to the domain, organizational units (OUs), and Active Directory sites. Because user and computer objects are stored in these containers, it is logical that the objects in a container where a GPO is linked will receive those settings, by default of course!

Group Policy Includes Security Settings

A distinct area of interest to the entire computing world, especially Microsoft, is security. When Group Policy was first introduced, it was important that an entire section within the GPO settings be dedicated to security. Throughout the life cycle of the current Group Policy ancestry, these security settings have expanded and evolved. Figure 1-1 illustrates the plethora of security settings that exist in a standard GPO.

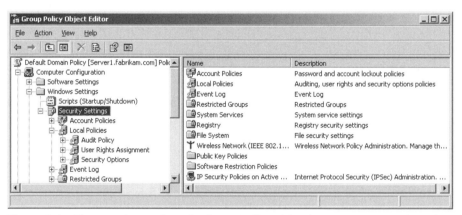

Figure 1-1   The security section of a Group Policy object has numerous settings that all target the security of the computer being configured.

These security settings have grown in numbers, as well as detail. For example, if you compare the anonymous controls from first-generation Group Policy with today's anonymous controls, you will see a dramatic difference in the level of detail that can be configured. Figure 1-2 shows what the original version of a Group Policy object included with regard to Anonymous controls.

Windows XP introduced the first "updated" security settings related to the Anonymous controls. These controls were a radical new approach to the security implications that an anonymous connection could expose to a computer running Windows. Now, in the newer Group Policy objects for the latest operating systems, you can get very granular with your anonymous controls, as shown in Figure 1-3.

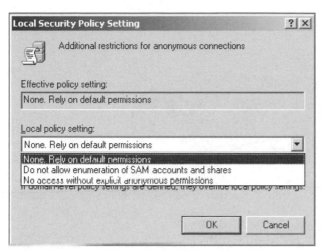

Figure 1-2   The Windows 2000 Group Policy object controls for anonymous connections were limited.

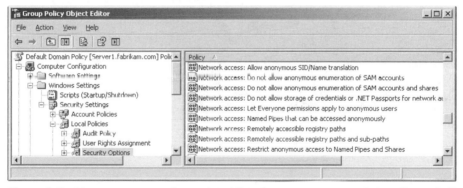

Figure 1-3   Here you can see the updated list of anonymous controls in a Group Policy object.

This example illustrates just some of the security settings that are available when using Group Policy. Other settings allow control over passwords, group membership, Internet Explorer, firewalls, and more. For more information about these other settings, see Chapter 13, "Settings Breakdown for Windows Server 2008 and Vista."

How It Works: Anonymous Connections

Anonymous connections can be made to any computer running Windows if the correct security settings are not in place. These connections can be made from any computer on the network, not just computers that have been joined to the domain. With this type of environment, an anonymous connection can be established by simply running the following command:

```
Net use \\<computer name or IP address>\ipc$ /u:"" ""
```

This establishes an anonymous connection to the exposed computer, as shown in Figure 1-4.

Figure 1-4   A successful anonymous connection can be made to a computer that does not have adequate security.

After the computer is protected, the attempt to make the anonymous connection shown in Figure 1-4 is no longer valid. Figure 1-5 shows the result when you attempt anonymous access to a protected computer.

Figure 1-5   An anonymous connection attempt will be unsuccessful when made to a computer that does not allow anonymous connections.

It should be noted that Windows XP, Windows Server 2003, Windows Vista, and Windows Server 2008 will not function in this manner. Because there are so many granular settings for anonymous connections, a connection will succeed, but the ability to access resources is limited by the settings that are made in the Group Policy.

Group Policy Includes Software Distribution

Another benefit of the evolution of Group Policy is software distribution. With the ability to distribute software using Group Policy and Active Directory, you can remove much of the complexity of other tools such as Systems Management Server (SMS) and System Center Configuration Manager. When the software distribution feature of Group Policy was developed, it was important that Microsoft Installer (MSI) packages could be distributed using this technology. This made Group Policy a valid alternative to other technologies that managed the installation of software.

There were, however, some limitations of software distribution using Group Policy that made the more robust solutions, such as SMS and System Center Configuration Manager, more attractive and viable. Group Policy software distribution was limiting to those companies and administrators that needed validation that the software installed successfully. Group Policy also lacked the ability to do reporting to show where software was installed. These limitations were not omissions from Group Policy; they were left out because other Microsoft solutions provided those services. In essence, Group Policy is designed to work for software distribution for smaller companies and for software that does not require validation or license reporting. If you need these features, you can purchase SMS and System Center Configuration Manager enterprise solutions.

Group Policy Helps Eliminate Tattooing

One of the most heralded features of Group Policy is an approach that fixes some issues around tattooing. The concept that registry settings would persist, even after an administrator deleted the GPO, became an ongoing issue. Because software, operating systems, system settings, and other aspects of the computer and user environment needed to be dynamic, tattooing needed to be "fixed."

Group Policy takes an entirely new approach toward tattooing by creating special areas in the registry that are updated when a GPO is deleted or the computer falls out of scope of management. These special areas are wiped clean and rebuilt during policy refresh so that tattooing is not an issue. Administrators can now use Group Policy to establish registry values that are more suited to how desktop and server administration was initially intended.

However, earlier versions of Group Policy did leave some aspects of registry management in a state of tattooing. These areas included the security settings and any custom registry settings exposed through custom ADM templates. In the most recent addition of policy settings in Windows Server 2008, registry policy options eliminate tattooing entirely.

The new settings available with Windows Server 2008 Group Policy Preferences allow you to configure virtually any registry value setting (even those that were previously not supported initially, such as multivalue and binary). Not only can you make the policy set these registry values, but you can make the entry nonpersistent. This means that when the policy is no longer in place, the registry value that you put in with the GPO will be removed, as shown in Figure 1-6.

> **Important**   If some registry values are removed, leaving the value blank, the computer might see the blank values as a critical error and generate a stop error. Before implementing any registry value modification, test the scenarios and outcomes. For more information, see Chapter 12, "Group Policy Preferences."

Group Policy Can Modify System Settings

Group Policy really progressed when the inclusion of system settings were exposed via a Group Policy object. These system settings are not in the registry or are not exposed through routine registry editing tools and techniques in most cases. These new settings in Group Policy work directly with the dynamic system settings on the computer, such as disabling the Administrator account.

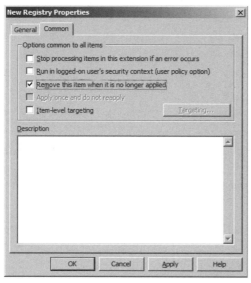

Figure 1-6   Group Policy Preferences now provides a registry policy, where entries can be nontattooing and volatile.

Before the release of Windows XP Service Pack 2, the default Administrator account could not be disabled, deleted, or otherwise modified so that it would not function on a computer. However, with these new settings in Group Policy, an administrator can disable this account on any computer with the use of a GPO, as shown in Figure 1-7.

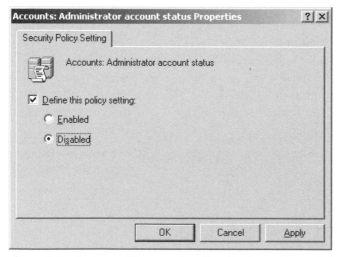

Figure 1-7   System settings can be altered using a Group Policy, as seen with this control over the Administrator account status.

> **Important**   Disabling the Administrator account is not something that you should do without tremendous forethought. Thoroughly consider the potential ramifications that this might cause on each computer being considered for this setting. This setting can affect desktops, servers, and even domain controllers, which would disable the Administrator account that controls the forest or domain.

Group Policy Is Extensible

Almost all of the features discussed in this section are "extensions" to Group Policy. That is, they are extensions that Microsoft made to Group Policy since its introduction with Windows 2000. In addition, anyone can extend Group Policy to add more settings and robust features. Numerous companies have built their entire suite of products around extending Group Policy. For example, the Group Policy Preferences extensions that now exists in Windows Server 2008 were not originally created by Microsoft; they were created by DesktopStandard, which is now a Microsoft subsidiary.

Extensions exist today that can contribute amazing functionality to Group Policy. Some companies provide extensions to do reporting on Group Policy; others configure third-party applications, and others allow for seamless integration of strict password policies for domain user accounts. The options for Group Policy extensibility are nearly endless, and the push to make Group Policy the central location for desktop configuration and management will grow as Group Policy continues to grow in popularity and effectiveness.

Group Policy Is Dynamic

Group Policy is dynamic compared to System Policy. Its dynamic environment is made possible by the constant background refreshes. These background refreshes are occurring on your network right now! They are built into Group Policy and occur approximately every 90 minutes on desktops and servers.

These background refreshes allow changes to GPOs to take effect without a reboot or logoff and logon by the user. This dynamic environment gives the administrators the advantage of efficiently managing the overall status and settings on any computer on the network. If a setting must be distributed to all computers in a short amount of time, the default Group Policy background refresh mechanism will suffice to get the job done.

Some settings do not adhere to the background refresh rules. These settings include options such as folder redirection, software distribution, and drive mappings. They are omitted from the background refresh because they could cause data corruption—without any warning to the user—if they were to change in the background. For example, you would not want your manager working on a letter in Microsoft Office Word addressing the reasons why you should get a raise, only to have a GPO remove Word before your manager can save and send the letter.

Much, Much More

If every feature were listed here, it would be the entire book! So just keep in mind that there are many features, new and seasoned, that are not listed here. When you think of Group Policy, you should be considering it for all aspects of your daily needs. New technologies associated with Group Policy Preferences and Microsoft Advanced Group Policy Management shed new and imaginative light on areas that were needing attention for a long time. You will be exposed to all aspects of Group Policy in this book . . . from the ground up and the outside in.

Group Policy's Future

The road to the current Group Policy has been filled with excitement and amazing new technology. It is very clear that Microsoft has made a bold statement that Group Policy is not only here to stay, but will become an increasingly integral part of managing a Windows environment over time. The Group Policy team has been a key driver in making sure that the Group Policy technology is alive and growing with each new revision.

The big question is: "Where will Group Policy be in 1, 3, and 5 years?" The answer to that is not completely solidified, but we can be assured that some new technologies will materialize. If you imagine where you would want Group Policy to be in the future, what would your list of features look like? Here are some ideas that have been suggested by Group Policy MVPs, Group Policy software companies, and even Microsoft employees.

Troubleshooting Tools

It is no secret that there are some deficiencies in the ability to troubleshoot Group Policy. Troubleshooting has improved over the years, but no one closely involved with the Group Policy community would stand up in a crowded room and boast about the impressive troubleshooting tools and power that currently exist for Group Policy.

The entire community receives frequent questions and suggestions regarding troubleshooting Group Policy. Here are some of the most persistent requests, which are most certainly on the "wish list" for the Group Policy team:

- Confirmation that Group Policy has refreshed for specific computers
- Confirmation that specific Group Policy settings were applied during the last refresh
- Database of current state and version of all computers and users regarding GPOs
- Ability to compare Resultant Set of Policies (RSoP) against actual configured policies

It is quite likely that you, too, have a troubleshooting need that you want to add to the wish list. There is a resources page in this book that lists e-mail addresses for many people associated with Group Policy. This is your big chance to contribute to the list by e-mailing them and describing the new troubleshooting features that you would like to see.

Enterprise Administration

Without question, the Group Policy Management Console (GPMC) provides an excellent view into the administration of Group Policy. With each domain specifically listed within the console, you can clearly see which GPOs are associated with the appropriate domain.

However, when it comes to having GPOs move, copy, and otherwise update settings across domain boundaries, the GPMC leaves room for improvement. Today, Group Policy is very domain specific. Migration tables help you "translate" security principals from one domain to another, but these tables can be difficult to work with.

The future of Group Policy will hopefully allow you to move GPOs across domains and even forests for easy duplication of your GPOs and settings. This will be especially useful for large organizations, multinational organizations, and organizations that have test domains and forests that duplicate the production environment.

Disaster Recovery

As you will see, the advent of Advanced Group Policy Management (AGPM) has brought Group Policy management and recovery to a respectable level in a short amount of time. AGPM provides off-line editing, roll-back, roll-forward, automatic backup and archiving, and change management in one easy tool.

However, an all-in-one disaster recovery solution with regard to Group Policy is still incomplete. There is still a need for control over access control lists (ACLs), filters, granular link control, and specific settings when recovering from a disaster tied to Group Policy. The goal is to provide as much granularity as possible when recovering from a disaster, similar to the level of granularity provided when using Ntdsutil to manage Active Directory recovery.

Such an elaborate disaster recovery suite of options is necessary because disasters can be caused by one of many things, such as a server failure, hard drive failure, or even the Group Policy settings. In any case, the more options that you have, the better your chances of getting all computers back and running in the shortest amount of time.

Reporting

Reporting is similar to troubleshooting in many cases, except that information is gathered for review, not to fix a problem. Therefore, some of the same reports used for troubleshooting would be nice to have for the purpose of gathering information. For example, you might want to query detailed settings and computer-related or user-related information. This would require that a database of information be created to store all of the information that you would want reported.

For example, say you want to run a report to determine which computers have had the local Administrator account renamed using Group Policy. You might also want a report that indicates how many computers, per new name, have been modified. With this type of reporting, you can get a very quick and useful report on a myriad of configurations that are made in a GPO.

Reporting will also delve deep into every aspect of Group Policy, such as settings, links, administration, management, processing, failures, and more. With developing technologies such as SMS and System Center Configuration Manager, this type of environment is not necessarily that far off. Reporting is certainly a feature that is both wanted and deserved by all who use Group Policy.

Instant Configuration

As you have seen and most likely already knew, policy settings were not always as instantaneous as they are today. There was a time when System Policy required a reboot or logoff and logon, whereas today Group Policy has an automatic background refresh. This refresh occurs approximately every 90 minutes, but it handles only some—not all—GPO settings.

The future of Group Policy will hopefully provide more control over "pushing" settings to one or more computers or users. This form of control creates an instant configuration that is useful in many scenarios. For example, there might be a security configuration that needs to be pushed out immediately, or a user might require a new configuration so that he or she can finalize a contract, trade, or other business deal. Regardless of the scenario, the ability to have instant configurations of Group Policy settings would make desktop and server administration even more efficient.

Is the Future Already Here?

Do not get the impression that some of these proposed features and improvements are not already available. That would be a false statement and one that could get everyone involved into a lot of trouble. Rather, be fully aware that many of these features and functions already exist. Yes, they already exist.

They just don't exist in the Microsoft suite of offerings. A handful of software vendors, small and large, have been producing amazing tools for Group Policy for years. Many of these vendors have driven changes that have occurred within Microsoft for the Group Policy efforts. Still today numerous companies and individuals provide valuable input into the present and future of Group Policy. You can find more information about these vendors and their tools in Appendix A, "Third-Party Tools."

Benefits of Group Policy

If you are a Windows administrator who is new to Group Policy, if you are not convinced that it is all that it could be, or even if you are a longtime administrator who has been exposed to all of the great benefits of Group Policy, you are in the right place. Here, you will be shown some of the most popular and heralded reasons that companies, administrators, and IT personnel use Group Policy.

If the list were short, there would be no reason to waste your time on the ins and outs of the benefits that Group Policy provides to a Windows network. However, the list is not short. In reality, this is an abridged list that highlights only the most important and useful benefits of Group Policy. Amazing and sometimes bizarre accounts have been brought up in conferences, seminars, and training rooms over the years on why and how companies use Group Policy. All have validity, but those outlined in this section rise to the top.

More Efficient Management

There is no doubt that centralized management of desktops and servers has saved millions of person-hours over the past few years. It may be hard to believe that we used to manage computers in a workgroup, requiring each computer in the enterprise to be "touched" every time something needed to be done. But you might still live in that world today, where you have to touch every computer to get software loaded, set a configuration, make changes to the registry, and so on.

Group Policy is the king of centralized management. The key to Group Policy's centralized management and efficiency is in the way in which it ties in with Active Directory. If Active Directory did not exist, Group Policy would not be as beneficial as it is. Group Policy is so efficient when paired with Active Directory because of the Active Directory structure. Active Directory provides you with the ability to create a hierarchy within the domain using organizational units. You can create single-level organizational units or deep nested levels. The ultimate goal of this hierarchy is to move computer, user, and group accounts into these organizational units so that you can then manage them in a like manner.

For example, you would want to manage IT staff computers differently than HR staff computers. These two computer categories would most likely belong to different organizational units. If you have different organizational units for these different computers, you can manage them separately. It is as simple as creating two different GPOs, both containing the appropriate settings for their type of computer. After this is completed, you just link the GPO to the respective organizational unit, and the operating systems and directory service take over from there.

Not only can you make initial settings efficient, but you can also make changes to the GPO dynamically, which in turn modifies the entire group of computers located in the organizational unit.

This type of efficiency can make thousands of computers seem like just a few. In essence, you just need to manage the "types" of computers, allowing Group Policy and Active Directory to handle the rest.

More Powerful Management

Group Policy comes with numerous settings. At latest count, the settings in a default GPO for Windows Server 2008 are hovering around 2500. With this many settings, the power is at your fingertips. There is almost nothing left out of the latest suite of GPO settings. For the few settings that are left out, another option is available with Windows Server 2008: Group Policy Preferences.

Group Policy Preferences alone adds thousands of settings to a GPO. How many, you might ask? That number has not been determined. There are so many settings and options that no one has taken the time to count them all.

All of these settings allow you to control key areas of a computer and user environment. The following is just a short list of areas that you can control with a GPO:

- Drive and printer mappings
- User password maintenance
- Local and domain group memberships
- Software installation
- Internet Explorer
- Windows Firewall
- My Documents

This list could go on and on, and it does later in the book (see Chapter 13, "Settings Breakdown for Windows Sever 2008 and Windows Vista"). With all of the new settings and areas of control, there is nothing left to manual or scripting maintenance. If you need to get something completed or configured on a desktop or server, a Group Policy can manage it for you in almost every case.

Reliability

Group Policy is one of the most reliable technologies that Microsoft has produced. With such a reliance on Active Directory, which has proven to be stable, strong, extensible, and reliable, Group Policy has had a fairly smooth ride to such a good reputation.

Active Directory has grown right along with Group Policy, and this makes the two equally responsible for the accolades that they have been given. Active Directory has numerous built-in fault-tolerant technologies, including the following:

- Multi-master domain controllers
- Multi-master DNS servers
- Active Directory replication
- Domain controller authentication algorithms

The reason that these Active Directory technologies are so important when discussing the reliability of Group Policy is that Group Policy relies on all of these technologies, too. The partnership that Group Policy has with Active Directory is seamless.

Group Policy is also very reliable because of the way in which the settings are delivered and processed by the target computers and users. With an automatic background refresh that occurs every 90 minutes or so, the settings that reside in a GPO reliably get delivered to the desktop in plenty of time for most networks.

Extensibility

Group Policy has always been customizable. As you just learned from the history of policy within Microsoft, System Policy was also customizable. Even back in the early days of System Policy, Microsoft provided an open platform to make policy not only customizable, but extensible. This extensibility allows third-party vendors, as well as Microsoft, to add to the technology and GPO settings with great ease. Put simply, this extensibility is primarily a result of a simple structure that Group Policy relies upon, which includes technology called *client-side extensions*.

Client-side extensions are the brains in the extensibility matrix. Really just DLLs, client-side extensions live on the target computer, where policy settings will be delivered from Active Directory. Within these DLLs reside code that can handle the information that is delivered to the target computer from the originating GPO.

The extensibility of Group Policy has been mastered by many third-party vendors, as well as by Microsoft. It seems like every service pack or major operating system release comes with a new set of policy settings, which are handled in most cases by an extension to Group Policy.

One of the best examples of Group Policy extensions is the acquisition of PolicyMaker, which is now called Group Policy Preferences. Group Policy Preferences add over 20 client-side extensions, which is nearly seamless to anyone who is not current on Group Policy technology. With these extensions, Group Policy now covers many new areas of configuration, not to mention the thousands of settings that the new client-side extensions add.

Security

Security is a two-fold benefit when it comes to Group Policy. Initially, Group Policy is a reliable and secure technology. There have been no reports or documented incidents of any issue arising from an attacker using Group Policy to elevate privileges or cause damage to a computer. This is a testimony to the rigorous efforts of the Group Policy and Active Directory teams over the years. However, the security benefits only start here.

Some of the many security benefits of Group Policy are just becoming available, such as the awesome and powerful security settings that are available through the new Group Policy Preferences. Three specific security settings make Group Policy shine above many other technologies:

- The ability to reset the local Administrator (and any other user, for that matter) password through a policy.

- The ability to control membership in local groups, such as the Administrators group, using Group Policy. This is a fantastic setting that allows you full granularity of the membership.

- The ability to reset service account passwords within the service itself. This promotes compliancy and security in an area in which passwords and security were once thought too complex and mundane a task.

Other areas in a GPO have also benefited from immense efforts by the Group Policy community. An entire section in a GPO is geared toward security settings. Here, settings help you control anonymous connections, digital signatures, authentication protocols, Server Message Block (SMB) signing, and much more. Still other areas help you control security related to Internet Explorer, Windows Firewall, file and folder ACLs, and so on.

With such an emphasis on security these days, Microsoft has not spared any effort in making sure all potential security settings are exposed in a GPO. By far, this is one of the most important benefits of using Group Policy.

Diversity

When developing a strategy for managing desktops and servers, it is always a good idea to categorize each type of computer. As you categorize, you should consider a variety of criteria for each computer type, some of which includes the following:

- Security settings
- Installed software
- User privileges
- User environment
- Internet Explorer settings
- Application settings

The resulting matrix of combinations of these criteria and the associated settings can become quite complex and daunting. However, when you start to organize these areas into the Group Policy framework for distributing the settings, the solution becomes very manageable.

Although each computer has a different set of needs and requires different configurations and settings to facilitate user productivity, Group Policy, combined with Active Directory structuring, makes managing these diverse settings easy. It is as simple as creating different GPOs for each type of computer, then applying those settings through Active Directory organizational units so that only the correct computers and users receive the settings.

Consistency

Consistency is defined as "adherence to the same form." In terms of computers, this means that all desktops and servers should maintain a baseline of settings that ensure security and stability, provide ease of management, and maintain reliability. Whether you are creating baseline settings to meet internal guidelines or external compliancy regulations, computers must be consistent.

Group Policy excels in ensuring that computers are maintained consistently. As we have seen in many of the other benefits regarding Group Policy, the design of Active Directory and the placement of computer and user objects within that structure is the foundation for reliability and consistency. When the GPOs are integrated into this structure, the inherent nature of Group Policy technology ensures that computers are consistent.

Without the Active Directory structure and constant refreshing of Group Policy in the background, the concept of consistency would not be as clean cut. The process for creating, maintaining, and delivering the settings would become very manual, and thus would break down the level of consistency that an automated process delivers.

Stability

The result of a secure, reliable, consistent, and managed desktop or server is stability; the alternative is potential chaos and instability. If you are not managing your computers tightly, your computers are managing you.

Time has shown that end users cause more damage and down time for their desktop than anyone can imagine. The more control administrators have over ensuring that desktops are configured properly, the more stable the desktop. The more secure the desktop, the more stable the desktop. Thus, the more an administrator can reduce the end user's privileges over the desktop, the greater the stability of the desktop.

Group Policy can do all of these things, and even more. With such a powerful and robust system aiding administrators in their overall quest to manage everything and anything on a desktop, the result is a more stable environment.

Group Policy Negatives

As you can see, the benefits of Group Policy are certainly clear and compelling. There are, however, some negatives (not disadvantages, though) of Group Policy. These negatives are not issues that should push you away from Group Policy, but they do make managing and maintaining some settings more of a challenge. You have seen many of these already, when we discussed the future of Group Policy. Of course, because these items are futuristic, we cannot call them benefits yet.

Limited Troubleshooting Tools

There are not as many tools and solutions for troubleshooting Group Policy as there need to be. Microsoft and other third-party vendors are spending thousands of person-hours trying to produce and perfect some tools, and within the next few years there will be amazing tools on the market that will move this topic from the negatives list to the benefits list.

Limited Testing Environment and Tools

Because Group Policy is so powerful and manageable, testing of its features is important. A single errant Group Policy setting can bring down a computer, department, or application, and potentially halt production. Therefore, more attention and better tools need to be provided for testing of Group Policy. There are some mechanisms built in, such as modeling, but more needs to be done. Modeling gets the testing to a certain point, but it does not complete the task. It has been suggested that a test environment be created to test all Group Policy settings and their interaction with computers before the GPOs are placed in production.

Limited Inter-Domain and Inter-Forest Support

If your company has a complex Active Directory environment, you have probably already seen some of the pain points related to Group Policy across your enterprise. One limitation of today's Group Policy is that it does not handle cross-domain and cross-forest interactions very well. There are tools and features designed to aide in this, such as the GPMC and migration tables, but still more needs to be developed. The Group Policy team is considering these solutions already, as are many of the Group Policy software vendors. In no time, there will be integrated and robust solutions, by Microsoft or other software vendors, to resolve this disadvantage.

Summary

Group Policy is not an infantile technology; it has developed into a full-fledged enterprise technology. The history of Group Policy proves that it has seen substantial growth and maturity over the many, many years that Microsoft has been producing policy-based management.

Radical and innovative additions to Group Policy for Windows Server 2008 and Windows Vista make this an exciting time for Group Policy. New technologies, new settings, new controls, and new possibilities allow administrators and companies to gain more control, resulting in more stable computers.

The future of Group Policy is just as exciting as the present Group Policy offering, maybe more so. Microsoft and other leading Group Policy software companies are daily making new products, new developments, and new features that allow Group Policy to become even more powerful than imagined.

Group Policy can benefit companies of any size. Whether there are just a few desktops or servers, or thousands of computers, Group Policy can scale to help manage them. The benefits of Group Policy are like any other management platform, but Group Policy is integrated with a technology that you rely on today—Active Directory. With Active Directory and Group Policy working together, the overall benefits of manageability, security, consistency, reliability, and stability are clearly evident.

Additional Resources

- The Microsoft Group Policy Web site, at *http://www.microsoft.com/grouppolicy*, includes more information on the benefits of Group Policy for Active Directory enterprises.

- Chapter 2, "What's New in Windows Vista and Windows Server 2008," includes information about new Group Policy features and settings with the newest operating systems.

- Chapter 13, "Settings Breakdown for Windows Server 2008 and Windows Vista," includes information about specific settings within a GPO.

- Appendix A, "Third-Party Group Policy Tools," includes information about other companies that have extended Group Policy.

Chapter 2

What's New in Windows Vista and Windows Server 2008

There has been a distinct push in recent years to make Group Policy a more integrated, reliable, stable, and useful product within Active Directory directory service. That is not to say that it has not been all of these things, but efforts within the Group Policy team and supporting teams have put great emphasis on making Group Policy even better in these areas.

Each iteration of Group Policy has brought something impressive. The continual improvement of technology is a testament to all of the teams working to make the technology work better and more efficiently for customers.

Remember When

If you look back at some of the major milestones in the life cycle of Group Policy, you will note that there have been distinct times of radical and amazing changes. Table 2-1 summarizes these milestones.

Table 2-1 Group Policy Technology Milestones

Place in Time	Feature
Windows 2000	Approximately 900 total Group Policy settings
Windows XP	Approximately 1,400 total Group Policy settings
Windows Server 2003	Group Policy Management Console 1.0 introduced as an add-in
Windows XP SP2	Approximately 1,600 total Group Policy settings
Windows Vista	Approximately 2,400 total Group Policy settings and Advanced Group Policy Management made available
Windows Server 2008	Group Policy Management Console 2.0 updated and added to Server Manager; Preferences added

Windows 2000 introduced Group Policy and accumulated about 900 settings before Windows XP shipped. When Windows XP shipped, there was a bit of "flux" in the industry as administrators tried to juggle the Windows 2000 settings, Windows XP settings, and ADM templates that shipped with each operating system. The Group Policy Management Console (GPMC) was a major improvement, because it moved the administration of Group Policy objects (GPOs) from the Active Directory Users and Computers snap-in to the GPMC snap-in. Of course, the GPMC also provided a lot of new functionality, which we will discuss in Chapter 7, "Using the GPMC."

Windows XP Service Pack 2 (SP2) was a milestone, not only for Group Policy, but for Microsoft as a company. The security efforts that came along with SP2 were revolutionary, and Microsoft continues to use these efforts as a baseline for any desktop operating system. Microsoft views Windows Server 2003 SP1, the partner to Windows XP SP2, as the baseline for server operating systems.

New and Now

Now that Windows Vista and Windows Server 2008 have arrived, so have some new and cool technologies for Group Policy. Don't fret. The same great features are still there; they have just been enhanced and made more spectacular. Settings are expanded, new features abound, and many features that members of the community have wanted for a long time have finally arrived.

Some of these features came with Windows Vista. Features such as ADMX files and the ADMX central store have already been used by those who use Windows Vista. Because Windows Vista was released quite a few months before Windows Server 2008, some of these technologies might be more familiar to you. Windows Server 2008 introduced some great new features tied into the GPMC that will make administrative life much simpler when working with Group Policy. Some of the new features include searching GPO settings, filtering GPO settings, and adding the Preferences to all GPOs. Other technologies , like PolicyMaker from DesktopStandard, will show up in a GPO as Group Policy Preferences. A final addition, Advanced Group Policy Management (AGPM), works with Windows Server 2008 and Windows Vista to ensure management of GPOs is secure, stable, and consistent. AGPM is available through the Microsoft Desktop Optimization Pack (MDOP).

New Group Policy Features in Windows Vista

Windows Vista arrived on the market in early 2007. The new features that it introduced have had a significant effect in the Group Policy community. Windows Vista not only provides some impressive new graphical enhancements, it also comes with some overall changes to Group Policy that can affect the entire network of desktops—not just single machines. (The exception is the Multiple Local GPO enhancements, which do affect just one desktop at a time.) The new features that can affect either one desktop or many desktops include the following:

- Network Location Awareness
- ADMX templates
- ADMX repository
- Improved logging

Multiple Local GPOs

Some historical background will help you understand what has changed with local GPOs on a Windows Vista desktop. In previous versions of Windows, there was a single local GPO on every server and desktop. Beyond the local GPO on the individual computers, there could be many GPOs in Active Directory linked to the domain, organizational units, and sites. The local GPO had no power over the Active Directory GPOs unless nonconflicting settings were established. In such a case, the local GPO settings would make their way through the maze of Active Directory GPOs to the Resultant Set of Policy (RSoP) that molded the final policy settings on the computer.

Multiple Local GPOs were put into place in Windows Vista to solve many issues. One of the biggest problems this feature solves involves handling the ability for both users and administrators to log on to the same desktop, but be treated differently. Before Windows Vista, if local GPOs were configured to constrain the user account, both the administrator accounts and regular user accounts would receive the constraining settings. This caused some very odd results, either allowing the user to have too many privileges or restricting the administrator too severely. If the administrator needed to run elevated tasks in a restricted environment like this, he or she was forced to use "Run As" or other privilege elevating technologies. Although this is an almost ideal situation, it can cause some issues in companies that do not want such restrictions on administrators logging on to desktops.

Windows Vista tackles all of these issues with new technology related to the local GPO. In reality, there is no longer just a single GPO on the local desktop, but three local GPOs, which Microsoft refers to as Multiple Local Group Policy objects (MLGPO). These three GPOs provide granular control over the users who log on to the desktop. Local GPOs can be used in a single-computer environment, home environment, small business environment, or even large corporate scenario.

The three local GPOs are designed to control desktop users in a hierarchical manner. This hierarchy allows control over the settings that will be configured in GPO. The three MLGPO options consist of the following, in their proper hierarchical order:

- Local Policy Object
- Administrators and Non-Administrators Local Group Policy
- User-specific Local Group Policy

Local Computer Policy Object   The Local Computer Policy Object is identical to the local GPO in Windows 2000 and Windows XP. It can be accessed by using the Group Policy Management Editor (by running Gpedit.msc from the Run dialog box) or using the Microsoft Management Console (MMC). In either case, you can control both Computer Configuration and User Configuration settings, as shown in Figure 2-1.

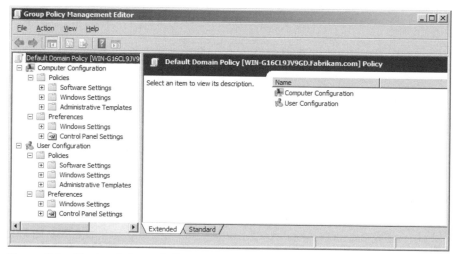

Figure 2-1   The local Group Policy can be opened in the Group Policy Management Editor by clicking Start, clicking Run, and then typing gpedit.msc in the Run dialog box.

Administrators and Non-Administrators Local GPOs   The Administrators local GPO and the Non-Administrators local GPO are new in Windows Vista. As their names indicate, the GPOs in this layer are designed to control two types of user accounts. The delineation is based on which users have membership in the local Administrators group.

> **Note**   User accounts that belong to the Power Users group are not considered Administrators and will not be affected by GPO settings under the Administrators local GPO. Rather, they will be affected by the GPO settings in the Non-Administrators local GPO.

The reason for this delineation is obvious. The settings for administrator-type accounts and nonadministrator-type accounts should be different on a desktop. Without these two options for local GPOs, it is nearly impossible to make a distinction between these two types of user accounts.

These two GPOs are not easy to access, however. To access these GPOs, you must use the MMC. This console exposes both of these GPOs so that administrators can manage them, as shown in Figure 2-2.

User-Specific Local GPO   The final local GPO layer is the user-specific local GPO. This GPO offers definitive granular control because it allows you to specify an individual user account to receive special GPO settings. Do not use this GPO option very often, because individual user account settings are typically discouraged from an administrative efficiency standpoint.

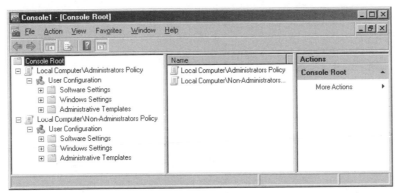

Figure 2-2   Both the Administrators local GPO and the Non-Administrators local GPO can be edited in the MMC.

This type of GPO is very useful on specialized desktops throughout the environment. Such desktops might include those functioning as a kiosk, those in a training or educational facility, or even those that have a shared user account. In such cases, the user account used to log on to these special desktops has a unique set of GPO settings, where all other user accounts are controlled by the Local Policy Object or even the Administrators or Non-Administrators local GPOs.

You do not access the administration of this type of GPO through the Group Policy Management Editor directly; rather, it is accessed through the MMC. When using the MMC to open this GPO, you select the GPO that is associated with any one of the local user accounts that are configured in the local Security Accounts Manager (SAM). After you add your GPO into the MMC, the interface will include only User Configuration settings. Because this local GPO affects user accounts only, the MMC removes Computer Configuration settings so that they do not confuse the administrator of the local GPO. This can be seen in Figure 2-3.

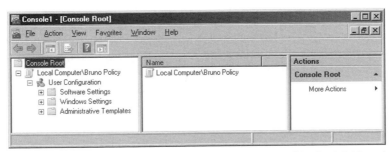

Figure 2-3   The local user-specific GPOs can be edited in the MMC and allow control over User Configuration settings only.

Precedence and Application   Now that there are Multiple Local GPOs to configure and choose from, it is important to understand how they are tiered in the hierarchy, in case there are ever any conflicting settings among them. The hierarchy of local GPOs is predetermined and creates the precedence for conflicting settings in different local GPOs. The most generic GPO has the least precedence, and the most specific GPO has the most precedence. Thus, the local GPO has the least precedence, the user-specific local GPO has the highest precedence, and the Administrators/Non-Administrators local GPOs fall between these two. The order of precedence from lowest to highest is summarized as follows:

- Local GPO
- Administrators/Non-Administrators
- User-specific local GPO

The hierarchy of the local GPOs must also coordinate with the GPOs that administrators link with Active Directory. The same rules apply here as before, where the local GPOs have the weakest precedence when compared to the GPOs from Active Directory.

Network Location Awareness

The Network Location Awareness technology that Windows XP delivered has been a successful solution for many aspects of the operating system and network connectivity. This technology allows the computer to be fully aware of its state and communication capabilities, thus allowing it to make intelligent decisions based on that state.

Group Policy has historically relied on dependable, yet not the most impressive, network identification technology. In the past, Group Policy has used the Internet Control Message Protocol (ICMP) to determine the state of the network, as well as network link speed. ICMP, which encompasses the PING command, is great for getting some network information, but it has not been ideal for helping Group Policy application.

Now that Group Policy relies on Network Location Awareness, the overall picture and state of Group Policy have been enhanced. Group Policy uses network location awareness in two primary fashions: it determines link speed, and it uses network location awareness to determine whether the computer needing to refresh Group Policy is connected to the domain.

For the first use of Network Location Awareness, Group Policy determines whether the link from the computer receiving GPO settings has a fast or slow connection to the domain and domain controllers. Because some GPO settings can take a long time to apply because of the amount of data being sent, determining link speed can be an indicator as to whether the data should be sent at all. Network Location Awareness provides this assistance by determining the bandwidth of a TPC connection. Group Policy can then use this information to make decisions regarding the settings that it should deliver based solely on the bandwidth available.

Group Policy also uses Network Location Awareness for background refreshes. Network Location Awareness indicates whether the computer has authenticated to a domain controller and whether the domain controller is available to the computer. This feature is important for computers that have failed to refresh Group Policy because the domain controller was not available. In the past, when Group Policy failed to apply, the computer would wait until the next refresh interval—90 to 120 minutes—to attempt to apply Group Policy. The domain controller might have been available only minutes after the failed refresh, but the system would wait the full refresh interval to apply the Group Policy updates. With Network Location Awareness, the Group Policy refresh occurs as soon as it detects the connection to the domain controller.

ADMX Templates

A change that surprised some, but was needed, was a new form of administrative template. The old ADM formatting was limiting in many ways, so a new format was developed. The new format, based on XML, has more flexibility and power than the old format. The new XML-based files have an .admx extension and have changed substantially from their predecessors. A sample of the new XML formatting is shown in Figure 2-4.

```
GroupPolicy.admx - Notepad                                              _ □ ×
File  Edit  Format  View  Help
<?xml version="1.0" encoding="utf-8"?>
<!--  (c) 2006 Microsoft Corporation  -->
<policyDefinitions xmlns:xsd="http://www.w3.org/2001/XMLSchema" xmlns:xsi="http://www.w
  <policyNamespaces>
    <target prefix="grouppolicy" namespace="Microsoft.Policies.GroupPolicy" />
    <using prefix="windows" namespace="Microsoft.Policies.Windows" />
  </policyNamespaces>
  <resources minRequiredRevision="1.0" />
  <categories>
    <category name="PolicyPolicies" displayName="$(string.PolicyPolicies)">
      <parentCategory ref="windows:System" />
    </category>
  </categories>
  <policies>
    <policy name="DisableLGPOProcessing" class="Machine" displayName="$(string.DisableL
      <parentCategory ref="PolicyPolicies" />
      <supportedOn ref="windows:SUPPORTED_WindowsVista" />
      <enabledValue>
        <decimal value="1" />
      </enabledValue>
      <disabledValue>
        <decimal value="0" />
      </disabledValue>
    </policy>
    <policy name="SyncWaitTime" class="Machine" displayName="$(string.SyncWaitTime)" ex
      <parentCategory ref="PolicyPolicies" />
```

Figure 2-4   The ADMX files are now based on XML for flexibility of language and ease of administration.

The XML formatting was adopted primarily for its language flexibility. ADM formatting did not translate into other languages, forcing other countries and languages to use English, which is not always feasible. During migration to the new format, the structure of the ADM files was radically enhanced also. With the ADM structure, all settings lived in five ADM files. Now there are 132 ADMX files that contain all of the administrative template policy settings. Figure 2-5 shows some of these policy settings.

Note   ADMX files, their structure, and additional details are described in Chapter 11, "Customizing ADM Templates and ADMX Files."

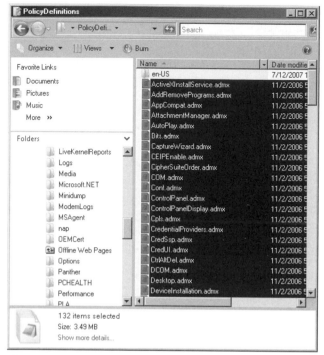

Figure 2-5   Now that the ADMX files are XML-based, 132 individual templates make up the Administrative Templates section of a GPO.

These new ADMX files reside by default on the local system drive of computers running Windows Vista and Windows Server 2008. The path to these ADMX files is %SystemRoot%\ PolicyDefinitions, which is usually the default C:\Windows folder that the operating system uses to store the system files.

ADMX Repository

In conjunction with the changes to the administrative template file structure and formatting, GPO administrators create and utilize the central store so that all ADMX files now reside in one location, instead of administrators spreading these files throughout the network on their local computers.

ADM templates were difficult to control and manage, which is one of the major reasons for the change. Another key reason involved how each GPO handled ADM templates. Every GPO that administrators created copied the entire set of default ADM templates into the location where GPO settings were maintained (referred to as the Group Policy template). The Group Policy template is located on domain controllers. Because there can be hundreds or thousands of GPOs, the space required to store these ADM templates was substantial. With each set of default ADM templates (coming in at a massive 4 MB of data) being stored on domain controllers, this could also add to replication traffic between domain controllers.

These negative aspects triggered the development of new technology for handling administrative template files. If an administrator does not create the repository, the local ADMX files will still be used to edit a GPO. This keeps the administration of GPOs consistent, even if the technology is not used. It should be noted, however, that the ADMX files are *not* stored in the Group Policy template. This change helps with storage of files on domain controllers, as well as the replication of those files between domain controllers.

> **Note**   ADM template management and the ADMX repository are described in detail in Chapter 10, "ADM Templates, ADMX Files, and the ADMX Central Store."

Improved Logging

It is no secret that managing logging and documentation has been a struggle for Group Policy over the years. Obtaining information from the old Event Log entries was a bit problematic. You needed to be an expert in Group Policy and Microsoft server technologies to get much from the logging that occurred in the Event Viewer. The other logs, such as Userenv.log, were better, but still not ideal.

All of this has changed with the latest installment of GPO logging. The changes are like many of the other changes: stunning and extraordinary. The new logging is built within the updated Event Log service that is available with Windows Vista. It disposes of Userenv.log and instead stores information in a Group Policy Operational log found in Event Viewer. You can find this log in Event Viewer by opening Applications and Services Logs and then browsing to Microsoft\Windows\GroupPolicy\Operational. The resulting log view is shown in Figure 2-6.

These new logs also provide specific new features that help with extraction of information. The logging technology provides for forwarding events to a central location; this is called *subscribing to an event*. Another benefit of the new log structure is the ability to filter views of specific events, making mining information from large log files more efficient.

There is much more to logging, as you will learn in Chapter 15, "Troubleshooting GPOs."

New Group Policy Features in Windows Server 2008

Windows Vista introduced many new features, but Windows Server 2008 offers a few more. These features allow for easier management and configuration of Group Policy settings and will change the way you work with Group Policy in Windows Server 2008.

Filters

If you have ever tried to decrypt the myriad settings in a GPO while trying to troubleshoot a problem, you know that it is a difficult task. There have been very few options for filtering the thousands of potential settings in a GPO, until now. Windows Server 2008 introduces an entire platform for searching and filtering the settings in a GPO. Of course, it includes the obvious search options, such as title text, explanation text, and comments, as shown in Figure 2-7.

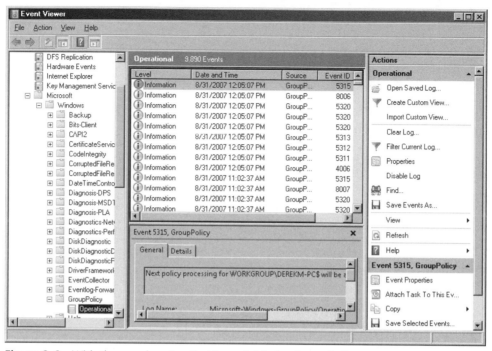

Figure 2-6 With the new logging that is available for Group Policy, new Group Policy events can be seen in the operational logs.

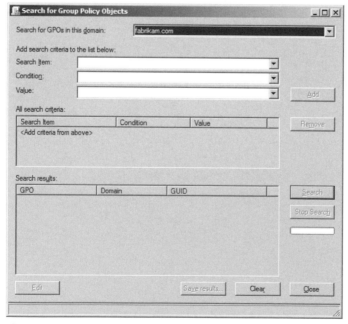

Figure 2-7 The new settings allow for basic searching and filtering of titles, explanation text, and comments within a GPO.

Additional options also allow you to search based on operating system platform support. With so many iterations of Group Policy, as discussed in Chapter 1, "Introduction to Group Policy," it is important to be able to identify which settings work on which operating system versions.

Another option for searching is based on the application and version supported. With the variety of versions of Microsoft Internet Explorer and Microsoft Office in use, it is important to know which versions the Group Policy settings will affect.

The filtering capability applies only to the Administrative Templates area in a GPO, the area that handles registry modifications. The filter can denote *managed* (policies) settings versus *unmanaged* (preferences) settings. These two types of registry settings make a difference when applied and controlled; it is nice to be able to search for settings by category. For more information about the differences between how registry settings are applied, see Chapter 10, "ADM Templates, ADMX Files, and the ADMX Central Store," and Chapter 13, "Settings Breakdown for Windows Server 2008 and Vista."

Finally, you can filter settings based on whether they are disabled or enabled. This is important when working with the new Group Policy Preferences settings. All of these configurations allow for the individual setting to either be enabled or disabled. The filter quickly allows you to see which settings in the GPO administrators have configured, which helps with both troubleshooting and management. Figure 2-8 illustrates how filtering settings based on their enabled or disabled status can make your administrative efforts more efficient.

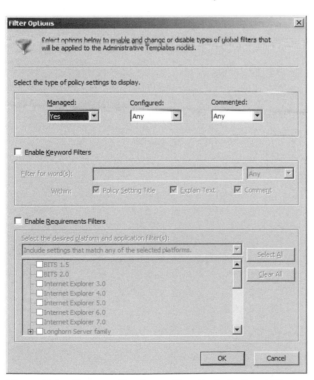

Figure 2-8   The new filtering options include the ability to search on enabled or disabled GPO settings.

Starter GPOs

You now have another tool in your toolkit if you are the lead GPO administrator or responsible for those who create GPOs in your environment. The new Starter GPOs provide an excellent way for you to create a baseline of settings within an off-line "Starter" GPO, which then can be copied to create a new GPO. The new GPO will contain all of the configurations and comments that were created in the Starter GPO.

The one small drawback to the use of Starter GPOs is that they can contain only Administrative Template settings. This is a bit limiting, but the ability to create a baseline of settings that can then be copied to create new GPOs is beneficial nonetheless. A sample Starter GPO is shown in Figure 2-9.

Figure 2-9   Starter GPOs allow you to configure any setting under the Administrative Templates section of a GPO.

> **Note**   If you want to create baseline GPOs that contain settings from any portion of a GPO, you can use AGPM. AGPM allows you to create GPO templates, which are in essence Starter GPOs that contain all areas of a GPO.

Another benefit of Starter GPOs is the ability to include them in your RSoP analysis. This gives you an inside look at the settings in the Starter GPO with regard to how they will interact with other GPOs that might have conflicting settings.

For more information on Starter GPOs, refer to Chapter 6, "GPMC Basics."

Commenting

Changes to Group Policy objects can have a significant impact on the computers in the environment. A single change to a Group Policy setting can affect all computers in your company. With such a powerful tool as Group Policy, some mechanism had to be developed to help maintain a documentation system for changes that occur to GPO settings.

One of those mechanisms is the ability to add comments to every GPO as a whole, as well as every GPO setting individually. This provides a more global and comprehensive way to track changes that occur to GPOs and their settings.

It is common for quick changes to occur to GPOs that are fixes to exploits on a computer that need to be deployed quickly. For example, an exploit might occur that an Internet Explorer setting or a custom registry entry fixes. Changes like these usually occur quickly and without any documented reasoning, and administrators who perform future audits or analysis are left wondering why the change occurred.

With commenting, all changes are tracked immediately when the modification to the GPO occurs. This provides a very detailed trail of the changes that occur to a GPO throughout its life cycle. Figure 2-10 shows some sample comments.

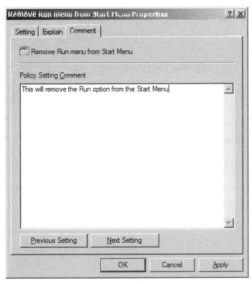

Figure 2-10   A GPO can include comments, allowing for administrators to document the changes that occur each time the GPO is altered.

Not all comments are created equal, though. The comments that are added to a new Starter GPO (at the GPO level) are not saved when a new GPO is created from that Starter GPO. The comments that are associated with the settings within the Starter GPO are copied and carried along to the new GPO.

The commenting mechanism is built this way to help senior administrators document information and details within the GPO for junior administrators who might use the Starter GPO to make a new GPO. Because the new GPO will carry along the settings configured in the Starter GPO, the comments associated with the settings go along with the GPO.

So, What About Those DesktopStandard Products?

In late 2006, Microsoft acquired many of the tools and employees from DesktopStandard. The acquisition was extremely valuable for the entire Group Policy landscape. The tools and products that DesktopStandard had to offer were leaders in the industry. These tools are now available in a variety of offerings by Microsoft.

Group Policy Preferences

Group Policy Preferences is scheduled for delivery to the market in early to mid-2008. This coincides with the release of Windows Server 2008, which Microsoft plans to release in early 2008.

For details about the technology and offerings that Group Policy Preferences will provide, read Chapter 12, "Group Policy Preferences," which is dedicated to Group Policy Preferences. However, there must be some introduction to Group Policy Preferences here, simply because it is a spectacular product that is coming with Windows Server 2008.

Group Policy Preferences will relate directly to the way in which standard Group Policy is managed and controlled. You will use the Group Policy Management Console, Group Policy Management Editor, and Advanced Group Policy Management, just like you do today. Group Policy Preferences contributes 22 client-side extensions to a GPO. These extensions include settings related to files, folders, user accounts, local groups, drive mappings, printer mappings, and much more.

Group Policy Preferences provide control over areas of a desktop and server that past Group Policy settings did not. The technology has been on the market for many years, and customers have loved what it can do for them. If Group Policy Preferences is something that could benefit you, Chapter 12 is where you should be looking now.

Advanced Group Policy Management (GPOVault)

The other product line that Microsoft acquired from DesktopStandard is Advanced Group Policy Management (AGPM). DesktopStandard called it GPOVault when they owned it.

Unlike the other Group Policy products and technologies, AGPM is offered through the Microsoft Desktop Optimization Pack (MDOP). MDOP is available only to those companies that have bought software assurance for desktops running Windows Vista. Software assurance provides 24-hour phone support, partner services, training, and IT tools for the life of the license. MDOP is an enormous package that offers a great value.

> **Note**   For more information on MDOP, refer to *http://www.microsoft.com/windows/products/windowsvista/enterprise/mdopoverview.mspx.*

AGPM itself brings tremendous value to the Group Policy management arena. Although Chapter 14, "Advanced GPO Management with AGPM," goes into the AGPM features and settings in full detail, the following is a list of benefits that AGPM can provide to your GPO management environment:

- Role-based delegation
- Roll back and roll forward to any GPO in the archive
- Off-line editing of GPOs
- Settings difference reports between two GPOs
- Workflow for GPO management tasks
- GPO templates for baseline configurations
- Built on GPMC
- Integrated change control for your Group Policy management environment

You can complete some of these tasks by using the GPMC and scripting, but AGPM performs these tasks seamlessly and automatically. AGPM is also a very lightweight installation, relying on a simple flat file structure and metadata to keep track of all of the changes within each GPO.

Summary

With every new operating system come new changes in every technology area. Group Policy is no different. Some exciting and amazing new technologies come with Windows Vista and Windows Server 2008. Windows Vista introduced some of these technologies, including local GPOs, Network Location Awareness, logging improvements, ADMX file format, and ADMX repository. New for Windows Server 2008 are many updates to GPMC, including searching, commenting, and filtering, as well as Group Policy Preferences technology. Last but not least is the new AGPM functionality, which makes management of Group Policy easier and more efficient.

Additional Resources

- The Microsoft Group Policy Web site, at *http://www.microsoft.com/grouppolicy*, includes more information on the new features and settings that are available in Windows Server 2008 and Windows Vista.

- The Microsoft TechNet article titled "Step-by-Step Guide to Managing Multiple Local Group Policy Objects," at *http://go.microsoft.com/fwlink/?LinkId=73759*, includes more information on multiple local Group Policy objects in Windows Vista.

- Chapter 14, "Advanced Group Policy Management with AGPM," includes information about installing AGPM, how to use AGPM, how to obtain AGPM, and the benefits of AGPM.

- Chapter 13, "Settings Breakdown for Windows Server 2008 and Windows Vista," includes information about specific settings within a GPO.

- Appendix A, "Third-Party Group Policy Tools," includes information about other companies that have extended Group Policy.

Chapter 3
Group Policy Basics

If you are new to Group Policy, it is important to receive a good introduction to the subject, especially with regard to Windows Server 2008 and Windows Vista. Group Policy can be a bit overwhelming and intimidating. However, with the right exposure and foundational concepts, Group Policy is not all that complex. This chapter will introduce some of the basic concepts of Group Policy to get you acquainted with the subject.

The goal of this chapter is to provide an overview of how Group Policy is structured so that you know what you are looking at when you get into the details. All GPOs have the same structure, so if you have seen one, you have essentially seem them all. After you understand the structure, you need only carry out the details of making the settings and performing the management of each GPO.

This chapter will also describe the two categories of GPOs that you have to work with: local GPOs and Active Directory–based GPOs. Now there are also three local GPOs that you can work with, so understanding each of them is important. The local GPOs provide flexibility for controlling the local desktop; before their introduction, it was very difficult to control different users logging on to the same desktop.

Beyond the local GPOs, some GPOs are configured and stored in Active Directory directory service. There are two of them in a default installation, and they are highly important to the Active Directory enterprise. These two default GPOs control security for domain controllers and the domain. Additional GPOs can be created, and they are in almost every Active Directory installation. These additional GPOs will help create and mold the desktop and security environment for servers, desktops, and users throughout the enterprise.

Group Policy Defined

Many technology terms can be confusing, especially when the terms are very similar to each other. Examples include Group Policy, Group Policy objects, policies, policy settings, and so on. An understanding of the Group Policy terminology will help when you are reading this book, as well as any other publication regarding Group Policy topics.

Group Policy is a technology that is built into Windows 2000 and later operating systems. Group Policy—broken down to the rawest form and definition—is defined as a mechanism for centralizing configurations for computers and user accounts.

Group Policy objects (GPOs) are "things" that are configured. These "things" will be defined in Chapter 4, "Architecture of Group Policy." For now, understand that Group Policy objects are the objects that the Group Policy technology uses to centralize the configurations. GPOs contain collections of policy settings, which the GPOs are in turn linked to Active Directory nodes (such as the domain, organizational units, or sites). The objects contained within the nodes receive the settings contained within the Group Policy Objects.

Policy settings are used in many different forms and definitions. Many administrators use policy settings to refer to any setting within a GPO. Others use the term to refer to those special settings in the registry that users do not have permission to modify. We will discuss this definition in more detail in Chapter 10, "ADM Templates, ADMX Files, and the ADMX Central Store."

Preference settings is a term that is not used often, but it is important. It is used in conjunction with the preceding term, policy settings. *Preferences* are registry settings that are not volatile. Preference settings "tattoo" the registry with settings. There is an entirely new section in a GPO within the Group Policy Management Editor that involves preferences, as shown in Figure 3-1.

Structural Overview of a GPO

Most administration of GPOs occurs with those that are stored in Active Directory. The local GPOs will be discussed later in this chapter; although these are important to an individual desktop, they will not be discussed here because they do not follow the "standard" GPO structure.

Active Directory–based GPOs use a common format and structure. First, all GPOs are accessed and administered in the same way. There are a few options here, but most use the Group Policy Management Console (GPMC) and the Group Policy Management Editor (GPME). For more information about the GPMC, refer to Chapter 6, "GPMC Basics," and Chapter 7, "Advanced GPMC Management," where al aspects of using and working with the GPMC are discussed. When you use the GPME, the GPO always has a distinct structure, shown in Figure 3-2.

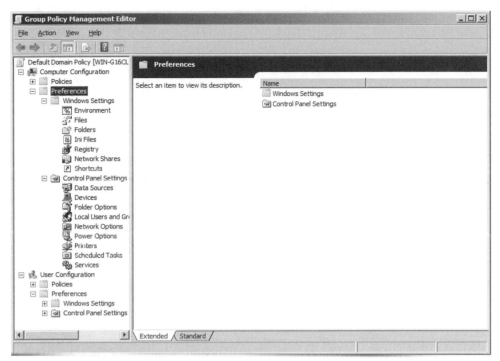

Figure 3-1   Windows Server 2008 GPOs have a new section in a GPO named *Preferences*.

Figure 3-2   A standard GPO opened in the GPME has the same format and structure as all GPOs stored in Active Directory.

Notice that there are two sections to the GPO: Computer Configuration and User Configuration. These sections are very important to keep separate, because they configure different object types. The Computer Configuration section controls computer accounts. In a like manner, the User Configuration section controls user accounts. Although a few settings fall under both sections, they do not cross the boundary of the two sections. If you have a setting that falls under both sections, and you want them both configured, you must configure both settings for users and computers to receive the settings.

Keep in mind that settings located under the Computer Configuration section apply to computer objects, regardless of the user. In a like manner, settings located under the User Configuration section apply to user objects, regardless of the computer.

Computer Configuration

Breaking down the two sections of the GPO reveals a very consistent structure that will help you get around in the GPO in the future. First, if you expand the Computer Configuration section, you will see the nodes shown in Figure 3-3.

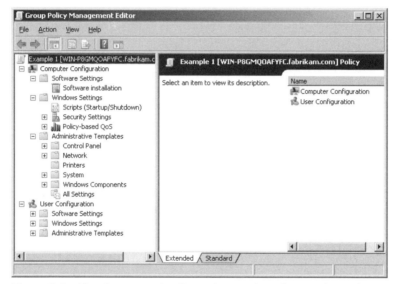

Figure 3-3   The Computer Configuration section of a GPO has a distinct structure that is similar to the User Configuration section.

Within this section, you have the following three primary nodes:

- Software Settings
- Windows Settings
- Administrative Templates

The Software Settings node is rather straightforward; it allows you to distribute software via .msi or .zap files.

The Windows Settings node goes a bit deeper, including many subnodes, as shown in Figure 3-4.

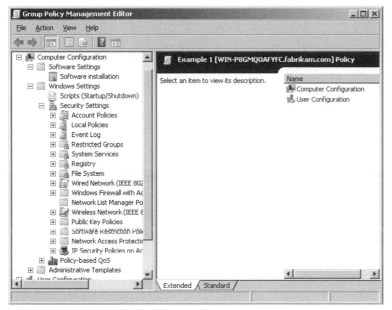

Figure 3-4   The major subnodes of the Windows Settings node include Scripts and Security Settings.

Within this section of the GPO, you have plenty of options to choose from. Account Policies control all aspects of user account passwords. Local Policies offer extensive control over auditing and user rights, as well as a variety of security settings. The security settings section alone includes over 75 individual policy settings.

Other settings include Windows Firewall, public key infrastructure (PKI), and IP security. In the Software Restriction Policies node, you can establish black lists and white lists of software that users can run. These policies can be set for hash rules, path rules, or certificate rules, as well as network zone rules. For more information on Group Policy settings, refer to Chapter 13, "Settings Breakdown for Windows Server 2008 and Windows Vista."

The Administrative Templates node is the final section of the Computer Configuration section, and the largest. This section covers a wide variety of settings for the computer, as shown in Figure 3-5.

Although there are only five major nodes within the Administrative Templates node, these nodes control over 1,250 individual settings. As you can see, the top-level nodes—including Control Panel, Network, Printers, System, and Windows Components—cover a wide range of areas for a computer. For more information about the settings available in a GPO, refer to Chapter 13, which covers the majority of the settings available in a GPO and includes references to documents that list all settings.

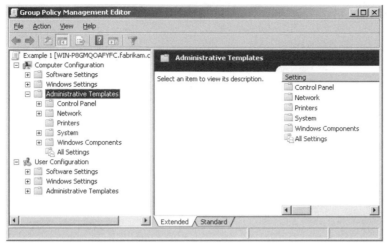

Figure 3-5   The Administrative Templates node within the Computer Configuration section contains several subnodes.

User Configuration

The User Configuration section is similar to the Computer Configuration section. The main difference is that the settings target user account settings, not computer account settings. If you expand the User Configuration section, as shown in Figure 3-6, you will see that there are three primary nodes:

- Software Settings
- Windows Settings
- Administrative Templates

As in the Computer Configuration section, you can create a policy in the User Configuration section that distributes software to user accounts. Both .msi and .zap files can be distributed using Group Policy.

The Windows Settings node within the User Configuration section is distinctly different from the Windows Settings node in the Computer Configuration section. Immediately you see that there are policies related to Remote Installation Services and Microsoft Internet Explorer maintenance. Expanding the Security Settings node shows that only public key policies are available, as shown in Figure 3-7.

The final node is Administrative Templates. With so few settings in the other two nodes, it is no surprise that this node contains the majority of the settings that fall under the User Configuration section of a GPO. After expanding this node, you will see that it contains more top-level nodes than the Computer Configuration section. Some of the subnodes are the same as in the Computer Configuration section, but many are different, as you can see in Figure 3-8.

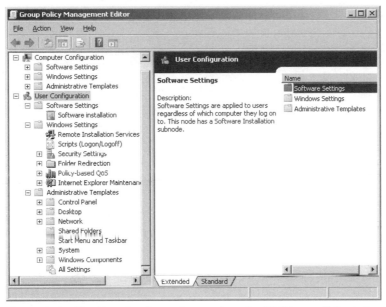

Figure 3-6 The User Configuration section of a GPO has a distinct structure that is similar to the Computer Configuration section.

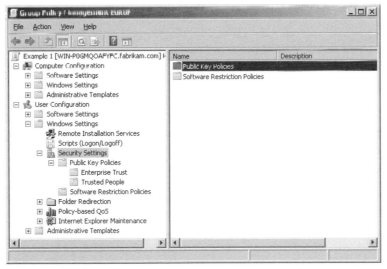

Figure 3-7 The Security Settings node of the User Configuration section of a GPO contains only Public Key Policies.

The settings in the Administrative Templates node are intended for controlling the user profile. The user profile maintains and controls the user desktop and overall "look and feel" of the desktop environment. Therefore, it is not surprising that this node contains nodes called Shared Folders and Start Menu and Taskbar.

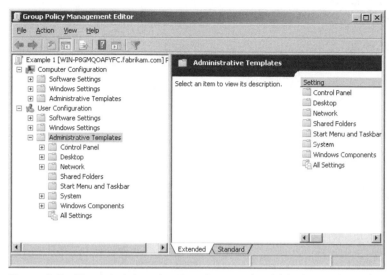

Figure 3-8   The Administrative Templates node within the User Configuration section of a GPO has more subnodes than it does in the Computer Configuration section.

Although some of the nodes exist within both the User Configuration and Computer Configuration sections, the settings could not be more different. This is because each section controls a different portion of the registry. The Administrative Templates node and subnodes in the User Configuration section contain over 1,200 policy settings—almost as many as in the Computer Configuration section.

Local GPOs

Windows Vista desktops and servers running Windows Server 2008 have three local GPOs. The addition of multiple local GPOs benefits anyone who has special computers in his or her company, as well as anyone who wants to configure a home or small business computer more easily.

The first of the three local GPOs is a generic one called the *Local Policy Object*. The second is really two GPOs, but only one of the two will apply to a user; the *Administrators GPO* applies to users in the local Administrators group, and the *Non-Administrators GPO* applies to any user outside of the local Administrators group. The third and final local GPO is not defined on the system by default. This local GPO is *user specific*, meaning it is associated with a local user account, after the local user account is created on the local desktop.

Accessing these local GPOs can be complex, and gaining a complete understanding of each control is not simple. The following sections examine each local GPO, describing how to access each one and discussing how each is designed to function.

Local Policy Object

This is the most generic of the three local GPOs. If you are familiar with earlier versions of GPOs, the basic premise of the Local Policy Object is identical to the original design of the local GPO for Windows 2000 or Windows XP Professional. This GPO should be used to include the generic settings that affect all users. Of the three local GPOs, it has the weakest precedence. Any settings in this GPO apply to all users who log on to the computer. Furthermore, if there is a conflicting setting with this GPO and any GPOs from Active Directory (or the other two local GPOs), this GPO will not take precedence for that setting.

To access this GPO, you use the Local Group Policy Editor. To access the Local Group Policy Editor, type **gpedit.msc** in the Run dialog box.

> **Note**   This is an administrative task; if you have User Account Control (UAC) enabled, you must agree to the permissions that opening the Local Group Policy Editor MMC snap-in requires.

The Local Group Policy Editor opens, exposing the Local Computer Policy, as shown in Figure 3-9.

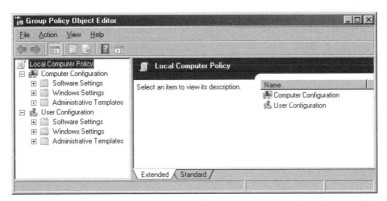

Figure 3-9   The Local Computer Policy can be opened in the Local Group Policy Editor by running gpedit.msc.

Note that this local GPO includes settings for both the computer and user accounts. This is not the case for all local GPOs. This GPO is used to configure all settings for the computer and user in a generic manner.

Administrators and Non-Administrators Local GPOs

One of the new local GPOs that comes with Windows Vista is not just one GPO, but two. Together, the Administrators and Non-Administrators local GPOs give you the ability to separate those users who are seen by the local desktop as administrators from standard users on the desktop.

This structure of local GPOs is ideal for both normal desktops and specialized desktops, such as kiosks, training room computers, and shared computers. The Administrators local GPO applies only to user accounts that have membership in the local Administrators group on the desktop. Because this group is controlled at the desktop level, each desktop can have a unique list of members. You use the Administrators Local GPO to override the Local Policy Object when the administrators need more privileges than other users and the Local Policy Object is too confining.

The Non-Administrators local GPO applies to all users who are not affected by the Administrators local GPO. By deduction, this includes all users who log on to the desktop who do not have membership in the local Administrators group. You use the Non-Administrators Local GPO to modify the Local Policy Object settings, or as an alternative to configuring the Local Policy Object.

Access to these local GPOs is not as simple as it is for the Local Policy Object. These GPOs are exposed by using the Microsoft Management Console (MMC). To access them for editing, follow these steps:

1. In the Run dialog box, type **MMC**.

> **Note**   This is an administrative task; if you have UAC enabled, you must agree to the permissions that opening the Local Group Policy Editor MMC snap-in requires.

2. In the MMC console, click File, and then click Add/Remove Snap-in.

3. Select Group Policy Management Editor from the Available Snap-ins list, and then click Add.

4. In the Welcome to the Group Policy Wizard page, leave Local Computer as the entry under Group Policy Object.

5. Click Browse.

6. In the Browse for a Group Policy Object dialog box, click the Users tab.

7. Select Administrators, and then click OK.

8. On the Welcome to the Group Policy Wizard page, click Finish.

9. In the Add/Remove Snap-ins dialog box, click OK.

10. In the console, expand the Local Computer\Administrators Policy node.

11. Repeat these steps for the Non-Administrators local GPO, replacing Non-Administrators with Administrators in the applicable steps.

Note that these two local GPOs have only User Configuration settings, not Computer Configuration settings, as shown in Figure 3-10. This is because a computer cannot have membership in the local Administrators group, so there is no way to differentiate between the two types of computers.

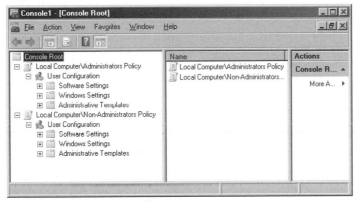

Figure 3-10   The Administrators local GPO and the Non-Administrators local GPO can be edited in the MMC; they offer control over User Configuration settings only.

Any settings that are configured in both the Local Policy Object and one of these Administrator GPOs are controlled by the Administrator-based GPO.

User-Specific Local GPOs

There are some instances in which you would like to have more precise control over the settings on a computer. This is not possible with the Local Policy Object, the Administrators GPO, or the Non-Administrators GPO. These GPOs are for "groups" of users, not specific users.

The final local GPO option is to specify a unique set of policy settings for a local user account. This is an ideal solution for controlling users logging on to kiosks or other specialized desktops throughout the enterprise. With user-specific local GPOs, you can create a custom environment that will allow for a more relaxed or more strict set of policy settings.

As with the Administrators local GPOs, access to user-specific GPOs requires the use of the MMC and involves several steps. Follow these steps to access the user-specific local GPOs:

1.   In the Run dialog box, type **MMC**.

> **Note**   This is an administrative task; if you have UAC enabled, you must agree to the permissions that opening the Local Group Policy Editor MMC snap-in requires.

2.   In the MMC console, click File, and then click Add/Remove Snap-in.

3.   Select Group Policy Management Editor from the Available Snap-ins list, and then click Add.

4. On the Welcome to the Group Policy Wizard page, leave Local Computer as the entry under Group Policy Object.

5. Click Browse.

6. In the Browse for a Group Policy Object dialog box, click the Users tab.

7. Select the desired user account from the list, and then click OK.

8. On the Welcome to the Group Policy Wizard page, click Finish.

9. In the Add/Remove Snap-ins dialog box, click OK.

10. In the console, expand the Local Computer\<username> Policy node.

As with the Administrators local GPOs, the user-specific local GPOs contain only User Configuration settings, as you can see in Figure 3-11.

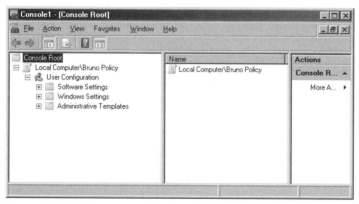

Figure 3-11   The user-specific local GPOs can be edited in the MMC; they offer control over User Configuration settings only.

> **Note**   It is essential to note that the only user accounts that can have a user-specific local GPO associated with them are those that have an account in the local Security Accounts Manager (SAM).

The user-specific local GPOs give you control over User Configuration settings, which is logical. Because these GPOs involve user accounts, it would not make sense for them to configure computer-related settings.

Precedence

If you review the local GPOs from the more generic to more specific, you will see the overall precedence structure. The most generic local GPOs have the weakest precedence, and the most specific local GPOs have the highest precedence. Table 3-1 lists the affected settings of each local GPO and their precedence in relation to local and Active Directory–based GPOs.

Table 3-1   Group Policy Object Settings and Precedence

Group Policy Object	Precedence	Settings in the GPO
Local Policy Object	6 (lowest precedence of all GPOs)	Computer Configuration User Configuration
Local Administrators and Non-Administrators GPO	5	User Configuration
User-specific local GPO	4 (highest precedence of all local GPOs)	User Configuration
GPO linked to Active Directory site	3 (lowest precedence of Active Directory GPOs)	Computer Configuration User Configuration
GPO linked to Active Directory domain	2	Computer Configuration User Configuration
GPO linked to Active Directory organizational unit	1 (highest precedence of all GPOs)	Computer Configuration User Configuration

Managing the Local GPOs

As stated earlier, only users who have membership in the local Administrators group can manage the local GPOs. This includes user from the local SAM or from Active Directory. In either case, if User Account Control (UAC) is enabled, the security dialog box from UAC will appear, forcing users with administrative privileges to agree to the privileges that opening the MMC snap-in requires.

Another new feature is the option to disable local GPOs. Through Active Directory–based GPOs, local GPOs can be disabled, and thus excluded from the evaluation of overall Resultant Set of Policy (RSoP). The policy that you would set is "Turn off Local Group Policy objects processing." This policy setting is located under Computer Configuration\Administrative Templates\System\Group Policy, as shown in Figure 3-12.

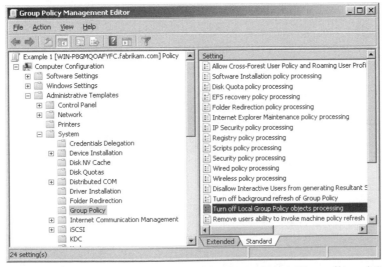

Figure 3-12   Local GPOs can be disabled by using the "Turn off Local Group Policy objects processing" setting in an Active Directory–based GPO.

GPOs in Active Directory

Although GPOs that are created in Active Directory can total into the hundreds or even thousands, they all follow the same regimen. To go a step beyond that, all GPOs in Active Directory are created, managed, and controlled through a central console. It is this centralization that gives Group Policy such power and control over the entire network of computers.

All GPOs that are stored in Active Directory have the same structure. You must use the GPMC to access one of these GPOs. Within the GPMC, you can expand the console to see the list of GPOs that are in Active Directory. To access this list, follow these steps:

1.   In the Run dialog box, type **gpmc.msc**.

2.   In the GPMC, expand the Forest and Domains nodes.

3.   In the Domains node, expand the Group Policy Objects node.

 Note   To run the GPMC, the computer must be a member of the domain. Also, if you are running the GPMC with Windows Server 2008, the GPMC is not installed by default and must be installed before it can be accessed. Refer to Chapter 6, "GPMC Basics," for more information regarding the GPMC.

You should see a list of GPOs, as shown in Figure 3-13.

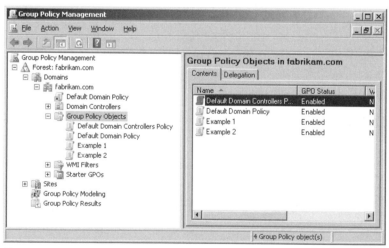

Figure 3-13   All of the GPOs that are stored in Active Directory can be seen by expanding the Group Policy node in the GPMC.

From this list, you can edit any of the GPOs to see the policy settings that are already set, or you can configure more settings. To edit a GPO, right-click it, and then click Edit. This launches the

Group Policy Management Editor with your selected GPO active in the interface, as shown in Figure 3-14.

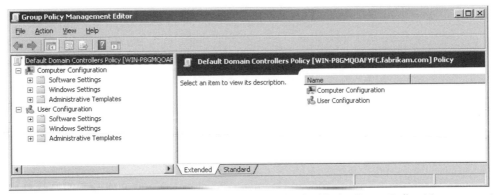

Figure 3-14   All Active Directory–based GPOs are edited with the Group Policy Management Editor.

All of the GPOs that are stored in Active Directory are available in this list through the GPMC. Note, however, that if you have multiple Active Directory domains, you will need to ensure that you are viewing the correct domain in the GPMC to see your GPO. GPOs are stored in only one domain. There is no mechanism to synchronize the settings between two GPOs in different domains.

For example, suppose that you wanted all domain controllers in all domains to have the same set of user rights. These settings would be established in the Default Domain Controllers Policy in each domain. If you made a configuration to the User Rights in DomainA, the Default Domain Controllers Policy in DomainB would not be updated. You would need to manually make this change in the DomainB GPO if you wanted the domain controllers in that domain to be updated.

After the creation and configuration of GPOs in Active Directory, one step remains before the GPO can perform any actions on computers or users on the network: you must link the GPO to an Active Directory node. Without this final linking step, the GPO is stored in Active Directory and on domain controllers, but it does not perform any action.

GPOs in Active Directory can be linked to the following nodes:

- Domain (for example, to the fabrikam.com node)
- Organizational Units
- Sites

It should be obvious that if a GPO is linked to the domain it will affect all computer and user accounts located in the domain by default. This is important to remember, because linking GPOs to the domain node or site nodes can potentially affect too many objects.

> **Important**   Most GPOs will be linked to organizational units. GPOs linked to the domain or sites can affect too many types of computer or user accounts. Some settings can be configured in a GPO linked to the domain, such as DNS suffix, password policies, account lockout policies, screen saver settings, and various Internet Explorer settings. Any settings that are set in the GPOs linked to sites are typically "network"-related settings. This might include firewall settings, proxy settings, Distributed File System (DFS), and software installation points.

The design and implementation of your organizational units is critical to a successful GPO deployment for two reasons: because the majority of GPOs in Active Directory will be linked to Organizational Units, and because there is only one organizational unit in a default installation of Active Directory.

> **More Info**   *Windows Server 2008 Active Directory Resource Kit* (Microsoft Press, 2008) covers this in great detail.

Default GPOs

When you install Active Directory, you are provided with the following two default GPOs:

- Default Domain Policy
- Default Domain Controllers Policy

These GPOs are extremely important, and they set up much of the security in a default installation of Active Directory. Their placement is also important, because they are precisely located within Active Directory to control certain aspects of domain controllers, servers, desktops, and even—indirectly—user accounts.

The inclusion of these two default GPOs is not new to Active Directory; they have been included since Windows 2000. However, there have been some slight changes to their settings over the years. With Windows Server 2008, the changes are slight and almost negligible. However, if you have never seen a dissection of these two default GPOs, it is vital that you know what they are configured to do.

> **Note**   If you want to add settings beyond what the Default Domain Policy or Default Domain Controllers Policy provide, it is a good idea to create new GPOs to implement these new settings. The default GPOs are very important and contain essential baseline information and settings. If the default GPOs ever need to be recovered, the new settings that you place in them might be lost.

Default Domain Policy

The Default Domain Policy is included for one primary reason, with some secondary reasons. The primary reason that the Default Domain Policy is included in Active Directory by default is to establish the Account Policies settings. The Account Policies settings control how user account passwords are defined in Active Directory, as well as in every SAM on every computer that joins the domain. Some of the many secondary reasons for the existence of the Default Domain Policy include autoenrollment settings for PKI, control of Encrypting File System (EFS), establishment of a company-wide screen saver lockout policy, and more.

Account Policies in the Default Domain Policy

From a security standpoint, one of the most important aspects of protecting the network is ensuring that user accounts have complex and secure passwords. The definition of complex and secure might not be the same everywhere, but there must be some form of baseline security regarding passwords on the network. The Default Domain Policy is responsible for defining that for a new Active Directory installation.

The question of where you can set user account password restrictions for an Active Directory domain has caused some confusion. The short answer is that you can establish password policies for domain user accounts in a GPO linked to the domain. By default, this is the Default Domain Policy. If you want to create a different set of password policies not in the Default Domain Policy, you can create a new GPO, configure your settings, link the GPO to the domain node, and then ensure that this GPO has higher precedence than the Default Domain Policy. For more information about how to modify GPO precedence, refer to Chapter 5, "Group Policy Processing," which covers all forms of precedence and inheritance with GPOs in the GPMC.

Here are some other restrictions regarding password policies within a GPO to control domain user account password restrictions:

- GPOs linked to organizational units will not affect the user accounts that are located in the organizational unit.

- There is no way to configure a single GPO containing Account Policies settings to control multiple domains.

How It Works: Account Policies

The Account Policies within the GPOs that control domain user account passwords can be a bit confusing. However, when you understand how they work and the technology behind the settings, it will make much more sense. Some of the confusion involves where these Account Policies can be configured to control domain user account passwords. The answer is simple: in a GPO at the domain level only. The settings do not need to reside in the Default Domain Policy, but they must be in a GPO that is linked to the domain.

Another point of confusion results from the desire to configure the Account Policies within a GPO that is linked to an Organizational Unit, expecting these settings to affect the user accounts that reside in the Organizational Unit. This will not work! If you look at the location of the Account Policies within the GPO, you will see that they are not User Configuration settings. Rather, these settings are under Computer Configuration, so they affect computer accounts only, not user accounts.

The user account does not control the password; the *location* where the user account is stored controls the password. For a domain, this is domain controllers and Active Directory. For desktops and servers, this is the local SAM. Thus, the Account Policies must affect computer accounts, because the user accounts and their passwords are stored on computers.

A final point of confusion involves administrators of large or complex organizations attempting to have a single set of Account Policies control all of their domains and the user accounts in them. This is also not possible. The Account Policies, and Group Policy in general, are domain centric. (GPOs linked to sites can span domains, but the GPO is still stored in only one domain.) There is no technology built into Windows that allows you to configure a single set of Account Policies that will span multiple domains.

Account Policies are divided into three sections within a GPO: Password Policy, Account Lockout Policy, and Kerberos Policy. These are shown in Figure 3-15.

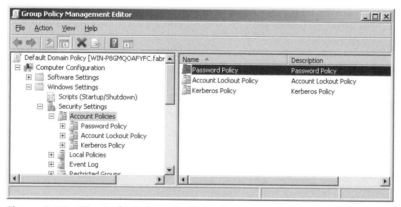

Figure 3-15   The Default Domain Policy is responsible for establishing the default Account Policies for the domain user accounts and all user accounts located on computers that join the domain.

Each of these sections provides options for controlling all areas of the user account password. Table 3-2 lists all of the possible policy settings that can be configured within these three sections.

Table 3-2 Default Domain Policy Default Account Policy Settings

Computer Configuration	Policy Setting	Default Value
Windows Settings \Security Settings \Account Policies \Password Policy	Enforce Password History	24 passwords remembered
	Maximum Password Age	42 days
	Minimum Password Age	1 days
	Minimum Password Length	7 characters
	Password must meet complexity requirements	Enabled
	Store passwords using reversible encryption	Disabled
Windows Settings \Security Settings \Account Policies \Account Lockout Policy	Account lockout duration	Not defined
	Account lockout threshold	0 invalid log-on attempts
	Reset account lockout counter after	Not defined
Windows Settings \Security Settings \Account Policies \Kerberos Policy	Enforce user log on restrictions	Enabled
	Maximum lifetime for service ticket	600 minutes
	Maximum lifetime for user ticket	10 hours
	Maximum lifetime for user ticket renewal	7 days
	Maximum tolerance for computer clock synchronization	5 minutes

Other Policy Settings in the Default Domain Policy

Still more default policies are set in the Default Domain Policy. The majority of the remaining settings are located within Computer Configuration\Windows Settings\Security Settings, as shown in Figure 3-16. These settings exist mainly to control the Public Key Infrastructure environment as a baseline.

The User Configuration section contains a few other settings, which control some of the options for using Remote Installation Services (RIS). Table 3-3 provides a full list of all Default Domain Policy settings outside of the Account Policies.

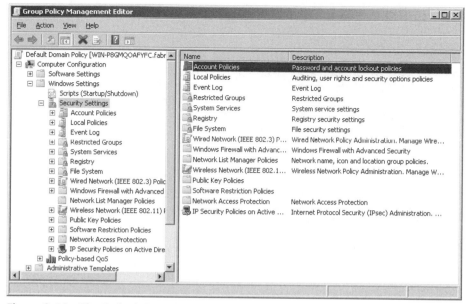

Figure 3-16   The Default Domain Policy configures some important security settings for all computers that join the domain.

Table 3-3   Default Domain Policy Default Configurations and Values

Computer Configuration	Policy Setting	Value
Windows Settings \Security Settings \Local Polices\Security Options	Network access: Allow anonymous SID/ Name translation	Disabled
	Network security: Do not store LAN Manager hash value on next password change	Enabled
	Network security: Force logoff when log-on hours expire	Disabled
Windows Settings \Security Settings \Public Key Policies \Encrypting File System	<Certificates>	Administrator is configured for File Recovery

Default Domain Controllers Policy

The Default Domain Controllers Policy is extremely important for establishing the default security on domain controllers. Windows stand-alone and member servers are not secured as thoroughly as domain controllers, because they need to have more backward compatibility with applications and services that might be running on them. Domain controllers need to be secured more tightly, and the Default Domain Controllers Policy is responsible for making those configurations. Figure 3-17 shows some of the settings in the Default Domain Controllers Policy.

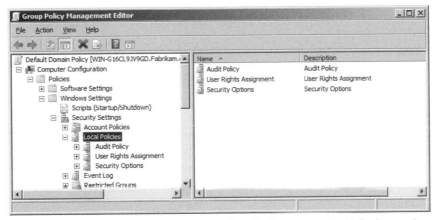

Figure 3-17   The Default Domain Controllers Policy creates the default security for all domain controllers that come into the domain.

Three main areas have settings within the Default Domain Controllers Policy. The first establishes the audit policies for the domain controllers. These settings ensure that the domain controllers are logging to the security event logs essential actions that occur. The second area is related to the user rights for the domain controllers. User rights establish which users can perform certain tasks on the computer. Because domain controllers need to be protected, the Default Domain Controllers Policy defines the user rights to create a baseline of security. Finally, some policies are defined to control network communication. The majority of these control whether data and communication will be digitally signed to increase security of the communication. One policy deals with the authentication protocols that the domain controllers will allow.

Table 3-4 lists all Default Domain Controllers Policy settings that are established by default. Note that user rights that are not filled in are either not defined or defined but left empty.

Table 3-4   Default Domain Controllers Policy Default Configurations and Values

Computer Configuration	Policy Setting	Value
Windows Settings\Security Settings\Local Policies \User Rights Assignment	Access this computer from the network	Administrators
		Authenticated Users
		ENTERPRISE DOMAIN CONTROLLERS
		Everyone
		Pre-Windows 2000 Compatible Access
	Add workstations to the domain	Authenticated Users

Table 3-4   **Default Domain Controllers Policy Default Configurations and Values**

Computer Configuration	Policy Setting	Value
	Adjust memory quotas for a process	Administrators
		LOCAL SERVICE
		NETWORK SERVICE
	Allow logon locally	Account Operators
		Administrators
		Backup Operators
		Print Operators
		Server Operators
	Back up files and directories	Administrators
		Backup Operators
		Server Operators
	Bypass traverse checking	Pre-Windows 2000 Compatible Access
		Authenticated Users
		Administrators
		NETWORK SERVICE
		LOCAL SERVICE
		Everyone
	Change the system time	Administrators
		Server Operators
		LOCAL SERVICE
	Create a pagefile	Administrators
	Debug programs	Administrators
	Enable computer and user accounts to be trusted for delegation	Administrators
	Force shutdown from a remote system	Administrators
		Server Operators
	Generate security audits	LOCAL SERVICE
		NETWORK SERVICE
	Increase scheduling priority	Administrators
	Load and unload device drivers	Administrators
		Print Operators
	Log on as a batch job	Performance Log Users
		Backup Operators
	Manage auditing and security log	Administrators
	Modify firmware environment variables	Administrators

Table 3-4   Default Domain Controllers Policy Default Configurations and Values

Computer Configuration	Policy Setting	Value
	Profile single process	Administrators
	Profile system performance	Administrators
	Remove computer from docking station	Administrators
	Replace a process level token	LOCAL SERVICE NETWORK SERVICE
	Restore files and directories	Administrators Backup Operators Server Operators
	Shut down the system	Administrators Backup Operators Print Operators Server Operators
	Take ownership of files or other objects	Administrators
Windows Settings\Security Settings\Local Policies\Local Polices\Security Options	Domain controller: LDAP server signing requirements	None
	Domain member: Digitally encrypt or sign secure channel data (always)	Enabled
	Microsoft network server: Digitally sign communications (always)	Enabled
	Microsoft network server: Digitally sign communications (if client agrees)	Enabled
	Network security: LAN Manager authentication level	Send NTLMv2 response only

Creating Additional GPOs

If you are reading this book, there is no doubt that you will be creating additional GPOs. The two GPOs that you get with Active Directory are good and effective, but you will need to create additional GPOs to control all aspects of desktops, servers, and users on the network.

Many ask the question, "How many GPOs can I create?" The question has not been answered in a production environment to date. Some companies have 3,000, some 4,000, and a few have over 5,000 GPOs in their production environments. These are very large implementations of Group Policy and by no means typical. In most cases, companies have between 100 and 500 production GPOs to control all areas of their environments.

Adding GPOs is very simple with the easy interface provided by the GPMC. When you add GPOs, it is important to know where they should be linked and what settings will be configured within them. Beyond that, the creation and implementation process is straightforward.

Privileges for Creating New GPOs

The first thing you will need before you create any new GPOs is privileges. By default, only members of the Domain Admins group have the privileges necessary to create new GPOs. This can and should be altered.

The GPMC provides a simple way to delegate the creation of GPOs to others beyond the Domain Admins group members. The reason you would want to do this is that some users who should have the privilege to create new GPOs might not need all of the privileges that a Domain Admin has. If someone should have all of the privileges of a Domain Admin and should be able to create GPOs, then you should certainly add them to the group. Otherwise, adding them to a group that has only delegated privileges to create GPOs is a better solution. For more information on delegation, refer to Chapter 9, "Security Delegation for Administration of GPOs," which covers the best practices and technology for securing administration of GPOs.

For example, you might have an administrator who is responsible for desktops. This administrator should be able to create and modify GPOs that will control and configure the desktops properly. This administrator should not be able to modify group membership or delete computer accounts from Active Directory. If such an administrator were to be added to the Domain Admins group, he or she would have these other capabilities.

Note   It is always ideal to separate duties for administrators. Delegation options exist that allow administrators to create a GPO, but not link it to a node in Active Directory. Although such administrators can do all of the setup and creation work, they cannot implement the settings without assistance from another administrator who has been granted the link delegation. For more information on delegation, refer to Chapter 9, which covers the best practices and technology for securing administration of GPOs.

Creating GPOs Correctly

The creation of a GPO is not especially difficult. Essentially, creating a GPO involves just right-clicking New. However, to make sure that you do not cause damage to the network and computers, caution should be taken when creating and configuring new GPOs. Like anything, there is a right way and a not-so-right way.

Initially, you must know exactly what the GPO will do, and you should also have considered which objects it should affect. If you have not carefully considered what the GPO will do, you are not ready to create a GPO. However, if you do know what you want the GPO to do, you can get started without knowing exactly which objects the GPO should affect.

This is possible because you can create a GPO that is not linked to any Active Directory node. In addition, if you feel the need to be especially cautious, you can also disable the GPO. To create a GPO that is not linked to a node, follow these steps:

1. In the Run dialog box, type **gpmc.msc**, and then click OK.

2. In the GPMC, expand the Forest and Domains nodes, and then expand the *<domain name>* node.

3. Right-click the Group Policy Objects node, and then click New.

4. In the New GPO dialog box, type a new name for the GPO, such as **test**, and then click OK.

> **Security Alert**   If the user attempting to create the GPO does not have the necessary privileges to do so, the New menu option will be dimmed. To read more about setting up this delegation, refer to Chapter 9, "Security Delegation for Administration of GPOs."

This will create a new GPO that is not linked to any node in Active Directory. You can consider this GPO as existing in Active Directory, but as inactive because it does not affect any objects. If you want to disable this GPO for extra assurance that it will not affect any object, follow these steps:

1. Find and select the GPO that you want to disable under the Group Policy Objects node in the GPMC.

2. On the Details tab, click the GPO Status list.

3. Click All Settings Disabled.

This is now a new GPO that is not linked to any node, has all settings disabled, and has no configured settings at all. This is a very safe and secure GPO!

When you know which objects you want your GPO to affect, you can link your GPO to the proper Active Directory node. Follow these steps to link your GPO to an Organizational Unit:

1. Under the *<domain name>* node in the GPMC, right-click the organizational unit that you want to link, and then click Link An Existing GPO.

2. In the Select GPO dialog box, select the GPO that will be linked from the Group Policy Objects list box.

> **Security Alert**   If the user attempting to Link the GPO to this Active Directory node does not have the necessary privileges to do so, the Link An Existing GPO menu option will be dimmed. To read more about setting up this delegation, refer to Chapter 9, "Security Delegation for Administration of GPOs."

At this point, nothing will happen as a result of linking the GPO. However, after a setting is made and the GPO is enabled, the GPO setting will apply to the target objects on the next background refresh of Group Policy.

> **Note**   You could also combine the creation and linking of a GPO into one step. This would be accomplished by right-clicking the appropriate Active Directory node to create the GPO, instead of the Group Policy Objects node. After doing this, you would see an option to "Create and Link a GPO Here."

Summary

With any technology, understanding the foundational concepts can help you understand the rest of the technology. Group Policy is no different, and this chapter defined the basic concepts of Group Policy. Group Policy has many components, and some of the technical terms can be confusing. Here, you received definitions and examples of these terms, as well as a clear view of the structure of a GPO. This information will be invaluable as you begin to implement settings in a GPO that has over 2,500 individual settings.

You will work with three local GPOs and as many GPOs within Active Directory as you want to deal with. In the end, you will likely have more GPOs than you want to manage. You will use two default GPOs to establish security for domain controllers, member servers, desktops, and network communications. You can create additional GPOs within Active Directory, provided that you have the correct privileges.

Additional Resources

- The Microsoft Group Policy Web site, at *http://www.microsoft.com/grouppolicy*, includes more information about local GPOs.

- Chapter 4, "Architecture of Group Policy," includes information about how GPOs are stored and managed.

- Chapter 9, "Security Delegation for Administration of GPOs," includes details about how to establish a best practice delegation model for administering GPOs.

- Chapter 10, "ADM Templates, ADMX Files, and the ADMX Central Store," includes information about registry-based settings in a GPO.

- Chapter 13, "Settings Breakdown for Windows Server 2008 and Windows Vista," covers the majority of the settings available in a GPO and includes references to documents that list all settings.

- *Windows Server 2008 Active Directory Resource Kit* (Microsoft Press, 2008), by Stan Reimer, Mike Mulcare, Conoan Kezema, and Byron Wright covers implementation, tool, and management of Group Policy with Acitve Directory.

Part II
Group Policy Structure

Chapter 4
Architecture of Group Policy

Like most technology, Group Policy is very logical and predictable. The structure of Group Policy has not changed much over the years, although some of the internal mechanisms have. Because Group Policy is such a stable and reliable technology, there has been no need for major changes.

With that said, there have been some radical changes to the underlying implementation of Group Policy with Windows Vista and Windows Server 2008. Although the core dependencies have not changed, the core engine of Group Policy has changed for the better. There is now a dedicated service for Group Policy, which gives Group Policy even more stability and efficiency.

Administration of your domain-based GPOs has not changed, either. The Group Policy Object Editor is now called the Group Policy Management Editor (GPME), but its functions and those of the Group Policy Management Console (GPMC) remain the same. The core architecture for updating domain-basedGPOs is important to understand and manage, as it has always been.

Understanding the storage of Group Policy in terms of the Group Policy template (GPT) and the Group Policy container (GPC) is critical to efficient management of the GPOs, ADM files, replication, and troubleshooting. Of course, the biggest change that Windows Vista and Windows Server 2008 offer with regard to architecture is the addition of ADMX templates and the central repository.

An architecture overview cannot be complete without a rigorous discussion on replication. Replication for Group Policy is not simple, but a good summary of the subject will help you tackle most problems that arise. Replication and Group Policy are important concepts to understand when you need to troubleshoot an issue.

Finally, this chapter will review the architecture of client-side extensions (CSEs). CSEs are the soul of Group Policy settings. You will get an inside glimpse into the different CSEs, what they do, and how they function with the information provided by the GPT and the GPC.

Group Policy Dependencies

Although Group Policy is a large and complicated service and technology, it also relies heavily on other complicated services and technologies. You must understand these other services and technologies to fully understand Group Policy, especially when you encounter trouble. Understanding Group Policy's dependencies will help you pinpoint the source of the problem, whether it be Group Policy or one of these services.

The services and technologies that Group Policy has direct dependencies on include the following:

- Active Directory
- Domain Name System (DNS)
- Active Directory replication
- Distributed File System Replication (DFSR)—formerly File Replication Service (FRS)
- DFS publishing
- Network Location Awareness (NLA)

As you can see from the preceding list, the services and technologies that Group Policy depends on are extremely important, not only to Group Policy, but to your network as a whole. Without these services and technologies, you would not have a fully functional enterprise.

Each of these services and technologies is responsible for a specific aspect of Group Policy. Understanding how each component fits into the bigger picture will help you with design, implementation, management, and troubleshooting of Group Policy.

Active Directory and Group Policy

Active Directory has the biggest role as a dependent technology with Group Policy. Most certainly, without Active Directory you would not have much of a Group Policy infrastructure to work with. Active Directory provides the foundation upon which Group Policy is embedded.

First, consider that Active Directory houses all of the user and computer objects for the domain or domains. It is these user and computer objects that Group Policy controls. Next, Active Directory creates the structure that the objects are placed within. The structure is made up of organizational units. The design of the organizational units is essential in the deployment of Group Policy—the user and computer objects located within the organizational unit where the GPO is linked, as well as those in child organizational units, are affected by the settings in the linked GPO by default.

Important A poorly designed Active Directory structure can make it very difficult to deploy Group Policy. It is always best to design Group Policy deployment into the initial Active Directory design. If the Active Directory design is too chaotic or disorganized, it might need to be completely redesigned before Group Policy can be correctly deployed.

A well designed Active Directory structure considers the user and computer object location within the organizational units. Because GPOs are linked primarily to organizational units, ensuring that the links are easy and efficient will help with the overall success and good design of Active Directory.

Note Active Directory should be designed to incorporate two important components: Group Policy and delegation of administration should be the two driving factors for your Active Directory design. As a best practice, delegation of administration should have the highest priority, because Group Policy can be filtered to apply to only certain objects in an organization unit.

GPOs can be linked to three Active Directory components. These include the domain, organization units, and sites. If Active Directory did not contain these components, GPOs would not be able to link to them.

As a side benefit, Active Directory allows for single sign-on for user accounts, which Group Policy can leverage because each user is unique within the Active Directory domain. Because each user is unique, administrators can mold and deploy the precise security settings, desktop settings, registry values, and profile environment for each user.

Note Local Group Policy objects can still be used without Active Directory, in a small business or home office environment, for example. In such cases, the Local Group Policy objects must be administered on each computer separately.

Domain Name System

You probably already know what the Domain Name System (DNS) is, but as a reminder, DNS is a distributed database that resolves DNS host names to Internet Protocol (IP) addresses. In Active Directory, DNS is the locator service that enables computers to find other computers, as well as important networking services.

For Active Directory networks, DNS has entries called Service Resource Records (SRVs) that are associated with different networking services. These include entries for Lightweight Directory Access Protocol (LDAP), Transmission Control Protocol (TCP), and Kerberos. These SRVs help computers in the Active Directory domain find the servers that are functioning as domain controllers. At a domain controller, they might get a listing of Group Policy Objects, update their Kerberos ticket, find a resource, and so on. When DNS is not working properly or is misconfigured, computers will not be able to use DNS to find this information. At this point, Group Policy will fail to work properly; all updates and refreshes will cease until DNS is functioning properly again.

DNS is also used for Distributed File System (DFS). DFS can be used within Group Policy to share applications or other resources. When a GPO is configured to direct a desktop or user to a DFS distribution point for accessing software, the computer must use DNS to find these installation points. If DNS is not configured properly, the computer will never find the DFS distribution point and the software will not be installed or updated.

Finally, DNS is important for managing Group Policy. As you will see later in this chapter, domain controllers are the computers that store GPOs. Therefore, when you are managing a GPO, a domain controller must be contacted. If DNS is not functioning properly, a domain controller cannot be found and an error will occur when trying to update or view a GPO.

From the Source: Group Policy Dependency on DNS

Here's the simplest explanation I found for why Group Policy depends on DNS. As stated earlier, Group Policy queries Active Directory for information about GPOs, user and computer locations, security groups, and other information needed for processing Group Policy. A TechNet article on DNS integration (*http://technet2.microsoft.com /WindowsServer/en/library/2c6fde55-8d99-4c2d-9f38-95d6446ebdb51033.mspx*) states, "Active Directory provides an information repository and services to make information available to users and applications. Active Directory clients send queries to domain controllers using the Lightweight Directory Access Protocol (LDAP). In order to locate a domain controller, an Active Directory client queries DNS. Active Directory requires DNS to function." There are instances in which Group Policy uses a fully qualified domain name (FQDN) for its naming, but when you are attempting to bind to a domain, the domain controller must be located, which requires a functioning DNS.

Judith Herman, Programming Writer

Microsoft

Replication

One of the more significant tasks of Group Policy is to ensure that each GPO is synchronized with each domain controller. Domain controllers are the command center of GPO distribution. As you will see a little later in this chapter, a GPO is not just a single entity. It is really made up of two separate parts: the Group Policy template (GPT), which is stored in the SYSVOL of each domain controller, and the Group Policy container (GPC), which is stored in Active Directory, again on each domain controller.

Both portions of the GPO must be replicated to every domain controller within the domain. If the GPOs do not synchronize to all domain controllers after a change is made, strange behavior will occur. This behavior might include differing settings on two desktops that should have the same settings, errant settings on a server caused by a missing GPO setting, failure to apply policy altogether, or a desktop that is not secure because of a failure of the GPO to replicate.

As you can see, replication is a significant factor for Group Policy. There is a small concern with Group Policy replication, however. The GPO is made up of two different parts, but the SYSVOL replication and the Active Directory replication are not driven or supported by the same replication technology.

SYSVOL replication is controlled by either the Distributed File System Replication (DFSR) or the File Replication Service (FRS), depending on the domain functional level. Domain controllers running Windows 2000 or Microsoft Windows Server 2003 cannot take advantage of DFSR for replication of the SYSVOL, so they must still use FRS. Windows Server 2008 does support DFSR for SYSVOL replication, but all domain controllers must be running Windows Server 2008 to take advantage of this new technology. If any domain controllers in the domain are running Windows 2000 or Windows Server 2003, the Windows Server 2008 domain controllers must also use FRS to support the limitations of the older operating systems.

Active Directory replication is not controlled by DFSR or FRS. Instead, Active Directory replication is controlled by its own replication service. Active Directory replication is responsible for replicating the entire Active Directory database, not just the GPC. Because changes occur with the other objects in the database more than the GPC, the technology and details of replication were designed for those other objects more so than for Group Policy. With this said, the replication of Active Directory is quite complex, with many moving parts and considerations. Later in this chapter, an in-depth overview of Active Directory replication will explain how it affects and controls the GPC.

DFS

Another service that Group Policy depends on is DFS. You might miss this service unless you consider how DFS assists Group Policy in many different areas. If you think that DFS publishing can assist Group Policy when software is delivered through a GPO, you are correct. However, Group Policy does not *depend* on this service in this regard—DFS is simply an enabling service in this scenario.

So, how exactly does DFS function with Group Policy as a dependant service? DFS is the service that makes the SYSVOL on the domain controllers available. Every domain controller has the SYSVOL shared. There are two folders named SYSVOL, and only one of them is shared. The path to the shared SYSVOL is C:\Windows\SYSVOL\Sysvol.

This share is not a routine share. Rather, it is a domain-based DFS share. This type of share is very useful in situations in which all computers in the domain need to access the same resource. If you are not familiar with domain-based DFS, it has some significant advantages.

With domain-based DFS shares, all computers access the share by using the domain name, instead of the domain controller's NetBIOS computer name or DNS fully qualified domain name (FQDN). Therefore, all computers that communicate with SYSVOL on the domain controllers (every computer in the domain) do so by using *domainname*\sysvol.

Although this might seem simplistic and limited in rewards, the power is in the technology behind the scenes. With this form of communication to the domain controller and SYSVOL, the names of the domain controllers are irrelevant. Domain controllers can be added, removed, changed, taken offline, brought back online, and so on without the existing connections and mapped drives. As long as there is at least one domain controller online for the computers to access, the computers on the network will be able to communicate with the domain-based DFS share.

This is possible because domain-based DFS shares are accessed through DNS. SRV records that help the computer find the nearest domain controller are automatically registered in DNS. The nearest domain controller is relative, because DNS uses Active Directory sites, which represent physical networks. When a computer receives a list of domain controllers from DNS, the domain controllers in the computers' sites are listed first, followed by the other domain controllers.

This process and technology allows computers to receive the GPT information for the GPOs from the domain controllers. The process is very efficient for both keeping track of the domain controllers and allowing the computers on the network to find the closest domain controller to retrieve the Group Policy information from SYSVOL.

New Group Policy Service

One of the major changes that came with Windows Vista and is now being leveraged in Windows Server 2008 is a new Group Policy service. Earlier operating systems used the WinLogon service to run Group Policy. There were no inherent problems with using WinLogon, but there are significant benefits to using a separate service to control Group Policy. Considering the emphasis that Microsoft is putting into Group Policy, with advanced technologies being included in Group Policy and new management tools, the move to a separate service was not surprising.

The new Group Policy service improves the overall stability of the Group Policy infrastructure and computer by completely isolating it from WinLogon. The Group Policy service uses a completely new architecture for performing notifications and processing Group Policy. Not only does the Group Policy service change the architecture, it also adds these benefits:

- New Group Policy–related files can be delivered to computers administrating GPOs and computers consuming GPO settings without requiring a restart of the operating system.

- Group Policy application is more efficient because fewer resources are required for background processing.

- Less memory is used for Group Policy on computers consuming GPO settings, increasing performance and eliminating the need to load Group Policy in multiple services.

- The Group Policy service is started automatically and cannot be disabled, which creates a more stable environment.

To find the service in running services, look for gpsvc, as shown in Figure 4-1.

```
Administrator: Command Prompt                                             _ |□| x|

C:\Users\Administrator>sc query gpsvc

SERVICE_NAME: gpsvc
        TYPE               : 20  WIN32_SHARE_PROCESS
        STATE              : 4   RUNNING
                                 (STOPPABLE, NOT_PAUSABLE, IGNORES_SHUTDOWN)
        WIN32_EXIT_CODE    : 0   (0x0)
        SERVICE_EXIT_CODE  : 0   (0x0)
        CHECKPOINT         : 0x0
        WAIT_HINT          : 0x0

C:\Users\Administrator>
```

Figure 4-1   The new Group Policy service runs as gpsvc and can be seen in a list of running services on a computer running Windows Vista or Windows Server 2008.

Domain Controller Selection During GPO Management

Consider a typical Active Directory environment that has multiple domain controllers. As you have seen, all domain controllers house a copy of each GPO. The replication of the GPOs is handled by the two replication technologies: DFSR and Active Directory replication. But which domain controller makes the initial changes to the GPOs?

The answer is quite simple. The domain controller that has the PDC emulator role is relied upon to make the changes to a GPO. Then this domain controller replicates the changes to the other domain controllers.

> **Note**   As a reminder, the first domain controller in each domain controls all three of the domain operation masters: PDC emulator, RID master, and infrastructure master.

In some instances, you either cannot or do not want to use the domain controller that has the PDC emulator role to make the initial changes, and you may want to use another domain controller to update the GPOs. For these reasons, there is a built-in ability to alter the default behavior.

Using the PDC Emulator

Every time a GPO is viewed or changed, the GPMC and the GPME locate the domain controller that is responsible for the PDC emulator role. It is the GPO from this domain controller that is viewed and updated. There is no inherent reason for choosing this domain controller by default; one domain controller must be selected, because changes must occur on one domain controller and then replicate to all domain controllers. Because the PDC emulator is already responsible for many other critical domain tasks, it makes sense to use this domain controller for GPO updates as well.

There are times when the domain controller running the PDC emulator role is not available or is not the ideal candidate for updating the GPOs. If the PDC emulator is not available when a change must be made to a GPO, the system displays an error message, as shown in Figure 4-2.

Figure 4-2   When the domain controller running the PDC emulator role is not available for editing the GPO, an error message appears.

Note that not only does the system display a dialog box indicating that the domain controller is not available, it also gives you the option to choose a different domain controller. In most cases, selection of the domain controller for updating a GPO has no effect on the result of updating a GPO. Sometimes, however, selecting a different domain controller will result in faster or slower GPO deployment situations. This is because of the way in which a computer receives information regarding domain controllers during initial bootup. Computers receive a list of domain controllers from DNS that prioritizes them based on network location. The domain controllers in the computers own site are first; then the other domain controllers follow. If you make a change to a GPO that is initially updated on a domain controller that is not in the target computer's site, it can take a while to replicate to the domain controller in the computer's site. This could cause a delay in the processing of the GPO until all replication converges.

Selecting the Domain Controller for GPO Editing

To eliminate the processing delay described in the previous section, you can select a domain controller that is in the computer's site. Of course, you must know which site the target computers are in, as well as which domain controllers correspond to that site.

You can also control which domain controller is used when you edit a GPO within the GPMC. Again, this is beneficial when you want to update a specific domain controller to ensure the fastest and most reliable application of the policy settings. To change the domain controller used for editing GPOs from within the GPMC, follow these steps:

1. Right-click the domain name in the GPMC window.

2. Click Change Domain Controller.

3. Make your selection from the list of possible domain controller options, as shown in Figure 4-3.

The next time you edit a GPO from within the GPMC, you will be using the domain controller that you selected. Do not forget that you changed the domain controller in the interface.

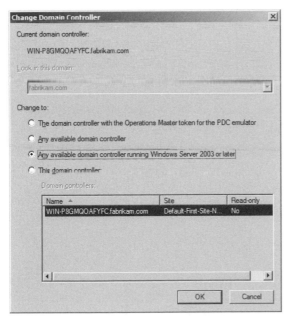

Figure 4-3 The domain controller used to edit GPOs can be selected from within the GPMC to optimize the application of the settings configured in the GPO.

> **Note** One Group Policy setting allows you to configure the domain controller that will be used when editing GPOs. The setting, "Group Policy domain controller selection," is under User Configuration\Administrative Templates\System\Group Policy, as shown in Figure 4-4. This policy setting is a bit out of date; it does not offer the same options as the GPMC, and it includes an option for using the domain controller that is being used by the snap-in, which refers to Active Directory Users and Computers.

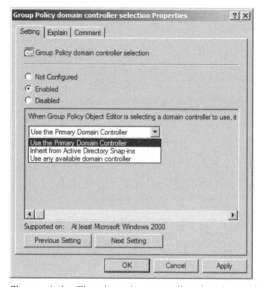

Figure 4-4 The domain controller that is used for editing GPOs can be configured in a GPO, located under User Configuration\Administrative Templates\System\Group Policy.

Architectural Parts of a GPO

A GPO is not as straightforward as you might think. The GPO is made up of two independent parts. These parts are not stored in the same location, they do not have the same structure, and they do not store the same information. If you were to look at the two parts separately, it would be hard to tell that they are related through Group Policy. However, they both perform very important duties for Group Policy and the storage of policy settings.

The first component is the GPT, which is responsible for storing the settings that are made in the GPO. The structure of the GPT can be very complex, because it is a dynamic set of folders and files. The information stored in the files is delivered to the target computers during Group Policy processing.

The second component is the Group Policy container (GPC). The GPC is the "glue" that ensures that all references, paths, network locations, Active Directory objects and paths, and so on are accounted for and correct. The contents of the GPC are usually limited or blank. The details for the GPC are in the Active Directory properties that are associated with each GPC.

Group Policy Template

The Group Policy template (GPT) is the portion of the GPO that is stored in the SYSVOL folder on the domain controllers. The GPT is not a single file or folder, but rather a suite of folders and files that are used to store and maintain the settings that are established in a GPO. The GPT is very dynamic, yet very simple.

Each GPO has a unique GPT where the files are stored. The GPT is kept unique between GPOs by its GUID (globally unique identifier). When a GPO is initially created, a new folder is created under the %windir%\SYSVOL\sysvol\<*domainname*>\Policies folder. This new folder is named the same as the GPO's GUID, as you can see in Figure 4-5.

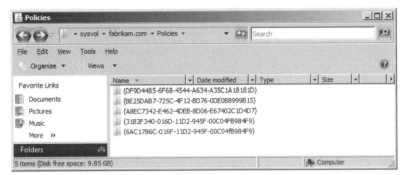

Figure 4-5   All Group Policy templates are stored in a unique folder named after the GPO's GUID; they are all stored in the SYSVOL\Policies folder on each domain controller.

During the creation of the GPT main folder, additional folders and files are created under this root folder. These folders and files include:

- **Group Policy folder**   Holds the GPE.ini file. The GPE.ini file tracks the GUIDs for the CSEs that are referenced in the GPO. As settings within the GPO are added or removed, the associated GUID for the CSE controlling the setting is added or removed from this file.

- **Machine folder**   Stores all GPO settings that are configured under the Computer Configuration node in the GPO.

- **User folder**   Stores all GPO settings that are configured under the User Configuration node in the GPO.

- **Gpt.ini file**   Tracks the GPO version number. The version number changes each time the GPO is modified.

Figure 4-6 illustrates the default folders and files that exist in the GPT.

As settings are created in the GPO, additional folders and files are created in the appropriate folder, depending on whether a Computer Configuration setting or a User Configuration setting is made.

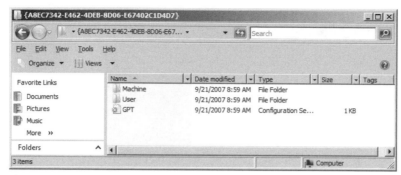

Figure 4-6   Newly created GPOs have only two default folders and one default file that make up the GPT in SYSVOL.

Not all settings create the same type of files. The different portions of the GPO make up the different client-side extensions supported in the GPO. When a setting is made for each client-side extension, the file in which it is stored within the GPT is also different. Table 4-1 shows the client-side extension in addition to the files used within the GPT for that extension. For more information about client-side extensions, refer to the section later in this chapter on the topic.

Table 4-1   Group Policy Template Files

Client-Side Extension	Folder Structure in GPT	File Name and Extension in GPT
Software Installation	Machine\Applications User\Applications	<GUID>.aas
Scripts	Machine\Scripts\Startup Machine\Scripts\Shutdown User\Scripts\Logon User\Scripts\Logoff	Varies (typically with .vbs, .bat, .cmd, .exe extension)
Security	Machine\Microsoft\Windows NT\SecEdit	GptTmpl.inf
Windows Firewall and Advanced Security	Machine	Registry.pol
Public Key Policies	Machine User	Registry.pol
Software Restriction Policy	Machine User	Registry.pol
Network Access Protection	Machine	Registry.pol
Policy Based QoS	Machine User	Registry.pol
Registry	Machine	Registry.pol
Remote Installation Services	Microsoft\RemoteInstall	Oscfilter.ini

Table 4-1   Group Policy Template Files

Client-Side Extension	Folder Structure in GPT	File Name and Extension in GPT
Folder Redirection	User\Documents & Settings	Fdeploy1.ini
Internet Explorer Maintenance	User\Microsoft\IEAK	Various folders and files
Group Policy Environment	Machine\Preferences \EnvironmentVariables User\Preferences\EnvironmentVariables	EnvironmentVariables.xml
Group Policy Data Sources	Machine\Preferences\DataSources User\Preferences\DataSources	DataSources.xml
Group Policy Devices	Machine\Preferences\Devices User\Preferences\Devices	Devices.xml
Group Policy Files	Machine\Preferences\Files User\Preferences\Files	Files.xml
Group Policy Folder Options	Machine\Preferences\Options User\Preferences\Options	Options.xml
Group Policy Folders	Machine\Preferences\Folders User\Preferences\Folders	Folders.xml
Group Policy Local Users and Groups	Machine\Preferences\Groups User\Preferences\Groups	Groups.xml
Group Policy Ini Files	Machine\Preferences\IniFiles User\Preferences\IniFiles	IniFiles.xml
Group Policy Network Options	Machine\Preferences\NetworkOptions User\Preferences\NetworkOptions	NetworkOptions.xml
Group Policy Network Shares	Machine\Preferences\NetworkShares User\Preferences\NetworkShares	NetworkShares.xml
Group Policy Power Options	Machine\Preferences\PowerOptions User\Preferences\PowerOptions	PowerOptions.xml
Group Policy Printers	Machine\Preferences\Printers User\Preferences\Printers	Printers.xml
Group Policy Registry	Machine\Preferences\Registry User\Preferences\Registry	Registry.xml
Group Policy Scheduled Tasks	Machine\Preferences\ScheduledTasks User\Preferences\ScheduledTasks	ScheduledTasks.xml
Group Policy Services	Machine\Preferences\Services User\Preferences\Services	Services.xml
Group Policy Shortcuts	Machine\Preferences\Shortcuts User\Preferences\Shortcuts	Shortcuts.xml

Table 4-1   Group Policy Template Files

Client-Side Extension	Folder Structure in GPT	File Name and Extension in GPT
Group Policy Applications	User\ Preferences\Applications	Applications.xml
Group Policy Drive Maps	User\ Preferences\Drives	Drives.xml
Group Policy Internet Settings	User\ Preferences\InternetSettings	InternetSettings.xml
Group Policy Regional Options	User\ Preferences\RegionalOptions	RegionalOptions.xml
Group Policy Start Menu	User\ Preferences\StartMenuTaskbar	StartMenuTaskbar.xml

Figure 4-7 illustrates what a complex set of GPO settings might look like through the files and folders that are created in the GPT.

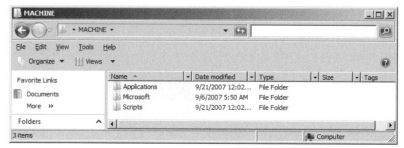

Figure 4-7   When a GPO has many settings configured in different areas of the GPO, folders and files may be created in the GPT.

As you can see, the GPT is responsible for housing all of the raw settings that are made in a GPO. Each setting is stored in a unique file structure, which correlates with the client-side extension under which it is categorized. The files that are stored in the GPT are delivered to the target computer during Group Policy processing.

Group Policy Container

The Group Policy container (GPC) is the portion of the GPO that is stored in Active Directory. The subfolder format of the GPC is similar to that of the GPT, but the GPC is radically different in content and overall use. The GPC has a suite of Active Directory properties associated with it, giving it the same feel as a typical Active Directory object, such as a user or computer object.

The GPC is also similar to the GPT, in the way in which it is tracked in the system; the GPC is also named after the GPO's GUID. You can find the GPC by using one of many tools that display the Active Directory objects. By using Active Directory Users and Computers, you can access the full list of GPCs by following these steps:

1.   In Active Directory Users and Computers, expand the domain node.

2.   Expand the System node.

3. Expand the Policies node to expose the list of GUIDs that represent the GPCs, as shown in Figure 4-8.

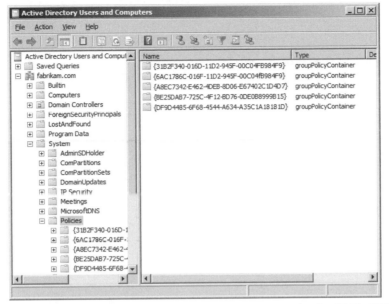

Figure 4-8   All GPCs are stored in Active Directory under the GPO's GUID, allowing the system to keep each GPO unique and distinguishable.

> **Note**   To see the System folder in Active Directory Users and Computers, you must first enable the Advanced Features option. To enable this option, click the domain node in Active Directory Users and Computers. Then click the Tools menu and select the Advanced Features menu option.

During the creation of the GPC, two main folders are created: Machine and User. These folders are empty by default; you can see nothing from the Active Directory Users and Computers interface with regard to the GPC. However, if you create some policy settings, you can see some folders and content within the Active Directory Users and Computers. Table 4-2 lists the folders and files associated with the policies that update the GPC.

Table 4-2   GPC Files

Client-Side Extension	Folder Structure in GPC	File Name and Extension in GPC
Software Installation	Machine\Class Store\Packages User\Class Store\Packages	<*GUID*>, which is a packageRegistration object
IP Security	Machine\Microsoft\Windows	IPSEC, which is an ipsecPolicy object
Wireless Network (IEEE 802.3) Policies	Machine\Microsoft\Windows \IEEE8023	<*policyname*>, which is a ms-net-ieee-8023-GroupPolicy object
Wireless Network (IEEE 802.11) Policies	Machine\Microsoft\Windows \Wireless	<*policyname*>, which is a msieee80211-Policy object

If you want to see details of the GPC, you can use Active Directory Users and Computers or an LDAP tool, such as ADSIEdit, which allows you to see the properties associated with the GPC. These properties help Active Directory and Group Policy apply the appropriate settings and point to the correct GPT and any other network location that might be configured within the GPO. Table 4-3 shows the default properties associated with the GPC.

Table 4-3   GPC Active Directory Properties

Property	Default Value
adminDescription	<not set>
adminDisplayName	<not set>
cn	(GUID of GPO)
defaultClassStore	<not set>
description	<not set>
displayName	(Name of GPO)
displayNamePrintable	<not set>
distinguishedName	CN={GUID of GPO}
dSASignature	<not set>
dSCorePropagationData	0x0 = ( )
extensionName	<not set>
flags	0
fSMORoleOwner	<not set>
gPCFileSysPath	\\<domainname>\SysVol\<domainname>\Policies
gPCFunctionalityVersion	2
gPCMachineExtensionNames	<not set>
gPCUserExtensionNames	<not set>
gPCWQLFilter	<not set>
instanceType	0x4 = (WRITE)
isCriticalSystemObject	<not set>
isDeleted	<not set>
lastKnownParent	<not set>
mS-DS-ConsistencyChildCount	<not set>
mS-DS-ConsistencyGuid	<not set>
msDS-NcType	<not set>
msDS-ObjectReference	<not set>
Name	(GUID of GPO)
objectCategory	CN=Group-Policy-Container,CN=Schema, CN=Configuration, DC=<domainname>, DC=<domain name extention>

Table 4-3   GPC Active Directory Properties

Property	Default Value
objectClass	Top;container;groupPolicyContainer
objectGUID	GUID of GPO
objectVersion	<not set>
otherWellKnownObjects	<not set>
partialAttributeDeletionList	<not set>
partialAttributeSet	<not set>
proxiedObjectName	<not set>
proxyAddresses	<not set>
replPropertyMetaData	<Octet string table>
replUpToDateVector	<not set>
repsFrom	<not set>
repsTo	<not set>
revision	<not set>
schemaVersion	<not set>
showinAdvancedViewOnly	TRUE
subRefs	<not set>
systemFlags	<not set>
url	<not set>
uSNChanged	Dynamic numeric variable
uSNCreated	Dynamic numeric variable
uSNDSALastObjRemoved	<not set>
USNIntersite	<not set>
uSNLastObjRem	<not set>
uSNSource	<not set>
versionNumber	0
wbemPath	<not set>
wellKnownObjects	<not set>
whenChanged	Date of change
whenCreated	Date of creation
wWWHomePage	<not set>

Figure 4-9 shows what the GPC looks like when viewed with ADSIEdit.

The GPC is not responsible for storing the settings that are in the GPO—that is the job of the GPT. The GPC ensures that all network links, resources, and paths are correct and tracked. When Group Policy processing occurs, the GPC properties are used to find all of the pertinent information for the GPT, software installation nodes, and so on.

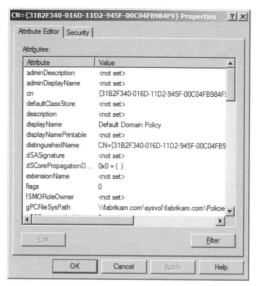

Figure 4-9   Each GPO is represented with a GPC, which in turn has a suite of Active Directory object properties that store information about the GPO resources.

GPO Replication

You just saw that a single GPO is not a single entity. A GPO has two major parts: the GPT and the GPC. Earlier in this chapter, we briefly discussed how Group Policy relied on replication services to move GPO settings from one domain controller to another. These replication services are essential for the success and efficiency of Group Policy application. Because Group Policy models the concept of a multi-master environment, changes to a GPO are made on only one domain controller. The replication services are responsible for making sure that the changes to the GPO get to all domain controllers.

The two parts of the GPO could not be more different, nor could the replication services that synchronize the parts on domain controllers. Understanding how the replication services are dissimilar can make you a troubleshooting expert. In many cases, failed Group Policy processing is the result of failed or errant replication of either the GPC or the GPT.

Group Policy Template and SYSVOL Replication

SYSVOL replication in Windows 2000 and Windows Server 2003 was driven by the File Replication Service (FRS). FRS was a stable and reliable service, but it had some issues for large organizations. FRS was difficult to troubleshoot, and when broken, it was hard to get running again.

With Windows Server 2008, a new replication service ensures that SYSVOL is synchronized among all domain controllers. The new service is the Distributed File System Replication (DFSR). DFSR was introduced with Windows Server 2003 R2, but this version did not support replication of SYSVOL. The current version of DFSR in Windows Server 2008 supports replication of SYSVOL for Windows Server 2008 domain controllers, but it does not support Windows Server 2003 and earlier. The only way to use DFSR to replicate the SYSVOL is to raise your Windows Server 2008 domain to the Windows Server 2008 domain functional level. The service is installed and started by default, but the upgrade to the domain functional level will trigger it to control replication.

How It Works: Enabling DFSR for Your Active Directory Domain

Enabling DFSR will benefit your entire Active Directory infrastructure because it is much more efficient than the old FRS replication. The first step is to ensure that all of your domain controllers are running Windows Server 2008. This is a requirement for replicating the SYSVOL using DFSR, because only domain controllers running Windows Server 2008 support this form of replication of the SYSVOL. The second step is to raise the domain level to Windows Server 2008 functional level. The process is very similar to the process for raising the level of the domain in Windows 2000 and Windows Server 2003. Open the Active Directory User and Computers interface and do the following:

1. In the console tree pane, locate the domain name.

2. Right-click the domain name, and then click Raise Domain Functional Level, as shown in Figure 4-10.

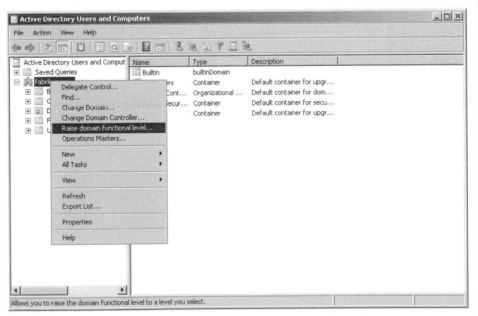

Figure 4-10   The Active Directory Users and Computers interface allows you to configure the domain functional level, including Windows Server 2008.

3. In the Domain Functional Level dialog box, select Windows Server 2008.

4. To Convert your SYSVOL from FRS to DFSR, you must run the dfsrmig command on all domain controllers to properly convert the SYSVOL to DFSR. After you do this, you will not have the option to convert back to FRS.

> **Warning**   After you upgrade to a new functional level, you cannot revert back to the original level. For more information about functional levels in Windows Server 2008 Active Directory, refer to the article titled "Appendix of Functional Level Features" at *http://technet2.microsoft.com/windowsserver2008/en/library /34678199-98f1-465f-9156-c600f723b31f1033.mspx?mfr=true.*

DFSR provides additional benefits over its predecessor, FRS, such as the following:

- Bandwidth throttling and replication scheduling
- Support for replication groups
- Replication of GPO differences only
- File and subfolder filtering

Note that DFSR and FRS follow state-based replication schedules. This means that as soon as a change occurs in the SYSVOL, SYSVOL will replicate the changes to the replication partners. This state-based replication does not adhere to any Active Directory site topology, so the convergence of the changes is rather fast compared to schedule-based replication technologies.

> **Note**   DFSR does provide for scheduling and manipulating of the service, but it is a best practice to leave the replication of SYSVOL at the default values.

Active Directory Replication

Active Directory replication is controlled by...Active Directory replication. The underlying services that control Active Directory replication include the Knowledge Consistency Checker (KCC) and the Inter-Site Topology Generator (ISTG) services. The KCC is in charge of all Active Directory replication, whereas the ISTG is responsible only for replication of Active Directory between domain controllers in different sites.

Because the GPC is stored in Active Directory, it is important to understand how this replication differs from DFSR replication. First, Active Directory replication is not state based. There is a schedule associated with the replication of Active Directory, which is set in the Active Directory Sites and Services tool, as shown in Figure 4-11.

Note that the replication value available for configuration shown in Figure 4-11 is only for replication between sites. The replication of Active Directory between domain controllers in the same site is not available for configuration. This replication, intra-site replication, is set to 15 seconds by default. The maximum time that a change to Active Directory should take to converge to all domain controllers in the same site is 45 seconds, which is a three-hop maximum between replication partners.

Figure 4-11   Site links have a schedule for Active Directory replication between sites, which is configured in Active Directory Sites and Services.

In Figure 4-11, you can see that a much longer convergence time could occur with domain controllers between sites. The default value is 180 minutes, with simple conversion to three hours. This is only the replication of the domain controllers chosen to replicated between sites (*bridgehead servers*), not the replication within the site between domain controllers. If multiple site hops must be completed, the convergence time could be substantially higher.

> **Note**   It has become a best practice for most companies to set the intra-site replication schedule to 15 minutes. This is because most site links are a high-bandwidth scenario. If your bandwidth is significantly less than 10 Mbps, you should consider keeping the replication schedule interval between 60 and 180 minutes.

As you can clearly see, Active Directory replication can lag behind DFSR replication substantially. This has caused dramatic effects in the past, but since the release of Windows XP, this lag in convergence of the two replication technologies has been almost eliminated because Group Policy processing now checks for version numbers in a different way. For more information about Group Policy processing with regard to the version numbers of the GPT and GPC, refer to Chapter 5, "Group Policy Processing." For more information on troubleshooting replication issues with Group Policy, refer to Chapter 15, "Troubleshooting GPOs."

Client-Side Extensions

Client-side extensions (CSEs) provide much of the intelligence behind Group Policy. CSEs are files that must reside on the computer that is consuming Group Policy settings. The CSEs are divided into logical categories that match the nodes within the GPO, which can be seen in the structure of the GPO in the GPME. For example, the Security Settings node and all of the settings under it are controlled by the security CSE. The Drive Maps policy under the Preferences nodes is controlled by its own CSE, the Group Policy Drive Maps CSE.

The CSEs are .dll files that contain code that applies the settings to the target computer. The settings are delivered from the domain controllers to the computer receiving the policy settings during Group Policy processing. The data delivered to the target computer is the information stored in the files that makes up the GPT of the GPO. When these raw settings are delivered to the target computer, the appropriate CSEs perform the correct action on the target computer. Each CSE is tracked and managed by a GUID. The GUID ensures that the CSE is unique—we saw earlier that the GPC tracks the correct CSE in the *gPCMachineExtensionNames* and *gPCUserExtentionNames* attributes.

Table 4-4 provides information about all of the CSEs that are supported in Windows Server 2008 and Windows Vista. The CSEs are referenced in the registry, where this information is kept and tracked. You can see the full list of CSEs in the registry at HKLM\Software\Microsoft\Windows NT\CurrentVersion\Winlogon\GPExtensions.

Table 4-4   Group Policy Client-Side Extensions

Client-Side Extension	CSE DLL	GUID
Wireless Group Policy	Wlgpclnt.dll	{0ACDD40C-75AC-47ab-BAA0-BF6DE7E7FE63}
Group Policy Environment	Gpprefcl.dll	{0E28E245-9368-4853-AD84-6DA3BA35BB75}
Group Policy Local Users and Groups	Gpprefcl.dll	{17D89FEC-5C44-4972-B12D-241CAEF74509}
Group Policy Device Settings	Gpprefcl.dll	{1A6364EB-776B-4120-ADE1-B63A406A76B5}
Folder Restriction	Fdeploy.dll	{25537BA6-77A8-11D2-9B6C-0000F8080861}
Microsoft Disk Quota	Diskquota.dll	{3610eda5-77ef-11d2-8dc5-00c04fa31a66}
Group Policy Network Options	Gpprefcl.dll	{3A0DBA37-F8B2-4356-83DE-3E90BD5C261F}
QoS Packet Scheduler	Gptext.dll	{426031c0-0b47-4852-b0ca-ac3d37bfcb39}
Scripts	Gpscript.dll	{42B5FAAE-6536-11d2-AE5A-0000F87571E3}
Internet Explorer Zonemapping	Iedkcs32.dll	{4CFB60C1-FAA6-47f1-89AA-0B18730C9FD3}
Group Policy Drive Maps	Gpprefcl.dll	{5794DAFD-BE60-433f-88A2-1A31939AC01F}
Group Policy Folders	Gpprefcl.dll	{6232C319-91AC-4931-9385-E70C2B099F0E}
Group Policy Network Shares	Gpprefcl.dll	{6A4C88C6-C502-4f74-8F60-2CB23EDC24E2}
Group Policy Files	Gpprefcl.dll	{7150F9BF-48AD-4da4-A49C-29EF4A8369BA}
Group Policy Data Sources	Gpprefcl.dll	{728EE579-943C-4519-9EF7-AB56765798ED}

Table 4-4   Group Policy Client-Side Extensions

Client-Side Extension	CSE DLL	GUID
Group Policy Ini Files	Gpprefcl.dll	{74EE6C03-5363-4554-B161-627540339CAB}
Windows Search Group Policy Extension	Srchadmin.dll	{7933F41E-56F8-41d6-A31C-4148A711EE93}
Security	Scecli.dll	{827D319E-6EAC-11D2-A4EA-00C04F79F83A}
Deployed Printer Connections	Gpprnext.dll	{8A28E2C5-8D06-49A4-A08C-632DAA493E17}
Group Policy Services	Gpprefcl.dll	{91FBB303-0CD5-4055-BF42-E512A681B325}
Internet Explorer Branding	Iedkcs32.dll	{A2E30F80-D7DE-11d2-BBDE-00C04F86AE3B}
Group Policy Folder Options	Gpprefcl.dll	{A3F3E39B-5D83-4940-B954-28315B82F0A8}
Group Policy Scheduled Tasks	Gpprefcl.dll	{AADCED64-746C-4633-A97C-D61349046527}
Group Policy Registry	Gpprefcl.dll	{B087BE9D-ED37-454f-AF9C-04291E351182}
EFS Recovery	Scecli.dll	{B1BE8D72-6EAC-11D2-A4EA-00C04F79F83A}
802.3 Group Policy	Dot3gpclnt.dll	{B587E2B1-4D59-4e7e-AED9-22B9DF11D053}
Group Policy Printers	Gpprefcl.dll	{BC75B1ED-5833-4858-9BB8-CBF0B166DF9D}
Group Policy Shortcuts	Gpprefcl.dll	{C418DD9D-0D14-4efb-8FBF-CFE535C8FAC7}
Microsoft Offline Files	Cscobj.dll	{C631DF4C-088F-4156-B058-4375F0853CD8}
Software Installation	Appmgmts.dll	{c6dc5466-785a-11d2-84d0-00c04fb169f7}
IP Security	Polstore.dll	{e437bc1c-aa7d-11d2-a382-00c04f991e27}
Group Policy Internet Settings	Gpprefcl.dll	{E47248BA-94CC-49c4-BBB5-9EB7F05183D0}
Group Policy Start Menu Settings	Gpprefcl.dll	{E4F48E54-F38D-4884-BFB9-D4D2E5729C18}
Group Policy Regional Options	Gpprefcl.dll	{E5094040-C46C-4115-B030-04FB2E545B00}
Group Policy Power Options	Gpprefcl.dll	{E62688F0-25FD-4c90-BFF5-F508B9D2E31F}
Group Policy Applications	Gpprefcl.dll	{F9C77450-3A41-477E-9310-9ACD617BD9E3}
Enterprise QoS	Gptext.dll	{FB2CA36D-0B40-4307-821B-A13B252DE56C}

You can see from Table 4-4 that some CSEs use the same file to store the code needed to apply settings delivered from the domain controller.

Note   If a target computer is missing a CSE during Group Policy processing, the settings that are delivered from the domain controller will not apply to the computer.

Important   The CSEs for the Group Policy Preferences must be installed on all computers running Windows XP SP2, Windows Server 2003 SP1, and Windows Vista that will consume these settings. You can download the CSEs from here: *http://technet.microsoft.com/en-us /windowsserver/grouppolicy/default.aspx*. The CSEs are all contained in one .dll file. The file is best distributed using Group Policy, because it is wrapped up in an .msi file. The .dll CSE files are stored in the C:\Windows\System32 folder. For more information about Group Policy Preferences, refer to Chapter 12, "Group Policy Preferences," which provides details on these settings.

Each CSE is defined and tracked in the registry and includes a set of registry values that define and control its behavior. Clicking a CSE GUID in the registry will expose the registry settings that are configured by default and can be modified, as shown in Figure 4-12. The full list of possible registry value settings is shown in Table 4-5.

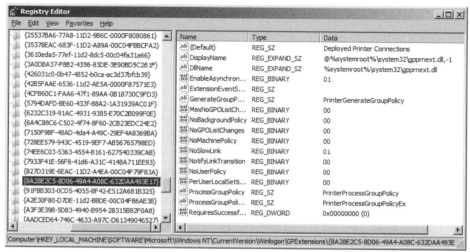

Figure 4-12 Each CSE in the registry has a set of values that control the behavior of the CSE.

> **Warning** Modifying a registry value for a CSE could cause instability or operating system failure. Be sure to test all changes to any setting in the registry before deploying to any production computer. For more information about the registry values for the CSEs, refer to Table 4-4 and the TechNet article "NoSlowLink Entry," at *http://technet.microsoft.com/en-us /windowsserver/grouppolicy/default.aspx*, which covers all registry entries and supported values for each.

Table 4-5 Table 4-5 Possible Group Policy Extension Registry Values

Registry Value	Value Type	Possible Values
(Default)	REG_SZ	<Name of Group Policy>
DisplayName	REG_EXPAND_SZ	@<CSE DLL>, -1 to -????
DLLName	REG_EXPAND_SZ	Name or path to DLL
EnableSynchronousProcessing	REG_DWORD	<0 or 1>
EnableAsynchronousProcessing	REG_BINARY or REG_DWORD	<0 or 01>
ExtensionDebugLevel	REG_DWORD	<0 or 1>
ExtensionEventSource	REG_SZ	Varies
ExtensionRsopPlanningDebugLevel	REG_DWORD	<0 or 1>
EventSources	REG_MULTI_SZ	Varies
GenerateGroupPolicy	REG_SZ	Varies
MaxNGPListChangesInterval	REG_DWORD	<0 or 1>

Table 4-5   Table 4-5 Possible Group Policy Extension Registry Values

Registry Value	Value Type	Possible Values
NoBackgroundPolicy	REG_DWORD	<0 or 1>
NoGPOListChanges	REG_DWORD	<0 or 1>
NoMachinePolicy	REG_DWORD	<0 or 1>
NoSlowLink	REG_DWORD	<0 or 1>
NotifyLinkTransition	REG_DWORD	<0 or 1>
NoUserPolicy	REG_DWORD	<0 or 1>
PerUserLocalSettings	REG_DWORD	<0 or 1>
ProcessGroupPolicy	REG_SZ	Varies
ProcessGroupPolicyEx	REG_SZ	Varies
RequireSuccessfulRegistry	REG_DWORD	<0 or 1>

Summary

Group Policy can stand alone as a technology, but it also has many dependencies on other services and technologies; its close relationship with Active Directory explains these dependencies. Group Policy also runs under a new service, which provides a more reliable, flexible, and feature-rich environment.

Administration of Group Policy is mandatory, and understanding how GPOs are updated is essential. Understanding that the PDC emulator role domain controller is used for editing GPOs is important, as is the fact that you may choose a different domain controller. Selecting the domain controller in the correct site, as a best practice, will make Group Policy application more efficient.

Each GPO consists of two parts: the GPC and the GPT. Both parts are stored on a domain controller, but they have completely different structures and content, as well as different replication services, making the architecture of a GPO somewhat complex. Knowing that the DFSR service and the Active Directory replication have different schedules and mechanisms for replicating content can help with troubleshooting issues.

Client-side extensions are the working mechanism for configuring GPO settings on the target computer. The CSE DLL takes the information from the GPO and makes the setting on the computer. Windows Server 2008 provides over XZY CSEs, which is a large increase from the 13 that were available in Windows Server 2003.

Additional Resources

- The Microsoft TechNet article titled "How the Active Directory Replication Model Works," at *http://technet2.microsoft.com/WindowsServer/en/Library /1465d773-b763-45ec-b971-c23cdc27400e1033.mspx?mfr=true*, includes information about Active Directory replication.

- The Microsoft TechNet article titled "Appendix of Functional Level Features," at *http://technet2.microsoft.com/windowsserver2008/en/library/34678199-98f1-465f-9156-c600f723b31f1033.mspx?mfr=true*, includes information about Windows Server 2008 functional levels for Active Directory.

- Chapter 3, "Group Policy Basics," includes information about configuring local Group Policy Objects.

- Chapter 5, "Group Policy Processing," includes information about how Group Policy processes settings.

- Chapter 12, "Group Policy Preferences," includes information about the Preferences settings in a GPO.

- Chapter 15 "Troubleshooting Group Policy," includes information about how DNS can affect Group Policy application and how to troubleshoot Group Policy replication issues.

Chapter 5
Group Policy Processing

Group Policy processing is one of the primary elements that makes Group Policy so powerful and popular. Changes in a GPO are processed automatically in the background, without forcing the user to log off or the computer to restart. Processing allows administrators to make configurations centrally and rely on the technology to implement the settings.

In this chapter, you will learn how multiple GPOs and conflicting settings are handled by Group Policy processing. When all GPO settings from all GPOs apply to a target user or computer, the result is referred to as the *Resultant Set of Policy (RSoP)*. All of the objects that receive the settings from a GPO fall under that GPO's scope of management. Controlling scope of management is an important topic that this chapter will discuss in detail.

The default processing behavior of GPOs can be altered by using different techniques and configurations. We will discuss Windows Management Instrumentation (WMI) filters, enforcement of GPO settings, blocking inheritance of GPO application, and security filtering. All of these techniques can help administrators control which objects will receive specific GPO settings.

Scope of Management

Scope of management (SOM) is a foundational concept that can make administration of Group Policy significantly easier. Understanding how Group Policy determines which objects to apply to simplifies the management and design of the Group Policy infrastructure and settings within the GPO.

To evaluate the scope of management of a GPO, you must know not only which objects, user, and computer are in the path of the GPO, but also which of those objects have the capability of applying the settings in the GPO. To determine the list of objects that are under the scope of management, you must perform three steps:

1. Based on the settings in the GPO, determine which objects are in the path of the GPO within the Active Directory directory service structure.

2. Create a list of objects that have permission to apply the settings in the GPO.

3. Determine which objects are on both lists to produce a final list of objects that fall under scope of management.

To better understand this concept, let's look at a quick example. Figure 5-1 illustrates a simple Active Directory structure. We will look at three organizational units: Finance, Marketing, and Corp Groups.

Figure 5-1   This figure shows a sample Active Directory structure to illustrate the concept of scope of management.

The group membership matrix is as follows in Table 5-1.

Table 5-1   Example Group Matrix

Group Name	Group Members
Finance	Bruno
	Barbara
Marketing	Maria
Managers	Bruno
	Maria

Notice in Figure 5-1 that two users and a computer account appear under the Finance organizational unit, and a single user and computer account appear under the Marketing organizational unit. The Corp Groups organizational unit contains three groups.

In this example, a GPO named GPO1 is linked to the Finance organizational unit. Within GPO1, a single setting is configured—the Remove Help Menu From Start Menu setting, which is located under User Configuration\Policies\Administrative Templates\Start Menu and Taskbar. The setting is configured as disabled, so any objects that fall under the scope of management of the GPO will not appear on the Help and Support menu accessed from the Start menu.

To determine the scope of management for our example, you must first perform step 1, which is:

Based on the settings in the GPO, determine which objects are in the path of the GPO within the Active Directory structure.

In our example, that list would contain both Bruno and Barbara. Because the user Maria is not in the Active Directory path of the linked GPO, she will not be on this list. The computers named Desktop1 and Desktop2 are not on our list, because the setting we configured is under User Configuration, and only user objects can apply these settings

After you determine the list of objects, you must evaluate the permissions on GPO1. The permissions on GPO1 have been changed from the default, and the new permissions are shown in Figure 5-2.

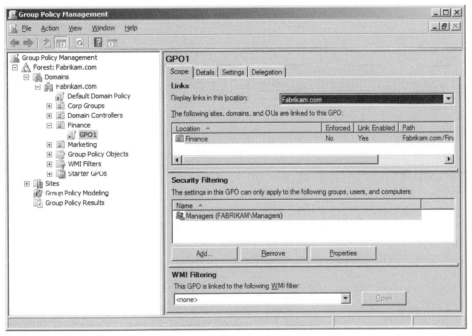

Figure 5-2   With these example permissions for GPO1, the Managers group has the ability to apply the GPO and its settings.

Now that we have our list from step 1 and the permissions for the GPO, we must perform step 2, which is:

Create a list of objects that have permission to apply the settings in the GPO.

By reviewing the group matrix from Table 5-1, we can see that both Bruno and Maria have permission to apply the settings in the GPO.

Our final step is to do the following:

Determine which objects are on both lists, to produce a final list of objects that fall under scope of management.

Table 5-2 summarizes our lists from the first two steps and includes the final list of objects that are under the scope of management for our example. You can see that the settings from GPO1 will apply only to the user Bruno.

Table 5-2   Example Group Matrix

Step 1 List of Objects	Step 2 List of Objects	Step 3 Final List of Objects Under SOM
Bruno	Bruno	Bruno
Barbara	Maria	

To give you an idea of how the scope of management could change, here are some examples that would occur if objects moved or group membership changed:

- If Barbara were added to the Managers group, she would fall under the scope of management.

- If Maria were moved to the Finance organizational unit, she would fall under the scope of management.

- If the default group were put back on the permission list for GPO1, which is the Authenticated Users group, Bruno and Barbara would both fall under the scope of management, but Maria would not.

Group Policy Processing

If only a single GPO could be created, the application of the settings would be rather easy to understand. However, GPOs can be linked to many different nodes within Active Directory, which does not even include the local GPOs that are available on desktops running Windows Vista. These nodes include: domain, organizational units, and sites.

When there is more than one GPO in your Active Directory enterprise, you must determine which GPO will have precedence over the others in the scope of management. This is because any conflicting settings (the same GPO setting configured in two different GPOs) must be resolved to a single value.

How It Works: GPO Settings with No Conflicts

If there are no conflicting settings in the GPOs that are in the scope of management, all of the settings will be applied. For example, GPO1 is linked to the domain node, GPO2 is linked to the HR organizational unit, and GPO3 is linked to the Payroll

---

organizational unit (which is a suborganizational within HR). Each GPO has the following settings:

- GPO1: Remove Run Menu From Start Menu (set to enabled)
- GPO2: Remove Help Menu To Start Menu (set to disabled)
- GPO3: Enable Active Desktop (set to enabled)

For a user account that resides in the Payroll organizational unit, all three settings will be applied to the user because there are no conflicting settings.

Precedence is the hierarchical order in which GPOs resolve conflicting settings. Precedence must be considered in two scenarios: when GPOs are linked to different nodes within Active Directory, and when multiple GPOs are linked to the same node within Active Directory.

GPO Precedence for GPOs Linked to Different Nodes

GPOs can be linked to many different nodes within the Active Directory structure. The design of the organizational units and the deployment strategy of the GPO settings will dictate where the GPOs are linked. One of the considerations for the deployment of GPO settings is precedence of the GPOs that are in the scope of management. GPOs can be linked to the following Active Directory nodes:

- Domain
- Organizational unit
- Site

Also, multiple local GPOs reside on desktops running Windows Vista. These are always resident on the desktops and must be considered when determining precedence of GPO settings, as well as the RSoP. The rules of precedence for applying GPO settings are as follows:

- Local GPOs apply first and have weaker precedence than all GPOs linked in Active Directory.
- Local GPO precedence, strongest to weakest, is: user specific, Administrator/ Non-Administrator, local Group Policy.
- Active Directory GPOs apply after the local GPOs and have stronger precedence than all local GPOs.
- The Active Directory GPO precedence, strongest to weakest, is: organizational unit, domain, site.

Altogether, the precedence of all GPOs considered is as follows, with the strongest precedence at the top:

- GPO linked to organizational unit
- GPO linked to domain
- GPO linked to site
- Local GPO for specific user
- Local GPO for Administrators/Non-Administrators
- Local GPO for local Group Policy

For more information about the local GPOs, refer to Chapter 3, "Group Policy Basics," which covers all aspects of local GPOs.

When considering overall precedence, it is also important to remember the following:

- A user or computer can belong to only one domain.
- Organizational units can have child organizational units, grandchild organizational units, and so on.
- A computer can belong to only one site.

These points are important to consider when determining precedence, because they indicate that you only ever need to consider one domain and one site at a time. However, you do need to consider the organizational unit structure and where the user or computer object is located.

For example, imagine that you have the following domain structure:

Fabrikam.com
   HR
     Payroll

In this example, the GPOs and settings are linked to the Active Directory nodes, and the local GPOs are configured on Desktop1, which is located in the Payroll organizational unit, as listed in Table 5-3.

Table 5-3   Example GPO Settings and Links

GPO Name	GPO Link or Scope	GPO Setting	GPO Setting Value
GPO1	Fabrikam.com	Remove Run Menu From Start Menu	Enabled
GPO2	HR	Remove Help Menu From Start Menu	Disabled
GPO3	Payroll	Remove Run Menu From Start Menu	Disabled
LGPO	General	Remove Pictures Icon From Start Menu	Enabled
LGPO	Non-administrators	Remove User's Folders From The Start Menu	Enabled
LGPO	Bruno	Remove Music Icon From Start Menu	Enabled

If you apply the rule that local GPOs apply first and have the weakest precedence with the concept that GPOs linked to the Active Directory nodes have precedence of site, domain, organizational unit (weakest to strongest), the GPOs would be applied as listed in Table 5-4, with the strongest at the top of the list.

Table 5-4   Example GPO Precedence Order

GPO Name	GPO Link or Scope	GPO Setting	GPO Setting Value
GPO3	Payroll	Remove Run Menu From Start Menu	Disabled
GPO2	HR	Remove Help Menu From Start Menu	Disabled
GPO1	Fabrikam.com	Remove Run Menu From Start Menu	Enabled
LGPO	Bruno	Remove Music Icon From The Start Menu	Enabled
LGPO	Non-administrators	Remove User's Folders From The Start Menu	Enabled
LGPO	General	Remove Pictures Icon From Start Menu	Enabled

The RSoP for Bruno (who is in the Payroll organizational unit), logging onto Desktop1, would be as listed in Table 5-5.

Table 5-5   Example GPO Precedence RSoP

GPO Setting	GPO Setting Value	GPO Name
Remove Run Menu From Start Menu	Disabled	GPO3
Remove Help Menu From Start Menu	Disabled	GPO2
Remove Music Icon From Start Menu	Enabled	LGPO
Remove User's Folders From The Start Menu	Enabled	LGPO
Remove Pictures Icon From Start Menu	Enabled	LGPO

Notice that all of the GPOs in our example that did not have a conflicting setting were applied. Only the conflicting setting did not apply all settings. In this instance, GPO3 had a stronger precedence than GPO1, so GPO3 won the conflict and its setting was carried through to the RSoP.

GPO Precedence for GPOs Linked to the Same Node

When more than one GPO is linked to any single Active Directory node, additional considerations must be made for precedence. In such a case, the GPO settings that are linked to the same node must be resolved if there are any conflicting settings.

 Note   Additional local GPOs cannot be created on any desktop or server.

For example, imagine that you have multiple GPOs linked to the HR organizational unit from the previous example, with the settings listed in Table 5-6.

Table 5-6   Example GPO Settings and Links to One Node

GPO Name	GPO Link or Scope	Link Order	GPO Setting	GPO Setting Value
GPO4	HR	1	Remove Music Icon From Start Menu	Disabled
GPO2	HR	2	Remove Help Menu From Start Menu	Disabled
GPO5	HR	3	Remove Music Icon From Start Menu	Enabled

In this scenario, the GPOs that are linked to the HR organizational unit will be applied with the GPO with the highest link order having the strongest precedence. Thus, the two conflicting GPOs and settings, GPO4 and GPO5, must be resolved to a single setting for the Remove Music Icon From Start Menu setting. Because GPO4 has a stronger precedence, this GPO and setting will win the conflict and the setting will be set to Disabled.

Group Policy Processing Events

There are two types of policy processing events: background policy processing and foreground policy processing. Both types have unique characteristics that make them important to the overall processing of GPOs.

Background GPO Policy Processing

Group Policy settings can be applied without requiring the computer to reboot or the user to log off, in a process referred to as background policy processing. Background policy processing is a default feature that is very important for the application of policy settings. The default interval for background policy processing is 90 minutes, with up to a 30-minute offset for all computers except domain controllers. Domain controllers have a background policy refresh interval of five minutes.

If you need to alter the background policy processing for servers, you can do so by using the appropriate policy under the Computer Configuration\Policies\Administrative Templates\System\Group Policy node:

- Group Policy Refresh Interval For Computers
- Group Policy Refresh Interval For Domain Controllers

For user-based policy settings, that background refresh is also 90 minutes with up to a 30-minute offset. That value can be modified under the User Configuration\Policies\Administrative Templates\System\Group Policy node and is the Group Policy Refresh Interval For Users policy.

> **Warning**   The background refresh interval should be reduced only after considering the effect of the increased network traffic on the overall network. With thousands of desktops, the additional network traffic could be detrimental.

Foreground Group Policy Processing

Foreground policy processing is processing of GPO settings when the computer is rebooted or when the user logs off and then logs back on. Foreground processing is an important factor in the overall processing of Group Policy because not all GPO settings can process in the background. All GPO settings can apply in the foreground. GPO settings that apply only with a foreground refresh include the following:

Computer Configuration\Policies\Windows Settings\Security Settings\Local Policies\Security Options

- Audit: Audit The Access Of Global System Objects
- Audit: Audit of the Use Of Backup And Restore Privilege
- Audit: Shut Down System Immediately If Unable To Log Security Audits
- Domain Controller: Allow Server Operators To Schedule Tasks
- Microsoft Network Client: Digitally Sign Communications (Always)
- Microsoft Network Client: Digitally Sign Communications (If Server Agrees)
- Microsoft Network Client: Send Unencrypted Password To Third-Party SMB Servers
- Microsoft Network Server: Amount Of Idle Time Required Before Suspending Session
- Microsoft Network Server: Digitally Sign Communications (Always)
- Network Access: Named Pipes That Can Be Accessed Anonymously
- Network Access: Restrict Anonymous Access To Named Pipes And Shares
- Network Access: Shares That Can Be Accessed Anonymously
- Network Security: LDAP Client Signing Requirements
- User Account Control: Run All Administrators In Admin Approval Mode
- Shutdown: Clear Virtual Memory Pagefile
- System Cryptography: Force Strong Key Protection For User Keys Stored On The Computer
- System Objects: Require Case Insensitivity For Non-Windows Subsystems
- System Objects: Strengthen Default Permissions Of Internal System Objects (e.g., Symbolic Links)
- System Settings: Optional Subsystems

Computer Configuration\Policies\Administrative Templates\Windows Components

- Desktop Window Manager\Do Not Allow Desktop Composition
- Desktop Window Manager\Do Not Allow Flip3D Invocation

- Desktop Window Manager\Do Not Allow Window Animations
- Desktop Window Manager\Window Frame Coloring\Do Not Allow Color Changes
- Desktop Window Manager\Window Frame Coloring\Specify A Default Color
- Terminal Services\Terminal Server\TS Session Broker\Join TS Session Broker
- Terminal Services\TS Licensing\License Server Security Group
- Windows Logon Options\Report When Logon Server Was Not Available During User Logon
- Windows Media Player\Prevent Video Smoothing
- Shutdown Options\Turn Off Legacy Remote Shutdown Interface
- Windows Defender\Turn Off Windows Defender

Computer Configuration\Policies\Administrative Templates\System

- Remove Boot/Shutdown/Logon/Logoff Status Messages
- Verbose Vs. Normal Status Messages

User Configuration\Policies\Administrative Templates\Windows Components

- Windows Media Player\Networking\Configure MMS Proxy
- Windows Media Player\Networking\Configure Network Buffering
- Desktop Window Manager\Do Not Allow Window Animations
- Desktop Window Manager\Do Not Allow Desktop Composition
- Desktop Window Manager\Do Not Allow Flip3D Invocation
- Desktop Window Manager\Window Frame Coloring\Specify A Default Color
- Desktop Window Manager\Window Frame Coloring\Do Not Allow Color Changes
- Windows Media Player\User Interface\Do Not Show Anchor
- Windows Media Player\Networking\Hide Network Tab
- Windows Logon Options\Report When Logon Server Was Not Available During User Logon
- Windows Logon Options\Set Action To Take When Logon Hours Expire
- Tablet PC\Touch Input\Turn Off Tablet PC Touch Input
- Backup\Client\Turn Off Restore Functionality

User Configuration\Policies\Administrative Templates\System

- Custom User Interface

In addition to these GPO settings, specific client-side extensions (CSEs) also adhere to foreground-only policy processing. The GPO CSEs that apply only with foreground policy processing include the following:

- Deployed Printer Connections
- Folder Redirection
- Group Policy Drive Maps
- Group Policy Printers
- Internet Explorer Branding
- Scripts (Policy Processes)
- Microsoft Offline Files
- Software Installation

> **Note**   You can also trigger a background refresh of Group Policy manually by using the GPUpdate utility. GPUpdate emulates a background refresh. For more information on GPUpdate, refer to Chapter 15, "Troubleshooting GPOs."

Asynchronous vs. Synchronous Policy Processing

In addition to foreground and background processing, you must also consider whether Group Policy processing should occur asynchronously or synchronously. In general terms, these options determine whether the user must wait for all of the policies to process before receiving their desktops. The two options are described as follows:

- **Asynchronous processing**   Windows does not wait for the network stack to initialize before starting and the letting the user receive the desktop.

- **Synchronous processing**   Windows waits for the network stack to initialize, and all Group Policy foreground processing occurs before the user receives the desktop.

To control whether a computer will run asynchronously or synchronously, you need only modify the following GPO setting:

Computer Configuration\Policies\Administrative Templates\System\Logon\Always Wait For The Network At Computer Startup And Logon

Configuring this setting as Enabled forces the computer to process GPO settings synchronously. Disabling this setting allows the computer to process GPO settings asynchronously.

When considering asynchronous and synchronous policy processing in conjunction with foreground and background policy processing, you must also consider the cycles of policy processing to understand how each setting will process. For example, Software Installation can apply only during a foreground refresh. If the computer does not wait for the software to install before giving the user access to the desktop (asynchronous processing), the software will not be installed until the computer reboots or the user logs off and back on. This is because all foreground policy processing ceases to work after the user receives the desktop.

Table 5-7 lists all of these policy processing parameters and indicates how each CSE will behave.

Table 5-7   CSE Processing Matrix

CSE	Runs during Foreground Synchronous	Runs during Foreground Asynchronous	Runs during Background Asynchronous
Wireless Group Policy	Yes	Yes	Yes
Group Policy Environment	Yes	Yes	Yes
Group Policy Local Users And Groups	Yes	Yes	Yes
Group Policy Device Settings	Yes	Yes	Yes
Folder Redirection	Yes	No	No
Microsoft Disk Quota	Yes	Yes	Yes
Group Policy Network Options	Yes	Yes	Yes
QoS Packet Scheduler	Yes	Yes	Yes
Scripts	Yes	No	No
Internet Explorer Zonemapping	Yes	Yes	Yes
Group Policy Drive Maps	Yes	Yes	No
Group Policy Folders	Yes	Yes	Yes
Group Policy Network Shares	Yes	Yes	Yes
Group Policy Files	Yes	Yes	Yes
Group Policy Data Sources	Yes	Yes	Yes
Group Policy Ini Files	Yes	Yes	Yes
Windows Search Group Policy	Yes	Yes	Yes
Security	Yes	Yes	Yes
Deployed Printer Connections	Yes	No	No
Group Policy Services	Yes	Yes	Yes
Internet Explorer Branding	Yes	No	No
Group Policy Folder Options	Yes	Yes	Yes
Group Policy Scheduled Tasks	Yes	Yes	Yes
Group Policy Registry	Yes	Yes	Yes
EFS Recovery	Yes	Yes	Yes
802.3 Group Policy	Yes	Yes	Yes
Group Policy Printers	Yes	No	No
Group Policy Shortcuts	Yes	Yes	Yes
Microsoft Offline Files	Yes	Yes	Yes

Table 5-7   CSE Processing Matrix

CSE	Runs during Foreground Synchronous	Runs during Foreground Asynchronous	Runs during Background Asynchronous
Software Installation	Yes	No	No
IP Security	Yes	Yes	Yes
Group Policy Internet Settings	Yes	Yes	Yes
Group Policy Start Menu Settings	Yes	Yes	Yes
Group Policy Regional Options	Yes	Yes	Yes
Group Policy Power Options	Yes	Yes	Yes
Group Policy Applications	Yes	Yes	Yes
Enterprise QoS	Yes	No	No

Note Security policy can be applied to a computer during background refresh, but some security policy settings may not take effect without a reboot. Additionally, some of the CSEs listed in Table 5-7 apply only to the user or only to the computer, so background asynchronous processing might mean something different depending on the circumstances. For example, if no user is logged on to a computer, no user-specific background processing occurs.

Using GPUpdate

The standard background and foreground refreshing of Group Policy is built in to the system and occurs without any configuration or setup. However, there may be times when the refresh interval is not frequent enough for settings to be applied; in such cases, you need another option for applying settings faster, preferably in real time.

The solution is the GPUpdate utility. GPUpdate is a standard command-line utility on all computers running at least Windows XP Professional.

Note Computers running Windows 2000 must run the Secedit command to refresh policy manually. For more information about the Secedit command, refer to *http://support.microsoft.com/kb/227448*.

The GPUpdate utility manually performs a background Group Policy processing refresh. You must run the utility from the computer that you want to refresh; it does not work remotely. By default, the utility refreshes both the user and computer portions of the GPO. You can, however, target just one of the two sections of the GPO by adding the /Target switch and indicating User or Computer. The other switch options are useful, but in most cases you can use GPUpdate without any switches. All of the switches and their uses are listed in Table 5-8.

Table 5-8   GPUpdate Utility Switches

Switch	Description of Use
/Target: {Computer | User}	Specifies that only User or only Computer policy settings are refreshed. By default, both User and Computer policy settings are refreshed.
/Force	Reapplies all policy settings. By default, only policy settings that have changed are applied.
/Wait: {value}	Sets the number of seconds to wait for policy processing to finish. The default is 600 seconds. The value '0' means not to wait. The value '-1' means to wait indefinitely. When the time limit is exceeded, the command prompt returns, but policy processing continues.
/Logoff	Causes a logoff after the Group Policy settings have been refreshed. This is required for those Group Policy client-side extensions that do not process policy on a background refresh cycle but do process policy when a user logs on. Examples include user-targeted Software Installation and Folder Redirection. This option has no effect if there are no extensions called that require a logoff.
/Boot	Causes a reboot after the Group Policy settings are refreshed. This is required for those Group Policy client-side extensions that do not process policy on a background refresh cycle but do process policy at computer start-up. Examples include computer-targeted Software Installation. This option has no effect if there are no extensions called that require a reboot.
/Synch	Causes the next foreground policy application to be done synchronously. Foreground policy applications occur at computer boot and user logon. You can specify this for the user, computer, or both by using the /Target parameter. The /Force and /Wait parameters will be ignored if specified.

Note   The GPUpdate utility cannot perform a foreground refresh. The only two options that do this are rebooting for computer settings and logging off and back on for user settings. The /Force switch does not perform a foreground refresh.

The security CSE behaves somewhat differently from the other CSEs. If a GPO has not changed since the last time it was processed, settings will not reapply at the next refresh interval. If the settings in the registry have been modified manually on the target computer, those settings will remain until the GPO is modified. For security settings, this could leave the computer in a nonsecure state.

Because of this possibility, the security CSE processes security settings every 16 hours on nondomain controllers and every five minutes on domain controllers, regardless of any changes that have occurred in the GPO for security settings.

This interval of 16 hours can be modified, up or down, depending on needs of the computer being controlled. The value in the registry that modifies this interval can be found at:

HKEY_LOCAL_MACHINE\SOFTWARE\Microsoft\Windows NT\CurrentVersion\Winlogon
GPExtensions\{827D319E-6EAC-11D2-A4EA-00C04F79F83A}\MaxNoGPOListChangesInterval

The default value is 960 (hex 0x3c0), which is in minutes. This value should not be modified unless there is a valid business reason. In general, it is a best practice to leave the value in the default state; you could, however, modify a highly secure group of computers to have a smaller value. Reducing this value for a large number of computers is not recommended, because the processing and network overhead could become a problem.

> **Note**   If you want to modify this value on all computers on the network, you have three options. You can create a custom .adm template, you can create a custom ADMX/ADML file, or you can use the Registry Preference to modify the registry setting. Refer to Chapter 11, "Customizing ADM Templates and ADMX Files," and Chapter 12, "Group Policy Preferences," for more information about customizing these settings.

You can find additional information regarding the security CSE and processing of this extension at *http://technet2.microsoft.com/windowsserver/en/library/f546e58e-8473-4985-a05d-0b038dea4a9f1033.mspx?mfr=true*.

Version Checking During Updates

Group Policy processing and settings updates are based on the GPO version number. GPO version numbering is based on how many changes have occurred for both user and computer settings. As each change occurs within the GPO, the version numbers of both the Group Policy template (GPT) and Group Policy container (GPC) are updated. For more information about the GPT and GPC, refer to Chapter 4, "Architecture of Group Policy."

The GPO version is cached on the computer when the settings are applied. Upon the next refresh interval, foreground or background, the cached version is compared to the version number on the domain controller that is offering the GPO processing. If the version numbers differ, Group Policy settings will apply. If they are the same, processing is not performed.

GPO Version Numbers on the Client

When a GPO applies to a computer, information regarding the GPO is stored on the computer. The client must know the version numbers of both the GPT and the GPC so that information is stored along with the other information about the applied GPOs. To see the current state of the GPOs that are affecting the computer, you would access the registry at HKEY_LOCAL_MACHINE\SOFTWARE\Microsoft\Windows\CurrentVersion\Group Policy\State, as shown in Figure 5-3.

This registry location contains two sections. One is related to the computer and is named Machine. The other is user related and is listed by the user's security identifier (SID). Both sections have a GPO-List node, which stores information about the applied GPOs.

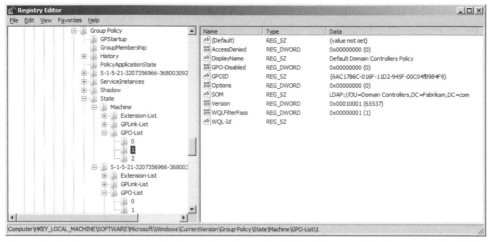

Figure 5-3 Computers store information about the GPOs that are affecting them, including the version number.

In Figure 5-3, notice the entry for the listed GPO named Version. This number represents the GPT and GPC. The first four digits of the number represent the version number of the GPT, and the last four digits represent the version number of the GPC. When the Group Policy refresh occurs, these values are compared to the current values of the GPT and GPC. If they differ, Group Policy is applied. If they are the same, no changes have occurred to the GPO in Active Directory, so no update is necessary.

GPO Version Numbers on the Domain Controller

The client compares the GPO version numbers stored locally with those stored on the domain controller for each GPO. The domain controller stores the version number for each GPO in two locations. The first is the in GPT, which is under the appropriate GUID for the GPO, located under the %systemroot%\SYSVOL\sysvol\<*domainname*>\Policies folder. The version number is stored in a file called GPT.ini. The second location is in Active Directory, which is referred to as the GPC. Here, the version number is stored as an attribute of the GPO object.

Both of these version numbers are referenced during Group Policy refreshes. The client compares the local version number to these and updates policy based on whether the numbers are different or the same.

Refer to Chapter 4 for more information about storage of the GPO version number in the GPC and GPT.

NLA Refresh in Windows Vista and Windows Server 2008

Network Location Awareness (NLA) is the replacement technology that helps Group Policy identify slow links. Internet Control Message Protocol (ICMP) (the protocol that supports

PING) is no longer used within Group Policy because NLA is more reliable and accurate. NLA ensures that all computers are aware and can respond more precisely to changes in network conditions and available network resources.

NLA provides many benefits, including the following:

■ Computer start-up times are faster and more efficient. NLA accurately determines the state of the network and processes Group Policy accordingly. If the adapter is disabled or disconnected, NLA causes Group Policy to shorten the wait time for the network.

■ If the computer has been offline or the network has not been available for some time, NLA helps the computer recognize when a domain controller becomes available. This helps with virtual private network (VPN) sessions, recovering from hibernation (and standby), exiting quarantine, and laptop docking.

■ NLA provides more control over how the computer responds to Group Policy, the network state, and the boot process for GPO application. Refer to Chapter 13, "Settings Breakdown for Windows Server 2008 and Windows Vista," for more information.

How It Works: VPN Connections Using NLA

When a computer is disconnected from the corporate network but is still running, Group Policy refreshes will fail. These failures will continue until a domain controller is available and the network connection is established. When a VPN connection is established, NLA helps the computer detect the availability of a domain controller. Because the last Group Policy refresh cycle failed, Group Policy will initiate a background refresh, updating both the computer and user sections of the GPOs that should apply. NLA makes this happen efficiently, without requiring the computer to reboot or the user to log off for the computer to update the changes over the VPN.

Altering Default GPO Processing and Inheritance

The default inheritance and processing of GPOs is very reliable. It is a best practice to keep the default settings as they are, but if you need to alter the way in which GPOs process and affect users and computers, you can use additional settings to control this behavior. You have numerous options, as discussed in the following sections.

Block Policy Inheritance

Blocking policy inheritance is a function that you configure on the domain or organizational units. This setting can block the application of GPOs that are higher in the Active Directory structure than where the setting is configured. When configured on a top-level organizational unit, this setting blocks all GPOs from the site and domain from applying to objects located in the organizational unit where it is configured, and below.

> **Note**   The Block Inheritance option does not block the application of local GPOs. If you want to block local GPOs, it is a best practice to disable them using a GPO.

For example, assume you had the Active Directory structure and links shown in Table 5-9.

Table 5-9   Example Active Directory Structure and GPO Links

Active Directory Node	Linked GPO
Fabrikam.com	Default Domain Policy
	GPO_Domain_Security
Finance organizational unit	GPO_Finance_Security
AccountsPayable organizational unit (child under Finance)	GPO_AP_Security
	GPO_AP_Applications

All of the GPOs in Table 5-9 have computer-related settings, not user-related settings. The standard Group Policy inheritance and processing would apply all five of these GPOs to the computer objects located in the AccountsPayable organizational unit, as shown in Figure 5-4.

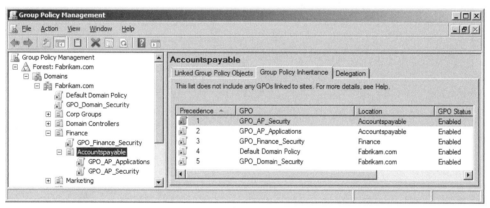

Figure 5-4   This figure shows GPO inheritance on the AccountsPayable organizational unit before any blocking of policy inheritance is applied.

There are desktop computers located in the AccountsPayable organizational unit. To block policy inheritance, you configure the setting at the AccountsPayable organizational unit, as shown in Figure 5-5. To configure Block Inheritance, right-click the organizational unit, and then click Block Inheritance.

After the Block Inheritance options configured for the AccountsPayable organizational unit, the new set of GPOs that will affect the objects appears as shown in Figure 5-6.

> **Important**   Note that all settings in all blocked GPOs will be blocked. The Block Inheritance option cannot block just some settings in GPOs with weaker precedence—it blocks all settings in all GPOs.

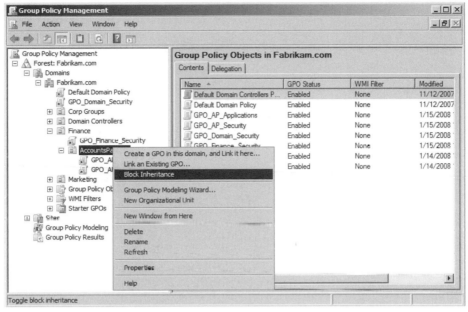

Figure 5-5 You apply the Block Inheritance option by right-clicking the node where the inheritance should be stopped.

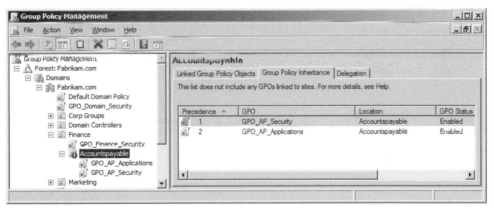

Figure 5-6 This figure shows GPO inheritance on the AccountsPayable organizational unit after blocking of policy inheritance is applied.

Enforce

The Enforce option for Group Policy is slightly different than the setting to block inheritance. Enforcement of a GPO and its settings occurs at the GPO level, not the Active Directory node level. When a GPO is set to be enforced, the GPO cannot be blocked with any other setting. The GPO also gains the strongest precedence of all GPOs.

Continuing with the Block Inheritance example, we will now investigate how enforcing a GPO affects the situation. Figure 5-6 illustrates the current GPO application based on the blocking of policy inheritance at the AccountsPayable organizational unit. If the Default Domain Policy were set to be enforced, the result would appear as shown in Figure 5-7. To configure the Enforce option on a GPO, right-click the GPO link, and then click Enforce.

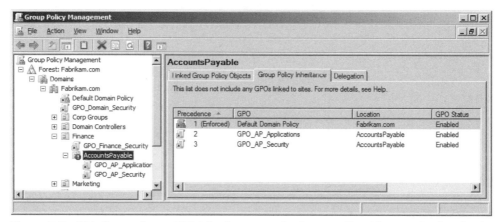

Figure 5-7   This figure shows GPO inheritance on the AccountsPayable organizational unit after the Enforce option and the Block Inheritance option have been configured.

You can clearly see that after the Default Domain Policy is set to be enforced, the GPO applies through the Active Directory structure. Also, the Default Domain Policy is now at the top of the precedence list of all GPOs. This means that all settings configured in this GPO will win any conflict with any other GPO in the scope of management for an object.

> **Note**   If multiple GPOs are set to be enforced, the GPOs that are higher in the Active Directory structure will have stronger precedence. So if the GPO_AP_Security GPO is set to be enforced, it will have a weaker precedence than the enforced Default Domain Policy.

Security Filtering

Security filtering is modification of the security permissions on the GPO itself. To receive the settings in a GPO, an object must have both the Read and Apply Group Policy permissions. You configure the permissions to establish security filtering per GPO in the details pane after you have selected the GPO in the Group Policy Management Console (GPMC). To access this security permission list box, follow these steps:

1.   Select the GPO under the Group Policy Objects node in the GPMC.

2.   In the details pane, select the Scope tab.

3.   To add a user or group to the security permission list, click Add in the Security Filtering section. To remove a user or group from the security permission list, click Remove in the Security Filtering section.

Warning The inclusion of a user account or group account in the Security Filtering section does not mean that a user or computer will receive the settings in the GPO. An object must be both in the scope of management of a GPO and included in the Security Filtering list. For more details about GPO processing for an object, refer to the "Scope of Management" section, earlier in this chapter.

How It Works: Detailed Security Permissions on a GPO

When a user or group is configured with permission in the Security Filtering section of the Scope tab of a GPO, two permissions are actually configured for that object—Read and Apply Group Policy. To see this level of permission, you must use the Advanced permissions view of the GPO. To access the Advanced permissions view, click the Delegation tab, and then click Advanced, which displays the Security Settings dialog box, as shown in Figure 5-8. Notice that the Authenticated Users group has both permissions; this is the default setting for all GPOs.

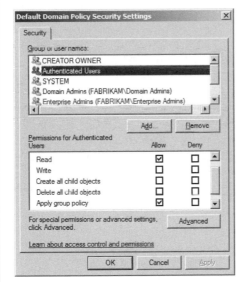

Figure 5-8 The Security Settings dialog box for a GPO displays the detailed permissions configured for security filtering and delegations.

WMI Filters

Windows Management Instrumentation (WMI) is a management technology that can query a computer to determine one or many attributes of the computer. For example, a WMI query can be created to determine the operating system of a computer or the hard disk space available on a computer hard drive.

A WMI filter consists of one or more queries and is associated with a GPO. The query returns either true or false. If the query returns true, the settings in the GPO where the WMI filter is linked will be applied. If the query returns false, the settings will not apply.

> **Note**   WMI filters are not supported on operating systems earlier than Windows XP.

To configure a WMI filter, you must understand WMI query language. If you want to learn more about WMI query language, refer to the Windows Management Instrumentation Web site at *http://msdn2.microsoft.com/en-us/library/aa286547.aspx* and the WMI Classes page at *http://msdn2.microsoft.com/en-us/library/aa394554.aspx*.

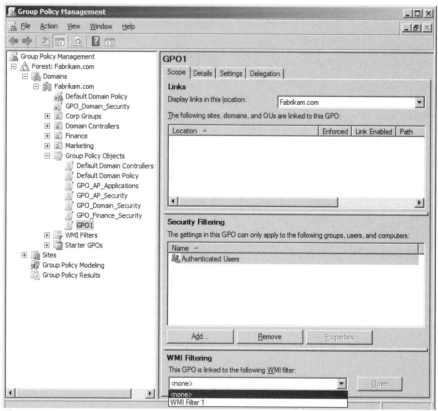

Figure 5-9   WMI Filters are linked to GPOs in the GPMC on the Scope tab in the WMI Filtering section.

To create a WMI filter and link it to a GPO, follow these steps:

1. In the GPMC, expand the domain name node to expose the WMI Filters node.

2. Right-click the WMI Filter node, and then click New. The New WMI Filter dialog box appears.

3. Type a name in the Name box and a description in the Description box for the filter, and then click Add. The WMI Query dialog box appears.

4. In the WMI Query dialog box, ensure that the namespace is root\CIMv2.

5. Enter the WMI query in the Query box, and then click OK. Here is an example:

    ```
    Select * from Win32_LogicalDisk where FreeSpace > 104857600 AND Caption = "C:"
    ```

6. Click Save to save the filter and close the New WMI Filter dialog box.

7. In the GPMC, click the GPO to which you want to link the WMI filter.

8. Select the Scope tab in the details pane.

9. From the drop-down list in the WMI Filtering section, click the WMI filter that you just created, as shown previously in Figure 5-9.

10. A Group Policy Management dialog box appears asking if you want to change the WMI filter to the WMI you have selected. Click Yes.

Group Policy Preferences

The only option that can alter default GPO processing at the GPO setting level is related to Group Policy Preferences settings. The technology that makes this possible is item-level targeting. Item-level targeting allows for one or more decision criteria to be configured to ensure that the settings apply to the correct computers and users. There are over 25 item-level targeting criteria, as shown in Figure 5-10.

For more information about Group Policy Preferences, item-level targeting, and creating the criteria for the target, refer to Chapter 12.

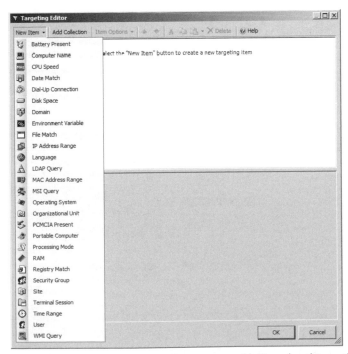

Figure 5-10   Group Policy Preferences provide item-level targeting to ensure that GPO settings apply to the correct users and computers.

Summary

Group Policy processing is the most important aspect of the Group Policy technology. If processing does not occur, no settings apply. The default processing of GPOs considers that a GPO can be linked to a site, the domain, or an organizational unit. It also considers the local GPO.

Without altering the default Group Policy processing behavior, all computers and users that are in the scope of management of the GPO will receive the appropriate settings contained within it.

If you alter the processing of GPOs and their settings, you can specify which GPOs and settings affect specific computers and users. Blocking policy inheritance, enforcing GPOs, WMI filters, security filtering, and Group Policy Preferences provide granular control over Group Policy processing.

Additional Resources

- The Microsoft TechNet article titled "How Security Settings Extension Works," at *http://technet2.microsoft.com/windowsserver/en/library/f546e58e-8473-4985-a05d-0b038dea4a9f1033.mspx?mfr=true*, includes information about the security CSE and its processing.

- Chapter 3, "Group Policy Basics," covers information regarding LGPOs.

- Chapter 4, "Architecture of Group Policy," includes information about the structure of GPO storage and CSEs.

- Chapter 11, "Customizing ADM Templates and ADMX Files," covers information about customizing registry settings using ADMX files.

- Chapter 12, "Group Policy Preferences," includes information about item-level targeting for Group Policy Preferences.

- Chapter 13, "Settings Breakdown for Windows Server 2008 and Windows Vista," includes information about the settings that control slow links.

- Chapter 15, "Troubleshooting GPOs," includes information about Group Policy processing and fixing issues related to replication and application of policy.

Part III
Administering Group Policy

Chapter 6
Using the GPMC

The Group Policy Management Console (GPMC) has been around for a long time, in technology years anyway. Microsoft introduced the GPMC as a revolutionary free tool soon after the release of Windows Server 2003. The tool has not seen many advancements, until now. With Windows Vista and Windows Server 2008, the GPMC provides new functions and features that administrators have desired for a long time.

The GPMC now provides a better interface for viewing the huge variety of Group Policy settings. The new filters and searching capabilities allow for a more efficient view of the Group Policy settings; they also allow you to focus on nearly every possible scenario within the GPO, such as enabled, disabled, configured, operating system supported, and so on.

One of the most significant and proven benefits of the GPMC is the ability to see the entire Group Policy infrastructure in one simple view. The GPMC is ideal for creating, editing, linking, and managing nearly every aspect of every GPO in the environment. With Windows Server 2008 and Windows Vista, the GMPC also supports a new feature called Starter GPOs. Starter GPOs are tools that administrators use to create baseline settings for the GPOs they configure for the different computers, users, departments, and scenarios in your company.

Getting Around in the GPMC

To ensure that you are familiar with the GPMC, the following sections provide a firm foundation in GPMC basics, including descriptions of some new features and functions.

Launching the GPMC from Windows Server 2008

To access the GPMC from a computer running Windows Server 2008, you should first ensure that the GPMC is installed on your computer before trying to run it from the command prompt or Run menu option. With Windows Server 2008, you can access the GPMC locally without any additional installations. The easiest way to do this is to perform one of the following two tasks:

Option 1:

1. On the taskbar, click Start, and then click Run.

2. In the Run dialog box, type **gpmc.msc**.

Option 2:

1. On the taskbar, click Start, and then click Administrative Tools.

2. On the Administrative Tools menu, click Group Policy Management.

> **Note**   Windows Server 2008 does not come with the GPMC installed on nondomain controllers. For these computers, you must install it from the Server Manager.

Launching the GPMC from Windows Vista

To launch the GPMC from a computer running Windows Vista, you must first consider the service pack you are running. With no service packs, Windows Vista comes with the older version of the GPMC installed and ready to go, similar to Windows Server 2008. However, because of the dramatic GPMC advancements shipping with Windows Server 2008, Service Pack 1 for Windows Vista removes the GPMC, providing a clean slate for the improved GPMC that is compatible with Windows Server 2008. To access the new GPMC for Windows Vista, you must download and install the Remote Server Administrative Tools (RSAT).

Domain Views in the GPMC

The GPMC allows you to view your entire Group Policy infrastructure, whether you have a single domain, a single forest that includes multiple domains, or multiple forests. By default, the GPMC displays the domain in which the administering computer has membership. For example, if you are using Windows Vista to manage GPOs, the GPMC will default to the domain of which the Windows Vista machine is a member.

If you want to add additional domains from the same forest to the GPMC interface, you can do so in just a few clicks:

1. In the GPMC, expand the forest node in which you want to add a domain.

2. Right-click the Domains node, and then click Show Domains.

3. In the Show Domains dialog box, select the check box for each domain that you want to add to the GPMC.

This process allows you to add all of the domains within the forest to the GPMC for centralized management of all Group Policy for the entire forest.

Forest Views in the GPMC

The GPMC offers the ability to add additional domains from other forests for Group Policy management. The process is a bit different for these domains because they fall outside of the current forest and therefore require additional security measures.

To add a domain from another forest into the GPMC, some form of trust must be established with the other domain or forest. Microsoft Windows Server 2003 introduced the ability to establish forest trust. A forest trust is not required to manage domains from another forest, but it provides the greatest flexibility and efficiency for managing all domains in another forest; a domain trust is simply a one-to-one connection to a single domain. The following options and configurations provide access to a domain in another forest for managing Group Policy from within the GPMC:

- Forest trust between the resident forest and the desired forest containing the domain you want to manage. This requires Windows Server 2003 or greater domain and forest functional levels.

- Two-way trust between the resident domain and the domain that you want to manage.

- One-way trust between the resident domain and the domain that you want to manage. In addition to the trust, the trust detection configuration must be disabled, as shown in Figure 6-1.

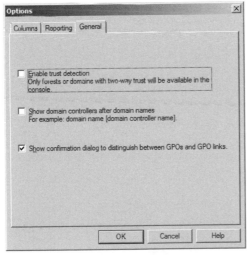

Figure 6-1   To administer GPOs from another forest's domain with a one-way trust, you must disable the trust detection option in the GPMC.

With one of these options configured, you can add a domain from another forest to the GPMC for administration by following these steps:

1. In the GPMC, right-click the Group Policy Management node, and then click Add Forest.

2. In the Add Forest dialog box, type the domain name for the forest you want to add; this should be the DNS domain name.

> **Note**   Administrators must establish appropriate permissions and delegations to administer any object, including GPOs, from another domain. Ensure that the delegations are correct before attempting to administer GPOs from another domain.

Site Views in the GPMC

By default, no sites are present in the GPMC. The most obvious reason for this might be that there are no GPOs linked to any sites by default. This is because there are only two default GPOs, which are linked to the domain node and the Domain Controllers Organizational Unit (OU).

The GPMC does not show sites by default because it is a best practice to limit the number of GPOs that administrators link to sites. Because sites are IP based, linking GPOs to sites is not the most logical or straightforward method for deploying GPO settings.

However, if you do want to add sites to the GPMC, you can do so by following these steps:

1. In the GPMC, expand the forest node in which you want to add a domain.

2. Right-click the Sites node, and then click Show Sites.

3. In the Show Sites dialog box, select the check box next to each site that you want to add to the GPMC.

GPMC Management Limitations

Unlike with many other interfaces for managing Active Directory directory service objects, files and folders, and other similar objects, the GPMC does not automatically create objects in the environment simply by adding them to the GPMC. Because of this behavior, many of the following limitations are characteristics of the GPMC, even though other Active Directory management tools provide the features:

- Adding a domain to the GPMC will not create the domain in Active Directory.

- Adding a forest to the GPMC will not create a new forest or domain in Active Directory.

- Adding a site to the GPMC will not create a new site in Active Directory.

- Because forests do not have names in Active Directory, a forest added to the GPMC will be named after the forest root domain.

- When you add a forest to the GPMC, only one domain is added at a time. Additional domains must be added separately.

- Sites are not added by default in the GPMC. They must be added explicitly.

- Group Policy is not inherited across domains or forests, even if multiple domains and forests are added to the same GPMC.

Selecting Domain Controllers for Administration of GPOs

Within the GPMC, you have complete control over which domain controller you use for management of GPOs. As you saw in Chapter 4, "Architecture of Group Policy," the domain controller that contains the PDC (primary domain controller) emulator role is the default domain controller for updating GPOs. Within the GPMC you can select the domain controller for both the domain and the site for managing GPOs.

To select the domain controller you want to use for managing GPOs related to the domain, follow these steps:

1. In the GPMC, expand the forest node in which you want to add a domain.

2. Right-click the *<domainname>* node, and then click Change Domain Controller.

3. In the Change Domain Controller dialog box, select the option associated with the domain controller that you want to use.

The Change Domain Controller dialog box provides many options, as shown in Figure 6-2.

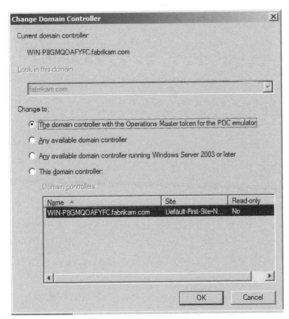

Figure 6-2   You can select the domain controller used to manage GPOs for the domain node in the GPMC.

Each of these options offers benefits:

- **The domain controller with the Operations Master token for the PDC emulator**   This is the default option. In most cases with small to medium-sized companies, it is best to keep the default domain controller configuration, to simplify troubleshooting of Group Policy.

■ **Any available domain controller**   When the domain controller with the PDC emulator role is not available, or the specific domain controller that you picked is not available, this option selects a domain controller that is online. By far, this is the most generic of the four settings, ensuring that you can connect to any domain controller that is online.

■ **Any available domain controller running Windows Server 2003 or later**   Group Policy tools are aware that different operating system versions provide additional features in the GPMC. This option is available to help the Group Policy tools that are aware that different operating system versions provide additional features. In some cases, schema extensions or files may be in a different location, so the version of the operating system is important. For example, with Windows Vista and Windows Server 2008, the GPMC looks for the ADMX files located in the PolicyDefinition folder. Pointing the tool to a domain controller with the correct information is important in such a scenario.

■ **This domain controller**   When you want to optimize the placement of a setting on a domain controller that is close to a target computer that will receive a GPO setting, this option is ideal. This is the most precise of all of the options, allowing you to target the modification of a GPO setting to a specific domain controller.

> **Note**   You can also select the domain controller that you want to use for modeling of GPOs. This is discussed later in this chapter in the "Group Policy Modeling" section.

Administering GPOs

The management of GPOs occurs entirely within the GPMC, the command center for GPOs. Administrators can complete a variety of tasks within the GPMC, some of which you might not be familiar with because the features are either new or somewhat hidden. The most basic task is creating a GPO, but the management of GPOs goes well beyond that.

GPO management includes control of the GPO from design through implementation—and troubleshooting if required. The GPMC helps with all aspects of the overall management of GPOs. After you create a GPO, you must link it to a node within Active Directory. You must then manage the GPO, which includes configuring security, enabling the GPO, and potentially deleting the GPO if necessary. Backing up GPOs is essential, in case of a disaster. Finally, a new feature added with Windows Server 2008 is the ability to create Starter GPOs. Starter GPOs are excellent for baselining and for making overall GPO creation and management easier.

Creating GPOs

The creation of GPOs should not occur without serious consideration of two aspects of your enterprise. First, you should know exactly which settings you want to create in the GPO. The creation of a GPO that has no purpose or has settings that are not well conceived or documented could cause damage or network downtime if incorrectly linked. Second, you should know where the GPO will be linked and which objects it should target. Again, having errant GPOs within your Active Directory infrastructure can cause significant issues if not managed.

Before you start creating GPOs, you must design them into the environment. The design of GPOs consists of the following tasks:

■ Determine which objects will be controlled.

■ Determine whether the current organizational unit structure can support default GPO processing and inheritance, or whether filtering or targeting must be used. For more information about filtering and targeting, refer to Chapter 5, "Group Policy Processing," and Chapter 12, "Group Policy Preferences."

■ Select the settings that must be configured in each GPO required.

> **Note**   For more information about designing GPO deployment, refer to "Designing a Group Policy Infrastructure" at *http://technet2.microsoft.com/windowsserver/en/library/ c75e3e6f-c322-4220-b205-46c6e9ba76741033.mspx?mfr=true*.

After your design of the GPO is complete, implementation of the GPO starts with its creation. The creation of a GPO is very simple and has some characteristics that can help you manage all newly created GPOs. All new GPOs have these characteristics:

■ Blank, with no settings configured (unless you use a Starter GPO)

■ Enabled by default

■ Configured to affect all user and computer accounts in the scope of management, through the Authenticated Users group

Creating a GPO involves just a few clicks within the GPMC. To create a new GPO that you do not link to an Active Directory node, follow these steps:

1. In the GPMC, expand the forest node, and then expand the domain node.

2. Right-click the Group Policy Objects node, and then click New.

3. In the New GPO dialog box, type the name of the new GPO.

4. (Optional) Select the Starter GPO that you want to use from the Source Starter GPO list. Starter GPOs are discussed later in this chapter.

Another way to create a new GPO is to have it linked to an Active Directory node upon creation. This process helps eliminate the issue of creating test or random GPOs that are not linked to any node and never seem to get configured. Creating and linking a GPO in one step can help eliminate random, empty GPOs. To create a GPO that is linked to an Active Directory node upon creation, follow these steps:

1. In the GPMC, expand the forest node, and then expand the domain node.

2. Right-click the Active Directory node to which you want to link the new GPO (*<domainname>*, organizational unit, or site), and then click Create A GPO In This Domain, And Link It Here.

3. In the New GPO dialog box, type the name of the new GPO.

4. (Optional) Select the Starter GPO that you want to use from the Source Starter GPO list.

Although these two processes for creating a new GPO are similar, the end result is substantially different: Any setting that you make in the GPO that is linked to an Active Directory node will immediately be distributed to the target objects located in that scope. For example, if you link a GPO to the HR organizational unit, the user and computer objects in the HR organizational unit will be affected by the settings you make in the GPO.

> **Note**   The ability to create GPOs is not available to every user or administrator by default. Only a few accounts can create GPOs by default. For more information about granting delegation permission to create GPOs, refer to Chapter 9, "Security Delegation for Administration of GPOs."

Linking GPOs

Whether you want a GPO to affect a few objects or numerous objects, the GPO and the settings contained within it will only do so after you link the GPO to an Active Directory node. Linking GPOs within Active Directory is limited in scope to the major Active Directory structural components. Within Active Directory, you can link a GPO to the following node types:

- Domain, such as fabrikam.com
- Organizational Unit, such as Domain Controllers
- Site, such as *Default-first-site-name*

Linking a GPO to the other object types that exist in Active Directory will not work. Linking GPOs to individual user accounts, computer accounts, or group accounts is not possible.

You can link a GPO to a node either when the GPO is created or at a later time. Linking the GPO at the time of creation is discussed in the previous section, "Creating GPOs." If you want to link an existing GPO to a site, the domain, or an organizational unit, follow these steps:

1. In the GPMC, expand the forest node, and then expand the domain node.

2. Right-click the Active Directory node to which you want to link the existing GPO (*<domainname>*, organizational unit, or site), and then click Link An Existing GPO.

3. In the Select GPO dialog box, select the domain from which you want to link the GPO from the Look In This Domain list (the default domain listed is typically the domain that you want to use).

4. Select the GPO or GPOs to which you want to link from the Group Policy Objects box.

After you have linked the GPO, the objects under the scope of the node will be affected by the policy settings in the GPO. Of course, if you have configured any other settings to alter the default processing or inheritance of processing the GPO, you will need to consider these settings.

The GPMC provides two ways to view GPO links to Active Directory nodes. The first option is to view the Active Directory nodes to which a specific GPO is linked. To view the links per GPO, follow these steps:

1. In the GPMC, expand the forest node, and then expand the domain node.

2. Expand the Group Policy Objects node.

3. Select the GPO for which you want to see links.

4. In the right pane, click the Scope tab.

5. Under "The following sites, domains, and OUs are linked to this GPO," you will see the full list of Active Directory nodes, as shown in Figure 6-3

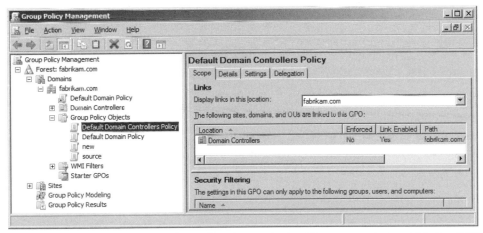

Figure 6-3   The Scope tab displays a list of every Active Directory node to which the GPO is linked.

The second option is to view all of the GPOs that are linked to a specific Active Directory node. This will give you an excellent idea of the most directly linked GPOs that will affect the objects in scope. To view the GPOs linked to a specific Active Directory node, follow these steps:

1. In the GPMC, expand the forest node, and then expand the domain node.

2. Select the Active Directory node for which you want to view GPO links.

3. In the right pane, click the Linked Group Policy Objects tab.

4. The GPO column displays the full list of GPOs that are linked to this node, as shown in Figure 6-4.

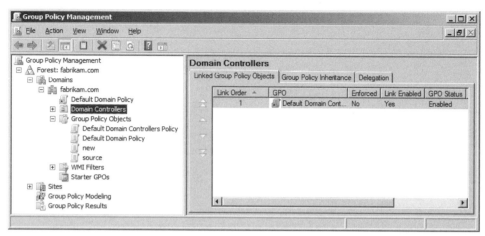

Figure 6-4   You can view all of the GPOs linked to a specific Active Directory node.

> **Note**   The ability to link GPOs to Active Directory nodes is not available to every user or administrator by default. Only a few accounts can link a GPO to an Active Directory node by default. For more information about granting delegation permission to link GPOs, refer to Chapter 9.

Managing GPO Configurations

The GPMC can do a lot to expose configurations that can be made for GPOs. Although this section does not discuss all aspects of the configurations, it covers the areas that do not fall into other categories. However, to give you an idea of what is covered here and elsewhere, Table 6-1 provides direction for GPMC/GPO configurations and where you will find the information in this book.

Table 6-1   GPMC/GPO Configuration Reference

GPMC/GPO Configuration	Chapter
Add Forest, Domain, or site to GPMC	Chapter 5
Manage Migration Tables	Chapter 5
Manage GPO Backups	Chapter 5
Creating GPOs	Chapter 5
Linking GPOs	Chapter 5
Blocking Inheritance	Chapter 4
Group Policy Modeling and Results	Chapter 5

Table 6-1   GPMC/GPO Configuration Reference

GPMC/GPO Configuration	Chapter
Changing Domain Controllers for GPMC	Chapter 5
Editing GPOs	Chapters 2, 3, 8
Enforcing GPOs	Chapter 4
Enabling/Disabling GPOs	Chapter 5
Import Settings into GPOs	Chapter 5
WMI Filters	Chapter 4
Starter GPOs	Chapter 5
GPO Security Filtering	Chapter 4
GPMC Delegation	Chapter 8
Searching GPOs	Chapter 5

This section helps you find all areas of Group Policy management, and it also describes some management features that are not covered elsewhere in this book. The three tasks that are critical to Group Policy management but do not fit into other areas are described in the following sections.

Enabling and Disabling GPOs

Some believe that disabling a portion of a GPO can increase the performance of Group Policy processing. However, some review and log analysis shows that is really not true. Even with a portion of a GPO disabled, the server must still analyze it to some degree during processing. To enable or disable a portion of the GPO, follow these steps:

1. In the GPMC, expand the forest node, and then expand the domain node.

2. Expand the Group Policy Objects node.

3. Select the GPO that you want to enable or disable.

4. Select the Details tab in the details pane.

5. In the GPO Status list, select the enable or disable option that you want.

How It Works: Processing of Disabled GPOs

Let's say you disable the computer portion of a GPO. During processing, this is basically equivalent to finding the GPO with a version of 0. The client must still query Lightweight Directory Access Protocol (LDAP) to determine whether that side is disabled, so performance is not increased significantly; the effect would be the same if the portion of the GPO were not disabled. From a performance perspective, there is little value in this function, but it may offer user convenience. That is, this feature allows you to "turn off" some policies without having to unlink the GPO from the node.

Renaming GPOs

There might be a time when you need to rename a GPO for some reason. You can do so easily by using the GPMC. The system does not rely on the name of the GPO, but rather on the GUID of the GPO; the GPO name is really just an alias. To change the name of a GPO using the GPMC, follow these steps:

1. In the GPMC, expand the forest node, and then expand the domain node.

2. Expand the Group Policy Objects node.

3. Right-click the GPO that you want to rename, click Rename, and then type the new name for the GPO.

4. Press Enter.

Enabling and Disabling a GPO Link

There might be a time when you want to disable just one of the nodes that a GPO is linked to. For example, you might want to disable a GPO link for a short time only; in an instance such as this, you can disable a GPO link but keep it active. This might seem like an insignificant configuration, but it allows you to maintain the overall link strategy. The maintenance of the strategy will help prevent situations in which GPOs become orphaned from any links to nodes in Active Directory. When you want the GPO to be active again for that link, you can easily re-enable the link.

To disable or enable a GPO link, follow these steps:

1. In the GPMC, expand the forest node, and then expand the domain node.

2. Right-click the Active Directory node for which you want to alter the GPO link, and then click Link Enabled.

> **Note**   If the Link Enabled menu option is selected, the link is enabled; if cleared, it is disabled.

Managing GPO Backups

The GPMC provides some amazing features, but some of these are not automated. One of the best and most important features of the GPMC is the ability to protect your Group Policy investment by backing up the GPOs. You have complete control over restoring your backups in case of a disaster.

> **Note**   If you want to automate the process of backing up GPOs when an administrator edits them, you should consider the Microsoft Advanced Group Policy Management (AGPM) tool. Chapter 14, "Advanced GPO Management with AGPM," describes the tool and explains how it automatically backs up the GPO being edited every time it is modified.

Backing Up GPOs

When you back up a GPO, all of the settings that you have implemented are archived; this is valuable in case of a disaster or in case an older version of the GPO is needed in the future. The backup routine also backs up other essential aspects of the GPO. These other areas include:

- Security filtering
- Delegation of administration
- Windows Management Instrumentation (WMI) filter links

For more information about WMI filters, refer to Chapter 5.

The areas of a GPO that are not included in the backup and restore routine include:

- WMI filter files
- IPsec policies
- Links to sites, domains, and organizational units

To perform a backup of a single GPO, you must have Read permissions on the GPO and Write permissions on the folder containing the GPO backup. Then follow these steps:

1. In the GPMC, expand the forest node, and then expand the domain node.

2. Expand the Group Policy Objects node, right-click the GPO that you want to back up, and then click Back Up.

3. In the Back Up Group Policy Object dialog box, type the path and name of the folder where you want to store your GPO backups in the Location box.

4. (Optional) Enter a description for the backed-up GPO in the Description box.

5. Click Back Up.

> **Note** If you have not already configured a path and folder for backing up your GPOs, click Browse in step 3 to create a folder in which you want to store your GPO backups. To secure the backed-up GPO, ensure that only authorized administrators have permission to access the folder to which you are exporting the GPOs.

Of course, if you choose to back up your GPOs in this manner, you must perform these steps for each GPO if you want to back up all of the GPOs for the domain. A much more efficient option is to select the option to back up all of the GPOs. This is the default option in the GPMC interface. To back up all of your GPOs at one time, follow these steps:

1. In the GPMC, expand the forest node, and then expand the domain node.

2. Right-click the Group Policy Objects node, and then click Back Up All.

3. In the Back Up Group Policy Object dialog box, type the path and name of the folder where you want to store your GPO backups.

4. Click Back Up.

5. After the GPO is backed up, click OK.

Figure 6-5 shows the confirmation of a successful backup.

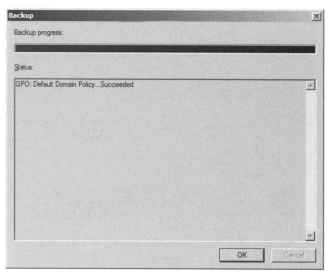

Figure 6-5   If the GPO is backed up successfully, you will receive a confirmation that the action was a success.

> **Best Practices**   It is a best practice to back up a GPO before and after you modify it. This ensures that you have a functioning copy of the GPO before you alter it. The GPMC backup program allows you to restore GPOs that you have backed up.

Restoring GPOs

You might need to recover a GPO because of an incorrect configuration that must be undone, or for a variety of other reasons. Regardless of the reason, the restoration process is easy and straightforward. You can restore a GPO that still exists, or one that you have deleted. This is possible because the system backs up the GPO's GUID, settings, and WMI filter links. The process for restoring a GPO that still exists in the GPMC is slightly different from the process for restoring one that has been deleted, but the end result is the same, which are all of the aspects of the GPO that were backed up (see list of items backed up above).

Restoring an Existing GPO   To restore a GPO that still exists in the GPMC and has been backed up, follow these steps:

1. In the GPMC, expand the forest node, and then expand the domain node.

2. Expand the Group Policy Objects node.

3.   Right-click the GPO that you want to restore from the backup archive, and then click Restore From Backup. The Restore Group Policy Object Wizard appears.

4.   On the Welcome to the Restore Group Policy Object Wizard page, click Next.

5.   On the Backup Location page, select the folder that contains the backed-up GPO from the Backup Folder list, and then click Next.

6.   On the Source GPO page, select the GPO that you want to restore from the Backed Up GPOs list box, and then click Next.

7.   Click Finish to complete the Restore Group Policy Object Wizard, as shown in Figure 6-6.

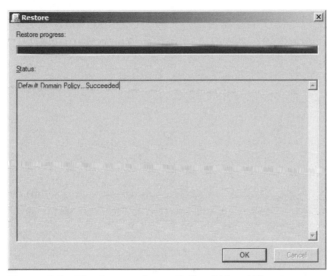

Figure 6-6   The Restore Group Policy Object Wizard presents a summary of the GPO that was restored during the restoration process.

 Warning   Restoration of an existing GPO will overwrite the existing GPO.

Restoring a Deleted GPO   If an administrator has already deleted a GPO, or it no longer exists in the domain but has been backed up in the past, you can restore it by following these steps:

1.   In the GPMC, expand the forest node, and then expand the domain node.

2.   Right-click the Group Policy Objects node, and then click Manage Backups.

3.   In the Manage Backups dialog box, select the GPO that you want to restore from the Backed Up GPOs list, as shown in Figure 6-7.

4.   Click Restore, and then, in the Group Policy Management message box, click OK to confirm the restoration.

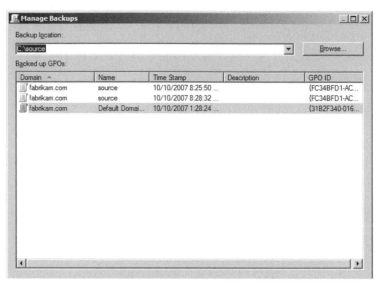

Figure 6-7   The Manage Backups dialog box allows you to restore a GPO that has been previously backed up.

Viewing the GPO Settings of a Backed-Up GPO   If you have been following the best practices for backing up your GPOs, you will have numerous copies of your GPOs in the backup archive. With so many GPOs listed in the archive, it is difficult to know which GPO has the settings that you want to restore. The GPOs include the timestamp when they are archived, but over time this will not help you remember the exact settings that were in the GPO at the time of the backup.

To help you remember the settings in the backed-up GPOs, you can access a settings report from within the GPO archive. To view the settings of any backed-up GPO, follow these steps:

1. In the GPMC, expand the forest node, and then expand the domain node.

2. Right-click the Group Policy Objects node, and then click Manage Backups.

3. In the Manage Backups dialog box, select the GPO for which you want to view the settings from the Backed Up GPOs list.

4. Click View Settings.

> **Note**   If a Microsoft Internet Explorer dialog box appears regarding security of the Web page you are attempting to view, you can either close the dialog box and view the content on a limited basis or add the page to the trusted sites list.

The ability to view the settings of a backed-up GPO is also extremely useful when you are restoring a GPO. The View Settings button is available during the selection of the GPO when you are restoring it. It is always a good idea to look at the GPO settings before restoration, to ensure that you do not deploy an incorrect or damaging setting into production.

Starter GPOs

A new GPMC feature in Windows Server 2008 is the Starter GPO. Starter GPOs provide a mechanism for Group Policy administrators to establish a set of policy settings that can serve as a baseline for all newly created GPOs. The Starter GPOs not only allow you to produce a baseline of settings—they also promote the establishment of best-practice Group Policy settings within each GPO that you create.

There can be many Starter GPOs to accommodate a wide variety of different GPOs. For example, you might have Starter GPOs for security, Internet Explorer, desktop profiles, wireless, and so on. The Starter GPOs contain recommended settings, which you can alter within each new GPO that you create from them. Starter GPOs are designed so that anyone can create and share them with the Group Policy administrators.

Creating Starter GPOs

To create a Starter GPO, follow these steps:

1. In the GPMC, expand the forest node, and then expand the domain node.

2. Right-click the Starter GPOs node, and then click New.

> **Note**   If you have not created any Starter GPOs, you must first click the Create Starter GPOs Folder on the Contents tab in the right pane.

3. Select the Starter GPOs node to view your new Starter GPO in the right pane, as shown in Figure 6-8.

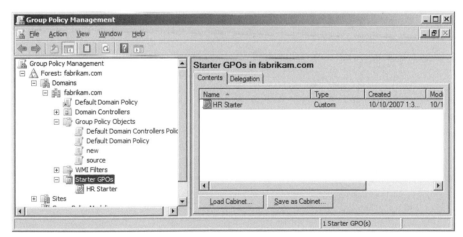

Figure 6-8   Starter GPOs allow you to configure baseline settings for the creation of new GPOs.

The primary reason for creating Starter GPOs is to establish a baseline of settings from which new GPOs can be created. There are two methods for doing this. You can either create the new

GPO by right-clicking the Starter GPO, or you can select a Starter GPO during the creation of a new GPO.

To create a new GPO from the Starter GPO, follow these steps:

1. In the GPMC, expand the forest node, and then expand the domain node.

2. Click the Starter GPOs node.

3. In the list of Starter GPOs in the right pane, right-click the Starter GPO that you want to use, and then click New GPO From Starter GPO.

4. In the New GPO dialog box, type the name of the new GPO in the Name box.

To create a new GPO by selecting a Starter GPO during the creation process, follow these steps:

1. In the GPMC, expand the forest node, and then expand the domain node.

2. Right-click the Group Policy Objects node, and then click New.

3. In the New GPO dialog box, select the Starter GPO that you want to use from the Source Starter GPO list.

4. Type the name for the new GPO in the Name box, and then click OK.

Editing Starter GPOs

The process for editing a Starter GPO is almost identical to the process for editing a standard GPO, with some slight differences. The most notable difference is that a Starter GPO does not contain all areas of a standard GPO. Instead, a Starter GPO contains only the Administrative Template settings. To edit a Starter GPO, follow these steps:

1. In the GPMC, expand the forest node, and then expand the domain node.

2. Expand the Starter GPOs node.

3. Right-click the Starter GPO that you want to edit, and then click Edit. The Group Policy Starter GPO Editor appears.

4. Configure your settings in the Group Policy Starter GPO Editor.

5. Exit the Group Policy Starter GPO Editor.

Backing Up Starter GPOs

The GPMC not only provides you with the new Starter GPOs—it is also a complete mechanism for backing them up. The backup routine for Starter GPOs is similar to that for a normal GPO, but you can select a different archive folder for them. This is recommended, because the folder that houses the backed-up GPOs controls access to them. If you allow too many users and administrators to access the Starter GPO archive and it shares the space with the normal GPOs, you are exposing the normal GPOs to too many users.

To back up the Starter GPOs, follow these steps:

1. In the GPMC, expand the forest node, and then expand the domain node.

2. Click the Starter GPOs node.

3. In the details pane, right-click the Starter GPO that you want to back up, and then click Back Up.

4. Type the path and name of the folder where you want to store your backups in the Location box.

5. (Optional) Enter a description for the backed-up GPO in the Description box.

6. Click Back Up.

> **Note**   If you have not already configured a path and folder for backing up your Starter GPOs, click Browse in step 4 to create a folder where you want to store your GPO backups.

You can also back up all Starter GPOs with just a few clicks, instead of backing up each one individually. This can make your administration time more efficient and also provide a standard backup routine for your Starter GPOs. To back up all Starter GPOs at one time, perform the following steps:

1. In the GPMC, expand the forest node, and then expand the domain node.

2. Right-click the Starter GPOs node, and then click Back Up All.

3. In the Back Up Starter GPO dialog box, type the path and name of the folder where you want to store your GPO backups in the Location box.

4. Click Back Up.

Working with Starter GPO Cabinet Files

Starter GPOs are meant to help administrators with the overall administration and baselining of new GPOs. They can ensure that all GPOs meet a specific level of security, as well as any other company requirements. Starter GPOs can also be used in other domains, forests, and companies, and they can be shared between IT professionals through the use of cabinet files.

Any Starter GPO can be placed into a cabinet file (CAB file). CAB files are what make Starter GPOs portable so that administrators can share them among different environments. CAB files contain all of the important information for the Starter GPO, including:

■ Settings for both Computer and User

■ Name of Starter GPO

■ Type of Starter GPO

- Version of both Computer and User parts of the GPO
- Author
- Product

To load a Starter GPO from a CAB file, follow these steps:

1. In the GPMC, expand the forest node, and then expand the domain node.
2. Click the Starter GPOs node.
3. In the details pane, click Load Cabinet.
4. In the Load Starter GPO dialog box, click Browse For CAB.
5. Select the CAB file from the list, and then click Open.
6. In the Load Starter GPO dialog box, click OK to load the Starter GPO.
7. In the Group Policy Management message box, click OK to verify that you want to overwrite the settings of an existing Starter GPO in the domain with that of the loaded CAB file.

If you have a Starter GPO that you want to share with someone or move to another environment, you can create your own CAB file containing your Starter GPO. To create a Starter GPO CAB file, follow these steps:

1. In the GPMC, expand the forest node, and then expand the domain node.
2. Click the Starter GPOs node.
3. In the details pane, select the Starter GPO that you want to place in a CAB file.
4. Click Save As Cabinet. The Save Starter GPO as Cabinet dialog box appears.
5. In the File Name box, type the name of the CAB file (if different from the Starter GPO name).
6. Click Browse Folders to select the location where you want the CAB file to be created.
7. Ensure that Starter GPO Cabinet File is selected in the Save As Type list.
8. Click Save.

Summary

The GPMC is almost a requirement for Group Policy management with Active Directory. The tool is secure, stable, and efficient, and it provides benefits for managing GPOs that no other solution provides within the Microsoft solutions. The GPMC is built in to Windows Server 2008 and is an easy download and install for Windows Vista Service Pack 1.

The GPMC provides an easy view of all domains, in the same forest or in different forests. This allows for easy administration of GPOs across all domains, even migration of GPOs from one domain to another.

With the GPMC, administrators can create, link, back up, and manage all aspects of the GPOs for the enterprise. The new Starter GPOs provide for an easy method of establishing baselines of settings, which new GPOs can use for efficient setting management.

The new GPMC also provides advanced management features such as searching, filtering, and commenting. All of these features make management and troubleshooting of GPOs more efficient and controllable.

Combine of all of these features with the capabilities of Group Policy Results and Group Policy Modeling, and the GPMC provides nearly everything that you might want for Group Policy management. If you do need to take a GPO from one domain to another, the migration tables provide an easy and straightforward method to accomplish this. GPOs can be migrated from one domain to another, even across forest boundaries.

Advanced Group Policy Management (AGPM) is an additional utility that can be included with the GPMC. AGPM provides additional advanced features that the GPMC does not provide, such as offline editing, change management, and further delegation of administration of GPOs. For more information about AGPM, refer to Chapter 14.

Additional Resources

- A Microsoft TechNet article at *http://technet2.microsoft.com/WindowsServer/en/library/ b98e4746-da0d-4da5-9fa8-1b2d69c9cad81033.mspx?mfr=true* includes information about migration tables.

- The Microsoft TechNet article titled "Administering Group Policy with Group Policy Management Console Abstract," at *http://www.microsoft.com/windowsserver2003/gpmc/ gpmcwp.mspx*, includes information about using user accounts in two domains simultaneously.

- Chapter 8, "Controlling Group Policy via Scripts and Automation," includes information about scripting migration tables and Group Policy management.

- Chapter 9, "Security Delegation for Administration of GPOs," includes information about security, delegation, and management of Group Policy.

- Chapter 14, "Advanced GPO Management with AGPM," includes detailed information on how to combine AGPM with the GPMC for in-depth GPO management.

- Chapter 15, "Troubleshooting GPOs," includes information about Group Policy events in the event viewer.

Chapter 7
Advanced GPMC Management

The Group Policy Management Console (GPMC) includes some advanced features that go beyond the basic management of Group Policy. Using these features might become daily tasks for some administrators, but for others, the tasks might occur only once a year, if ever.

The GPMC provides the robust capability to analyze your Group Policy structure with the Group Policy Modeling option and the Group Policy Results option. These options provide a method of testing the interaction of GPO settings and verifying that the settings meet the desired results before you place any GPO into production.

The GPMC also provides overall management of a large infrastructure of Group Policy. The GPMC provides a backup tool that gives you options for managing the backed-up GPOs, restoring them, and even viewing the settings before restoration.

If you need to move a GPO from one domain or forest to another, migration tables provide a mechanism to translate all user, group, and computer accounts from one environment to another.

Working with GPOs

After a GPO is created and you have settings configured, there is still work to be done. For example, you may need to locate settings, report on settings, troubleshoot a GPO setting, modify a specific GPO setting, and so on. With so many GPO settings available, there will be a time when you need to find or view only a few settings among the thousands available.

With the GPMC come new features that make working with GPOs and GPO settings efficient. A new search option allows you to find what you need very quickly and precisely, and special filtering options allow you to view the Administrative Template settings (which is where the majority of all settings exist) with many different filter options.

In addition to the searching and filtering options, you can also view a GPO and its settings from many different administrative standpoints. One option allows you to document the GPO and the settings very quickly and efficiently, and another provides the ability to determine what a suite of GPO settings will do to a computer or user account before it is put into production. The Group Policy Modeling Wizard allows you to select almost every possible scenario to learn what will happen to the Resultant Set of Policy (RSoP) for a computer and user account. If you just want to see the current settings for a computer or user account, the Group Policy Logging Wizard will get the job done.

Searching GPOs

If you want to find a specific GPO setting, whether it is configured or not, the GPMC search tool is perfect for you. The new search feature allows you to find nearly any setting, based on almost any criteria. Because Group Policy settings are so complex and numerous, a search tool needs to accommodate almost any scenario. The GPMC search tool fulfills these requirements.

The search tool can search all GPOs in all domains in the forest, or just a single domain of GPOs. To access the search tool, you can right-click either the Forest node or the *<domainname>* node in the GPMC. Both of these options present a Search option, which will open the Search for Group Policy Objects dialog box, shown in Figure 7-1.

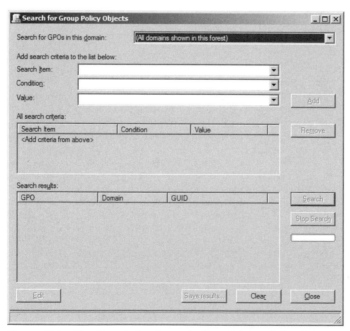

Figure 7-1   The Search for Group Policy Objects dialog box can be accessed from either the Forest node or the *<domainname>* node in the GPMC.

The search tool allows you to search on nearly every possible detail within a GPO. Each element of the search tool is described here.

- **Search Item**   This allows you to target specific areas of the GPO and Group Policy infrastructure. You can select from one of many global areas of Group Policy. When configuring the Search Item, you have the following choices:

  - ❑ GPO Name
  - ❑ GPO-links
  - ❑ Security Group
  - ❑ Linked WMI Filter
  - ❑ User Configuration
  - ❑ Computer Configuration
  - ❑ GUID

  Each of these selected items will determine a more specific setting. After configuring the Search Item, you define a Condition and Value, described next.

- **Condition**   Conditions are dynamic entries based on the Search Item that you selected. Conditions allow you to indicate more specifically which GPOs the search returns. Table 7-1 describes the Conditions available for each Search Item. After selecting the Condition, you will have more options to refine your search. This refinement is accomplished by configuring the Value option, described next.

Table 7-1 GPMC/GPO Configuration Reference

Search Item	Condition Options	Value Options
GPO Name	Contains	<Text entry>
	Does not contain	<Text entry>
	Is exactly	<Text entry>
GPO-links	Exist in	<domainname>
		[All Sites]
	Do not exist in	<domainname>
		[All Sites]
Security Group	Has this explicit permission	Apply settings
		Edit settings
		Edit settings, delete, modify security
		Read settings
	Does not have this explicit permission	Apply settings
		Edit settings
		Edit settings, delete, modify security
		Read settings
	Has this effective permission	Apply settings
		Edit settings
		Edit settings, delete, modify security
		Read settings

Table 7-1   GPMC/GPO Configuration Reference

Search Item	Condition Options	Value Options
	Does not have this effective permission	Apply settings
		Edit settings
		Edit settings, delete, modify security
		Read settings
Linked WMI Filter (domain only)	Is	\<WMI Filter name\>
	Is not	\<WMI Filter name\>
User Configuration	Contains (same as Does not Contain)	Deployed Printer Connections
		Folder Redirection
		Group Policy Data Sources
		Group Policy Device Settings
		Group Policy Drive Maps
		Group Policy Environment
		Group Policy Files
		Group Policy Folder Options
		Group Policy Folders
		Group Policy Ini Files
		Group Policy Internet Settings
		Group Policy Local Users and Groups
		Group Policy Network Options
		Group Policy Power Options
		Group Policy Printers
		Group Policy Regional Options
		Group Policy Registry
		Group Policy Scheduled Tasks
		Group Policy Services
		Group Policy Shortcuts
		Group Policy Start Menu
		Internet Explorer Branding
		Internet Explorer Zonemapping
		Microsoft Offline Files
		Policy-based QoS
		Registry
		Scripts
		Software Installation

Table 7-1   **GPMC/GPO Configuration Reference**

Search Item	Condition Options	Value Options
Computer Configuration	Contains (same as Does not Contain)	802.3 Group Policy
		Deployed Printer Connections
		EFS recovery
		Group Policy Data Sources
		Group Policy Device Settings
		Group Policy Drive Maps
		Group Policy Environment
		Group Policy Files
		Group Policy Folder Options
		Group Policy Folders
		Group Policy Ini Files
		Group Policy Internet Settings
		Group Policy Local Users and Groups
		Group Policy Network Options
		Group Policy Power Options
		Group Policy Printers
		Group Policy Regional Options
		Group Policy Registry
		Group Policy Scheduled Tasks
		Group Policy Services
		Group Policy Shortcuts
		Group Policy Start Menu
		Internet Explorer Zonemapping
		Internet Protocol Security Policies
		Microsoft Disk Quota
		Microsoft Offline Files
		Policy-Based QoS
		QoS Packet Scheduler
		Registry
		Scripts
		Security
		Software Installation
		Windows Search Group Policy Extension
		Wireless Group Policy
GUID	Equals	\<Text entry\>

- **Value**   Values are specified based on the Search Item and Condition selected. The Value allows the search tool to become very granular and detailed in the search for GPOs. Each Condition selected has a specific Value that can be configured. Table 7-1 includes all of the possible Values for each Condition that is specified.

The combination of Search Item, Condition, and Value make a full entry for the search criteria. You may enter many search criteria into the search tool to restrict the results of your search. This type of combined search is a powerful way to avoid the GPOs that you do not want to view and restrict results when troubleshooting the application of GPOs.

Filtering Administrative Templates in the GPME

The search tool is designed to find specific GPOs that match specified criteria. As an alternative to using the search tool, you can also filter settings within a GPO to restrict what you see in the Group Policy Management Editor (GPME). As stated, the filter tool is per GPO, whereas the search tool is per forest or domain, so the scope of the two tools is quite different.

Within the GPME, you can filter on Administrative Template settings only. If you right-click the Administrative Templates node in the GPME, you can click Filter Options to open the Filter Options dialog box, as shown in Figure 7-2.

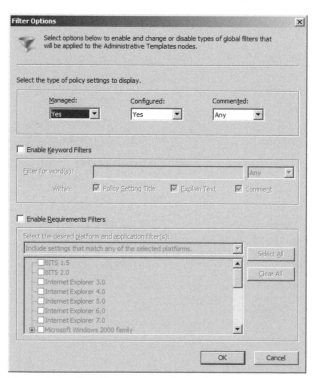

Figure 7-2   The Filter Options dialog box allows you to limit the number of Administrative Template settings you view within the GPME for optimized configuration of GPO settings.

Filter Options

The filter tool allows you to search on nearly every possible detail within the Administrative Templates settings, both Computer and User. Each element of the filter tool is described here.

- **Managed**   These are GPO settings that fall under the Policies categories for both Computer Configuration and User Configuration. These settings are volatile because they are located in a special part of the registry that is dynamic. The setting allows you to focus on GPO settings that are managed or not managed.

- **Configured**   By default, no GPO settings are configured. They appear as Not Configured in the interface. As soon as a setting is enabled, disabled, or set to anything but Not Configured, they will appear in the Configured category.

- **Commented**   All GPO settings can have a comment associated with them. These comments are excellent for tracking, documenting, and troubleshooting. Not all GPOs need to have comments, which is why it is good to have a filter that allows you to view only those settings that have a comment associated with them.

- **Enable Keyword Filters**   The keyword filter allows you to search for settings that are more general. For example, you might want to find all settings that contain the words *Internet*, *security*, or *desktop*. This filter can examine the Policy Setting Title, Explain Text, and Comment and allows you to specify any combination of these settings for searching.

- **Enable Requirements Filters**   The requirements filter allows you to focus on the technology that the policy setting controls, such as Microsoft Internet Explorer, as well as the version of the technology supported. The possible platforms that can be configured for the requirements filter include: options related to BITS, Internet Explorer, the Windows Server 2008 family, the Microsoft Windows Server 2003 family, the Windows 2000 family, the Windows XP family, the Windows Vista family, Windows Installer, Windows Media Player, and more.

Filter Option Operators

Each section in the Filter Options dialog box has a set of operators that also must be configured. These options allow you to include or exclude GPO settings from your filter. Table 7-2 lists the operators available for each filter area.

Table 7-2   Filter Options Operators

Type of Policy Setting	Operators
Managed	Any
	Yes
	No
Configured	Any
	Yes
	No

Table 7-2   Filter Options Operators

Type of Policy Setting	Operators
Commented	Any
	Yes
	No
Enable Keyword Filters	Any
(for keyword text that is entered)	All
	Exact
Within	Policy Setting Title
	Explain Text
	Comment
Enabled Requirements Filters	Include settings that match any of the selected platforms.
	Include settings that match all of the selected platforms.

Reporting on GPOs

You can use two different methods to run reports on GPOs within the GPMC. The first is a real-time view of the GPO settings that are currently configured in the GPO, which lets you view settings without having to search through the GPO for them. The second view is a slightly different view of the GPO, including not just the settings, but also the links, delegation, filtering, and so on. This view is excellent for documentation of the GPO's current state.

The first view of the GPO is built directly into the interface. It is referred to as the Settings report and is located in the details pane of the GPMC window. To view the Settings report for any of the GPOs, follow these steps:

1. In the GPMC, expand the forest node, and then expand the domain node.

2. Expand the Group Policy Objects node.

3. Select the GPO for which you want to see a report.

4. In the details pane, click the Settings tab.

5. In the Internet Explorer warning dialog box, click Close or Add. (This step might be optional, depending on your Internet Explorer security settings.)

You will see the full list of settings within the GPO, for both Computer Configuration and User Configuration, as shown in Figure 7-3.

The second report that you can run for a GPO is not as interactive as the Settings report, but it is more thorough and ideal for documentation of all GPOs.

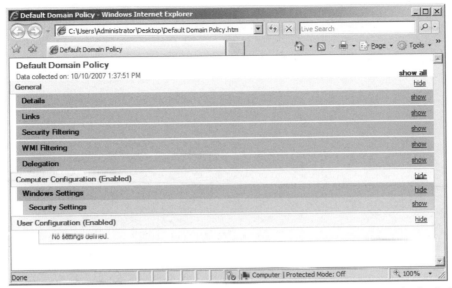

Figure 7-3 The Settings report summarizes all of the settings in the GPO, for both Computer Configuration and User Configuration.

> **Best Practices** It is a good idea to save reports for every GPO periodically, for documentation and disaster recovery of all GPOs. Because the saved reports of a GPO include all essential information about the GPO, they provide an excellent tool for troubleshooting in case of an errant setting or even complete disaster of your Group Policy infrastructure. You should print the reports and keep them in a binder in the server room for quick reference. You could also use the HTML reports on a secure intranet site that only the administrators and Help desk staff have access to for remote access to the settings in all GPOs.

To run a report that you can save to HTML or XML format, follow these steps:

1. In the GPMC, expand the forest node, and then expand the domain node.

2. Expand the Group Policy Objects node.

3. Right-click the GPO for which you want to save a report, and then click Save Report. The Save GPO Report dialog box appears.

4. Click Browse Folders, select the location where the report will be saved, type a name for the report in the File Name box, and then select a file type (HTML or XML) from the Save As Type list.

5. Click Save.

After the report is saved, browse to the location where you saved it and double-click it to open it in Internet Explorer. HTML reports are extremely useful for routine viewing of the GPO and the settings. Figure 7-4 shows what a typical report includes.

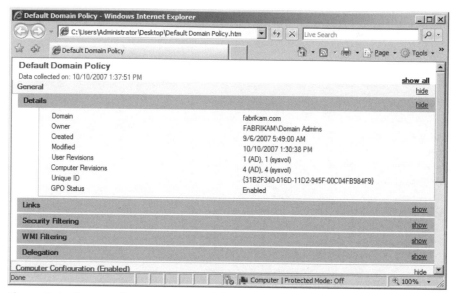

Figure 7-4   Reports that are generated from the GPMC contain essential information about the GPO, excellent for disaster recovery or troubleshooting.

Note that the report contains almost every bit of information that you would want to document for the GPO. Table 7-3 lists the contents of the saved GPO report.

Table 7-3   Saved Report Information

Report Section	Details Included
General - Details	Domain affiliation
	Owner of GPO
	Created and modified dates of GPO
	User and computer versions
	GUID of GPO
	Status of GPO
General - Links	List of all GPO links to the domain node or organizational units (not including links outside the current domain or to sites)
General - Security Filtering	Access control list of users and groups that will be affected by GPO
General - WMI Filtering	List of Windows Management Instrumentation (WMI) filters linked to GPO
General - Delegation	Security delegation for GPO, including permissions for each user or group
Computer Configuration	All GPO settings that fall under the Computer Configuration portion of the GPO, listed by section
User Configuration	All GPO settings that fall under the User Configuration portion of the GPO, listed by section

There is little else that you would want to document that the saved report does not provide.

Group Policy Results

Group Policy Results is a built-in utility that allows an administrator to view the settings for a specific user or computer, as well as for any object located in a specific organizational unit. The tool is built directly into the GPMC and models what the RSoP tool does locally on a computer.

To generate a report of the results, you must enter some information into a simple wizard. To generate a report, follow these steps:

1. In the GPMC, right-click the Group Policy Results node, and then click Group Policy Results Wizard.

2. On the Welcome to the Group Policy Results Wizard page, click Next.

3. On the Computer Selection page, choose the computer, if any, for which you want to generate a report, and then click Next.

   You can use the current computer or browse Active Directory directory service for a different computer. If you do not want to see any computer-related information in the report, select the Do Not Display Policy Settings For The Selected Computer In The Results (Display User Policy Settings Only) check box.

4. On the User Selection page, choose the user, if any, for whom you want to generate a report, and then click Next.

   You can use the current user or choose a user account from the list of users that have logged on to the computer before. If you do not want to see any user-related information in the report, select the Do Not Display User Policy Settings In The Results (Display Computer Policy Settings Only) check box.

5. On the Summary of Selections page, review your choices, and then click Next.

6. On the Completing the Group Policy Results Wizard page, click Finish to complete the Group Policy Results Wizard.

Results Pane for Group Policy Results

After you generate a report to see the Group Policy settings that will apply to a user or user/computer combination, you can see the results in the right pane. Each report that you generate will appear in the Group Policy Results node in the GPMC, and each will have three tabs that appear when you click them: Summary, Settings, and Policy Events.

Summary   The Summary tab displays all of the essential information that you will need regarding the objects that were selected, the location of the objects, and the GPOs that affected them, as shown in Figure 7-5.

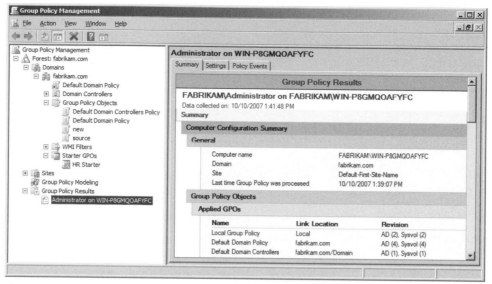

Figure 7-5 The Summary tab for Group Policy Results provides information regarding both the user and computer objects that were included in the report.

The important sections of this tab include the following:

- Computer Configuration Summary
  - ❏ General
  - ❏ Group Policy Objects
  - ❏ Security Group Membership when Group Policy was applied
  - ❏ WMI Filters
  - ❏ Component Status
- User Configuration Summary
  - ❏ General
  - ❏ Group Policy Objects
  - ❏ Security Group Membership when Group Policy was applied
  - ❏ WMI Filters
  - ❏ Component Status

Settings The Settings tab is similar to the Settings tab that you read about earlier. This tab is for the GPOs that affected the user and computer that were specified in the generation of the report.

Policy Events The Policy Events tab displays all of the Group Policy–related events that result from events generated by the system. This list is a summary of all of the Event Viewer events that Group Policy generates. SceCli and Group Policy are the primary events that you will see, as shown in Figure 7-6. For more information about events related to Group Policy, refer to Chapter 15, "Troubleshooting GPOs."

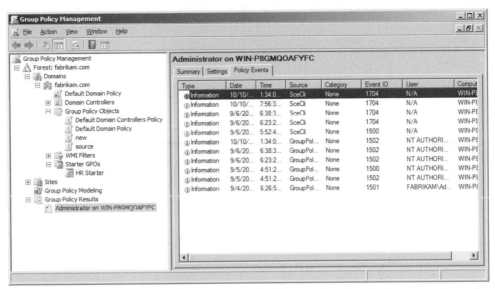

Figure 7-6 The Policy Events tab summarizes all of the events related to the computer and user that were used in the Group Policy Results report.

Controlling Results of Group Policy Reports

After you generate a report using Group Policy Reports, you have some advanced options for working with the results. The options are not advanced, but they do allow you to keep the results fresh and updated. Three options are available when you right-click the result under the Group Policy Results node.

Advanced View   This option displays the results in the traditional RSoP format, which organizes the settings like they are in the GPME, as shown in Figure 7-7

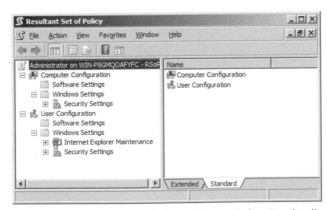

Figure 7-7 The Advanced view of Group Policy Results displays the settings in the traditional format, as in the GPME.

Rerun Query   You have the option to rerun the query, in case the user or computer object moves from one organizational unit to another. This option is available so you can keep the report and results up to date for troubleshooting purposes.

Save Report   This option allows you to document the output of the report. This is very similar to saving reports for a GPO, described earlier in this chapter. When you save a report, you need only specify the name of the file, the format of the file (HTML or XML), and the location where you want to save the file, as shown in Figure 7-8. The default location for the file is the Documents folder for the user who is generating the report.

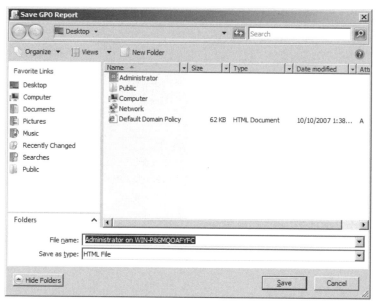

Figure 7-8   You can save a report for the output of each of the Group Policy Results that you generate.

Group Policy Modeling

Group Policy Modeling is a feature of the GPMC that allows administrators to see what settings will apply to a specific user or computer if that object is placed in a specified location in Active Directory. This allows the administrator to see and evaluate the potential GPO settings, before the settings actually apply to the object. This modeling can make administrative tasks much more efficient and reduce downtime that could result from settings causing negative effects on the target objects.

The Group Policy Modeling utility is a built-in feature of the GPMC that you can easily configure with a wizard. The wizard helps with all of the important configurations necessary to model the environment of the user or computer object when it is moved to a different location in Active Directory. To generate a report using the Group Policy Modeling utility, follow these steps:

1. In the GPMC, right-click the Group Policy Modeling node, and then click Group Policy Modeling Wizard.

2. On the Welcome to the Group Policy Modeling Wizard page, click Next.

3. On the Domain Controller Selection page, select the domain from the Show Domain Controllers In This Domain list and the domain controller from the Process The Simulation On This Domain Controller options that you want to use for the model, and then click Next.

> **Note** Ensure that you select a domain controller running Windows Server 2003 or later if you want to include settings and results that only Windows 2003 is aware of. Examples of these settings include wireless settings and some security settings.

4. On the User and Computer Selection page, select information about the user and computer objects, and then click Next.

   You can choose information about both types of objects, or just one of them. Here, you can choose an Active Directory path (using the LDAP syntax, such as CN=OU1, DC–fabrikam, DC=com), or you can specify the exact object (using the domain name followed by a slash and the object name, such as FABRIKAM\Administrator). You can either type the information directly or click Browse to find the container or object that you want to use in the report.

> **Note** At this point, or after any of the subsequent dialog boxes, you can choose to collect information only to that point and run the report based on what you have collected. You can do this by selecting the check box labeled Skip To The Final Page Of This Wizard Without Collecting Additional Data, and then clicking Next.

5. On the Advanced Simulation Options page, you have the option to configure the following considerations, as shown in Figure 7-9:

   ❑ Slow links: Select the Slow Network Connection (For Example, A Dial-Up Connection) check box.

   ❑ Loopback: Select the Loopback Processing check box, and then select either Replace or Merge.

   ❑ Site GPOs: Select the appropriate Active Directory site from the Site list.

6. On the Alternate Active Directory Paths page, select an optional new network location for the user or computer. You can enter the path manually by using the LDAP syntax, or you can browse for the path by clicking Browse.

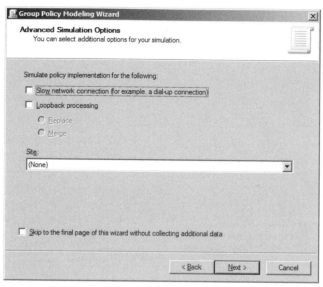

Figure 7-9   Advanced options for the Group Policy Modeling Wizard include consideration for slow links, loopback processing, and site GPOs.

7. On the User Security Groups page, click Add to include additional security groups that the user has membership in, or will have membership in when running the model. Click Remove to remove unwanted security groups from the list box. Then click Next.

8. On the Computer Security Groups page, click Add to include additional security groups that the computer has membership in, or will have membership in when running the model. Click Remove to remove unwanted security groups from the list box. Then click Next.

9. On the WMI Filters for Users page, select the WMI filters that should be considered for the user object in the model. You can select all of the WMI filters that are available or select just a few by selecting the Only These Filters option. Then click Next.

10. On the WMI Filters for Computers page, select the WMI filters that should be considered for the computer object in the model. You can select all of the WMI filters that are available or select just a few by selecting the Only These Filters option. Then click Next.

11. On the Summary of Selections page, review your selections, and then click Next.

12. On the Completing the Group Policy Modeling Wizard page, click Finish.

Results Pane for Group Policy Modeling

After you generate a report using the Group Policy Modeling utility, you can see the results in the details pane after clicking the Group Policy Modeling node in the GPMC. Each report displays information on three tabs: Summary, Settings, and Query.

Summary   The Summary tab displays all of the essential information that you need regarding the objects, the location of the objects, and the GPOs that affected them, as shown in Figure 7-10.

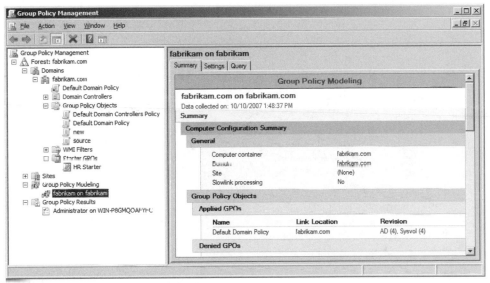

Figure 7-10   The Summary tab for the Group Policy Modeling utility provides information regarding both the user and computer objects that were included in the report.

The important sections of this tab include:

- Computer Configuration Summary
  - General
  - Group Policy Objects
  - Simulated security group membership
  - WMI Filters
  - Component Status
- User Configuration Summary
  - General
  - Group Policy Objects
  - Simulated security group membership
  - WMI Filters
  - Component Status

Settings   The Settings tab is similar to the Settings tab that you read about earlier. This tab is for the GPOs that affected the user and computer that were specified in the generation of the report.

Query   The Query tab summarizes all of the settings that you made while completing the wizard. Because you can skip information within the wizard, it is important to know which settings were selected and are associated with the results. You cannot change the settings here, but you can generate another report based on the existing settings by right-clicking the node you want to alter under the Group Policy Modeling node, and then clicking Create New Query From This One.

Controlling Results of Group Policy Modeling Post Query

After you generate a report using Group Policy Modeling, you have some advanced options for working with the results. The options are similar to the Group Policy Results options, with some variation. Four options are available when you right-click the result under the Group Policy Modeling node.

Advanced View   This option displays the results in the traditional RSoP format, which organizes the settings like they are in the GPME.

Rerun Query   You have the option to rerun the query. This will be important if there are any new settings in a GPO that affect the objects, or if there are any new GPOs that are linked to the nodes in Active Directory that would affect the objects.

Create New Query From This One   Some queries can be quite complex, so it is nice to be able to use the existing settings and modify them slightly. This allows for efficient control over the modeling of user and computer objects that are in different locations in Active Directory or that have membership in different groups.

Save Report   This option allows you to document the output of the report. When you save a report, the Save GPO Report dialog box appears from which you need only specify the name of the file, the format of the file (HTML or XML), and the location where you want to save the file.

> **Best Practices**   The Group Policy Modeling Wizard is a newer version of the RSoP wizard MMC snap-in available in Windows Server 2003, running in Planning mode. Because all RSoP functionality provided by the RSoP MMC snap-in is included in the GPMC, along with new functionality such as HTML reporting of RSoP data, it is recommended that users access all RSoP functionality primarily through the GPMC, rather than the stand-alone RSoP MMC snap-in.

Resultant Set of Policy Provider

This is the service that runs on the domain controller to simulate the application of Group Policy for Group Policy Modeling. The Resultant Set of Policy Provider (RSPP) passes the simulated results to the domain controller's client-side extensions (CSEs). All of this information is stored in a WMI database, which displays the report and retains the model for future use.

The RSPP works in conjunction with a WMI provider to perform the same function that the Group Policy service provides. The RSPP accepts the information regarding which portion of Active Directory should be considered, security group memberships, and any WMI filters. The RSPP runs under the system context to perform the report.

Comments

One of the new GPMC features shipping with Windows 2008 is the ability to place comments in GPOs and certain GPO settings. As GPOs are updated, administrators can enter information regarding why settings have changed, what the GPO is for, issues observed with the GPO, and so on. Comments can be made in the following GPOs and settings:

- Starter GPOs
- Standard GPO
- Administrative Template settings

Starter GPO Comments

Comments can be made in Starter GPOs so that all administrators who use them know what the initial intent was with the GPO and where it should be used. To make comments in a Starter GPO, follow these steps:

1. In the GPMC, expand the Starter GPO node.
2. Right-click the Starter GPO that you want to add a comment to, and then click Edit.
3. Right-click the name of the Starter GPO in the Group Policy Starter GPO Editor, and then click Properties.
4. Enter your comment on the Comment tab, shown in Figure 7-11.
5. Click OK and exit the Group Policy Starter GPO Editor.
6. Right-click the Starter GPO to which you just added a comment, and then click Refresh to see the comment on the Details tab, which is in the details pane of the GPMC, as shown in Figure 7-12.

> **Note** Comments made at this location in the Starter GPO will not be copied to a new GPO made from this Starter GPO. This comment is only for use in the Starter GPO. Any new GPO made from the Starter GPO will have a unique location for a comment. Comments made for any setting in the Starter GPO will be copied to a new GPO.

Figure 7-11   Comments for a Starter GPO are added to the property sheet for the GPO from within the Group Policy Starter GPO Editor.

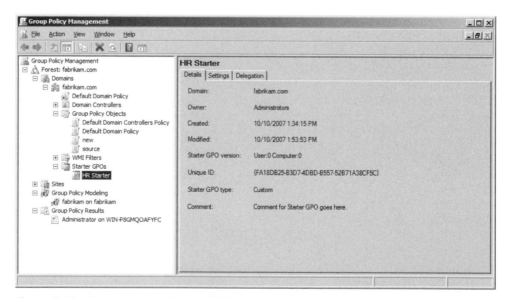

Figure 7-12   Comments made to a GPO appear on the Details tab in the right pane of the GPMC.

Production GPO Comments

Production GPOs (GPOs created in the live environment) can also have comments, very similar to those in a Starter GPO. As with Starter GPOs, comments inform all Group Policy administrators of the reason for the GPO and any issues that might need to be addressed. To add a comment to a production GPO, follow these steps:

1. In the GPMC, expand the Group Policy Objects node.

2. Right-click the GPO to which you want to add a comment, and then click Edit.

3. Right-click the name of the GPO in the GPME, and then click Properties.

4. On the Properties dialog box, type your comment on the Comment tab, and then click OK.

5. Exit the GPME.

6. Right-click the GPO to which you just added a comment, and then click Refresh to see the comment on the Details tab, which is in the details pane of the GPMC.

Comments for Administrative Template Settings

You can also be more specific when you add comments to a GPO by adding them directly to individual settings. The only caveat is that not all settings can support comments; only the settings under the Administrative Templates node in the GPME or Group Policy Starter GPO Editor support comments. To configure a comment for any of these settings, follow these steps:

1. In the GPMC, expand the GPO node.

2. Right-click the GPO to which you want to add a comment, and then click Edit.

3. Expand the Administrative Templates node under Computer Configuration or User Configuration until you find the policy setting to which you want to add a comment.

4. Right-click the policy setting, and then click Properties.

5. Enter your comment on the Comment tab, shown in Figure 7-13.

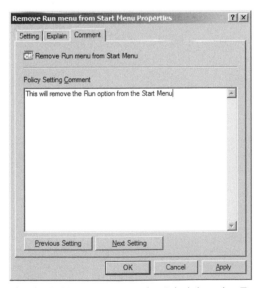

Figure 7-13   Comments for Administrative Template settings can be added to each setting on the Comment tab.

6. Type the comment on the Comments tab, and then click OK.

7. Exit the GPME.

8. Right-click the GPO to which you just added a comment, and then click Refresh to see the comment on the Settings tab, which is in the details pane of the GPMC, as shown in Figure 7-14.

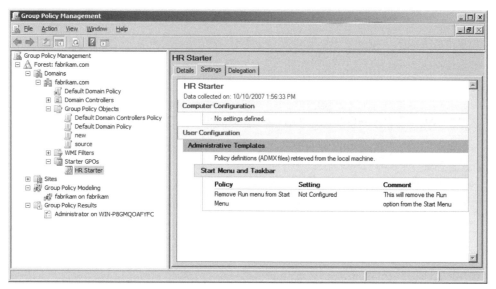

Figure 7-14   Comments for Administrative Template settings appear on the Settings tab of the GPO that was updated.

Migrating GPOs

The migration of GPOs from one environment to another is important for optimal setup of GPOs, troubleshooting of GPOs, and consistency between like environments. The problem with moving a GPO from one environment to another is that not all settings are the same in both environments, specifically some settings that are configured in the GPO itself. To migrate a GPO from one environment to another, you must consider the settings that need to be translated, which environments need this attention, and how you will perform the migration of the GPO and the settings.

Reasons for Migrating GPOs

A company may want to move a GPO and its settings from one environment to another for numerous reasons. Examples of GPO migrations might include the following:

- Production domain A to Production domain B

- Test domain A to Production domain A

- Production domain A in Forest A to Production domain B in Forest B

Any combination of these examples is also a valid reason for a GPO to be migrated from one domain to another.

Requirements for Migrating GPOs between Domains

A GPO cannot be migrated between domains without the correct configurations in place and the correct permissions established, because rogue GPOs could appear in your domain without your knowledge or approval. Such a situation usually leads to a trust relationship between the domains, but that is not necessary. There does not need to be a trust between domains to migrate GPOs from one to the other.

If a trust is not in place to perform the migration, you must consider one of the following alternatives:

- Perform an import of the GPO from the source domain. This requires that the GPO be backed up from the source domain and then made available to the target domain for importing.

- Use the Stored User Names and Passwords utility. This allows for simultaneous access to both domains, thus allowing a copy operation to be made from the source domain to the target domain.

 Note For more information about Stored User Names and Passwords in Windows XP, refer to *http://www.microsoft.com/windowsserver2003/gpmc/gpmcwp.mspx*.

Settings in a GPO That Require Translation

Many areas of a GPO refer to unique settings or objects in a domain. These unique settings or objects typically have a path or identifier that make them unique for that domain. When a GPO setting is migrated from one domain to another, even in the same forest, these settings must be translated. The translation takes the identifier from the source domain and converts it to the corresponding identifier in the new target domain.

The settings and objects that must be translated include security principals and paths, which are located in specific settings in a GPO, and will require a translation of the setting if configured in both the source and target domain.

The following settings contain security principals and must be updated during migration, if required:

- User Rights Assignment
- Restricted Groups
- System Services
- File System
- Registry

- Folder Redirection
- Security filtering on the GPO itself
- Access control list on software installation objects

The following settings can contain Universal Naming Convention (UNC) paths, which must be updated to new values as part of the migration process:

- Folder Redirection
- Software Installation
- Scripts

Migrating GPOs Across Domains

The GPMC offers two options for migrating a GPO from one domain to another. You can either use the Copy and Paste combination, or you can use the Backup and Import combination. Both options offer the ability to control certain aspects of the GPO and the settings during the operation.

Migrating a GPO Using Copy and Paste

To use the copy and paste method to migrate a GPO, first ensure that you have permissions in both domains. Then you must include both domains in the GPMC at the same time. This allows you to see both domains, copying the GPO from one domain and pasting it to the other.

The benefit of using the copy and paste method is that you can control the permissions of the GPO during the pasting process, as you can see in Figure 7-15.

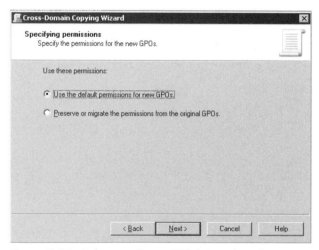

Figure 7-15   When pasting a GPO into a domain, you can control which permissions are used—the default permissions or permissions from the copied GPO.

The process of copying a GPO from one domain to another is similar to a standard copy and paste of a file. To copy and paste a GPO from one domain to another, follow these steps:

1.   Ensure that both the source domain and the target domain are added to the GPMC.

> **Note**   For information about how to add a domain to the GPMC, refer to Chapter 6, "GPMC Basics."

2.   Expand the Group Policy Objects node in the source domain.

3.   Right-click the GPO that you want to migrate, and then click Copy.

4.   Right-click the Group Policy Objects node in the target domain, and then click Paste. The Cross-Domain Copying Wizard appears.

5.   On the Cross-Domain Copying Wizard page, click Next.

6.   Select an option to control permissions from the source GPO to the target GPO:

     ❏   Choosing to use the default permissions for new GPOs will configure the GPO with the default permissions of any new GPO in the domain.

     ❏   Choosing to preserve or migrate the permissions from the original GPOs will allow you to select a migration table.

7.   On the Migrating References page, choose whether to preserve or migrate the permissions:

     ❏   Choosing to copy them identically from the source will leave all security principals and UNC paths in the new GPO the same as the source GPO.

     ❏   Choosing to use the migration table to map them to new values in the new GPOs will allow you to choose a migration table to use as part of the migration.

     ❏   The option to use the migration table exclusively is available if you choose to use a migration table. This option verifies all security principals and UNC paths found in the GPO and in the migration table. If the GPO has a security principal or UNC path that is not mapped in the migration table, the migration will fail.

8.   On the Completing the Cross-Domain Copying Wizard page, click Finish.

After the migration is complete, you will have a new GPO in the target domain. The permissions will be as you migrated them in the wizard, and you will have a fully functioning GPO. The GPO is not linked to any Active Directory node initially. After you link the new GPO to the domain, organizational unit, or site, the settings will start to apply to the objects under the scope of management of the GPO.

Migrating a GPO Using Backup and Import

The backup and import method for migrating GPOs is another option for getting your GPOs from one domain to another, quite different from the copy and paste method. Of course, you still must have the appropriate permissions in both domains to perform the backup from the source domain and the import in the target domain.

With this method, the specified target GPO must already exist. This is because the Import function takes the settings from the backed-up GPO and copies them into the existing GPO.

To perform the migration using the backup and import method, follow these steps:

1. In the GPMC, expand the Group Policy Objects node in the source domain.

2. Right-click the GPO that you want to migrate, and then click Backup.

Note   For information about backing up a GPO, refer to the section "Managing GPO Backups" in Chapter 6.

3. Expand the Group Policy Objects node in the target domain after the backup completes.

4. Right-click the GPO that you will import the settings into, and then click Import Settings. The Import Settings Wizard appears.

5. On the Welcome to the Import Settings Wizard page, click Next.

6. Click Backup to perform a backup of the settings in this GPO. When the backup is complete, click Next.

Note   For information about backing up a GPO, refer to Chapter 6.

Best Practices   When using the backup and import method, it is best to use a new GPO as the target GPO, instead of an existing GPO that has settings. This will eliminate the need to perform a backup of the GPO in the Import Settings Wizard.

7. On the Backup Location page, select the folder from the Backup Folder list to which you backed up the source GPO in step 2. You may click Browse to find this folder. Click Next.

8. On the Source GPO page, select the GPO that you will use as the source GPO from which you want to import settings, and then click Next.

9. On the Scanning Backup page, note whether any security principals or UNC paths need to be considered in the translation, as shown in Figure 7-16, and then click Next.

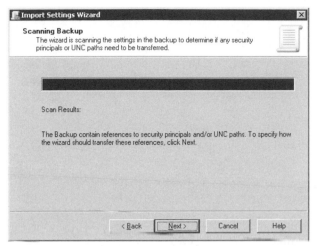

Figure 7-16   During the import process, the system indicates whether any security principals or UNC paths need to be considered for translation during the import.

10.   Select the option for handling the security principals or UNC paths on the Migrating References page:

❑   Choosing to copy them identically from the source will leave all security principals and UNC paths in the new GPO the same as the source GPO. Selecting this option takes you immediately to the Summary page of the Import Wizard.

❑   Choosing to use the migration table to map them to new values in the new GPOs will allow you to choose a migration table to use as part of the migration. Selecting this option forces you to take further steps in selecting the migration table.

❑   The option to use the migration table exclusively is available if you choose to use a migration table. This option verifies all security principals and UNC paths found in the GPO and in the migration table. If the GPO has a security principal or UNC path that is not mapped in the migration table, the migration will fail.

If you choose to use a migration table, you must also select the migration table on the Migrating References page. Select your migration table from the list or by clicking Browse.

11.   On the Migrating References page, click Next.

12.   On the Import progress page, click OK.

13.   On the Copy progress page, click OK.

As with the copy and paste method, the migrated GPO is not linked to an Active Directory node. After the GPO is linked to the domain, organizational unit, or site, it will start to affect all objects in the scope of management.

Migration Tables

Migration tables are used to translate security principals and UNC paths from one domain to another. Because these objects and paths differ in different domains (either in the same forest or a different forest), the values must be updated when a GPO is migrated from the source domain to the target domain.

Migration tables can be updated manually, automatically, or by using the Migration Table Editor. The manual method is not suggested, because the migration table is stored in XML format and syntax is extremely important; one minor mistake could make the migration fail. Migration tables are saved with a .migtable extension and can be located anywhere on the system that you desire. However, users who want to use a migration table must have the appropriate permissions to the file during the migration process.

A migration table itself is simple, containing only three variables: source name, source type, and destination name. Figure 7-17 illustrates what a typical migration table looks like in the Migration Table Editor through the GPMC.

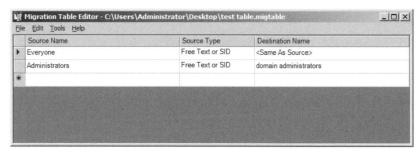

Figure 7-17   The Migration Table Editor allows you to add, delete, and update any of the three sources of information required to translate GPO references from one domain to another.

- **Source name**   The source name is the name of the security principal or UNC path in the source GPO. If the source name does not match the entry in the source GPO, the migration might fail. The syntax for the source name is important; Table 7-4 provides examples of what each source name would look like for the different source types.

Table 7-4   Source Name Syntax

Object Type	Example Syntax
User	UPN: bruno@fabrikam.com
	SAM: FABRIKAM\Bruno
	DNS: Fabrikam.com\Bruno
Domain Global Group	UPN: Domain Admins@fabrikam.com
	SAM: FABRIKAM\Domain Admins
	DNS: Fabrikam.com\Domain Admins

Table 7-4   Source Name Syntax

Object Type	Example Syntax
Domain Local Group	UPN: Administrators@fabrikam.com
	SAM: FABRIKAM\Administrators
	DNS: Fabrikam.com\Administrators
Universal Group	UPN: Enterprise Admins@fabrikam.com
	SAM: FABRIKAM\Enterprise Admins
	DNS: Fabrikam.com\Enterprise Admins
Computer	UPN: Client1$@fabrikam.com
	SAM: FABRIKAM\Client1
	DNS: Fabrikam.com\Client1
UNC Path	\\Server1\Data
Free Text or SID	"PilarA"
	"S-1-5-21-1473733259-1489586486 3363071491-1005"

> **Note**   SIDs cannot be referenced in the destination name field.

- **Source type**   The source type depicts the type of entry that is in the table. This is either a security principal or UNC path. There are many source types that can be configured. The following are all of the source types that can be included in a migration table:
  - ❑ User
  - ❑ Computer
  - ❑ Domain Local Group
  - ❑ Domain Global Group
  - ❑ Universal Group
  - ❑ UNC Path
  - ❑ Free Text or SID

- **Destination name**   The destination name refers to the name that is used in the target domain for the source name translation. For example, there might be a group in the source domain named HRAdmins, whereas in the target domain it is named HRAdministrators. The source name would be HRAdmins and the destination name would be HRAdministrators. You have a few options in the destination name field, other than the explicit name of the destination object. Table 7-5 lists a few of the other entries and their meanings.

Table 7-5   Destination Name Entries

Destination Name Entry	Description
Same as source	This will not modify the security principal or UNC path during the migration.
None	This will remove the entry from the source GPO when it is migrated to the target GPO (cannot be used with UNC path).
Map by relative name	This will be a translation based on name, such as DomainA\user1 to DomainB\user1 (cannot be used with UNC path).
Explicitly specify value	This is where a name is typed into the destination name, providing the exact literal value.

To create a migration table, it is best to use the Migration Table Editor, which allows you to work with the migration entries directly. The most efficient solution is to populate the migration table directly from the GPO in production or a GPO that has been backed up. To populate the migration table from a GPO that is in production, follow these steps:

1. In the GPMC, right-click the Group Policy Objects node, and then click Open Migration Table Editor.

2. In the Migration Table Editor, click Tools, and then click Populate From GPO.

3. Select the domain in which the GPO resides from the Look In This Domain list.

4. Select the GPO from the Group Policy Objects list.

> **Note**   If you want to include the security permissions that are configured on the GPO itself, you must also select the check box labeled During Scan, Include Security Principals From The DACL On The GPO.

5. Click OK, and review the results from the scan in the Migration Table Editor, as shown in Figure 7-18.

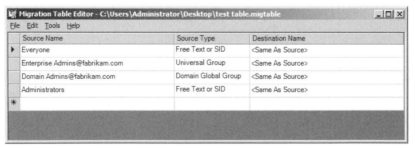

Figure 7-18   After a scan of a GPO for security principals and UNC paths, the results are imported into the Migration Table Editor for further refinement and saved to a file.

You can save a migration table and validate its entries. You save the table like any other file—click File, and then click Save. To validate the file and entries, click Tools, and then click Validate Table. The Validation Results dialog box indicates whether there are any issues with the table, as shown in Figure 7-19.

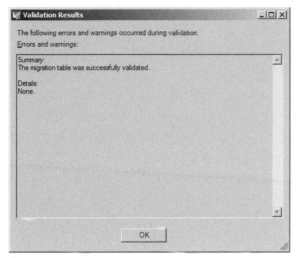

Figure 7-19   Validating the migration table will help eliminate simple errors and ensure the migration of the GPO.

Migration tables can also be controlled by using scripts. For more information regarding scripting of migration tables, refer to Chapter 8, "Controlling Group Policy via Scripts and Automation."

Summary

The GPMC provides advanced management features such as searching, filtering, and commenting. All of these features make management and troubleshooting of GPOs more efficient and controllable.

Combine all of these features with the capabilities of Group Policy Results and Group Policy Modeling, and the GPMC provides nearly everything that you might want for Group Policy management. If you do need to take a GPO from one domain to another, the migration tables provide an easy and straightforward method to accomplish this. GPOs can be migrated from one domain to another, even across forest boundaries.

Additional Resources

- The Microsoft TechNet article at *http://technet2.microsoft.com/WindowsServer/en/ library/b98e4746-da0d-4da5-9fa8-1b2d69c9cad81033.mspx?mfr=true* includes information about migration tables.

- The Microsoft TechNet article titled "Administering Group Policy with Group Policy Management Console Abstract," at *http://www.microsoft.com/windowsserver2003/ gpmc/gpmcwp.mspx*, includes information about using user accounts in two domains simultaneously.

- Chapter 8, "Controlling Group Policy via Scripts and Automation," includes information about scripting migration tables and Group Policy management.

- Chapter 9, "Security Delegation for Administration of GPOs," includes information about security, delegation, and management of Group Policy.

- Chapter 14, "Advanced GPO Management with AGPM," includes detailed information about combining AGPM with the GPMC for in-depth GPO management.

- Chapter 15, "Troubleshooting GPOs," includes information about Group Policy events in the Event Viewer.

Chapter 8

Controlling GPOs with Scripts and Automation

As a result of significant effort and time, Group Policy is the centralized mechanism for Windows configuration management. Equal amounts of effort and time are being spent on automating the management of Group Policy. Scripts that control much of the overall capabilities that the Group Policy Management Console (GPMC) provides have existed for a long time and have proven to be very useful.

The GPMC scripts duplicate the overall management capabilities that administrators can perform within the GPMC graphical user interface (GUI). You can manage links, permissions (delegation), reporting, and backups in an automated fashion by leveraging the GPMC scripts. With the correct syntax and details, nearly all GPMC management tasks can be automated.

Most administrators prefer Microsoft Windows PowerShell for automating Group Policy management. Windows PowerShell provides a unique and powerful environment for not only managing the GPOs like a GPMC script would, but also for modifying the GPO settings, using third-party solutions.

GPMC Scripts

Most administrators use the GPMC to manage GPOs. The GPMC GUI provides the ability to create, link, manage, delete, configure, and back up GPOs. For simple management of a GPO or a few GPOs, the GUI interface will suffice. However, when you must perform larger management tasks, automating the task is more efficient.

Microsoft provides a large number of prebuilt scripts that you can use immediately, without having to customize the automation of Group Policy. The scripts cover all areas of GPO management with the GPMC, with the exception of GPO settings modification (a task too complex for the GPMC scripts to handle).

The GPMC scripts cover many areas of GPMC management, described in the following sections. The scripts are very easy to acquire and use; this section of the book is designed to help you understand how to use the scripts with the correct syntax. As with any scripting or automation option, the correct syntax can control the success of the script.

The scripts can be downloaded and installed from *http://www.microsoft.com/downloads/ details.aspx?familyid=38c1a89b-a6d2-4f2a-a944-9236999aee65*. You can use them immediately after installation.

> **Note**   When referring to a script, you must change directories to where the script is located to just use the script and extension name, or you must add the path to the script, including the script name and extension. Similarly, you must include the full path to any and all target or source locations that you reference.

Backing Up and Restoring GPOs

Whether you want to back up a single GPO or the entire group of GPOs for the domain, there are scripts to handle these tasks. Not only can you back up GPOs, you can also use the script to restore them. Other scripts allow you to see the backup location where the GPOs have been archived.

BackupGPO.wsf

This script backs up a single GPO in the current domain or defined domain. A backup location is required; the Comment and Domain switches are optional. The script stores each GPO in a separate folder, which is uniquely named after the Backup IDs. This is to ensure that each GPO remains autonomous. The Comment switch becomes more useful when you are viewing saved versions with other GPMC scripts.

Syntax
```
Usage: BackupGPO.wsf GPOName BackupLocation [/Comment:value] [/Domain:value]
GPOName: GPO name or ID. Note: Use double quotes if the policy name has multiple words,
as in the following example.
BackupLocation: File system or UNC share location to back up to.
Comment: This switch is optional. Use " " for spaces with comment text.
Domain: DNS name of domain; if left blank, it will default to the current domain.
```

Example & Output   This example backs up only the Default Domain Policy to the Universal Naming Convention (UNC) path of \\server1\gpobackup.

```
cscript BackupGPO.wsf "Default Domain Policy" \\server1\gpo-backup /comment:"Default Domain
Policy 11/2/2007"
Microsoft (R) Windows Script Host Version 5.7
Copyright (C) Microsoft Corporation. All rights reserved.
Found GPO 'Default Domain Policy'

Done.
```

```
Backed up GPO Default Domain Policy with the following properties:
GPO ID: {31B2F340-016D-11D2-945F-00C04FB984F9}
Timestamp: 11/2/2007 9:43:44 AM
Backup ID: {A19258BC-2584-4081-80C6-24E5F6BD19F2}
```

BackupAllGPOs.wsf

This script backs up all of the GPOs in the current domain or defined domain. A backup location is required; the Comment and Domain switches are optional. This script stores the GPOs in separate folders with unique names using the Backup ID. The comment switch is useful for documenting any essential information regarding the GPO, which can then be leveraged using other scripts.

Syntax

```
Usage: BackupAllGPOs.wsf BackupLocation [/Comment:value] [/Domain:value]
BackupLocation: File system or UNC share location to back up to.
Comment: Comment switch is optional. Use " " if you have multiple words.
Domain: DNS name of domain; if left blank, it will default to the current domain.
```

Example & Output   In this example, we use the script to back up all of the GPOs in the current domain to the GPO-Backup share on Server1.

```
cscript BackupAllGPOs.wsf \\server1\gpo-backup
Microsoft (R) Windows Script Host Version 5.7
Copyright (C) Microsoft Corporation. All rights reserved.

== Found 2 GPOs in fabrikam.com to backup ==
Backed up GPO 'Default Domain Policy' with the following properties:
GPO ID: {31B2F340-016D-11D2-945F-00C04FB984F9}
Timestamp: 10/31/2007 10:43:04 PM
Backup ID: {4C02A6A1-3571-4D9E-9796-3A3401280197}

Backed up GPO 'Default Domain Controllers Policy' with the following properties:
GPO ID: {6AC1786C-016F-11D2-945F-00C04FB984F9}
Timestamp: 10/31/2007 10:43:20 PM
Backup ID: {8A9A15DB-01EC-485E-BEE3-7F0B06AA18B1}
Backup succeeded for 2 GPOs.
Backup failed for 0 GPOs.
```

RestoreGPO.wsf

This script restores a single GPO from the backup location. If you have archived the GPO multiple times to the same backup location, the script restores only the most recent backup. When you do not specify a domain or a domain controller, the restore occurs in the current domain.

Syntax

```
Usage: RestoreGPO.wsf BackupLocation BackupID [/Domain:value] [/DC:value]
BackupLocation: File system location where the backup is located.
BackupID: GPO name or backup ID (GUID) of the backup to use.
Domain: DNS name of domain.
DC: Netbios name of domain controller to use.
```

Example & Output   This script restores the Default Domain Policy from the share named gpo-backup.

```
cscript RestoreGPO.wsf \\server1\gpo-backup "Default Domain Policy"
Microsoft (R) Windows Script Host Version 5.7
Copyright (C) Microsoft Corporation. All rights reserved.
Backup found:
        ID: {A19258BC-2584-4081-80C6-24E5F6BD19F2}
        Timestamp: 11/2/2007 9:43:44 AM
        GPO ID: {31B2F340-016D-11D2-945F-00C04FB984F9}
        GPO Name: Default Domain Policy
        Comment: Default Domain Policy 11/2/2007

Restoring GPO Default Domain Policy from \\server1\gpo-backup\\{A19258BC-2584-40
81-80C6-24E5F6BD19F2} in domain Fabrikam.com.
GPO 'Default Domain Policy' has been restored.
```

RestoreAllGPOs.wsf

This script restores all GPOs from the backup location. If you have archived numerous GPOs in the backup location for a single GPO, the script will restore only the most recent backup for each GPO. If you do not specify a domain, the restore occurs in the current domain.

Syntax

```
Usage: RestoreAllGPOs.wsf BackupLocation [/Domain:value]
BackupLocation: File system location containing the GPO backups.
Domain: DNS name of domain.
```

Example & Output   This script simply restores all of the GPOs that have been archived in the gpo-backup share location to the domain.

```
cscript RestoreAllGPOs.wsf \\server1\gpo-backup
Microsoft (R) Windows Script Host Version 5.7
Copyright (C) Microsoft Corporation. All rights reserved.

2 backups found at location \\server1\gpo-backup.
Processing backed up GPO 'Default Domain Policy'
The restore operation completed successfully.

Processing backed up GPO 'Default Domain Controllers Policy'
The restore operation completed successfully.

Restore succeeded for 2 GPOs.
Restore failed for 0 GPOs.
```

QueryBackupLocation.wsf

This script provides a view into the location on the file system where you have backed up GPOs. It allows you to see which GPOs are archived to a specific location on the file system, whether the backup scripts ran (BackupAllGPOs.wsf and BackupGPO.wsf), and detailed information about the archived GPOs if the Verbose switch is used.

Syntax

```
Usage: QueryBackupLocation.wsf BackupFolder [/Verbose]
BackupFolder: File system location to query.
Verbose: Displays detailed information about each backup.
```

Example #1 & Output   This script queries the backup location in the gpo-backup share and returns a list of all GPOs that have been archived there.

```
cscript QueryBackupLocation.wsf \\server1\gpo-backup
Microsoft (R) Windows Script Host Version 5.7
Copyright (C) Microsoft Corporation. All rights reserved.

The following GPOs are backed up at \\server1\gpo-backup:
-- Summary --
{31B2F340-016D-11D2-945F-00C04FB984F9} - Default Domain Policy
{6AC1786C-016F-11D2-945F-00C04FB984F9} - Default Domain Controllers Policy
```

Example #2 & Output   This script queries the backup location in the gpo-backup share and returns a list of all GPOs that have been archived there, including full details about each of the archive points, including dates, descriptions, and Backup IDs.

```
cscript QueryBackupLocation.wsf \\server1\gpo-backup /verbose
Microsoft (R) Windows Script Host Version 5.7
Copyright (C) Microsoft Corporation. All rights reserved.

The following GPOs are backed up at \\server1\gpo-backup:
-- Summary --
    {31B2F340-016D-11D2-945F-00C04FB984F9} - Default Domain Policy
    {6AC1786C-016F-11D2-945F-00C04FB984F9} - Default Domain Controllers Policy

-- Details --
GPO Name: Default Domain Policy
GPO ID: {31B2F340-016D-11D2-945F-00C04FB984F9}

2 backup(s)

BackupID: {A19258BC-2584-4081-80C6-24E5F6BD19F2}
Timestamp: Fri Nov 2 09:43:44 EDT 2007
Comment: Default Domain Policy 11/2/2007

BackupID: {4C02A6A1-3571-4D9E-9796-3A3401280197}
Timestamp: Wed Oct 31 22:43:04 EDT 2007
Comment:

GPO Name: Default Domain Controllers Policy
GPO ID: {6AC1786C-016F-11D2-945F-00C04FB984F9}

1 backup(s)

BackupID: {8A9A15DB-01EC-485E-BEE3-7F0B06AA18B1}
Timestamp: Wed Oct 31 22:43:20 EDT 2007
Comment:
```

Copying and Importing GPOs

To efficiently utilize existing GPOs and their settings, you can use the copy and import features within the GPMC and the following scripts. The copy option allows a company to move GPOs efficiently from a test domain to a production domain, without having to manually duplicate the settings from one environment to the other.

CopyGPO.wsf

This script copies a GPO from one domain to another. This is ideal for moving GPOs from a test domain to production domain, or any other situation in which two domains need duplicate GPOs. If the GPO contains UNC paths or security principal references, the migration tables must be used to translate them from one domain to another.

Syntax

```
Usage: CopyGPO.wsf SourceGPO TargetGPO [/SourceDomain:value] [/TargetDomain:value]
[/SourceDC:value] [/TargetDC:value] [/MigrationTable:value] [/CopyACL]
SourceGPO: Name of the source GPO.
TargetGPO: Name of the target GPO.
SourceDomain: DNS name of the source domain.
TargetDomain: DNS name of the target domain.
SourceDC: Domain controller to use in the source domain.
TargetDC: Domain controller to use in the target domain.
MigrationTable: Migration table to use.
CopyACL: Copies the ACL on the GPO.
```

Example   This script copies the contents of GPO1 from the test.fabrikam.com domain and places the contents into GPO1 located in the production.fabrikam.com domain.

```
cscript CopyGPO.wsf GPO1 GPO1 /SourceDomain:test.fabrikam.com
/TargetDomain:production.fabrikam.com
```

> **Note**   For more information about using migration tables, refer to Chapter 7, "Advanced GPMC Management," which covers all aspects of creating and using migration tables using the GPMC.

ImportGPO.wsf

This script imports the settings from a backed-up GPO into an existing (target) GPO. If there is more than one version of the backed-up GPO, the latest is used. If you want to use a version other than the latest backed-up GPO for importing the settings, you must specify the Backup ID in the script. If you do not specify a target GPO, the target will be the name of the GPO backup. If a GPO exists with that name, the script imports the information into the existing GPO. If a GPO does not exist with that name, and you use the CreateIfNeeded switch, the script will create a new GPO in that name. You can use a migration table to handle any UNC paths or security principals must be translated during the import to the existing GPO.

Importing a GPO does not restore delegation information. To restore delegation information for a GPO, use the RestoreGPO.wsf script.

Syntax

```
Usage: ImportGPO.wsf BackupLocation BackupID [TargetGPO] [/MigrationTable:value]
[/CreateIfNeeded] [/Domain:value]
BackupLocation: File system location where the backup is located.
BackupID: GPO name or backup ID (GUID) of the backup to use.
```

```
TargetGPO: Target GPO in which to import settings.
MigrationTable: Optional migration table to use when importing.
CreateIfNeeded: Creates a new GPO if the specified target GPO does not exist.
Domain: DNS name of domain.
```

Example   This script takes the contents from the GPO with the specified GUID and copies them to a new GPO, named GPO1. The script specifies that the new GPO should be created if it does not already exist.

```
cscript ImportGPO.wsf \\Server1\gpo-backup {73624CC9-E8F2-4F05-88D2-193FAE8773CE} GPO1
/CreateIfNeeded
```

ImportAllGPO.wsf

This script creates a new GPO for every GPO that you have backed up in the reference backup location. The script uses only the latest version of the GPO from the backup location. The new GPO will maintain the same name as the GPO that you backed up. This script will not account for duplicate GPO names, so if there are existing target GPOs with the same name as those in the backup location, the script will overwrite the existing GPOs with the new GPO you are importing. Any settings you created in the existing GPO will be lost.

Syntax
```
Usage: ImportAllGPOs.wsf BackupLocation [/MigrationTable:value] [/Domain:value]
BackupLocation: File system location containing the GPO backups.
MigrationTable: Optional Migration table to use when importing.
Domain: DNS name of domain.
```

Example   This script takes all GPOs that have been archived to the gpo-backup share and imports the settings into existing (or new) GPOs, using the settings in the migration table named MigrationTable1.xml.

```
cscript ImportAllGPOs.wsf \\Server1\gpo-backup /MigrationTable:"G:\MigrationTable1.xml"
```

Creating GPOs and Other GPMC Objects

GPMC scripts allow you to create objects, such as a new GPO or a file that will duplicate the entire GPO environment. These tasks are very powerful and excellent for disaster recovery of the GPO infrastructure. You can also perform cleanup of the GPOs by using a script that allows you to delete them.

CreateGPO.wsf

This script creates a new GPO with the name you specify.

Syntax
```
Usage: CreateGPO.wsf GPOName [/Domain:value]
GPOName: Name of the GPO to create.
Domain: DNS name of domain.
```

Example & Output   This script creates a GPO named Hardened Server GPO.

```
cscript CreateGPO.wsf "Hardened Server GPO"
Microsoft (R) Windows Script Host Version 5.7
Copyright (C) Microsoft Corporation. All rights reserved.
Created GPO 'Hardened Server GPO'
```

CreateXMLFromEnvironment.wsf

This script reads the live GPO environment (organizational units, GPOs, GPO links, and so on) and creates an XML file representing that environment. Administrators often use this script in conjunction with CreateEnvironmentFromXML.wsf to back up and restore environments for GPOs.

Note that you must specify the TemplatePath location as an existing fully qualified path. The script will not create this location for you.

Syntax
```
Usage: CreateXMLFromEnvironment.wsf OutputFile /TemplatePath:value [/Domain:value]
[/DC:value] [/StartingOU:value] [/ExcludePermissions] [/IncludeAllGroups] [/IncludeUsers]
OutputFile: Name of the XML file to create.
TemplatePath: Storage location of the GPO templates (backups) containing the policy settings.
Domain: DNS name of domain. If you do not specify a domain, the script assumes it uses the
computer's domain.
DC: Domain controller to use.
StartingOU: Distinguished Name (DN) path to the starting organizational unit (OU), as an
alternative to processing the entire domain.
ExcludePermissions: Excludes policy-related permissions in the XML file.
IncludeAllGroups: Includes groups from the 'Users' container and the domain root, instead of
just OUs.
IncludeUsers: Includes user accounts as well as groups.
```

Example & Output   This script creates the FabrikamDomain.xml file, which will contain the information related to all GPOs located in the gpo-backup share, as well as the Group Policy information for the domain as listed in the output.

```
cscript CreateXMLFromEnvironment.wsf FabrikamDomain.xml /TemplatePath:\\server1\gpo-backup
Microsoft (R) Windows Script Host Version 5.7
Copyright (C) Microsoft Corporation. All rights reserved.

===================================================
Processing Environment
Output XML: FabrikamDomain.xml
Domain: Fabrikam.com
DC: Server1.Fabrikam.com
===================================================

Processing domain Fabrikam
Processing OU Domain Controllers
Done.
Backed up GPO Default Domain Policy with the following properties:

GPO ID: {31B2F340-016D-11D2-945F-00C04FB984F9}
Timestamp: Mon Nov 5 13:33:22 EST 2007
Backup ID: {118C096A-EEDE-47AB-87DB-2572D562DC99}
```

```
** Domain Admins has custom permissions. These will be dropped. **
** Enterprise Admins has custom permissions. These will be dropped. **

Warning: Some security permissions for GPO {31B2F340-016D-11D2-945F-00C04FB984F9}
were not recorded.
Processing GPO Default Domain Controllers Policy

Done.

Backed up GPO Default Domain Controllers Policy with the following properties:

GPO ID: {6AC1786C-016F-11D2-945F-00C04fB984F9}
Timestamp: Mon Nov 5 13:33:24 EST 2007
Backup ID: {96761225-7D4C-4171-B311-CCF106B0535B}

** Domain Admins has custom permissions. These will be dropped. **
** Enterprise Admins has custom permissions. These will be dropped. **

Warning: Some security permissions for GPO {6AC1786C-016F-11D2-945F-00C04fB984F9}
were not recorded.
Processing GPO Desktop GPO
Done.
Saved XML to FabrikamDomain.xml.
```

CreateEnvironmentFromXML.wsf

This script populates objects into Active Directory, OUs, users, security groups, GPOs, and permissions on GPOs from an XML file. You can create the XML file manually, or you can create it with the GPMC script CreateXMLFromEnvironment. In most cases, you will work with an existing XML file that was created with a script, instead of manually creating the file.

Syntax
```
Usage: CreateEnvironmentFromXML.wsf /XML:value [/Undo] [/Domain:value] [/DC:value]
[/ExcludeSettings] [/ExcludePermissions] [/CreateUsersEnabled] [/PasswordForUsers:value]
[/MigrationTable:value] [/ImportDefaultGPOs] [/Q]
XML: XML file to process.
Undo: Deletes the objects specified in the XML instead of creating them.
Domain: DNS name of domain.
DC: Domain controller on which to perform all operations.
ExcludeSettings: Does not import GPO settings from templates specified in the XML.
ExcludePermissions: Ignores any permissions specified for GPOs and SOMs.
CreateUsersEnabled: Creates any user objects as enabled, instead of disabled.
PasswordForUsers: Password to use for any user objects that do not have passwords in the XML.
MigrationTable: Migration table to use when mapping security principals and paths across
domains.
ImportDefaultGPOs: Imports settings into the default domain GPOs if specified in the XML.
Q: Quiet mode - no confirmation warning will be displayed.
```

Example & Output   The output for this script is very large. This example has been truncated to show only the significant parts of the output. You can see that the example script here creates the entire environment of the Fabrikam.com domain XML file.

```
cscript CreateEnvironmentFromXML.wsf /XML:FabrikamDomain.xml
Microsoft (R) Windows Script Host Version 5.7
Copyright (C) Microsoft Corporation. All rights reserved.


=====================================================
Processing environment
XML: FabrikamDomain.xml
Forest: fabrikam.com
Domain: fabrikam.com
DC: Server1.fabrikam.com
=====================================================
Warning! This script is intended primarily for use in a test environment.
=====================================================
Processing WMI Filter nodes...
=====================================================
=====================================================
Processing GPO nodes...
=====================================================
=====================================================
Processing OU nodes...
=====================================================
=====================================================
Processing User nodes...
=====================================================
=====================================================
Processing SecurityGroup nodes...
=====================================================
=====================================================
Processing the Domain Root node...
=====================================================
=====================================================
Processing permissions on OU nodes...
=====================================================
=====================================================
Processing GPO permissions...
=====================================================


Importing settings from \\server1\gpo-backup\{D3B77E91-CA0B-4C34-B99F-40FC14B7ACF7}
to GPO Desktop GPO in domain fabrikam.com.

The import operation completed successfully.

Done processing XML.
```

CreateMigrationTable.wsf

This script creates a migration table XML file that can be edited and used for mapping UNC
paths and security principals when performing import and copy operations.

Syntax
```
Usage: CreateMigrationTable.wsf TableName [/GPO:value] [/BackupLocation:value] [/AllGPOs]
[/Overwrite] [/MapByName] [/Domain:value]
TableName: File name of the migration table the script will create.
GPO: Name of a GPO to process when building the migration table.
```

```
BackupLocation: File system location where backups are located.
AllGPOs: If specified, indicates that the script should process all GPOs in the domain.
Overwrite: If specified, overwrites an existing XML file instead of appending to it.
MapByName: If specified, sets the default destination to map by relative name.
Domain: DNS name of domain.
```

Example & Output   In this example, the migration table is a file called WGTable.xml, which was created in the C:\Backup folder. The path to the file was necessary for successful creation.

```
cscript CreateMigrationTable.wsf c:\backup\WGTable.xml /AllGPOs /Overwrite /
Domain:Fabrikam.com
Microsoft (R) Windows Script Host Version 5.7
Copyright (C) Microsoft Corporation. All rights reserved.


Processing GPO 'Hardened Server GPO'
Processing GPO 'Server GPO'
Processing GPO 'Default Domain Policy'
Processing GPO 'Default Domain Controllers Policy'
Processing GPO 'Desktop GPO'
Processing GPO 'TestServer'
Done. Migration table 'c:\backup\WGTable.xml' was created.
```

Deleting GPOs

DeleteGPO.wsf

This script deletes the GPO with the name you specify in the command. It also deletes all links to the GPO in the specified domain and related sites. If you prefer that the links remain intact, specify the KeepLinks switch in the command.

Syntax
```
Usage: deletegpo.wsf GPOName [/KeepLinks] [/Domain:value]
GPOName: Name or GUID of the GPO to delete.
KeepLinks: Deletes the GPO but does not delete the links.
Domain: DNS name of domain.
```

Example & Output   This script deletes the GPO named New Group Policy Object.

```
cscript deletegpo.wsf "New Group Policy Object"
Microsoft (R) Windows Script Host Version 5.7
Copyright (C) Microsoft Corporation. All rights reserved.

Deleted GPO {305C5727-64AD-4FF1-AD7E-560655C7C39F}

Deleting links for GPO 'New Group Policy Object' in domain 'Fabrikam.com'
No links found.
```

GPO Reporting

Whether you are auditing the environment or just documenting the GPO infrastructure, you will want to report on a variety of aspects of the GPO environment. These scripts allow you to report on individual GPOs, their settings, and the GPO environment.

DumpGPOInfo.wsf

This script reports, or *dumps*, information regarding the specified GPO or GUID and then prints information about that GPO on the screen.

Syntax

```
Usage: dumpgpoinfo.wsf GPOName [/Domain:value]
GPOName: GPO name or ID.
Domain: DNS name of domain.
```

Example & Output   This script gathers information about the Default Domain Policy and lists it on the screen.

```
cscript dumpgpoinfo.wsf "Default Domain Policy"
Microsoft (R) Windows Script Host Version 5.7
Copyright (C) Microsoft Corporation. All rights reserved.


================================================
Name: Default Domain Policy
ID: {31B2F340-016D-11D2-945F-00C04FB984F9}

-- Details --
Created: 10/31/2007 9:26:20 PM
Changed: 10/31/2007 9:26:20 PM
Owner: FABRIKAM\Domain Admins

User Enabled: True
Mach Enabled: True

-- Version Numbers --
User DS: 0
User Sysvol: 0
Mach DS: 1
Mach Sysvol: 1

-- Who this GPO applies to --
Authenticated Users

-- Who can edit this GPO --

-- Who can edit settings, modify security and delete this GPO --
SYSTEM
-- Who only has Read access --
ENTERPRISE DOMAIN CONTROLLERS

-- Who has custom permissions --
Domain Admins
Enterprise Admins
-- where this GPO is linked (Sites,Domain,OU) --
Fabrikam.com (Domain)
```

DumpSOMInfo.wsf

This script takes a specified scope of management (SOM) and outputs policy information about it. It displays the linked GPOs and the policy permissions regarding the node in Active Directory about which you are inquiring. The SOMName can be the domain name, an organizational unit, or a site. If you also want to show the inherited GPO links, you can use the ShowInheritedLinks switch.

Syntax

```
Usage: dumpsominfo.wsf SOMName [/ShowInheritedLinks] [/Domain:value]
SOMName: Name of the SOM to query.
ShowInheritedLinks: Shows inherited GPO links for the SOM.
Domain: DNS name of domain.
```

Example & Output   This script focuses on the organizational unit named Servers OU, reporting on all of the GPOs that are associated with it, including the links that are inherited from other nodes above it in the Active Directory structure.

```
cscript dumpsominfo.wsf "Servers OU" /ShowInheritedLinks
Microsoft (R) Windows Script Host Version 5.7
Copyright (C) Microsoft Corporation. All rights reserved.


==========================================================
Name: Servers OU
Type: Organizational Unit
Path: OU=Servers,DC=Fabrikam,DC=com

-- Inherited GPO Links --
1 Server GPO
2 Default Domain Policy

-- Who can link GPOs to this OU --
Domain Admins
SYSTEM
Enterprise Admins
Administrators

-- Who can generate RSoP logging data for this OU --
Domain Admins
SYSTEM
Enterprise Admins
Administrators

-- Who can generate RSoP planning data for this OU --
Domain Admins
SYSTEM
Enterprise Admins
Administrators
```

GetReportsForAllGPOs.wsf

This script dumps all GPO information from all GPOs in the domain into XML and HTML files at the location you specify. The output is everything from all four tabs in the details pane of the GPMC when you click a GPO: Scope, Details, Settings, and Delegation.

Syntax

```
Usage: GetReportsForAllGPOs.wsf ReportLocation [/Domain:value]
ReportLocation: File system location to save reports to.
Domain: DNS name of domain.
```

Example & Output   This script gathers information about all GPOs in the domain and places the resulting reports in the C:\gpo-reports folder.

```
cscript GetReportsForAllGPOs.wsf c:\gpo-reports
Microsoft (R) Windows Script Host Version 5.7
Copyright (C) Microsoft Corporation. All rights reserved.

== Found 2 GPOs in Fabrikam.com

Generating XML report for GPO 'Default Domain Policy'
Generating HTML report for GPO 'Default Domain Policy'

Generating XML report for GPO 'Default Domain Controllers Policy'
Generating HTML report for GPO 'Default Domain Controllers Policy'

Report generation succeeded for 4 reports.
Report generation failed for 0 reports.
```

GetReportsForGPO.wsf

This script dumps the GPO information of the specified GPO into XML and HTML files at the location you specify. The output is everything from all four tabs in the GPMC when you click a GPO: Scope, Details, Settings, and Delegation.

Syntax
```
Usage: GetReportsForGPO.wsf GPOName ReportLocation [/Domain:value]
GPOName: GPO name or ID.
ReportLocation: File system location for saving the reports.
Domain: DNS name of domain.
```

Example & Output   This script gathers information about the Default Domain Policy and places the reports in the C:\gpo-reports folder.

```
cscript GetReportsForGPO.wsf "Default Domain Policy" c:\GPO-Reports
Microsoft (R) Windows Script Host Version 5.7
Copyright (C) Microsoft Corporation. All rights reserved.

Generating XML report for GPO 'Default Domain Policy'
Generating HTML report for GPO 'Default Domain Policy'
```

ListAllGPOs.wsf

This script lists all of the GPOs in the domain, but not the settings. The Verbose switch (/v) provides more detailed information about each GPO in your listing.

Syntax
```
Usage: ListAllGPOs.wsf /v
/v: Verbose, for detailed information.
```

Example & Output   This script lists information about all the GPOs in the domain.

```
cscript ListAllGPOs.wsf
Microsoft (R) Windows Script Host Version 5.7
Copyright (C) Microsoft Corporation. All rights reserved.
```

```
** For detailed info use the '/v' switch **
== Found 2 GPOs in Fabrikam.com ==
Name: Default Domain Policy
ID: {31B2F340-016D-11D2-945F-00C04FB984F9}
Name: Default Domain Controllers Policy
ID: {6AC1786C-016F-11D2-945F-00C04fB984F9}
```

Example #2 & Output

```
cscript ListAllGPOs.wsf /v
Microsoft (R) Windows Script Host Version 5.7
Copyright (C) Microsoft Corporation. All rights reserved.


-= Found 2 GPOs in Fabrikam.com ==
Name: Default Domain Policy
ID: {31B2F340-016D-11D2-945F-00C04FB984F9}
-- Details --
Created: 10/31/2007 9:26:20 PM
Changed: 11/2/2007 3:10:54 PM
Owner: FABRIKAM\Domain Admins
User Enabled: True
Mach Enabled: True
-- Version Numbers --
User DS: 0
User Sysvol: 0
Mach DS: 1
Mach Sysvol: 1
-- Who this GPO applies to --
Authenticated Users
-- Who can edit this GPO --
GPO Admins
-- Who can edit settings, modify security and delete this GPO --
SYSTEM
-- Who only has Read access --
ENTERPRISE DOMAIN CONTROLLERS
-- Who has custom permissions --
Domain Admins
Enterprise Admins
-- Where this GPO is linked --
Fabrikam.com (Domain)
Name: Default Domain Controllers Policy
ID: {6AC1786C-016F-11D2-945F-00C04fB984F9}
-- Details --
Created: 10/31/2007 9:26:20 PM
Changed: 11/2/2007 3:10:56 PM
Owner: FABRIKAM\Domain Admins
User Enabled: True
Mach Enabled: True
-- Version Numbers --
User DS: 0
User Sysvol: 0
Mach DS: 1
Mach Sysvol: 1
-- Who this GPO applies to --
Authenticated Users
-- Who can edit this GPO --
GPO Admins
-- Who can edit settings, modify security and delete this GPO --
```

```
SYSTEM
-- Who only has Read access --
ENTERPRISE DOMAIN CONTROLLERS
-- Who has custom permissions --
Domain Admins
Enterprise Admins
-- Where this GPO is linked --
Domain Controllers (OU)
```

ListSOMPolicyTree.wsf

This script outputs the Active Directory structure, indicating where GPOs are linked to the domain, organizational units, and sites.

Syntax
Usage: `ListSOMPolicyTree.wsf`

Example & Output   The following is an example of generic use of this script to output SOM information about GPOs.

```
cscript ListSOMPolicyTree.wsf
Microsoft (R) Windows Script Host Version 5.7
Copyright (C) Microsoft Corporation. All rights reserved.

=== GPO Links for domain Fabrikam.com ===
DC=Fabrikam
        GPO=Default Domain Policy
    OU=Domain Controllers
        GPO=Default Domain Controllers Policy
    OU=Servers
      OU=Model Office
          GPO=Hardened Server GPO
      OU=Production
          GPO=Hardened Server GPO
      OU=Test
    OU=Groups

=== GPO Links for sites in forest DC=Fabrikam,DC=com ===
CN=Default-First-Site-Name
```

Finding GPOs Based on Parameters

Sometimes you know what you are looking for, but you are not certain which GPOs contain the information. These scripts allow you find GPOs based on general criteria.

FindDisabledGPOs.wsf

This script lists GPOs for which all or part of the GPO is disabled, including the computer settings, the user settings, or the entire GPO.

Syntax
Usage: `finddisabledgpos.wsf`

Example & Output   This script lists all GPOs that are disabled.

```
cscript finddisabledgpos.wsf
Microsoft (R) Windows Script Host Version 5.7
Copyright (C) Microsoft Corporation. All rights reserved.

== GPOs that are completely disabled ==
{1EED9871-27D9-4741-91AF-13821272BDDA} - Hardened Server GPO
== GPOs with the computer settings disabled ==
== GPOs with the user settings disabled ==
```

FindDuplicateNamedGPOs.wsf

This script finds GPOs with duplicate names. Neither Microsoft Windows Server 2003 nor Windows Server 2008 permits duplicate names.

Syntax
Usage: **FindDuplicateNamedGPOs.wsf**

Example & Output   This script finds all duplicated GPO names.

```
cscript FindDuplicateNamedGPOs.wsf
Microsoft (R) Windows Script Host Version 5.7
Copyright (C) Microsoft Corporation. All rights reserved.

Looking for GPOs with duplicate names in Fabrikam.com
No duplicate named GPOs found.
```

FindGPOsByPolicyExtension.wsf

This script searches for all GPOs in the specified domain that have defined settings for the specified policy extension. The policy extension can be either the friendly name or the GUID for the client-side extension (CSE).

Syntax
Usage: **FindGPOsByPolicyExtension.wsf ExtensionID** [**/PrintCSEList**] [**/Domain:value**]
ExtensionID: GUID or friendly name of the client-side extension (CSE) for which to query.
PrintCSEList: Prints the list of available CSEs.
Domain: DNS name of domain.

Example & Output   This script lists the name and GUID for all configured CSEs in the GPOs within the domain.

```
cscript FindGPOsByPolicyExtension.wsf /PrintCSEList
Microsoft (R) Windows Script Host Version 5.7
Copyright (C) Microsoft Corporation. All rights reserved.

The following client side extensions are registered locally:
{0ACDD40C-75AC-47ab-BAA0-BF6DE7E7FE63} - Wireless Group Policy
{25537BA6-77A8-11D2-9B6C-0000F8080861} - Folder Redirection
{35378EAC-683F-11D2-A89A-00C04FBBCFA2} - Registry
{3610eda5-77ef-11d2-8dc5-00c04fa31a66} - Microsoft Disk Quota
{426031c0-0b47-4852-b0ca-ac3d37bfcb39} - QoS Packet Scheduler
```

```
{42B5FAAE-6536-11d2-AE5A-0000F87571E3} - Scripts
{4CFB60C1-FAA6-47f1-89AA-0B18730C9FD3} - Internet Explorer Zonemapping
{7933F41E-56F8-41d6-A31C-4148A711EE93} - Windows Search Group Policy Extension
{827D319E-6EAC-11D2-A4EA-00C04F79F83A} - Security
{8A28E2C5-8D06-49A4-A08C-632DAA493E17} - Deployed Printer Connections
{A2E30F80-D7DE-11d2-BBDE-00C04F86AE3B} - Internet Explorer Branding
{B1BE8D72-6EAC-11D2-A4EA-00C04F79F83A} - EFS recovery
{B587E2B1-4D59-4e7e-AED9-22B9DF11D053} - 802.3 Group Policy
{C631DF4C-088F-4156-B058-4375F0853CD8} - Microsoft Offline Files
{c6dc5466-785a-11d2-84d0-00c04fb169f7} - Software Installation·
{e437bc1c-aa7d-11d2-a382-00c04f991e27} - Internet Protocol Security Policies
{FB2CA36D-0B40-4307-821B-A13B252DE56C} - Policy-based QoS
```

FindGPOsBySecurityGroup.wsf

This script prints a list of all GPOs on which a given security group has the permission you specify in the command line. If you want to find just the list of GPOs that have a specified permission for that security group, you can input the permission level "Read," "Apply," "Edit," "Full Edit," or "None."

Syntax

```
Usage: FindGPOsBySecurityGroup.wsf GroupName /Permission:value [/Effective] [/None]
[/Domain:value]
GroupName: Security principal on which to search.
Permission: Permission level to find. Can be "Read," "Apply," "Edit," "FullEdit," or "None."
Effective: Displays effective permissions, taking group membership into account.
None: Displays the GPOs for which the security principal does not have the specified permission
level.
Domain: DNS name of domain.
```

Example & Output   This script lists all GPOs that have the Server Operators security group listed with the Edit permission on any GPO in the domain.

```
cscript FindGPOsBySecurityGroup.wsf "Server Operators" /Permission:Edit /effective
Microsoft (R) Windows Script Host Version 5.7
Copyright (C) Microsoft Corporation. All rights reserved.

Searching for all GPOs with effective Edit permissions for Server Operators
== 2 GPOs found ==
Hardened Server GPO
{00713EC8-BFE8-435F-93A4-E287A067EBA9}
Server GPO
{28EC2415-CF96-46AE-9301-CA60011D5F19}
```

FindGPOsWithNoSecurityFiltering.wsf

This script lists all of the GPOs that are not configured to apply to objects. This is determined based on whether the Apply Group Policy permission is set. This is useful for finding GPOs that might have been created for testing but are were designed to be functional in the production domain after the test was completed.

Syntax

```
Usage: FindGPOsWithNoSecurityFiltering.wsf
```

Example & Output   This script lists all GPOs that do not affect any object, as a result of omission of the Apply Group Policy permission.

```
cscript FindGPOsWithNoSecurityFiltering.wsf
Microsoft (R) Windows Script Host Version 5.7
Copyright (C) Microsoft Corporation. All rights reserved.

GPOs in Fabrikam.com that are missing 'Apply' rights:
{D0A29BFC-1109-4449-A138-B1533DD86EE3} - TestServer
```

FindOrphanedGPOsInSysvol.wsf

Finds and prints all GPOs in SYSVOL with no corresponding Active Directory portion of the GPO. Although this is not a common issue, if the Active Directory portion of the GPO is deleted in some manner, the GPO will fail to process and be functional.

Syntax
```
Usage: FindOrphanedGPOsinSysvol.wsf /Domain:value
Domain: DNS name of domain.
```

Example   This script lists all GPOs that are missing the GPC portion of the GPO.

```
cscript FindOrphanedGPOsinSysvol.wsf /Domain:fabrikam.com
```

FindSOMsWithExternalGPOLinks.wsf

This script searches for SOMs with links to GPOs that exist in different domains. This will most commonly appear for sites, which can have links to GPOs from other domains.

Syntax
```
Usage: FindSOMsWithExternalGPOLinks.wsf
```

FindUnlinkedGPOs.wsf

This script finds any GPOs that are not linked to the domain or OU within Active Directory. Site links and links to other domain nodes are not included in the results.

Syntax
```
Usage: FindUnlinkedGPOs.wsf
```

Example & Output   This script list all GPOs that exist in the domain but are not linked to any nodes within Active Directory.

```
cscript FindUnlinkedGPOs.wsf
Microsoft (R) Windows Script Host Version 5.7
Copyright (C) Microsoft Corporation. All rights reserved.

== GPOs that are not linked anywhere in Fabrikam.com ==
NOTE: links to sites, as well as external domains, will not be checked.
{8771E61D-7E96-4887-926B-10CAD1FEFBF1} - Test Group Policy Object
```

GPO Security

Some of the most powerful GPMC scripts, GPO security scripts allow you to create, modify, and delete security permissions on all aspects of the Group Policy environment. These scripts can really help when you need to alter many GPOs at one time to ensure that the environment is secure.

How It Works: GPO Security

Security can be configured in many areas within the GPMC. It can be a bit confusing to determine where to configure the different security settings, depending on the task you want to allow or deny. If you examine the delegations and security configurations in the GPMC, you will see that the following tasks and their permissions can be configured:

■ Creating GPOs

■ Linking GPOs

■ Editing GPOs

■ Performing a full edit of GPOs

■ Running Resultant Set of Policy (RSoP)

■ Modeling the GPO environment

To understand all of these delegations of security, you need to know the scope of each within the environment. Scoping is evident within each script that sets security—you will need to indicate the scope of management (SOM) for the permission. Table 8-1 indicates where each of these delegations must be set.

Table 8-1   GPMC Delegation of Permission Scope

Delegation	Scope
Creating GPOs	Domain level
Linking GPOs	Domain, organizational unit, or site
Editing GPOs	Individual GPO
Full Edit Capabilities	Individual GPO
Running RSoP	Domain, organizational unit
Modeling GPO environment	Domain, organizational unit

GrantPermissionOnAllGPOs.wsf

This script grants the specified security permission level to a user or group for all GPOs in the domain, even GPOs not linked to an Active Directory node. The Replace switch is very useful—it can remove the existing permissions and replace them with new permissions. If you specify a permission for a security group that already exists on the permission list for the GPO, the higher of the two permissions will be placed on the security group (unless you used the Replace switch).

Syntax

```
Usage: GrantPermissionOnAllGPOs.wsf GroupName /Permission:value [/Replace] [/Q]
[/Domain:value]
GroupName: Security principal to grant permissions to.
Permission: Permission level to set. Can be "Read," "Apply," "Edit," "FullEdit," or "None."
Replace: Specifies that any existing permissions should be replaced.
Q: Quiet mode - no warning will be displayed before executing the script.
Domain: DNS name of domain.
```

Example & Output   This script configures the GPO Admins security group with Edit permission on all GPOs in the domain.

```
cscript GrantPermissionOnAllGPOs.wsf "GPO Admins" /Permission:Edit
Microsoft (R) Windows Script Host Version 5.7
Copyright (C) Microsoft Corporation. All rights reserved.

Warning! By executing this script, all GPOs in the target domain will be updated with the
desired security setting.

Both the Active Directory and Sysvol portions of the GPO will be updated. This will result in
the Sysvol contents of every GPO being copied to all replica domain controllers, and may cause
excessive replication traffic in your domain.

If you have slow network links or restricted bandwidth between your domain controllers, you
should check the amount of data on the Sysvol that would be replicated before performing
this task.

Do you want to proceed? [Y/N] y
Updated GPO 'Default Domain Policy' to 'Edit' for GPO Admins
Updated GPO 'Default Domain Controllers Policy' to 'Edit' for GPO Admins
```

Note   For more information about the importance of resetting the permissions on GPOs in the GPMC, refer to Chapter 14, "Advanced GPO Management with AGPM," which covers how to configure the permissions for GPOs after Microsoft Advanced Group Policy Management (AGPM) is installed.

SetGPOCreationPermissions.wsf

This script grants or removes the ability to create GPOs in a domain for a given security group or user.

Syntax

```
Usage: SetGPOCreationPermissions.wsf Group [/Remove] [/Domain:value]
Group: Security group to grant GPO creation rights to.
Remove: Removes the permission instead of granting it.
Domain: DNS name of domain.
```

Example & Output   This script grants the GPO Admins security group the ability to create GPOs in the domain.

```
cscript SetGPOCreationPermissions.wsf "GPO Admins"
Microsoft (R) Windows Script Host Version 5.7
Copyright (C) Microsoft Corporation. All rights reserved.

Added 'GPO Admins' as having GPO creation rights in Fabrikam.com.
```

SetGPOPermissions.wsf

This script sets permissions on the defined GPO for the defined group. This script will error out if you do not define the arguments for it. All of the other scripts will list the script's syntax or generate the output.

Syntax

```
Usage: SetGPOPermissions.wsf <GPOName> <GroupName> /Permission:<PermissionLevel> [/Replace]
[/Domain:<DNSDomainName>]
GPOName: The name of the GPO to process.
GroupName: The security principal to grant permissions to.
Permission: Permission level to set. Can be "Read," "Apply," "Edit," "FullEdit," or "None."
Replace: Specifies that any existing permissions should be replaced.
Domain: DNS name of domain.
```

Example & Output   This script configures the Server Operators security group with Edit permission only on the GPO named Hardened Server GPO.

```
cscript SetGPOPermissions.wsf "Hardened Server GPO" "Server Operators" /Permission:Edit
Microsoft (R) Windows Script Host Version 5.7
Copyright (C) Microsoft Corporation. All rights reserved.

Modified GPO Hardened Server GPO to give Server Operators Edit rights.
```

SetGPOPermissionsBySOM.wsf

This script grants the specified permission for the security principal specified to all GPOs in the SOM of the site, domain, or organizational unit targeted. Complete control is allowed with this script and switches; the Replace, None, and Recursive options allow you to tailor your permission and scope of the permission.

Syntax

```
Usage: SetGPOPermissionsBySOM.wsf SOM Group /Permission:value [/Replace] [/Recursive]
[/Domain:value]
SOM: Name of the site, domain, or OU to process.
Group: Name of the group or user to grant permissions to.
Permission: Permission to grant. Can be "Read," "Apply," "Edit," "FullEdit," or "None."
Replace: Replaces any existing permissions for the specified trustee. Otherwise, the script
simply ensures that the trustee has at least the permission level specified.
Recursive: Applies the changes to all child OUs as well.
Domain: DNS name of domain.
```

Example & Output   This example contains an error. The /Recursive switch was used, but there was not a linked GPO in Test OU.

```
cscript SetGPOPermissionsBySOM.wsf Servers "Server Operators" /Permission:Read /Recursive
Microsoft (R) Windows Script Host Version 5.7
Copyright (C) Microsoft Corporation. All rights reserved.
Updating all GPOs linked to OU Servers to give Read rights to Server Operators

Updating all GPOs linked to OU Model Office to give Read rights to Server Operators

Updating permissions on linked GPO 'Hardened Server GPO'

Updating all GPOs linked to OU Production to give Read rights to Server Operators
Updating permissions on linked GPO 'Hardened Server GPO'

Updating all GPOs linked to OU Test to give Read rights to Server Operators
Error getting SOM CN=Servers,CN=Default-First-Site-
Name,CN=Sites,CN=Configuration,DC=Fabrikam,DC=com
```

SetSOMPermissions.wsf

This script targets the delegation that can be set for the Active Directory nodes where you can link GPOs. Because this is a function that affects only the appropriate permissions, there must be a domain controller running Windows Server 2003 or Windows Server 2008 so you can leverage the RSoP Planning permission.

Syntax
```
Usage: SetSOMPermissions.wsf SOM Group /Permission:value [/Inherit] [/Domain:value]
SOM: Name of the site, domain, or OU to process.
Group: Name of the group or user to grant permissions to.
Permission: Permission to grant. Can be "LinkGPOs," "RSOPLogging," "RSOPPlanning," "All,"
or "None."
Inherit: Specifies that the permission should be inherited by all child containers.
Domain: DNS name of domain.
```

Example #1 & Output   In Example #1, you add RSOPLogging to all of the GPOs for the Server Operators group. In Example #2, you add RSOPPlanning to all of the GPOs for the Server Operators group.

```
cscript SetSOMPermissions.wsf Servers "server operators" /Permission:RSOPLogging /inherit
Microsoft (R) Windows Script Host Version 5.7
Copyright (C) Microsoft Corporation. All rights reserved.

Added the 'RSoP Logging Mode' permission for server operators.
```

Example #2 & Output
```
cscript SetSOMPermissions.wsf Servers "server operators" /Permission:RSOPPlanning /inherit
Microsoft (R) Windows Script Host Version 5.7
Copyright (C) Microsoft Corporation. All rights reserved.

Added the 'RSoP Planning Mode' permission for server operators.
```

> **Note**   For more information about GPMC RSoP and Modeling, refer to Chapter 7, which describes how to run an RSoP and model within the GPMC. For more information about GPMC permissions, refer to Chapter 9, "Security Delegation for Administration of GPOs," which covers the security delegation options in the GPMC and AGPM.

Direct from the Source: The Scripting Group Policy Landscape

GPMC provides an important interface into Group Policy management. You may be familiar with the GPMC GUI, but the GPMC scripts provide a great tool for automating management of Group Policy objects themselves. All of the tasks that you can perform with the GUI can also be automated by using the supplied GPMC scripts; you can also create custom scripts by using the scripting model that GPMC provides. Automation tasks also include management of GPOs as a whole. That is, you create and delete GPOs, link them to Active Directory containers, back them up and restore or import them, and even generate Group Policy Results reports—all from scripts.

If you are a Windows PowerShell scripter, you can also leverage the GPMC scripting interfaces from that scripting environment, because they are just COM objects that you can call directly from your Windows PowerShell scripts by using the New-Object cmdlet. In addition, a set of free Windows PowerShell cmdlets makes it easy to leverage much of the GPMC functionality from Windows PowerShell. You can find these at *www.sdmsoftware.com/freeware.php*.

The GPMC is lacking, however, when it comes to modifying the settings within GPOs via scripts or some other automated mechanism. There are no scripting interfaces into Group Policy settings. Microsoft does provide the IGroupPolicyObject C++ interface (for more details, you can search for that interface name on *http://msdn.microsoft.com*) for programmatically accessing some parts of Group Policy, namely registry policy, but this interface is not easily accessible via Microsoft Visual Basic, Scripting Edition (VBScript) or other COM-based scripting languages.

The SDM Software GPExpert™ Scripting Toolkit for PowerShell exposes Group Policy settings to scripting interfaces. It supports VBScript (although it is designed to work primarily with Windows PowerShell), and it provides a mechanism for reading, searching, and writing settings within most of the supported policy areas in Windows Vista, Windows XP, Windows Server 2003, and Windows Server 2008.

Darren Mar-Elia Microsoft MVP, Group Policy, CTO & Founder, SDM Software, Inc.

VBScript Scripting

If you use VBScript, you may find it difficult to create custom scripts beyond the GPMC scripts for Group Policy management. Although you can create VBScript scripts to control and manage Group Policy, it is not a simple task.

If you want to manage the GPOs, link to GPOs, set permissions on the GPOs, set permissions on the Active Directory nodes, and so on, you would be better off just using the GPMC scripts covered earlier. Those scripts are fully functional and already proven. You can use those scripts in other scripts; just send a function call to them.

If you want to manage the GPO settings, however, the GPMC provides no programming interfaces into the Group Policy settings. To manage those settings with the GPMC, you have to understand how the Group Policy settings for each policy area are configured, stored, and tracked, because each policy uses a different format when being stored.

Solutions are available that apply this level of investigation. These solutions include scripting interfaces that you use to make, change, and delete settings from GPOs.

The most prevalent solution is an SDM Software product for making changes to GPO settings using Windows PowerShell. The GPExpert Scripting Toolkit for PowerShell allows you to automate the modification of Group Policy settings across all GPOs in a domain, not just one at a time manually. It also supports modification of local GPOs. You can register and download an evaluation version of the product at *http://www.sdmsoftware.com/products2.php*.

> **Note**   For more details on third-party tools, refer to Appendix A, "Third-Party Group Policy Tools."

Windows PowerShell

Windows PowerShell is one of the hottest topics and technologies for management of Windows today. This new technology was created from the ground up for Microsoft operating systems and it is proving to be a powerful, easy-to-follow, and widely used solution for Windows command-line automation.

Unfortunately, Windows PowerShell does not currently include native support for Group Policy. Although this is a limitation at first glance, it is quickly fixed with some of the other capabilities that it provides for Group Policy management. Windows PowerShell can call on COM objects directly, allowing you to manage Group Policy.

Windows PowerShell allows you to manage the settings in a GPO, as well as leverage better control over the GPOs compared with the GPMC scripts. Windows PowerShell derives its power from the *pipeline*, or the ability to "pipe" objects between Windows PowerShell cmdlets. This pipeline or piping is the ability of Windows PowerShell to carry out instructions to objects through a sequence of stages between cmdlets. For example, Windows PowerShell allows you to get a list of GPOs, determine which has a certain parameter (for example, the HRAdmins that have Edit permission delegated to them), and then pipe that list to a cmdlet that lets you alter just the GPOs that have this permission with a new set of permissions for the group. You can usually do this with one line of script by using Windows PowerShell.

The foundation has already been laid for you as well. Many example scripts and cmdlets have been generated for Windows PowerShell to control Group Policy. These cmdlets allow you to perform tasks on Group Policy and GPOs in a more efficient automated manner. For a list of Windows PowerShell–enabled scripts and cmdlets, visit the following links:

http://www.microsoft.com/technet/technetmag/issues/2007/05/GroupPolicy/default.aspx

http://www.sdmsoftware.com/freeware.php

Note   For more information detailing third-party tools and references, refer to Appendix A, "Third-Party Group Policy Tools."

As an example of the capabilities and simplicity offered by Windows PowerShell, Figure 8-1 shows you a Windows PowerShell cmdlet that reports on significant information from a GPO within the domain.

```
PS C:\> $gpo=get-sdmgpobject -gponame "gpo://cpandl.com/E98A1A41-481C-40F5-AC06-
PS C:\> $gpo

GPName                          : gpo://cpandl.com/E98A1A41-481C-40F5-AC06-42CCD201
UserName                        :
Password                        :
AuthEnum                        : None
OpenByName                      : False
CentralStore                    :
Containers                      : {Computer Configuration, User Configuration}
GPCComputerVersion              : 0
GPCUserVersion                  : 6
GPTComputerVersion              : 0
GPTUserVersion                  : 6
Name                            : GPSI test
Guid                            : e98a1a41-481c-40f5-ac06-42ccd2011d6b
DisableComputerConfiguration    : False
DisableUserConfiguration        : False
Type                            : AD
ADRoot                          : System.DirectoryServices.DirectoryEntry
FSPath                          : \\sdm1.cpandl.com\SYSVOL\cpandl.com\Policies\{e98
                                  6-42ccd2011d6b}\
PolFileManager                  : GPOSDK.Providers._Common.PolFileManager
AdmManager                      : GPOSDK.Providers._Common.AdmManager

PS C:\>
```

Figure 8-1   Windows PowerShell cmdlets allow you to gather information regarding GPOs.

In another example, shown in Figure 8-2, Windows PowerShell is used to control not only the GPO, but also the settings within the GPO. This is a very difficult task using a script, but Figure 8-2 illustrates how the GPExpert Scripting Toolkit for PowerShell can alter a GPO setting.

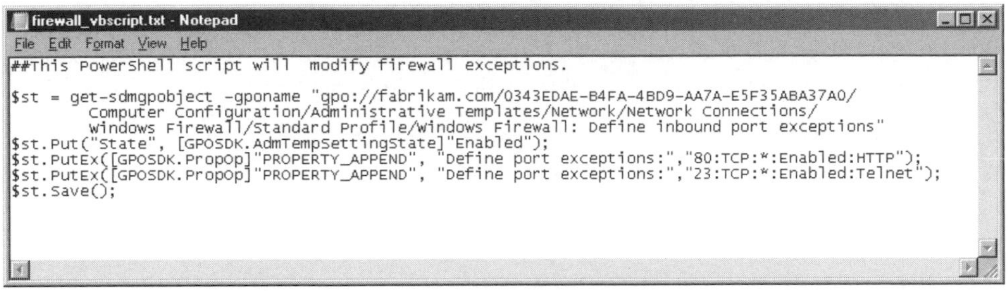

```
firewall_vbscript.txt - Notepad                                    _□×
File  Edit  Format  View  Help
##This PowerShell script will  modify firewall exceptions.

$st = get-sdmgpobject -gponame "gpo://fabrikam.com/0343EDAE-B4FA-4BD9-AA7A-E5F35ABA37A0/
       Computer Configuration/Administrative Templates/Network/Network Connections/
       windows Firewall/Standard Profile/windows Firewall: Define inbound port exceptions"
$st.Put("State", [GPOSDK.AdmTempSettingState]"Enabled");
$st.PutEx([GPOSDK.PropOp]"PROPERTY_APPEND", "Define port exceptions:","80:TCP:*:Enabled:HTTP");
$st.PutEx([GPOSDK.PropOp]"PROPERTY_APPEND", "Define port exceptions:","23:TCP:*:Enabled:Telnet");
$st.Save();
```

Figure 8-2 The firewall settings in a GPO can be altered by using Windows PowerShell.

Summary

Windows automation technology is growing at an exponential rate. Automation is very popular and is making administration easier and more efficient. Options for Group Policy automation have been limited over the years. When Microsoft first released the GPMC, it included a set of scripts that essentially duplicated the capabilities within the GPMC GUI, but in command-line format. These GPMC scripts allowed administrators to optimize the power of scripting to perform a task in mere minutes that would take hours if done manually in the GUI.

VBScript is a powerful tool for automation. Custom VBScript scripts can perform nearly any task. As a Group Policy administrator, you might not be fully educated on the finer points of VBScript, which might be a limiting factor in using it for Group Policy automation. In addition, most of the tasks that you would want to perform using VBScript are already scripted in the GPMC scripts, so the usefulness of VBScript for Group Policy management is limited.

Windows PowerShell has grown in usefulness and popularity. Although it does not natively support Group Policy, cmdlets have been created that perform actions similar to what you can do with the GPMC scripts. With the ability to pipe commands using PowerShell, this new method of automating Group Policy management is very powerful.

Finally, some third-party tools (some already existing and some still in production) allow you to not only manage Group Policy, but also create, modify, and remove policy settings within the GPO. This is the final piece of the GPO management space; before the existence of tools like the GPExpert Scripting Toolkit for PowerShell, you could not access the GPO to alter the settings.

Additional Resources

- The Microsoft Advanced Group Policy Management Web site, at *http://www.microsoft.com/windows/products/windowsvista/enterprise/agpm.mspx*, includes more information about Advanced Group Policy Management.

- The Group Policy Management Console Sample Scripts download page at *http://www.microsoft.com/downloads/details.aspx?familyid=38c1a89b-a6d2-4f2a-a944-9236999aee65&displaylang=en&tm* allows you to download the GPMC scripts.

- The Microsoft Windows PowerShell Web site, at *http://www.microsoft.com/ windowsserver2003/technologies/management/powershell/default.mspx*, includes more information about Windows PowerShell, including how to use it and how to customize it.

- The article titled "Simplify Group Policy Administration with Windows PowerShell," at *http://www.microsoft.com/technet/technetmag/issues/2007/05/GroupPolicy/ default.aspx*, includes more information and sample scripts regarding Windows PowerShell scripts and cmdlets.

- The SDM Software Web site, at *http://www.sdmsoftware.com*, includes information and sample Windows PowerShell scripts and cmdlets.

- Chapter 6, "GPMC Basics," includes information about the functionality and features of the GPMC.

- Chapter 7, "Advanced GPMC Management," includes information on how to delegate administration of Group Policy management.

- Chapter 14, "Advanced GPO Management with AGPM," includes information about the functionality and features of AGPM.

- Appendix A, "Third-Party Group Policy Tools," includes information about how third-party tools can improve management and control over GPOs.

Part IV
Implementing Security

Chapter 9
Security Delegation for Administration of GPOs

Group Policy is a diverse and complex technology. Any organization could contain from one to hundreds of Group Policy administrators. If your company has more than just a few Group Policy administrators, you should establish Group Policy delegation. Delegation allows the infrastructure to be managed by many administrators, while limiting what each administrator can do to the GPOs.

The delegation options in the Group Policy Management Console (GPMC) are far superior to anything that was available for Group Policy delegation before the release of the GPMC. Although GPMC delegation is somewhat limited and settings can be made to the production GPOs that could cause issues on the network, using the GPMC in conjunction with Microsoft Advanced Group Policy Management (AGPM) and its delegation options is an excellent solution for the overall management of Group Policy.

Understanding the strengths of the GPMC and AGPM tools will help you determine the delegation model you design and implement. This chapter presents many best practices that you can follow when designing and implementing your solution.

Default Security Environment

Windows Server 2008 offers only one tool for administering GPOs—the GPMC. As you saw in Chapter 6, "GPMC Basics," the GPMC is a broad and useful tool. In some cases, it is the only tool that you will need to administer your Group Policy infrastructure. The security and delegation within the GPMC is more than sufficient to secure the GPOs within your organization.

However, if you want more control and overall management of GPOs, AGPM is an essential tool. AGPM also comes with default security and delegation capabilities. Chapter 14, "Advanced GPO Management with AGPM," provides an in-depth discussion on how AGPM can enhance the overall management of Group Policy for your enterprise.

Understanding the default security model of both of these tools is important. You should be fully aware of what each tool can do and how the GPOs are controlled, as well as who can manage the GPOs.

Default Security of the GPMC

The default security configuration for administering Group Policy in Windows Server 2008 is similar to that in Microsoft Windows Server 2003. Of course, the changes from Microsoft Windows 2000 Server to Windows Server 2003 were substantial, because the GPMC was introduced with Windows Server 2003. The GPMC introduced a totally new set of delegations and methods of delegating administration over Group Policy management.

The GPMC is installed on a Windows Server 2008 domain controller by default with some default security delegation that existed in Windows Server 2003.

The default security for administration of Group Policy is divided into six categories:

- Create GPOs
- Link GPOs
- Edit, delete, and modify security of GPOs
- Edit GPOs (only)
- Model GPOs
- Perform Resultant Set of Policy (RSoP) of GPOs

For each of these delegations, Setup configures the default settings when it installs Active Directory directory service. Table 9-1 lists the default permissions for each of the delegations in the GPMC.

As you can see, unless you are in the Group Policy Creator Owners group or have membership in the Domain Admins group, you do not have permission to manage Group Policy by default.

Default Security of AGPM

AGPM adds an additional, yet integrated, level of delegation to your Group Policy management. Remember, AGPM is not a mandatory tool—it just makes the administration of GPOs much easier and adds functionality that the GPMC does not provide.

Table 9-1 **Default Delegations in the GPMC**

Delegation	Permission	User or Group
Create GPOs	Create GPO in the domain	Domain Admins
		Group Policy Creator Owners
		SYSTEM
Link GPOs	Link GPO to specified node in Active Directory only	Administrators
		Domain Admins
		Enterprise Admins
		SYSTEM
Edit settings, delete, modify security of GPOs	Edit GPO using GPME	Domain Admins
	Enable/Disable GPO and parts of GPO	Enterprise Admins
	Import Settings	SYSTEM
	Backup GPO	
	Restore from Backup	
	Link WMI Filters	
	Delete GPO	
	Modify Security Filtering	
	Modify Delegation on GPO	
Edit GPOs (only)	Edit GPO in GPME	
	Enable/Disable GPO and parts of GPO	
	Import Settings	
	Link WMI Filters	
Perform Group Policy Modeling analyses	Model GPOs for the specified Active Directory node	Administrators
		Domain Admins
		Enterprise Admins
		SYSTEM
Read Group Policy Results data	Determine RSoP for the specified Active Directory node	Administrators
		Domain Admins
		Enterprise Admins
		SYSTEM
Read (from Security Filtering)	View Settings	Authenticated Users
	Backup GPO to existing folder	

When you install AGPM, no GPOs are automatically added to the AGPM server for management. This could cause some undesired results, so the inclusion (or controlling) of GPOs in AGPM is left up to the AGPM administrator.

Some distinct delegations are set up during the installation of AGPM that are carried out through the initial use of AGPM and control of GPOs. Only two user accounts are even given control within AGPM as a default.

The first user account, agpmservice, is not used for logging in and managing AGPM; rather, it is a service account that the AGPM service uses when it accesses the GPOs on the production domain controller. This account is in essence the "proxy" account that does all of the work when production GPOs are in any way touched by AGPM. This account has privileges over creating new GPOs and the GPOs that it creates through its inclusion in the Group Policy Creator Owners group and its explicit permissions to the GPOs in SYSVOL of the domain controllers. As you can see, a real administrator does not use this user account; it is just the service account used by AGPM, as shown in Figure 9-1.

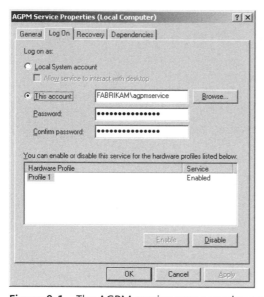

Figure 9-1   The AGPM service uses a service account
to connect to the domain controller and exchange information about the production GPOs.

The second user account used during installation will be used by a real administrator. This user account becomes the AGPM administrator and has full control over the AGPM environment, as shown in Figure 9-2. The AGPM administrator account can be an existing user account that will have full administrative privileges over all of AGPM, or it can be a dedicated AGPM administrator account used only for the initial setup of delegation in AGPM.

Best Practices   It is a best practice to use a dedicated user account when defining the AGPM administrator account during installation of AGPM. This simplifies administration and provides a more flexible delegation model for future configurations. If an existing user account, associated with an employee, is used, this account might not always be in control of GPOs, requiring the account to be changed when the user is no longer in charge of GPOs.

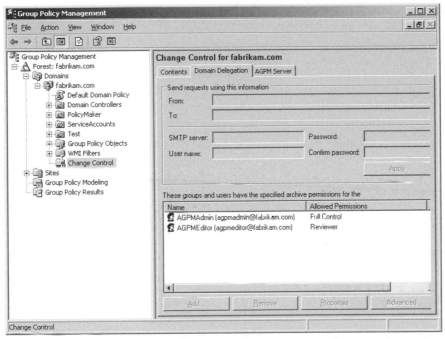

Figure 9-2   An AGPM administrator is determined at installation and is granted full control over AGPM for management and initial setup.

After you install AGPM, the AGPM administrator will log in and create the other delegations. At this time, you should configure another user account to have full control over the AGPM; multiple user accounts should have access to AGPM with this level of privilege so that administrators do not use the original AGPM administrator account on a regular basis. The list should be limited, however, as discussed later in the section "Best Practices."

Note   AGPM is not part of Windows Server 2008 or Windows Vista. AGPM is part of the Microsoft Desktop Optimization Pack (MDOP). For more information about MDOP, refer to *https://partner.microsoft.com/global/40043418*.

Group Policy Management Console Delegation

The default GPMC security is a baseline that is often modified by many organizations. The primary reason for this is that only those in the Domain Admins group have access to all areas of the GPMC delegation options. It is a best practice to utilize the delegation structure that is available within the GPMC to narrow the capabilities that come with membership in the Domain Admins group, as well as provide tight control over what GPO administrators can do to and with GPOs within the domain.

As mentioned earlier, a total of six GPMC delegations have default settings and therefore can be configured further. Of the six delegations, the creating, linking, and editing delegations are most important to control and configure. The other delegations provide "read only" access to the GPOs; this level of access will not allow any configurations or cause any destruction to the production network, but it could provide valuable insight into how things are configured, exposing vulnerabilities to a would-be hacker.

Thus, it is important to manage all areas of delegation in the GPMC. Management of delegation in the GPMC requires three important considerations: the scope of the delegation, the user or group receiving the delegation, and the permissions you are delegating. When you consider and determine all three of these factors, the delegation model is easy to implement.

Creating GPOs

The ability to create a GPO is controlled at the domain level. This makes sense, because all GPOs are domain centric and specific. The actual configuration of who can create a GPO is not implemented at the domain node in the GPMC, although it is a domain scope that is being considered.

Delegation of GPO creation in the domain is performed at the Group Policy Objects node in the GPMC, as shown in Figure 9-3.

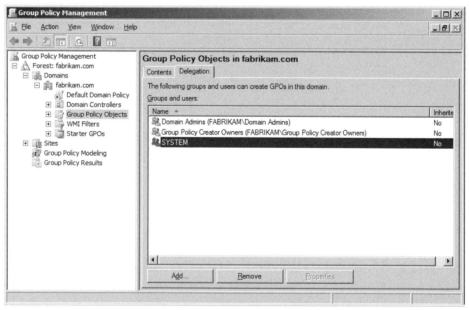

Figure 9-3   Delegation of administration over creating GPOs is performed at the Group Policy Objects node in the GPMC.

To delegate who can create GPOs for the domain, follow these steps:

1.   In the GPMC, expand the forest node, and then expand the domain node.

2.   Select the Group Policy Objects node.

3. Select the Delegation tab in the details pane.

4. To add members, click Add, and then select the user or group in the Select User, Computer, or Group dialog box.

5. To remove a member, select the member, and then click Remove. A Group Policy Management dialog box appears. Click OK.

The delegated privilege of creating a GPO in the domain gives the corresponding administrator some power. To create a GPO in the domain, follow these steps:

1. In the GPMC, expand the forest node, and then expand the domain node.

2. Right-click the Group Policy Objects node, and then click New.

3. In the New GPO dialog box, type a name for the new GPO in the Name box.

4. (Optional) Select a starter GPO from the Source Starter GPO list, as shown in Figure 9-4.

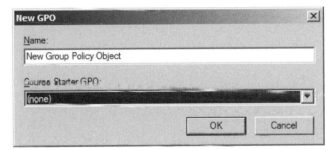

Figure 9-4   When a new GPO is created, it can be created with no settings, or it can use a Starter GPO that will include settings.

Although Starter GPOs are not production GPOs, there are delegations that control their creation, too. In a similar fashion to creating GPOs for the production domain, you will need to configure the groups that can create Starter GPOs for the domain. To delegate who can create Starter GPOs, follow these steps:

1. In the GPMC, expand the forest node, and then expand the domain node.

2. Select the Starter GPOs node.

3. Select the Delegation tab in the details pane.

4. To add members, click Add, and then select the user or group in the Select User, Computer, or Group dialog box.

5. To remove a member, select the member, and then click Remove. A Group Policy Management dialog box appears. Click OK.

After Starter GPOs are created in the domain, new GPOs in production can be created from them, as shown in Figure 9-5.

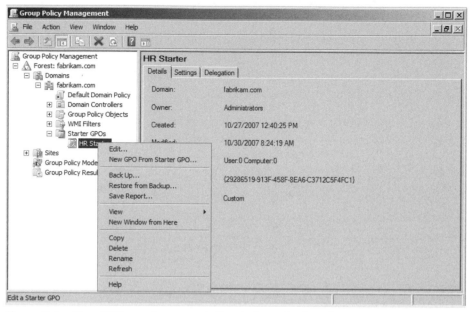

Figure 9-5   New GPOs can be created directly from the list of Starter GPOs, which can provide a baseline of settings.

Settings configured in the Starter GPO are used to create a baseline of settings in the new GPO when it is created. To create a new GPO using a Starter GPO, follow these steps:

1. In the GPMC, expand the forest node, and then expand the domain node.

2. Right-click the Group Policy Objects node, and then click New.

3. In the New GPO dialog box, select the Starter GPO you want to use from the Source Starter GPO list.

4. Type the name for the new GPO in the Name box, and then click OK.

> **Note**   Creation of a GPO does not include the ability to link the GPO. A user with the delegation to create GPOs in the domain can only create them from the Group Policy Objects node in the GPMC.

Note that new GPOs that do not use Starter GPOs are empty—they contain no configurations. Of course, if a new GPO uses a Starter GPO as the template for settings, those settings will be set in the new GPO.

> **Warning**   The security delegations set on Starter GPOs are not copied to new GPOs created from them. The default security on new GPOs is set, regardless of whether a Starter was used.

Linking GPOs

Linking GPOs to nodes in Active Directory is not a domain centric task. This is because GPOs can be linked to more than the domain node, which you most likely already know. GPOs can also be linked to Active Directory sites and organizational units. With this array of options, scoping of the delegation for linking GPOs is important.

Because each node within Active Directory can have unique administrators through the configuration of administration delegation within the Active Directory Users and Computers tool, it makes sense that the same format is followed within the GPMC. Each node (Site, Domain, and Organizational Unit) has a unique delegation for the list of administrators that can link a GPO to it.

> **Note**   Some containers in Active Directory, such as the default Users container and Computers container, cannot have GPOs linked to them. These containers do not appear in the GPMC for this reason. Organizational units, however, are containers that can support GPO links and appear in the GPMC.

To grant a user the delegation to link a GPO to an Active Directory node follow these steps:

1. In the GPMC, expand the forest node, and then expand the domain node.
2. Select the Active Directory node for which you want to set up delegation.
3. Select the Delegation tab in the details pane.
4. Ensure that the Link GPOs option is selected in the Permission list.
5. To add members, click Add, and then select the user or group.
6. To remove a member, select the member, and then click Remove.

An administrator who has been granted the delegation to link a GPO to a node in Active Directory can link any GPO in the domain to this node. To link an existing GPO to a site, the domain, or an organizational unit, follow these steps:

1. In the GPMC, expand the forest node, and then expand the domain node.
2. Right-click the Active Directory node to which you want to link the existing GPO (must be <*domainname*>, organizational unit, or site), and then click Link An Existing GPO.
3. In the Select GPO dialog box, shown in the following figure, select the domain from which you want to link the GPO from the Look In This Domain list (the default domain listed is typically the domain that you want to use), as shown in Figure 9-6.
4. Select the GPO, or GPOs, that you want to link from the Group Policy Objects list.

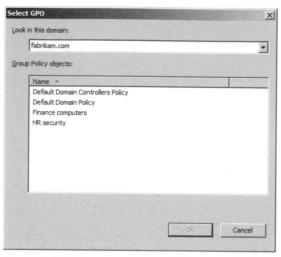

Figure 9-6   When you want to link an existing GPO to an
Active Directory node, you select the desired GPO from the full list of GPOs for the domain.

How It Works: Linking GPO Permission Configured for Active Directory Object

When an administrator is granted the delegation to link a GPO to a node, the GPMC is establishing nothing more than routine permissions on the node. If you open the Properties for the node in Active Directory Users and Computers and then view the Security tab, you will see the four permissions configured to allow this behavior. The first two permissions are Read gPLink and Write gPLink, located under Properties, and the other two permissions are Read gPOptions and Write gPOptions, configured under Properties For This Object And All Descendant Objects. Figure 9-7 shows these permissions.

Warning   When you re-deploy a GPO from AGPM, you have the option to restore the links to the Active Directory nodes with which it was originally configured. This is useful when a GPO is deleted and then restored, or when a GPO is rolled back or forward to another version. This action is performed by the AGPM service account on behalf of the AGPM administrator who has the deploy delegations in AGPM. The links can be restored to the Active Directory nodes even if the requesting AGPM user does not have the delegation within GPMC to link the GPO to the nodes selected in the deployment dialog box.

If a user is granted the ability to link a GPO to the node, but not create a GPO in the domain, this is the only task the user can perform in the GPMC. However, a user who is granted both delegations has another option available. This option combines both steps

Window Shop Books
P.O. Box 18283
Denver, CO 80218

PACKING SLIP

Order Date: 06/02/10	Ship Date:
Order Number: 104-8323386-8562617	Customer Contact: Jianxin_wang

Ship To:
SYED HYDER
17065 W BERNARDO DR
SAN DIEGO, CA 92127-1457

Item#:	Title	Qty	Ext Price	S&H	LOC
9780735625143	Windows® Group Policy Resource Kit: Windows Server® 2008 and Windows Vista®...	1	$6.50	$3.99	BB603

If you wish to contact us regarding this order, please email us at
sales@windowshopbooks.com.

Thank you for your order!

into a single step. To create a GPO and link it to an Active Directory node in the same action, follow these steps:

1. In the GPMC, expand the forest node, and then expand the domain node.

2. Right-click the Active Directory node to which you want to link the new GPO (must be *<domainname>*, organizational unit, or site), and then click Create A GPO In This Domain, And Link It Here.

3. In the New GPO dialog box, type the name of the new GPO in the Name box.

4. (Optional) Select the Starter GPO that you want to use from the Source Starter GPO list, and then click OK.

> **Note**   This method of creating a GPO and linking it to a node in Active Directory is possible only for those who have both the Create and Link delegations for the corresponding node where the GPO is being linked.

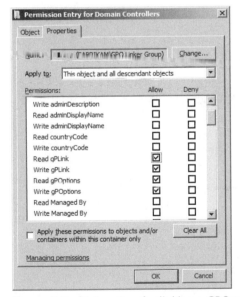

Figure 9-7   Delegation for linking a GPO to a node in Active Directory can be translated as individual permissions on that node.

Managing GPOs

The management of GPOs is not referred to as Management in the GPMC; rather, it is referred to as Edit Settings, Delete, Modify Security, as shown in the details pane in Figure 9-8. This level of delegation is very powerful—a user granted this delegation can do anything to the GPO, except create it and link it to a node.

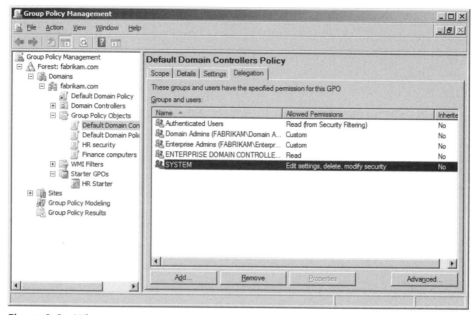

Figure 9-8   When you want a user to have management capabilities over a GPO, you can establish Edit Settings, Delete, Modify Security delegation.

Management over GPOs should be carried out with great care and consideration. If possible, only a few users should manage each GPO. As with everything else you have seen in this chapter, scoping of delegation is very important in the management of GPOs. Because each GPO is a stand-alone object, each has its own delegation for who can manage it.

To grant the delegation to manage a GPO, follow these steps:

1. In the GPMC, expand the forest node, and then expand the domain node.

2. Expand the Group Policy Objects node.

3. Select the GPO for which you want to set up delegation.

4. Select the Delegation tab in the details pane.

5. If the user or group is already listed in the Groups Or Users list, right-click the group or user for which you are setting up delegation, and then click the Edit Settings, Delete, Modify Security option.

6. To add members, click Add, and then select the user or group in the Select User, Computer, Or Group dialog box. When the Add Group or User dialog box appears, select the Edit Settings, Delete, Modify Security option from the Permissions list, and then click OK.

7. To remove a member, select the member, and then click Remove. When the Group Policy Management dialog box appears to confirm the deletion, click OK.

After the delegation has been performed, the user will be able to control many aspects of the GPO, including the following:

- Editing the GPO by right-clicking it and using the Group Policy Management Editor
- Configuring security on the GPO, specifying which user, group, or computer has the permission to apply the GPO

Note   For a user or computer to apply the settings in a GPO, the Read and Apply Group Policy permissions must both be set on the GPO for the target object. Permissions can either be set explicitly for the user or computer listed on the GPO or granted based on membership in a group with the permission.

- Deleting a GPO from the production environment, which removes all links to the GPO, the Group Policy template (GPT), and the Group Policy container (GPC) portions of the GPO

Warning   Without AGPM, any GPOs that are deleted using the GPMC are permanently deleted. This action can be undone only by restoring the GPO from the GPMC backup/restore tool or by performing a restore of the GPO from the System State. If the System State was not backed up or a manual backup of the GPO was not performed, the GPO is not recoverable. For more information about backing up GPOs using the GPMC, refer to Chapter 6.

Starter GPOs have the same delegation options as normal GPOs. The steps are the same for establishing the delegation on Starter GPOs as they are for normal GPOs—you just use the Delegation tab after selecting the Starter GPO that you want to configure.

Editing GPOs

Editing GPOs is another delegation that you must guard and selectively configure in the GPMC. This delegation is performed on individual GPOs so that control of the settings can be precisely set for each GPO.

If you need to give a user control over just the contents of a GPO, you should provide the editing delegation. The delegation to manage a GPO provides too much control for a user who simply needs to make setting changes within the GPO.

To delegate the editing of a GPO to a user, follow these steps:

1. In the GPMC, expand the forest node, and then expand the domain node.
2. Expand the Group Policy Objects node.
3. Select the GPO for which you want to set up delegation.
4. Select the Delegation tab in the details pane.

5. If the user or group is already listed in the Groups Or Users list, right-click the group or user for whom you are setting up delegation, and then select Edit Settings.

6. To add members, click Add, and then select the user or group in the Select User, Computer, or Group dialog box. When the Add Group or User dialog box appears, select the Edit Settings option from the Permissions list, and then click OK.

7. To a remove member, select the member, and then click Remove. When the Group Policy Management dialog box appears to confirm the deletion, click OK.

The edit delegation is targeted to only the specified GPO and tightly controls the delegate to only the specified GPO. No additional GPO permissions are granted to the delegate over the GPO. A user with the delegation to edit a GPO can do so by following these steps:

1. In the GPMC, expand the forest node, and then expand the domain node.

2. Expand the Group Policy Objects node.

3. Right-click the GPO that you want to edit, and then click Edit.

4. Configure your settings using the Group Policy Management Editor.

> **Warning**   A user who has been granted the manage or edit delegation over a GPO has great power. Editing GPOs directly within the GPMC, not using AGPM, affects the production GPOs. When a GPO setting is updated, the change occurs immediately to the GPT and is replicated to all of the domain controllers in the domain. A setting modification made using the GPMC will update a target user or computer as soon as the target object background refresh occurs. It is ideal to use AGPM, which can be easily configured to allow changes to the GPO without those changes affecting the production environment.

Starter GPOs also have the same delegation options as normal GPOs. The steps for Starter GPOs for delegation are the same as for normal GPOs, which are done using the Delegation tab after selecting the Starter GPO that you want to configure.

Modeling GPOs

The delegation to model the GPOs is useful for all IT staff members, including the Help desk, desktop management, and even personnel management. GPO modeling allows you to plan what the GPO settings would be for a user or computer if the objects were to be moved to a different organizational unit or have different settings applied to them, such as Windows Management Instrumentation (WMI) filters, loopback processing, site affiliation, and so on, as shown in Figure 9-9.

Group Policy Modeling of GPOs does not grant the user any control over the GPOs, just the ability to see the RSoP for users and computers that have membership in different groups, or that will be moved to a different organizational unit or configured with different GPO controls. For more information about modeling GPOs within the GPMC, refer to Chapter 7,

"Advanced GPMC Management," which describes the Group Policy Modeling Wizard and the steps for creating a model.

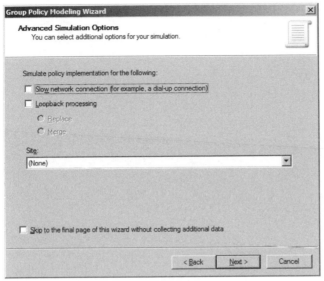

Figure 9-9 Modeling of a GPO includes configurations such as WMI filters, loopback processing, and site affiliation.

Delegation for modeling of GPOs is performed in the Active Directory node so that users can see the results of the modeling only for certain Active Directory organizational units. If users can see how GPOs are affecting users and computers elsewhere in the organization, they might be able to get important security or configuration information that could be used in a malicious way.

To configure the delegation for modeling of GPOs, follow these steps:

1. In the GPMC, expand the forest node, and then expand the domain node

2. Select the Active Directory node for which you want to set up delegation.

3. Select the Delegation tab in the details pane.

4. Ensure that the Perform Group Policy Modeling Analyses option is selected in the Permission list.

5. To add members, click Add, and then select the user or group in the Select User, Computer, or Group dialog box, then click OK.

6. When the Add Group or User dialog box appears, select the scope of the permission, either to the selected container only or to the selected containers and child containers. Then click OK

7. To remove a member, select the member, and then click Remove. When the Group Policy Management dialog box appears to confirm the deletion, click OK.

RSoP of GPOs

When delegating who can view RSoP data for users and computers, it is a good idea to include everyone who deals with management or support of GPOs. The tool does nothing more than determine the RSoP; however, it allows the RSoP to be seen from within the GPMC, instead of at the user's desktop or on a server with specific credentials.

For more information about using the Group Policy Results Wizard to see the RSoP in the GPMC, refer to Chapter 7, which describes the Group Policy Results Wizard and provides steps for creating an RSoP.

Granting delegation over the RSoP allows the user to see the RSoP for a specific location within Active Directory. Delegation of the RSoP is performed in each Active Directory node within the GPMC. To set up delegation for running the RSoP for a node, follow these steps:

1. In the GPMC, expand the forest node, and then expand the domain node.

2. Select the Active Directory node for which you want to set up delegation.

3. Select the Delegation tab in the details pane.

4. Ensure that the Read Group Policy Results Data option is selected in the Permission list.

5. To add members, click Add, and then select the user or group in the Select User, Computer, or Group dialog box; then click OK.

6. When the Add Group or User dialog box appears, select the scope of the permission, either to the selected container only or to the selected containers and child containers; then click OK

7. To remove a member, select the member, and then click Remove. When the Group Policy Management dialog box appears to confirm the deletion, click OK.

Advanced Group Policy Management Delegation

AGPM has its own unique set of delegations that must be configured in conjunction with the GPMC delegations. The overall goal of establishing AGPM delegations is to restrict GPO administrators from using the GPMC for the editing and management of GPOs in lieu of using AGPM.

For a list of best practice configurations for delegation when AGPM is installed, refer to the section "Best Practices" later in this chapter. This section describes how to merge the two delegation options, in the GPMC and AGPM, into a more complete delegation solution.

Full Control

When a user is granted full control over all GPOs in the domain or an individual GPO that has been controlled in AGPM, that user can control every aspect of the GPO. This includes editing, viewing, and approving changes and deployment of the GPO into production. The exact list of permissions is shown in Figure 9-10.

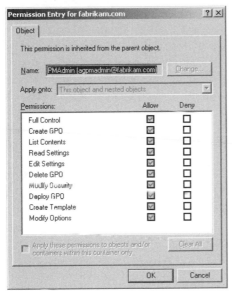

Figure 9-10   Full control delegation in AGPM consists of many detailed permissions that give a user complete control over the GPOs in AGPM.

The benefit of this level of delegation is that users can be granted full control privileges over a single GPO in AGPM, without having any other control over other GPOs in AGPM.

To set up full control delegation in AGPM for a single GPO, follow these steps:

1. In the GPMC, expand the forest node, and then expand the domain node.

2. Select the Change Control node.

3. Select the Controlled tab, located on the Contents tab in the details pane.

4. Select the GPO for which you want to set up delegation.

5. If the user or group is already listed as having the specified archive permissions for the selected GPO list, select the group or user for which you are setting up delegation. Then click Advanced to open the Permissions dialog box. Select the group or user name in the Group Or User Names list, and then select the Full Control check box in the Allow column.

6. To add members, click Add, and then select the user or group in the Select User, Computer, or Group dialog box. Set up the Full Control delegation in the Add Group or User dialog box after adding the object.

7. To remove a member, select the member, and then click Remove. When the Group Policy Management dialog box appears to confirm the deletion, click OK.

Editing

If you want to restrict the amount of control that a user has over a GPO in AGPM, but you still want that user to be able to make modifications to the GPO, you may want to delegate the edit privilege. This level of access in AGPM is referred to as Editor privileges. To set up Editor privileges for a group in AGPM, follow these steps:

1. In the GPMC, expand the forest node, and then expand the domain node.

2. Select the Change Control node.

3. Select the Controlled tab, located on the Contents tab in the details pane.

4. Select the GPO for which you want to set up delegation.

5. If the user or group is already listed as having the specified archive permissions for the selected GPO list, select the group or user for which you are setting up delegation. Then click Advanced to open the Permissions dialog box. Select the group or user name in the Group or User Names list box, and then select the Editor check box in the Allow column.

6. To add members, click Add, and then select the user or group in the Select User, Computer, or Group dialog box, setting up the Editor delegation after adding the object.

7. To remove a member, select the member, and then click Remove.

Like many other permissions for files, folders, and other NTFS-related objects in Windows, when you select the Editor check box, the Reviewer check box is also selected. This is because it is not possible to edit a GPO in AGPM without also having Reviewer (in essence, Read) access as well, as shown in Figure 9-11.

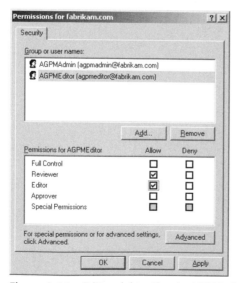

Figure 9-11   Editor delegation in AGPM also includes the Reviewer delegation, so users can list the contents of the AGPM, as well as edit the GPOs.

The Editor permission includes:

- List Contents
- Read Settings
- Edit Settings
- Create Template

After a user has been granted the Editor permission, one or more GPOs in the AGPM environment will be available for editing. Like the full control delegation, the Editor permission can be granted either at the domain level or at the individual GPO level. If granted at the domain level, under the Domain Delegation tab, the user can edit any GPO that is brought into AGPM. To edit a GPO from within AGPM, the user must follow these steps:

1. In the GPMC, select the Controlled tab in the details pane.
2. Right-click the GPO that you want edit, and then click Check Out.
3. Type an optional comment in the Comment box, and then click OK.
4. On the Controlled tab, right-click the GPO that you just checked out, and then click Edit.
5. Make any modification to the GPO, and then exit the GPMC.

> **Note**   To edit a GPO from within AGPM, the user must install both the GPMC and the AGPM client to expose the Change Control node in the GPMC (the area that controls the AGPM content). For more information about the AGPM client, refer to Chapter 14, which covers the installation and use of the AGPM client.

Approving

Only users who have been granted the Approver permission will be able to perform some of the more advanced actions in AGPM. The ability to create a new GPO and the ability to deploy a GPO to the production environment are both examples of tasks that require the Approver permission, such as approving a pending GPO, as shown in Figure 9-12.

To set up Approver permission or a group in AGPM, follow these steps:

1. In the GPMC, expand the forest node, and then expand the domain node.
2. Select the Change Control node.
3. Select the Controlled tab, located on the Contents tab in the details pane.
4. Select the GPO for which you want to set up delegation.
5. If the user or group is already listed as having the specified archive permissions for the selected GPO list, select the group or user for which you are setting up delegation. Then click Advanced to open the Permissions dialog box. Select the group or user name in the Group Or User Names list, and then select the Approver check box in the Allow column.

6. To add members, click Add, and then select the user or group in the Select User, Computer, or Group dialog box, setting up the Approver delegation after adding the object.

7. To remove a member, select the member, and then click Remove.

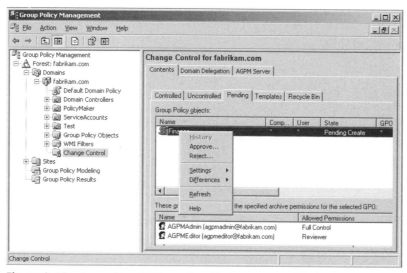

Figure 9-12   A pending GPO requires that someone with the Approver permission either approve it or reject it.

When you select the Approver check box, the Reviewer check box is also selected because it is a required permission for approving GPOs in AGPM. The Approver permission includes:

- Create GPO
- List Contents
- Read Settings
- Delete GPO
- Deploy GPO

After a user has been granted the Approver permission, his or her level of control over GPOs depends on whether the permission was granted at the domain level or the individual GPO level. If granted at the domain level, under the Domain Delegation tab, the user can approve any GPO that is brought into AGPM.

For more information about approving GPOs within AGPM, refer to Chapter 14, which describes the approval options within AGPM and provides steps for each option.

Reviewing

One of the benefits of AGPM is the ability to provide users with the option to see the settings in the GPOs, but not alter them in any way. Individuals such as managers, IT administrators (not related to Group Policy), and Help desk personnel can see the GPO settings and even compare two GPOs by using difference reporting.

> **Note**   To compare two GPOs, or to compare a GPO to a template, using difference reporting in AGPM, a user must be granted permissions over all GPOs being compared in the report. If the Reviewer permission has been granted at the domain level, permissions are automatically granted to GPOs that are controlled in the domain.

To set up Reviewer privileges for a group in AGPM, follow these steps:

1. In the GPMC, expand the forest node, and then expand the domain node.
2. Select the Change Control node.
3. Select the Controlled tab, located on the Contents tab in the details pane.
4. Select the GPO for which you want to set up delegation.
5. If the user or group is already listed as having the specified archive permissions for the selected GPO list, select the group or user for which you are setting up delegation. Then click Advanced to open the Permissions dialog box. Select the group or user name in the Group Or User Names list, and then select the Reviewer check box in the Allow column.
6. To add members, click Add, and then select the user or group in the Select User, Computer, or Group dialog box, setting up the Reviewer delegation after adding the object.
7. To remove a member, select the member, and then click Remove.

A user granted these permissions will be able to view the following, as shown in Figure 9-13:

- Settings report
- Difference report
- GPO history

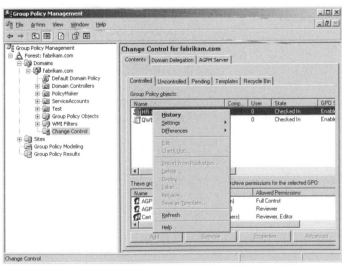

Figure 9-13   The Reviewer permission includes the ability to view the settings of a GPO.

For more information about viewing GPOs and their reports within AGPM, refer to Chapter 14, which describes the reporting options within AGPM and provides steps for each option.

Best Practices

As you have seen, both the GPMC and AGPM provide in-depth delegation capabilities. Unfortunately, the two delegations do not work in conjunction with one another natively. Therefore, when you decide to install AGPM and establish the delegations within both of the tools, some additional considerations are necessary. If you decide to *not* install AGPM, you must consider how the GPMC delegations can best be established to protect your Group Policy investment and infrastructure. The following best practice recommendations can help you establish your final delegation for Group Policy management.

Creating GPOs

The creation of GPOs is just the first step in establishing Group Policy settings, but the task should be limited to only a few administrators in the organization. Limiting the number of administrators will help you track all GPOs, because the number of GPOs will be kept to a manageable level with fewer administrators having the ability to create new GPOs.

Creating GPOs without AGPM

The ability to create a GPO within the GPMC is controlled on the domain-wide Group Policy Objects node. This is because you do not manage a GPO at the organizational unit level, but at the domain level.

Creating GPOs with AGPM

If AGPM is installed, it is a best practice to prevent administrators from creating GPOs from within the GPMC; this option should be available from AGPM only. This is because the GPMC works with production GPOs, whereas AGPM isolates the GPOs in the offline archive first, before they are deployed to production.

To follow this best practice, remove all but the AGPM service account from the GPMC delegation to create GPOs in the domain.

 Note   The SYSTEM account should also remain on the Delegation tab for the ability to create GPOs in the domain.

This configuration will limit the creation of GPOs in the production environment, without requiring the GPO to also be located in AGPM.

> **Warning**   When AGPM is installed, existing delegations in the GPMC are not altered. This means that users who could already perform actions such as create, link, and edit GPOs outside of AGPM will still have those capabilities. Removal of delegations from the GPMC options is a manual process.

Segregation of Group Policy Creation from Other Duties without AGPM

If AGPM is not installed and you will rely solely on the GPMC delegation, it is a best practice to segregate the duties of creating, linking, and editing the GPOs, as much as possible. In many environments, the organizational units in Active Directory have been designed for administration of the objects in the organizational unit. The administrators who have been granted control over the organizational units should have the ability to link GPOs to these nodes, but they may or may not have the ability to edit the GPOs that are being linked there. The reason for this limited control is that a GPO is domain based and could be linked to another node in Active Directory. Without a change management process, one change to a GPO linked to many nodes in Active Directory could cause negative results.

Editing GPOs

Editing of a GPO is the most powerful capability that someone can have, in either the GPMC or AGPM. Thus, this delegation must be the most strictly controlled. The best practices for editing of GPOs differ greatly depending on whether you have AGPM installed. This is because editing of GPOs in AGPM occurs offline, whereas GPMC editing occurs with a live production GPO.

Editing GPOs without AGPM

The only way to edit a GPO from the GPMC is in production, so some additional processes must exist to help protect the environment. To start, only a limited number of administrators should be able to edit the settings of each GPO. The following is a list of best practice settings and procedures that you should implement:

- Restrict membership in the Group Policy Creator Owners group.
- Restrict membership in the Enterprise Admins group.
- Restrict additional groups, and the group members, listed on the Delegation tab for each GPO for Editing GPOs configuration.
- Enforce the backup of each GPO before and after any edits.
- Create a backup script to back up all GPOs in the domain on a regular basis.
- Enforce a documentation procedure for editing GPOs. This should include when the GPO was updated, which settings were updated, why each setting was updated, and who performed the update.
- Ensure that the comment field is updated for information on the GPO, as well as for each setting that includes a comment field.

Editing GPOs with AGPM

As a best practice, you should remove the delegations for the users and groups that can edit GPOs using the GPMC natively. This is a manual process that can take a bit of time. After AGPM is installed, access every GPO listed under the Group Policy Objects node in the GPMC and remove all users and groups (except for the AGPM service account, SYSTEM, and Domain Controllers group) from the Delegation tab. This will restrict any user from editing a live production GPO.

Next, you should establish the delegation for editing GPOs in AGPM. This process consists of establishing delegation at the domain level and the individual GPO level. The best practice here is to limit the number of administrators for each level, giving domain delegations only to those who need to have this expansive privilege.

 Note   For more information about setting up delegation for editing GPOs in the GPMC and AGPM, refer to earlier sections in this chapter, which cover how to establish these delegations.

Linking GPOs

Because you do not link GPOs to Active Directory nodes by using AGPM, installation of AGPM does not alter the best practice recommendations for linking GPOs. As a best practice for establishing the delegation for this task, you should limit the number of administrators that can link per node. Ideally, you should implement the delegation to link GPOs in a way that mimics the overall administrative delegation for the rest of your Active Directory delegations.

Testing GPOs

There is no specific delegation permission for testing of GPOs. Over the years, administrators have implemented many strategies for testing GPOs. Each strategy has its own advantages and disadvantages, so there is no one strategy that works best. However, here are some possible solutions to use as best practices for testing of GPOs.

Testing GPOs without AGPM with a Production Organizational Unit

You can use existing Active Directory domains for testing GPOs by establishing a test organizational unit in the domain that has limited delegation over the linking of GPOs to it. Follow these steps to create the environment:

1. Create test users, computers, and groups in Active Directory, placing the user and computer accounts in the test organizational unit.

2. Create test GPOs, or copy production GPOs, that are linked to the test organizational unit.

3. Delegate the editing of the test GPOs to only those who should have control over the test environment.

4. Delegate linking of GPOs to the test organizational unit to only those that should be able to link a GPO to this area of Active Directory.

This environment isolates the production GPOs from the test area and also isolates any updated GPOs in production from the production users and computers. After you test the GPOs in the test area, you can duplicate the settings to the production GPOs by backing up and importing or manually updating the production GPOs.

Testing GPOs without AGPM with a Test Domain

Many companies and administrators do not like the idea of setting aside a portion of the production domain for testing. In this case, it is a best practice to create a test domain for testing of GPOs. As you can imagine, this is more expensive, takes more time, and requires more effort compared with testing GPOs in a test organizational unit located in production.

In this scenario, the goal is to create as much of the production domain as you need in the test domain, to fully test all GPO settings. This might include duplicating servers, applications, network topology, user accounts, groups, computer accounts, organizational units, and so on.

The testing process is very straightforward, because the test environment looks just like the production environment. The issue with this scenario is getting the GPOs from the test domain into the production domain. To accomplish this, you will need to use migration tables to handle the naming of users, groups, and UNC paths from the test domain to production. The best way to accomplish this is to use migration tables available in the GPMC. For more information on migration tables, refer to Chapter 6, which provides details about using migration tables.

Testing GPOs with AGPM with a Production Organizational Unit

With AGPM installed and running, you can take advantage of the built-in testing environment. The scenario is a bit different from your standard environment, because AGPM performs the editing out of the AGPM archive, not the production GPO. However, testing is possible, which can isolate and clean up your Group Policy environment automatically.

To test GPOs when you are using AGPM, follow these steps:

1. Create a test organizational unit in Active Directory.

2. Add test users and computers to the test organizational unit.

3. Check out the GPO that you want to test, using AGPM.

4. Edit the GPO that you have checked out.

5. Modify the GPO, with the settings that you want to verify or test on the test objects, leaving it checked out.

6. Link the GPO to the test organizational unit, as shown in Figure 9-14.

Note If you want to edit a GPO, AGPM requires that you first check it out, and then select the edit option for the GPO. When the GPO is checked out, a copy is created in the production environment. It is this temporary GPO that can be used for testing within the AGPM environment.

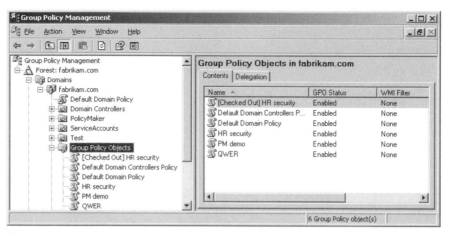

Figure 9-14 When a GPO is checked out from AGPM, a copy is created under the Group Policy Objects node in the GPMC, allowing you to link this temporary GPO to a test organizational unit.

7. Test the GPO settings by logging in as a user or by logging in on the computer that is under the scope of management. You can also run a Group Policy Modeling report or Group Policy Results report using the newly linked GPO.

8. After testing the GPO, check it back in; the GPO that was temporarily placed in production is deleted.

For more information about controlling GPOs by using AGPM, refer to Chapter 14, which covers all aspects of managing GPOs using AGPM.

Summary

Administration of Group Policy should be limited to just a few administrators in your company. Too many administrators of Group Policy objects can cause significant harm to the stability of the overall environment. By default and by design, the number of users who can administer Group Policy is very limited.

If you decide to alter the default delegations, your delegations should be well thought out. With different delegations for creating, editing, managing, and viewing Group Policy settings, the GPMC provides an excellent mechanism for you to establish nearly any administration model that you desire.

However, when you use only the delegations within the GPMC to administer Group Policy, all edits to GPOs are applied to production objects. There is no mechanism to modify and distribute a production GPO in an offline format. The GPMC also limits the management of GPOs by not automatically backing them up, not providing a change management environment, and not allowing for a different report of settings in two different GPOs.

AGPM enhances the manageability of Group Policy, and it also provides a secondary delegation model. AGPM can help you create a more stable and secure environment for updating and deploying GPOs from an offline environment to production. This environment allows you to modify, review, and test GPOs before they are placed in production. When placed in production, AGPM controls who can perform these offline tasks, and it also tracks all details regarding the GPO automatically.

If you follow the best practice recommendations for creating, editing, linking, and overall management of Group Policy detailed in this chapter, you should have a more efficient and more secure Group Policy management infrastructure.

Additional Resources

- The Microsoft Advanced Group Policy Management Web site at *http://www.microsoft.com/windows/products/windowsvista/enterprise/agpm.mspx* includes more information about AGPM.

- The Microsoft Desktop Optimization Pack Web site at *http://www.microsoft.com/ windows/products/windowsvista/enterprise/mdopoverview.mspx* includes more information about the Microsoft Desktop Optimization Pack.

- The Microsoft TechNet guide titled "Active Directory Backup and Restore," at *http://technet.microsoft.com/en-us/library/hh727048.aspx*, includes information about restoring System State data.

- Chapter 6, "GPMC Basics," includes information about the functionality and features of the GPMC.

- Chapter 14, "Advanced GPO Management with AGPM," includes information about the functionality and features of AGPM.

Part V
Using Registry-Based Policy Settings

Chapter 10

ADM Templates, ADMX Files, and the ADMX Central Store

One of the most powerful aspects of Group Policy is its utilization of .adm templates, ADMX files, and the new ADMX central store. Group Policy leverages these files and technologies to provide access to registry settings. Thousands of settings are exposed in a GPO through the use of administrative templates.

ADM templates are the legacy files that were used to create the Administrative Templates portion within the Group Policy Management Editor (GPME) for Windows 2000, Windows XP, and Microsoft Windows Server 2003. These files are no longer needed in Windows Vista and Windows Server 2008, but they are still supported for backward compatibility.

Instead of .adm templates, Windows Vista and Windows Server 2008 utilize ADMX files. These files use XML formatting and are more flexible and powerful than .adm templates. Use of the ADMX files in Windows Vista and Windows Server 2008 offers many benefits, including removal of SYSVOL bloat, multiple language support, and the ability to take advantage of the central store concept.

The central store for ADMX files is a popular and powerful technology that allows for centralization of ADMX files and their versions. The default and custom ADMX files can now be located centrally, where all GPO administrators can access them. After the central store is established, only the centralized versions of the ADMX files are used for the administration of GPOs. This has many benefits, primarily the elimination of version control and management of the ADMX files.

Administrative (.adm) Templates

Group Policy uses legacy files called .adm templates to display and configure registry settings. These files describe where registry-based policy settings are stored in the registry. Administrative template files, typically referred to as .adm templates, do not affect actual policy processing by the administrative template's client-side extension (CSE). The .adm templates affect only the display of the policy settings in the Group Policy Management Editor snap-in. If the .adm template is removed from a GPO, the settings corresponding to the .adm template will not appear in the GPME.

The .adm templates are Unicode text files that enable a user interface to allow modification of registry-based policy settings using the GPME. After a setting established by using the .adm templates is configured within the GPME, the setting information is stored in the Registry.pol file located in the Group Policy template (GPT) for the GPO. The actual policy settings are stored in the Registry.pol file, so the .adm template can be removed from the GPO, but the setting remains in the Registry.pol file and continues to apply to the appropriate target computer or user.

More than 1,300 administrative template settings are available, and administrators can add hundreds more custom settings. For more information on customizing .adm templates, refer to Chapter 11, "Customizing ADM Templates and ADMX Files," which describes how to create and implement custom settings using these files.

Default .adm Templates

Every computer running Windows 2000, Windows XP, or Windows Server 2003 comes with some default .adm templates. These files are used to create the default interface under the Administrative Templates portions of a GPO. The standard .adm templates are listed in Table 10-1.

Table 10-1   Standard .adm Templates

.adm Template	Features
Common.adm	Policy settings for the user interface common to Microsoft Windows NT 4.0 and Windows 9x. Designed to be used with System Policy Editor (Poledit.exe).
Conf.adm	Policy settings for configuring Microsoft NetMeeting. Conf.adm is loaded by default in Microsoft Windows 2000 Server, Windows XP, and Windows Server 2003. (It is not available with Windows XP Professional 64-bit edition or the 64-bit versions of the Windows Server 2003 family.)
Inetcorp.adm	Policy settings for dial-up, language, and control over Temporary Internet Files settings.
Inetres.adm	Policy settings for configuring Microsoft Internet Explorer. Ineteres.adm is loaded by default in Windows 2000 Server, Windows XP, and Windows Server 2003.
Inetset.adm	Policy settings for additional Internet properties: autocomplete, display settings, and some advanced settings.

Table 10-1   Standard .adm Templates

.adm Template	Features
System.adm	Policy settings for configuring the operating system. System.adm is loaded by default in Windows Server 2000, Windows XP, and Windows Server 2003.
Windows.adm	Policy settings for the user interface options specific to Windows 9x. Designed to be used with System Policy Editor (Poledit.exe) running on Windows 98 and Windows NT.
Winnt.adm	Policy settings for the user interface options specific to Windows NT 4.0. Designed to be used with System Policy Editor (Poledit.exe) running on Windows 98 and Windows NT.
Wmplayer.adm	Policy settings for configuring Windows Media Player. Wmplayer.adm is loaded by default in Windows XP and Windows Server 2003. (It is not available with Windows XP Professional 64-bit edition or the 64-bit versions of the Windows Server 2003 family.)
Wuau.adm	Policy settings for configuring Windows Update. Wuau.adm is loaded by default in Windows 2000 Service Pack 3 (SP3), Windows XP SP1, and Windows Server 2003.

The .adm templates that ship with Windows Server 2003, Windows XP Professional, and Windows 2000 Server are located in the %windir%\inf\ folder.

Additional .adm templates are available for security settings, Internet Explorer, Microsoft Office, and more. Some applications also come with their own .adm templates to help centralize administration and customization of the application. Table 10-2 lists the current Office 2003 and Internet Explorer .adm templates that you can obtain from the Microsoft Office Resource Kit and the Microsoft Windows Server 2003 Resource Kit.

Table 10-2   Office 2003 and Internet Explorer .adm Templates

Microsoft Office Template	Features
Aer_1033.adm	Office 2003 application error reporting client configuration.
Access11.adm	Office Access 2003 settings.
Dw20.adm	Old Office Application Reporting configuration file, replaced with Aer_1033.adm.
Excel11.adm	Office Excel 2003 settings.
Fp11.adm	Office FrontPage 2003 settings.
Gal11.adm	Microsoft Clip Organizer settings.
Inf11.adm	Office InfoPath 2003 settings.
Instlr11.adm	Microsoft Windows Installer settings.
Office11.adm	Common Office 2003 settings.
Onent11.adm	Office OneNote 2003 settings.
Outlk11.adm	Office Outlook 2003 settings.
Ppt11.adm	Office PowerPoint 2003 settings.
Pub11.adm	Office Publisher 2003 settings.
Word11.adm	Office Word 2003 settings.

Table 10-2   Office 2003 and Internet Explorer .adm Templates

Internet Explorer Template	Features
Aaxa.adm	Data binding settings.
Chat.adm	Microsoft Chat settings.
Inetesc.adm	Internet Explorer Enhanced Security Configuration settings.
Oe.adm	Microsoft Outlook Express Identity Manager settings. Use this to prevent users from changing or configuring identities.
Sp1shell.adm	Active Desktop settings.
Subs.adm	Offline Pages settings.
Wmp.adm	Windows Media Player, Radio Toolbar, and Network Settings customizations.

Working with .adm Templates

Acquiring an .adm template is only the first step in the process of updating the registry on a target computer or user account. You must then properly insert it into the GPO structure. You do this by importing the .adm template into the GPO that will target the computer or user accounts. The settings that are established in the .adm template will appear when the GPO is edited in the GPME, allowing the policy to be configured. Several default .adm templates are imported into every standard GPO, however, which creates the default administrative template section under both Computer Configuration and User Configuration.

Default Installed .adm Templates

Every new GPO has default Administrative Template sections. These sections are created by three or more .adm templates, depending on the operating system you are working with. The following is a list of the default .adm templates associated with each operating system:

- Windows 2000: Conf.adm, Inetres.adm, System.adm (Wuau.adm is also installed on computers running Windows 2000 SP3 or later.)

- Windows XP Professional: Conf.adm, Inetres.adm, System.adm, Wmplayer.adm (Wuau.adm is also installed on computers running Windows XP Professional SP1 or later.)

- Windows Server 2003: Conf.adm, Inetres.adm, System.adm, Wmplayer.adm, Wuau.adm

Each successive version of an operating system has more features that must be controlled. Windows XP includes an .adm template to control Windows Media Player. Windows Server 2003 adds a new .adm template for controlling the Windows Update and Software Update Service (SUS) features. From version to version, the standard .adm templates have changed slightly.

Before you add or remove any .adm templates, you can view a list of the default .adm templates used with all new GPOs created on a computer running Windows Server 2003, shown in Figure 10-1.

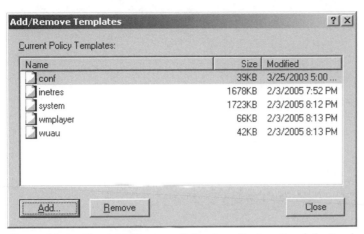

Figure 10-1 The Add/Remove dialog box displays the default .adm templates for Windows Server 2003 GPOs.

Importing .adm Templates

If you want to use a particular .adm template to configure some policy settings in a GPO, you must import it into the GPO. Here are some tips that will help the import process go smoothly:

- Make sure the syntax of the .adm template is correct. If it is incorrect, you will receive a message during the import process indicating that an error was recognized within the .adm template.

- A single .adm template can contain both computer and user registry-based settings. The GPME handles the separation of the two sections when it displays the GPO with the new .adm template inserted.

- You can store the .adm template anywhere you want before you import it into the GPO. During the import procedure, you can browse for the file on the local computer or on the network.

- After you import an .adm template into a GPO, it is available to be configured in that GPO only. If you want the .adm template settings to be available for different GPOs, you must import the .adm template into each GPO.

- The importing of the .adm template makes a copy of the file in the GPO structure stored in the SYSVOL of the domain controllers. The .adm template is copied into the ADM subfolder under the correct GPO folder represented by the GPO GUID.

Adding .adm Templates

Let's look at an example in which you need to add the Visio11.adm template to a GPO named OFFICE11. The Visio11.adm template is currently located on the desktop of the computer from which you are editing the GPO. To add the template, follow these steps after opening the OFFICE11 GPO in the GPME:

1.   Right-click the Administrative Templates node under the Computer Configuration section of the GPO, and then click Add/Remove Templates.

2.   In the Add/Remove Templates dialog box, click Add.

3.   In the Policy Templates dialog box, select Desktop in the console tree pane.

4.   Select the Visio11.adm template in the list. Click Open. You will see the Add/Remove Templates dialog box with the Visio11.adm template listed, as shown in Figure 10-2.

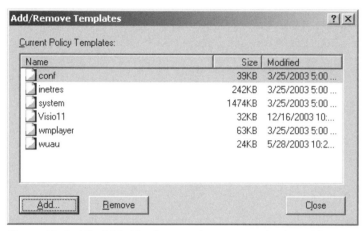

Figure 10-2   The Visio11.adm template appears in the Add/Remove dialog box after being added to a GPO.

After the .adm template has been imported to the GPO, you can see the Visio node and policy settings in the GPO, as shown in Figure 10-3.

How It Works: ADM Templates in the Group Policy Template

By default, newly created GPOs that have not been edited will create a new Group Policy template (GPT), but without any associated .adm templates or the ADM folder in the GPT folder structure. After the GPO is edited with the GPME, the .adm templates from the %windir%\Inf folder of the computer performing the administration are copied to the GPT. These .adm templates are placed in a newly created ADM folder. When additional .adm templates are added to the GPO, they are also uploaded to the GPT and placed in the ADM folder.

Removing .adm Templates

Sometimes you might need to remove an .adm template from a GPO. This action removes any settings from the GPME that were created by the .adm template.

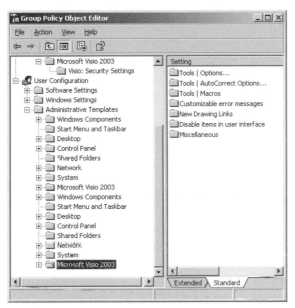

Figure 10-3   Policy settings for Office Visio 2003 are available after the Visio11.adm template is added to the GPO.

> **Note**   If a policy was configured using the settings in the .adm template before the .adm template was removed from the GPO, the policy setting will still be active in the GPO. Policy settings are not stored in the .adm template, but in the Registry.pol file. You should modify all settings made using the .adm templates as needed before you remove the .adm templates from the GPO.

Much like our example of adding an .adm template to a GPO, we will now walk through an example of removing an .adm template. Here we will remove the Visio11.adm template from the OFFICE11 GPO:

1. Right-click the Administrative Templates node under the Computer Configuration section of the GPO, and then click Add/Remove Templates.

2. In the Add/Remove Templates dialog box, select the Visio11.adm template in the list of templates, and then click Remove. The template is removed from the list.

Managing .adm Templates

Over time, you will make changes to the custom .adm templates that you have implemented within your GPOs. Built-in controls are available that help update new versions of the .adm templates. To make this process easier, it is best to have a dedicated workstation for creating and modifying GPOs.

Controlling Updated Versions of .adm Templates

The default behavior of controlling new versions of .adm templates ensures that the latest versions of the files are located in the GPT for the GPO. The .adm templates are updated and referenced in two steps. First, the .adm template timestamp is referenced. The timestamp of the local .adm template in the %windir%\Inf folder is compared to the .adm template in the GPT. If the local .adm template is newer than the GPT version, the local .adm template is copied to the GPT, replacing the current .adm template in the GPT. Second, the Group Policy Management Editor uses the .adm template from the GPT to create the interface within the Administrative Templates nodes in the GPO.

Two GPO settings control this behavior:

- Turn Off Automatic Updates Of ADM Files
- Always Use Local ADM Files For Group Policy Editor

Turn Off Automatic Updates Of ADM Files   This GPO setting can be found at the following location:

User Configuration\Administrative Templates\System\Group Policy

This policy controls whether the timestamps of the two .adm templates are compared and whether the latest one is placed in the GPT. By default, the timestamp is compared and the newer .adm template is placed in the GPT.

When this policy is set to Enabled, the .adm template timestamps are not checked for newer versions, so the GPT is not updated. When this policy is set to Disabled, the .adm templates are checked, and if the .adm template from the local computer performing the administration has a newer timestamp, the .adm template stored in the GPT of the GPO is updated.

Always Use Local ADM Files For Group Policy Editor   This GPO setting can be found at the following location:

Computer Configuration\Administrative Templates\System\Group Policy

This policy controls which .adm template is used to create the interface of the GPO when edited. By default, the .adm template stored in the GPT is used.

When this policy is set to Enabled, the .adm templates from the local computer are used. The results can be undesirable if the local .adm templates are updated without your knowledge. When this policy is set to Disabled, the .adm templates from the GPT of the GPO are used. This creates a safer environment for version control and ensures that all policies can be viewed consistently from any computer.

Tips for Working with .adm Templates

Over time and with the creation of new operating systems and features, the behavior of .adm templates has changed. Here are some tips for working with .adm templates:

- If the saved GPO contains registry settings for which there is no corresponding .adm template, these settings will not appear in the GPME. They will still be active, however, and will be applied to users or computers targeted by the GPO.

- Because of the importance of timestamps to .adm template management, you should not edit the standard .adm templates. If a new policy setting is required, create a custom .adm template.

- The Group Policy Management Console (GPMC) controls the .adm templates in a much different manner when it creates HTML reports, uses Group Policy Modeling, and generates Group Policy results.

- Windows XP Professional does not support the Always Use Local ADM Files For Group Policy Editor policy setting. Therefore, if your GPO administrative computer runs Windows XP Professional, you must use the .adm templates stored in the GPT.

Operating System and Service Pack Release Issues

Each operating system or service pack release includes a superset of the .adm templates provided by earlier releases, including policy settings specific to earlier versions of the operating system. For example, the .adm templates provided with Windows Server 2003 include all policy settings for all earlier versions of Windows, including settings relevant only to Windows 2000 or Windows XP Professional. This means that merely viewing a GPO from a computer with the new release of an operating system or service pack effectively upgrades the .adm templates for that GPO. Because later releases are a superset of previous .adm templates, this typically does not create problems (as long as the .adm templates being used have not been edited).

In some situations, an operating system or service pack release includes a subset of the .adm templates that were provided with earlier releases, potentially resulting in policy settings no longer being visible to administrators when they use GPME. However, the policy settings remain active in the GPO. Any active (either Enabled or Disabled) policy settings are not visible in the GPME. Because the settings are not visible, an administrator cannot easily view or edit them. To work around this issue, you must become familiar with the .adm templates included with each operating system or service pack release *before* using the GPME on that operating system. You must also keep in mind that the act of viewing a GPO is enough to update the .adm templates in the GPT when the timestamp comparison determines that an update is appropriate.

To plan for such potential issues in your environment, it is recommended that you do one of the following:

- Define a standard operating system and service pack for all viewing and editing of GPOs, making sure that the .adm templates being used include the policy settings for all platforms in your enterprise.

- Use the Turn Off Automatic Updates Of ADM policy setting for all Group Policy administrators to make sure that .adm templates are not overwritten in the SYSVOL by any GPME session, and make sure that you are using the latest .adm templates from Microsoft.

Policies vs. Preferences

Policies are registry-based settings that can be fully managed by administrators and Group Policy. These are also referred to as *true policies*. In contrast, registry-based settings that are configured by users or are set as a default state by the operating system at installation are referred to as *preferences*.

True policies are stored under approved registry keys. These keys are not accessible by users, so they are protected from being changed or disabled. The four approved registry keys are shown in Table 10-3.

Table 10-3   Approved Registry Key Locations for Group Policy Settings

Computer-Based Policy Settings	User-Based Policy Settings
HKLM\Software\Policies	HKCU\Software\Policies
HKLM\Software\Microsoft\Windows\CurrentVersion\Policies	HKCU\Software\Microsoft\Windows\CurrentVersion\Policies

Preferences are registry-based settings that are located in registry keys other than the approved registry keys listed in Table 10-3. Users can typically change their preferences at any time. For example, users can decide to set their wallpaper to a different bitmap. Most users are familiar with setting preferences through the operating system or application user interface.

You can create custom .adm templates that set registry values outside of the approved registry keys. When you create these preferences, you only ensure that a given registry key or value is set in a particular way. These preferences are not secured as true policies are; users can access these settings and modify them. Another issue with preferences is that the settings persist in the registry. The only way to alter preferences is to configure them using the .adm template or manually update the registry.

In contrast, true policy settings have access control list (ACL) restrictions to prevent users from changing them, and the policy values are removed when the GPO that set them goes out of scope (when the GPO is unlinked, disabled, or deleted). For this reason, true policies are considered to be policy settings that can be fully managed. By default, the GPME shows only true policy settings that can be fully managed. To view preferences in the GPME, you right-click the Administrative Templates node, click View, click Filtering, and then, in the Filtering dialog box, clear the Only Show Policy Settings That Can Be Fully Managed check box.

True policy settings take priority over preferences, but they do not overwrite or modify the registry keys used by the preferences. If a policy setting is deployed that conflicts with a preference, the policy setting takes precedence over the preference setting. If a conflicting policy setting is removed, the original user preference setting remains intact and configures the computer.

ADMX Files

ADMX files have replaced .adm templates in Windows Vista and Windows Server 2008. The purpose and result of the ADMX files are the same as the .adm templates, which is to provide an interface within the Group Policy Management Editor (GPME) so that registry-based settings can be configured. From a GUI experience, administration of a GPO will not be altered when using ADMX files compared to .adm templates.

The reasons for the change of file format, structure, and architecture are numerous. The legacy .adm templates were powerful and manageable, but limitations and negative behavior spurred the change to the ADMX file format. Some of the benefits of ADMX files include:

- Multiple language support

- Elimination of SYSVOL bloat

- Utilization of a central store

- More control over ADMX file versions

- Centralized management of default and custom ADMX files

> **Warning**   Because ADMX files were first introduced with Windows Vista, only two operating systems can manage GPOs using ADMX files: Windows Vista and Windows Server 2008. If a GPO is edited using a computer running Windows 2000, Windows XP, or Windows Server 2003, the local .adm templates will be copied from the computer performing the administration to the GPT for the GPO. Therefore, if you do not want to use .adm templates and want to keep the SYSVOL free of .adm templates, only edit GPOs using Windows Vista or Windows Server 2008. For more information about the GPT, refer to Chapter 4, "Architecture of Group Policy," which covers the GPT and all other related components of a GPO.

Default ADMX Files

Every installation of Windows Vista and Windows Server 2008 includes a complete set of ADMX files. These files create the two Administrative Template nodes under Computer Configuration and User Configuration in the GPME. There are 132 default ADMX files for Windows Vista and 146 default ADMX files for Windows Server 2008 and Windows Vista SP1. Each ADMX file has an associated ADML file located under one or more language-specific folders, such as EN-US for English.

The location of the default ADMX files is %windir%\PolicyDefinitions. There is only one default language-specific subfolder in this main folder, which is English in most cases.

Using Both .adm Templates and ADMX Files

Most companies will have to make decisions on how to incorporate the inclusion of both .adm templates and ADMX files when they move to Windows Server 2008 or Windows Vista. The reasons for using ADMX files rather than .adm templates are quite compelling, and many companies will want to take full advantage of the benefits that ADMX files provide.

If you have even one computer running Windows Vista or Windows Server 2008 in your environment, you can take advantage of these benefits. Domain controllers running Windows Server 2008 are not necessary; you need only the operating systems that can take advantage of ADMX files.

To help you gain a better understanding of how each operating system will function with .adm templates, ADMX files, and a mixture of operating systems performing administration on GPOs, the following scenarios explain how the GPO is affected depending on how it is edited. Each scenario has the following characteristics:

- Existing GPO that was created using Windows Vista

- Custom .adm template that has been manually added to the GPO and is currently located in the GPT

- Custom ADMX file that is only available on the original computer running Windows Vista

Scenario 1: Administration of GPO with Windows Vista

Both the .adm templates and the ADMX files will be added to the GPME when the GPO is edited.

- The Administrative Templates sections in the GPME will be created using the ADMX files resident on the computer running Windows Vista.

- Custom .adm template settings will be available in the GPME, because these files are already located in the GPT for the GPO.

- Custom ADMX file settings will be available in the GPME, because these files are located on the computer running Windows Vista.

Scenario 2: Administration of GPO with a Windows Server 2008 Domain Controller

Both the .adm templates and the ADMX files will be added to the GPME when the GPO is edited.

- The Administrative Templates sections in the GPME will be created using the ADMX files resident on the computer running Windows Server 2008.

- Custom .adm template settings will be available in the GPME, because these files are already located in the GPT for the GPO.

- Custom ADMX file settings will not be available in the GPME, because these files are not located on the computer running Windows Sever 2008.

> **Note**   If the ADMX files were stored in the central store, all default and custom ADMX files and their settings would be available to the computer running Windows Server 2008. For information about the creation and utilization of the central store for ADMX files, refer to the section "Creating and Using the ADMX Central Store," later in this chapter.

Scenario 3: Administration of GPO from a Windows XP Workstation

Only the .adm templates will be added to the GPME when the GPO is edited.

- The Administrative Templates sections in the GPME will be created using the local versions of the .adm templates resident on the computer running Windows XP.

- The .adm templates used to create the Administrative Templates sections in the GPME will be copied to the GPT of the GPO.

- Custom .adm template settings will be available in the GPME, because these files are already located in the GPT for the GPO.

- Custom ADMX file settings will not be available in the GPME, because these files are not supported by Windows XP.

How It Works: Cleaning Up .adm Templates from Existing GPOs

ADMX files and .adm templates are used to show the settings that can be configured in the GPME. For the existing GPOs that were created using .adm templates, the templates can be removed from the GPT. If the settings that are already configured in the GPO must be changed, the ADMX files can handle those settings. This solution updates the GPOs so that they use the ADMX files that come with Windows Server 2008 and Windows Vista instead of the .adm templates. It also eliminates the SYSVOL bloat that was enforced with the use of .adm templates. The .adm template files, totaling almost 4 MB for each GPT, can be removed, but the settings can still be managed with ADMX files.

Migrating .adm Templates to ADMX Files

Companies and administrators that have spent time creating custom .adm templates have two options for using those files in a Windows Server 2008 or Windows Vista environment. Because .adm templates are supported, they can be placed in the GPT of the GPO, and nothing else needs to be done. However, if you want to eliminate all .adm templates from the GPT of each GPO and still make the settings available to all administrators, the .adm templates and their settings must be migrated to an ADMX file.

Depending on the complexity of the .adm templates and the settings contained within them, the migration can either be very simple or quite complex. If only a few settings exist in an .adm template, it might be advantageous to manually migrate it to an ADMX file. However, if the .adm templates contain numerous settings that offer a complex array of setting options within the GPME, migrating them using the ADMX Migrator might be a better option.

Direct from the Source: Automatically Importing .adm Files into Windows Server 2008 and Windows Vista

If you copy your custom .adm file into the %windir%\inf directory, the GPME will automatically import into any GPO that is edited, relieving you of having to manually add the file to each GPO in which you want to use the custom settings. The disadvantage is that all GPOs that you edit will have the extra files added to the GPT.

Judith Herman, Programming Writer, Microsoft

File Syntax Conversion for .adm Template to ADMX Files

The syntax for an .adm template is similar to that of an ADMX file, but there are differences that need to be tracked and understood. Because both files create the interface within the GPME and define the registry information that will be updated, the settings will be a near duplication between the two formats. However, the two file formats use different syntax names, as defined in Table 10-4.

Table 10-4   File Syntax Conversion for .adm Template to ADMX

.adm Template Language Reference	.admx File Language Reference	.adml File Language Reference	Conversion Comments
Adm File Language Versions (#If Version)	revision	revision	Unlike ADM files, the ADMX file has versioning built in and is not tied to an operating system version.
comments (;)	Annotation <!-- -->	Annotation <!-- -->	For ADM files, all text following the ";" is considered a comment. For ADMX files, neither the Annotation element or the XML comments will not be processed by Group Policy tools.
Strings reference (!!)	string		In .adm templates, precede text with "!!" to reference a string.
<Strings> section of the .adm file		stringTable	
CLASS	class		ADMX files provide the ability to classify the policy definition as being for user, machine, or both. The "both" classification allows you to create a single policy definition that applies to the machine and user registry keys.

Table 10-4   File Syntax Conversion for .adm Template to ADMX

.adm Template Language Reference	.admx File Language Reference	.adml File Language Reference	Conversion Comments
CATEGORY	categories category parentCategory		ADM files assume categories are nested within the definitions. ADMX files specify a parentCategory element for each policy element defined in the ADMX file. An individual category is defined within the *categories* element.
Duplicate Category Sections allowed in different ADM files	Duplicate category sections are not allowed in different ADMX files.		If one .adm file includes a duplicate "CATEGORY" entry used in a different existing .adm file, the policy settings will be merged when the Group Policy object Editor processes the ADM files. ADMX files have unique namespaces. Defining the same *category* element names in two different ADMX files will cause the category to be displayed twice. For ADMX files, you must define the *category* element name once and then reference the category element name with the *using* element.
SUPPORTED	supportedOn		
POLICY	policies policy		In the ADMX file, the *policies* element contains individual *policy* elements that correspond to a policy setting.
PART	elements	presentation	In ADM files, the PART statement specifies various policy setting options, such as drop-down list boxes, text boxes, and text in the lower pane of the Group Policy snap-in. ADMX files aggregate policy setting options for one policy setting into the *elements* element in the ADMX file and the *presentation* element in the ADML file.
CHECKBOX	boolean	checkbox	
TEXT		text	The *text* element in the .adml file provides the string used as the parameter text prompt.
EDITTEXT	text	textBox	
NUMERIC	decimal	decimalTextBox	

Table 10-4   File Syntax Conversion for .adm Template to ADMX

.adm Template Language Reference	.admx File Language Reference	.adml File Language Reference	Conversion Comments
COMBOBOX	text	comboBox	
DROPDOWNLIST	enum item	dropdownList	
LISTBOX	list	listBox	
VALUEON	enabledValue		
VALUEOFF	disabledValue		
ACTIONLISTON	enabledList		
ACTIONLISTOFF	disabledList		
KEYNAME	key		
EXPLAIN	explainText		
VALUENAME	valueName		
CLIENTEXT	clientExtension		
END			XML syntax includes termination of all its elements. There is no need to use special syntax to terminate an element.
DEFCHECKED		defaultChecked	
Line Breaks \n or \n\n		Use link breaks or blank lines within the string definitions.	
Maximum string length for EXPLAIN text		Limited by available memory only.	
Maximum string length for CATEGORY EXPLAIN text		Limited by available memory only.	
Maximum string length for EDITTEXT string		Maximum string length for EDITTEXT string = 1023 characters.	

ADMX Migrator

The migration of .adm templates into ADMX files is not a simple task. The preceding information provides all of the details needed to migrate an .adm template to an ADMX file. However, as you can see, the process would not be simple because the structure, syntax, and formatting for each of the files is completely different.

One solution is to use ADMX Migrator, developed by FullArmor Corporation. At the time of publication, the tool is in version 1.2. It can be downloaded from the Microsoft Download Center at *http://www.microsoft.com/downloads/details.aspx?FamilyID=0f1eec3d-10c4-4b5f-9625-97c2f731090c&DisplayLang=en*.

The tool comes with two solutions, which provide two major functions:

- ADMX Editor
    - ❏ Edit ADMX files
    - ❏ Convert .adm templates to ADMX files
- ADMX Migrator Command Options

The ADMX Editor is an excellent interface for viewing and updating your ADMX files. It breaks down the ADMX file into the different areas of the XML formatted file. Figure 10-4 illustrates one of the default ADMX files viewed in the ADMX Editor, showing the areas of the file on the tabs.

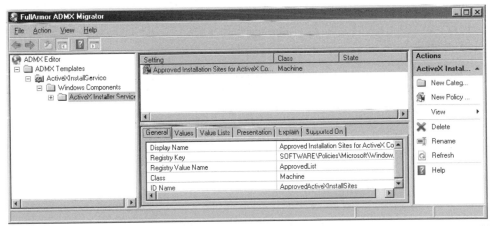

Figure 10-4   The ADMX Editor allows you to view and modify the contents of any AMDX file.

The ADMX Editor also allows you to migrate .adm templates to ADMX files. This process is quite simple: When you click the ADMX Editor node within the tool, the Generate ADMX From ADM option allows you to perform the conversion. Figure 10-5 shows the migration option, as well as the result of an .adm template that has been migrated to an ADMX file.

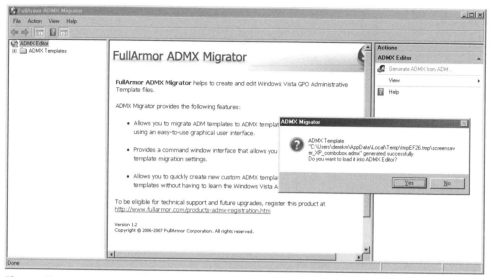

Figure 10-5 The ADMX Editor also provides support for migrating .adm templates to ADMX files.

Note that some conversion issues could arise. The most common issues are related to the areas listed in Table 10-5.

Table 10-5 ADMX Migrator Common Issues and Solutions

Migration Issue	Solution
Duplicate policy name	Edit the .adm template to ensure that POLICY names are unique from one another.
Missing "SUPPORTED" on values	Edit the .adm template and add the SUPPORTED on value with information for each POLICY entry.
Unresolved strings	Edit the .adm template and ensure that each string reference (!! syntax) has an associated string entry in the file.

Finally, ADMX Migrator provides you with a full suite of command-line tools and switches to migrate .adm templates to ADMX files. The tool allows you to control nearly every aspect of the migration. Table 10-6 lists the switches that can be used with the ADMX Migrator command-line feature.

Table 10-6 ADMX Migrator Command-Line Options

Switch	Function
Source	Specifies the name of the ADM template that you want to convert.
Targetpath	Specifies the target folder where you want to save the converted ADMX template. If you do not specify a target path, ADMX Migrator saves the converted ADMX template in the \Documents*UserName*\Local Settings\Temp folder, where *UserName* is the name of the user who is logged on to the computer on which you installed ADMX Migrator.
/X	Specifies ADMX as the type of the target file.
/L	Specifies ADML as the type of the target file.

Table 10-6   ADMX Migrator Command-Line Options

Switch	Function
/N:name	Specifies the display name XML element in the ADML file.
/D:description	Specifies the description XML element in the ADML file.
/R:revision	Specifies the revision number of the ADMX file. The Group Policy Object Editor checks this number when loading ADMX templates. The Group Policy Object Editor will not load ADMX templates with revision numbers that do not meet the requirements of the version of Group Policy Object Editor installed on the computer.
/P:prefix	Specifies the target element prefix used in the ADMX file.
/S:namespace	Specifies the namespace XML element in the ADMX file.
/U:prefix	Specifies the using element prefix used in the ADMX file.
/C:namespace	Specifies the namespace XML element in the ADMX file.

Creating and Using the ADMX Central Store

One benefit of using the ADMX files in Windows Vista and Windows Server 2008 is the option to centralize their management. ADMX files solve many issues that the legacy .adm templates created. Use of the central store makes the management of ADMX files easier and more efficient. The central store is beneficial to the management of Group Policy in the following ways:

- It centralizes management of all ADMX files.

- It allows Group Policy administrators to manage GPOs from anywhere on the network.

- It simplifies version management of updated ADMX files.

- It makes it easy to add new ADMX files so that all administrators have immediate access.

- It eliminates ADMX file version mismatch issues.

Creating the Central Store

To create a central store for ADMX files, you must have access to a domain controller as a Domain Admin. This is because the central store requires new folders to be created under the SYSVOL directory. Creation of the central store requires that a top-level folder named PolicyDefinitions be created under %systemroot%\sysvol\<*domainname*>\policies. This is where you will place a copy of the language-neutral ADMX files.

Best Practices   As a best practice, you should create the central store folder structure on the domain controller that controls the PDC Emulator role. This will ensure that the domain controller that Group Policy relies on is being updated first; then replication will ensure that the central store is copied to all domain controllers, because it is part of the Sysvol directory.

In addition to the PolicyDefinitions folder, you will also create additional subfolders within this folder for languages that are supported in your ADMX files. These subfolders will be used to hold the language-specific ADMX resource files, which have the extension .adml. To create these subfolders, you must use the ISO-style Language/Culture Names, which are listed in Table 10-7. If you needed to have two languages for your ADMX files, such as English and Spanish, you would create the following two subfolders:

%systemroot%\sysvol\<domainname>\policies\PolicyDefinitions\EN-US

%systemroot%\sysvol\<domainname>\policies\PolicyDefinitions\ES-ES

Table 10-7   ISO-Style Language/Culture Names

Language	Country Code
Afrikaans	AF
Arabic	AR
Basque	EU
Belarusian	BE
Bulgarian	BG
Catalan	CA
Chinese (China)	ZH, ZH-CN
Chinese (Taiwan)	ZH-TW
Croatian	HR
Czech	CS
Danish	DA
Dutch	NL
English (United Kingdom)	EN-GB
English (United States)	EN, EN-US
Estonian	ET
Faeroese	FO
Finnish	FI
French	FR, FR-FR
French (Canadian)	FR-CA
German	DE
Greek	EL
Hebrew	HE, IW
Hungarian	HU
Icelandic	IS
Indonesian	ID, IN
Italian	IT
Japanese	JA
Korean	KO

Table 10-7   ISO-Style Language/Culture Names

Language	Country Code
Latvian	LV
Lithuanian	LT
Neutral (use built-in word breaking)	NEUTRAL
Norwegian	NO
Polish	PL
Portuguese	PT
Portuguese (Brazil)	PT-BR
Romanian	RO
Russian	RU
Serbian	SR
Slovak	SK
Slovenian	SL
Spanish	ES, ES-ES
Swedish	SV
Thai	TH
Turkish	TR
Ukrainian	UK
Vietnamese	VI

Copying ADMX and ADML Files to the Central Store

After you manually create the PolicyDefinitions folder and the appropriate language-specific subfolders, you must copy the ADMX files to the central store. There is no user interface for performing this task, so you must manually copy the files into the relative folders.

If you had all of the correct ADMX files on the Windows Vista workstation from which you were administering Group Policy, you would perform the copy of the files by following these steps:

1.   Click Start, and then click Run.

2.   In the Run dialog box, type **cmd** in the Open box. The Command Prompt appears.

3.   Type **xcopy%systemroot%\PolicyDefinitions* %logonserver%\sysvol\ %userdnsdomain%\policies\PolicyDefinitions**.

You must then copy all of the ADMX language resource files, ADML files, to the central store, under the correct subfolder for that language. If you needed to do this for both English and Spanish, for example, you would use these commands:

```
xcopy %systemroot%\PolicyDefinitions\EN-US\*
%logonserver%\sysvol\%userdnsdomain%\policies\PolicyDefinitions\EN-US\
```

and

```
xcopy %systemroot%\PolicyDefinitions\ES-ES\*
%logonserver%\sysvol\%userdnsdomain%\policies\PolicyDefinitions\ES-ES\
```

> **Note**   If you want to use a free tool to help with the creation of the central store, visit
> *http://www.gpoguy.com/cssu.htm*. This simple utility creates the central store folder and copies
> the ADMX and ADML files into it for you.

How It Works: ADMX File Usage

By default, computers running Windows Vista and Windows Server 2008 use the local
ADMX files, from the C:\Windows\PolicyDefinitions folder, whether you are editing
the local GPO or a GPO that is stored in Active Directory directory service.

If you create the central store on the domain controllers, the ADMX files from the central
store are used. The two locations are not merged, so if there are local ADMX files that are
not in the central store, they will not be used.

If you want to include custom ADMX files, you must copy them either to the local
PolicyDefinitions folder or to the central store located on the domain controllers. When
these custom ADMX files are available in the PolicyDefinitions folder, the settings will
appear in the Group Policy Management Editor when you edit a GPO.

Summary

ADMX files and .adm templates are essential aspects of Group Policy. The majority of all
registry-based settings exposed through a GPO are controlled by these files. The files provide
two key functions for editing and deploying a GPO setting. The first is to display the policy
within the Group Policy Management Editor. The second is to provide the correct path and
value that will be modified in the registry when deployed.

For every operating system before Windows Server 2008 and Windows Vista, .adm templates
are legacy. However, they are still supported on every Windows operating system version that
you may be running today. If you have customized .adm templates, you can either continue to
use them as they are or convert them to ADMX files.

ADMX files solve many of the problems experienced with .adm templates. ADMX files come
with ADML files, which allow for the use of many languages for the configuration of default and
custom registry entries within a GPO. ADMX files also support the use of a central store, which
resolves problems with SYSVOL bloat, version control, and centralized ADMX file management.

If you want to convert .adm templates to ADMX files, you can use ADMX Migrator, a free
tool available from the Microsoft Download Center. It provides an ADMX editor, as well as
a GUI-based and command-line-based migration solution.

Additional Resources

- A Microsoft Help and Support article, at *http://support.microsoft.com/kb/816662*, includes information about managing .adm templates.

- The Microsoft TechNet article titled "Managing Group Policy ADMX Files Step-by-Step Guide," at *http://technet2.microsoft.com/WindowsVista/en/library/02633470-396c-4e34-971a-0c5b090dc4fd1033.mspx?mfr=true*, includes more information about managing ADMX files.

- You can download the ADMX Migrator at *http://www.microsoft.com/downloads/details.aspx?FamilyID=0f1eec3d-10c4-4b5f-9625-97c2f731090c&DisplayLang=en*.

- Chapter 4, "Architecture of Group Policy," includes information about the GPT, which stores the .adm templates by default.

- Chapter 11, "Customizing ADM Templates and ADMX Files," includes information about how to create custom .adm templates and ADMX files.

Chapter 11

Customizing ADM Templates and ADMX Files

You can use two file types to customize registry-based entries within a Group Policy Object in Windows Server 2008 and Windows Vista. The old file type, the .adm template, is still available; although it is not the preferred method for customizing your registry-based changes through Group Policy, many companies currently use them, and some might choose to continue doing so.

The new solution is the use of ADMX files. These files are XML based, language neutral, and can leverage many of the administrative features that Windows Server 2008 and Windows Vista provide for optimizing Group Policy management. The structure and creation of ADMX (and the associated ADML) files are nothing like they are with .adm templates, but the overall concepts are similar.

This chapter provides an inside look into customizing .adm templates, as well as customizing ADMX files. It includes conversion tables and high-level views of the construction of each table, as well as specific details on the syntax used for each table.

Creating Custom .adm Templates

In addition to the hundreds of default settings in the standard .adm templates, you will undoubtedly want more registry-based policy settings for applications and components installed on computers within your organization. Creating and implementing custom .adm templates involves the following steps:

1. Determine the specific registry path, value, and data. This step might not be as easy at it seems, considering the complexity of the registry and some of the registry value names. A good way to locate this information is to reference the standard .adm templates to find the correct registry path for similar settings.

> **Tip**   You can also use tools to help you locate registry values as they are changed from within the operating system or application. An excellent tool for this task is REGMON, which can be found in the Microsoft Diagnostics and Recovery Toolset at *http://www.microsoft.com/ windows/products/windowsvista/enterprise/dart.mspx.*

2. Develop the .adm template, including the information gathered in step 1. Custom .adm templates are created as Unicode text files that describe policy settings. A framework language is provided for .adm templates, as described in the section "Using .adm Template Language," later in this chapter.

3. Import the .adm template into a GPO. Each GPO can have a unique set of .adm templates, so you must do this for each GPO that will distribute the custom registry settings configured within the .adm template.

4. Use the Group Policy Management Editor (GPME) to view and configure the custom entries under the Administrative Templates nodes, which were created by the .adm template. This is where you establish the settings that will configure the user accounts or computers in the domain. To see the imported custom setting, you must ensure that all filters are off for the Administrative Templates node. Refer to Chapter 7, "Advanced GPMC Management," which describes how to set up filters.

> **Warning**   Any filters set up and enabled on the Administrative Templates node in the GPME will negate the viewing of Classic Administrative Templates.

> **Note**   Keep in mind that the .adm template does not actually apply any settings to the computer or user account. The policy within the GPO must be established first; then the target user or computer must have a corresponding component or application that responds to the registry value affected by the policy setting.

A Simple .adm Template

To get an idea of what an .adm template looks like, we will review a simple snippet from the System.adm template. You can look at the entire System.adm template to see what the code looks like for a complete .adm template.

```
CLASS USER
CATEGORY !!DesktopLockDown
   POLICY !!DisableTaskMgr
     EXPLAIN !!DisableTaskMgr_Explain
     VALUENAME "DisableTaskMgr"
     VALUEON NUMERIC 1
     VALUEOFF NUMERIC 0
     KEYNAME "Software\Policies\System"
   END POLICY
END CATEGORY
```

```
[strings]
DisableTaskMgr="Disable Task Manager"
DisableTaskMgr_Explain="Prevents users from starting Task Manager"
DesktopLockDown="Desktop Settings"
```

This policy setting defines the following behavior:

- When enabled, this policy setting creates a registry key called *DisableTaskMgr* and sets its value to 1. The VALUEON tag implements this behavior. After this policy is implemented, users cannot start Task Manager.

- When disabled, this policy setting creates a registry key called *DisableTaskMgr* and sets its value to 0. The VALUEOFF tag implements this behavior. After this policy is implemented, users can start Task Manager.

- In both cases, the *DisableTaskMgr* registry key is created below HKEY_CURRENT_USER\Software\Policies\System in the registry. Note that the key is created under CLASS USER and not under CLASS MACHINE, because this is a user policy setting. You will find this policy under the User Configuration\Administrative Templates\Classic Administrative Templates\Desktop Settings node within the GPME, as shown in Figure 11-1.

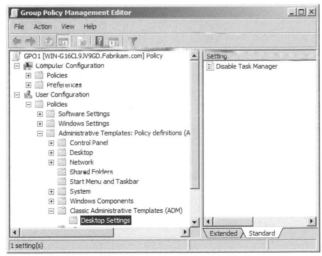

Figure 11-1   Custom .adm templates will place the GPO settings under the Classic Administrative Templates node in the GPME.

- When set to Not Configured, this policy setting deletes the registry key called *DisableTaskMgr*. In this case, users can start Task Manager. Note that in the Not Configured case, you will only see the deletion for a true policy setting, not a "preference," outside the true policy settings registry hive.

Using .adm Template Language

If you have a custom registry value that you need to distribute and configure to all or just a few computers in the organization, you should use custom .adm templates. To create these files, you must use and understand the .adm template language. Don't worry—the language is simple and easy to learn. This section provides all of the information you need to create your own .adm templates for importing into a GPO.

Structure of an .adm Template

An .adm template has two functions. The first function is to create the interface within the GPME for the registry values that you want configured on users or machines targeted by a GPO. This formatting is the same for all .adm templates, so you can use existing .adm templates as a guide. The second function of the .adm template is to format the registry path, value, and data that will be updated in the target computer's registry. Again, this syntax is the same for all .adm templates and is easy to follow.

> **Note**   Although the syntax is easy to follow for the registry path in the .adm template, the path must be accurate to avoid potential corruption of the registry on the target computer.

Look at the following .adm template example. It allows the computer to log on without any user input by using a predetermined username and password.

```
CLASS MACHINE
CATEGORY "Microsoft Custom ADM Entries"
   POLICY "Automatic Logon"
   KEYNAME "SOFTWARE\Microsoft\Windows NT\CurrentVersion\Winlogon"
      PART "Enable Auto Logon? (1=Yes, 0=No)" NUMERIC REQUIRED TXTCONVERT
      VALUENAME "AutoAdminLogon"
      MIN 0 MAX 1 DEFAULT "0" SPIN 1
      END PART
      PART "What is the name of the user?" EDITTEXT
      VALUENAME "defaultusername"
      END PART
      PART "What is the user's password?" EDITTEXT
      VALUENAME "defaultpassword"
      END PART
   END POLICY
END CATEGORY
```

You can see that the structure of the .adm template is very methodical. If you look closely at the example, you can see that some rules must be followed. One such rule is the inclusion of an END syntax for PART, POLICY, and CATEGORY entries.

Review the structure of the example to evaluate the components that you need to fully understand:

- **CLASS MACHINE**   Specifies that the registry HKEY that we are modifying is under HKEY_LOCAL_MACHINE.

- **CATEGORY**   Specifies the name that will be given to the folder that will appear in the GPME. In our example, it is Microsoft Custom ADM Entries.

- **POLICY**   Specifies the name we are giving to the policy that will appear in the GPME. In our example, it is Automatic Logon.

- **KEYNAME**   Specifies the path in the registry where the value that will be modified exists. Notice that KEYNAME does not include the HKEY name or the name of the value.

- **PART**   Specifies to the GPME that input will be required from the GPO administrator.

- **EDITTEXT**   Specifies that a text box will be presented to allow the administrator to type text for the data of the registry value.

- **VALUENAME**   Specifies the exact registry value that is being modified. Notice that VALUENAME is not the specified data for the registry value (the string or setting associated with the registry value); rather, it is the name of the registry value. The data for the registry value will be input through the GPME.

- **END PART**   Indicates to the GPME that the syntax related to this PART is done.

- **END POLICY**   Indicates to the GPME that the syntax related to this POLICY is done.

- **END CATEGORY**   Indicates to the GPME that the syntax related to this CATEGORY is done.

If you were to create a shell depicting a standard .adm template structure, it would look something like this.

```
CLASS (GPME and Registry)
CATEGORY (GPME)
KEYNAME (Registry)
POLICY (GPME)
PART (GPME)
VALUENAME (Registry)
```

To create your own .adm templates, you must build on this structure and understand all of the syntax that can be placed in the .adm templates. We will do this by breaking down the syntax into two categories: the interface for the GPME and the registry path and value inputs.

#if version

Instead of creating an .adm template for each set of operating system settings, you can use the *#if version* syntax within one .adm template to break up the settings. The *#if version* syntax breaks up the .adm template into zones, with each zone targeting a specific operating system range. The standard .adm templates use this method to create these zones, providing settings for older operating systems and newer operating systems in a single .adm template.

Each operating system matches up with a specific version number within the .adm template. The following chart specifies each operating system and the .adm template *#if syntax* version number associated with it.

Operating System	Version	Type
Microsoft Windows Server 2003 Service Pack 1 (SP1)	5.0	Group Policy
Windows XP SP2	5.0	Group Policy
Windows Server 2003 and Windows XP	4.0	Group Policy
Windows Server 2000	3.0	Group Policy
Microsoft Windows NT 3.*x* and 4.*x*	2.0	System Policy
Windows 95	1.0	System Policy

In some instances, the *#if version* syntax can be omitted and the .adm code can span multiple operating system generations. This is possible when the registry value and the location of the setting is the same for the different operating systems.

You can control the *#if version* syntax by adding operators to control ranges of operating systems that the .adm syntax should affect. Here are the operators that can be used with the *#if version* syntax.

>	Greater than
<	Less than
==	Equal to
!=	Not equal to
>=	Greater than or equal to
<=	Less than or equal to

Syntax for Updating the Registry

You know that the .adm template generates the interface for the GPME and specifies the registry path, value, and data. Specific syntax is used within the .adm template to handle all of these variables.

The syntax that builds the GPME interface is essential within the .adm template. If any syntax for one of these components is missing, the file will fail to load properly. The syntax used to build the registry path, value, and data includes CLASS, KEYNAME, VALUENAME, VALUEOFF/VALUEON, and PART.

CLASS

There are two CLASS options: MACHINE and USER. The CLASS syntax specifies two things within the .adm template. First it indicates which portion of the registry will be modified. If the MACHINE option is specified, the GPO will modify the HKEY_LOCAL_MACHINE handle in the registry. If the USER option is specified, the GPO will modify the HKEY_CURRENT_USER handle in the registry.

> **Note**   The registry contains only two primary handles: HKEY_LOCAL_MACHINE and HKEY_USERS. The other three handles are subsets of these two primary handles. The HKEY_CURRENT_USER handle is a subset of the HKEY_USERS handle. The HKEY_CURRENT_USER handle is the current user's profile that is placed in the registry when the user logs on.

You need to use the CLASS syntax only once for each of the MACHINE and USER options. All of the registry settings that fall under the HKEY_LOCAL_MACHINE handle will be grouped together, after you list the CLASS MACHINE syntax. The same is true for the registry settings that fall under the HKEY_CURRENT_USER handle and the CLASS USER syntax.

> **Note**   If an .adm template contains multiple CLASS MACHINE or CLASS USER sections, they will be merged together when the GPME interface is created.

If the .adm template you are creating will refer to only one of the registry handles, you list only that CLASS syntax in the .adm template.

The CLASS syntax also places the interface changes under Computer Configuration\classic administrative templates\ or User Configuration\classic administrative templates\, based on MACHINE or USER, respectively. When the GPME accesses the .adm template, it places the interface settings under the proper node.

> **Note**   There is no END CLASS statement associated with the CLASS syntax.

KEYNAME

The KEYNAME syntax is not optional within the .adm template. KEYNAME specifies the path from the HKEY to the registry value. KEYNAME comes after the CATEGORY syntax and either before or after the POLICY syntax, depending on how you choose to structure the .adm template. However, KEYNAME must come after the CLASS syntax and before the PART or VALUENAME syntax.

> **Note**   If you want to group multiple policy settings that reside under the same path in the registry, you can place the KEYNAME entry after the CATEGORY syntax. This results in a grouping of all the entries following the CATEGORY syntax under the same folder in the GPME.

The KEYNAME syntax indicates the path to the registry value. Do not include HKEY_LOCAL_MACHINE or HKEY_CURRENT_USER in the registry path—this is handled by the CLASS syntax. You also do not need to use an introductory slash (/) to start the path within the KEYNAME text. For our example, the KEYNAME entry is as follows:

```
KEYNAME SOFTWARE\Microsoft\WindowsNT\CurrentVersion\Winlogon
```

If a space follows the KEYNAME syntax within the path, you must put quotation marks (") around the entire path string, but do not include the KEYNAME word in the quotes. Here is an example of an entry that requires quotes:

```
KEYNAME "SOFTWARE\Microsoft\Windows NT\CurrentVersion\Winlogon"
```

> **Note**   There is no END KEYNAME statement associated with the KEYNAME syntax.

VALUENAME

VALUENAME references the registry value that will be updated. You must find the approved registry value name—you are not allowed to make up registry values. If the computer registry is updated with an incorrect registry value, the computer might experience a stop error. Values in the registry are typically cryptic words that are not found in a dictionary.

You can use two methods to modify the values specified with the VALUENAME syntax. These methods are controlled by the values that the registry can handle.

- Many registry values support only two numeric values: 0 and 1. If the numeric value is 0, the registry value is off. If the numeric value is 1, the registry value is on. When the registry value is controlled in this fashion, you use the VALUEOFF/VALUEON syntax.

- The other registry values require text or more than just 0 or 1 numeric values. These registry values are controlled using the PART syntax.

When you use the VALUEOFF/VALUEON syntax, you are directly affecting the behavior of the registry value. When you use the PART syntax, you are modifying the GPME, which allows for a more complex entry to be set for the registry value.

> **Note**   There is no END VALUENAME statement associated with the VALUENAME syntax.

VALUEOFF/VALUEON

The VALUEOFF/VALUEON syntax works like a switch. The registry value is either off or on, reflecting the simple use of binary values of 0s and 1s. When you look at many of the registry entries in the Registry Editor, you will see that they actually support the string data type, which is denoted at REG_SZ. This does not alter the behavior or the limited values that the registry value supports.

Here is an example of a standard .adm entry that uses VALUEON and VALUEOFF.

```
KEYNAME "Software\Microsoft\Windows\CurrentVersion\Policies\System"
VALUENAME "HideStartupScripts"
VALUEON NUMERIC 0
VALUEOFF NUMERIC 1
```

For this .adm entry, no input is required after you edit the setting in the GPME. You have only the ability to enable or disable the policy to toggle between the VALUEOFF and VALUEON numeric values. The GPME shows this policy with the standard interface, as shown in Figure 11-2.

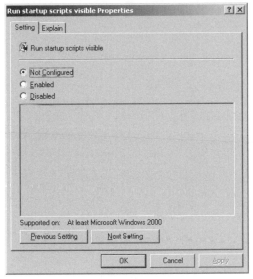

Figure 11-2 The GPME shows when a registry value is determined by the VALUEON/VALUEOFF syntax in the .adm template.

The policy setting includes the following three settings options:

- **Not Configured** Does not set any entry for the registry value; instead, it leaves the registry value as it is set on the computer.

- **Enabled** Sets the registry value to the VALUEON specified numeric value.

- **Disabled** Sets the registry value to the VALUEOFF specified numeric value.

You can use a second method that is indirectly associated with the VALUEOFF/VALUEON syntax, and that you use when you do not explicitly use the VALUEOFF and VALUEON statements. Here is an example of what that might look like:

```
POLICY!!EnableSlowLinkDetect
   EXPLAIN !!EnableSlowLinkDetect_Help
   KEYNAME "Software\Policies\Microsoft\Windows\System"
   VALUENAME "SlowLinkDetectEnabled"
END POLICY
```

Notice that there is no explicit use of VALUEON/VALUEOFF, but the behavior is similar. In this example, the three settings of the GPO policy behave in the following manner:

- **Not Configured** Changes nothing in the registry.

- **Enabled** Sets the registry value to a numeric value of 1.

- **Disabled** Deletes the registry value.

Note the policy-disabled state. The value is not written to the registry with the value of 0; instead, it is explicitly deleted. This means that a component reading the policy will not find the value in the registry and will revert to using the default in the code.

> **Note**   There is no END VALUEON/VALUEOFF statement associated with the VALUEON/VALUEOFF syntax.

Syntax for Updating the GPME Interface

The .adm templates do more than just indicate the registry path, value, and data that need to be updated. They also configure the interface of the GPME. The interface configurations are essential because the GPME interface is where the configurations are actually made.

Four main types of syntax create the interface within the Group Policy Management Editor:

- STRINGS
- CATEGORY
- POLICY
- PART

The CATEGORY and POLICY syntaxes are the only required entries in the .adm template, but the other two variables are important. The STRINGS syntax is used extensively in the standard .adm templates, but it is seldom used in custom .adm templates. The PART syntax is used when the registry value or values being referenced require more than an ON or OFF configuration.

STRINGS

The STRINGS syntax is used to help organize and logically format the string variables used within the .adm template. The STRINGS syntax is not mandatory, but it can help reduce the code within the main body of the .adm template to remove the clutter and make it easier to read. The STRINGS syntax allows for variables to be used for lengthy strings. Strings are used to create the interface within the GPME. The following example uses the STRINGS syntax whenever there is a string variable to create the interface.

```
CLASS MACHINE
CATEGORY !!CUSTOMADM
   POLICY !!Autologon
   KEYNAME "SOFTWARE\Microsoft\WindowsNT\CurrentVersion\Winlogon"
      PART !!Username
      EDITTEXT
      VALUENAME "autoadminlogon"
      END PART
      PART !!Password
      EDITTEXT
      VALUENAME "defaultpassword"
      END PART
   END POLICY
END CATEGORY
```

```
[STRINGS]
CUSTOMADM = "Microsoft Custom ADM Entries"
AutoLogon = "Automatic Logon"
Username = "what is the name of the user?"
Password = "What is the user's password?"
```

As you can see, the STRINGS syntax cleans up the main part of the .adm template. It also allows for easy administration of all of the string variables, because they are all located under the [STRINGS] section at the bottom of the .adm template. If a string variable is used more than once in the .adm template, you can just use the STRINGS syntax and the string variable name at each instance, which will point to the single instance of the actual string at the end of the .adm template. Within the main body of the .adm template, the strings are referenced by using the double exclamation point (!!) followed by the string variable name.

For smaller .adm templates, you might not need to use the STRINGS syntax. However, in larger .adm templates, the STRINGS syntax can help reduce the complexity of the main body of the .adm template. The STRINGS syntax is especially useful in conjunction with the EXPLAIN syntax. The EXPLAIN text is generally very lengthy and can clog up the main body of the .adm template. By using the STRINGS syntax within the main body of the .adm template, you can leave the longer strings to the STRINGS section at the bottom of the .adm template.

Tip   If you need to convert .adm templates to different languages, you should place all interface strings in the STRINGS section. You then need to convert only the STRINGS section to the different languages.

Note   The STRINGS syntax can be used with the CATEGORY, POLICY, PART, and EXPLAIN statements.

CATEGORY

The CATEGORY syntax produces the folders that you see in the GPME. Both the Computer Configuration and User Configuration sections in the GPME display these folders, so you use the CATEGORY syntax under both the CLASS MACHINE and CLASS USER entries. The CATEGORY syntax can be nested in a hierarchy, to generate subfolders. Each CATEGORY statement that you list produces a folder or subfolder in the GPME.

The following structure creates three folders in a hierarchy.

```
CATEGORY "First level"
   CATEGORY "Second level"
      CATEGORY "Third level"
      END CATEGORY
   END CATEGORY
END CATEGORY
```

If you want to display multiple policies under a single folder (CATEGORY statement), you can just list the policies after the CATEGORY syntax and before the END CATEGORY syntax.

> **Note**   The CATEGORY syntax must be combined with an END CATEGORY statement. This is required so that the GPME knows where to stop nesting folders, as well as where to stop placing policies within the folder.
>
> Additional syntax that you can use in conjunction with CATEGORY includes KEYNAME, CATEGORY, END, SUPPORTED, and POLICY.

POLICY

The POLICY syntax is used to identify a policy setting that the user can modify within the GPME. The POLICY syntax generates the "policy settings displayed" list of policies in the details pane of the GPME, under the folders, which are created by the CATEGORY syntax.

If you want different registry paths and values to appear under a single policy within the GPME, use the POLICY syntax followed by the KEYNAME syntax. However, if multiple registry paths and values that fall under the same KEYNAME must be placed under the same policy, the KEYNAME syntax must precede the POLICY syntax.

An example of the KEYNAME statement followed by the POLICY statement containing multiple registry values is shown here:

```
CLASS USER
CATEGORY "Microsoft Custom ADM Entries"
   POLICY "Controls hidden files."
   KEYNAME "SOFTWARE\Microsoft\Windows\CurrentVersion\Explorer\Advanced"
     PART "Do you want to see hidden files?" TEXT
     END PART
     PART "Hidden Files and Folders:" DROPDOWNLIST
     VALUENAME Hidden
        ITEMLIST
        NAME "Yes" VALUE Numeric 1
        NAME "No" VALUE Numeric 2
        END ITEMLIST
     END PART
     PART "Do you want to see Super Hidden files?" TEXT
     END PART
     PART "Super Hidden" DROPDOWNLIST
     VALUENAME Showsuperhidden
        ITEMLIST
        NAME "Yes" VALUE Numeric 1
        NAME "No" VALUE Numeric 0
        END ITEMLIST
     END PART
   END POLICY
END CATEGORY
```

> **Note**   The POLICY syntax requires an END POLICY to tell the GPME when to stop grouping the settings together. Additional syntax that you can use in conjunction with POLICY includes KEYNAME, ITEMLIST, VALUENAME, VALUEON, VALUEOFF, POLICY, PART, END, ACTIONLISTON, ACTIONLISTOFF, and CLIENTTEXT.

This .adm snippet generates the interface in the GPME, as shown in Figure 11-3.

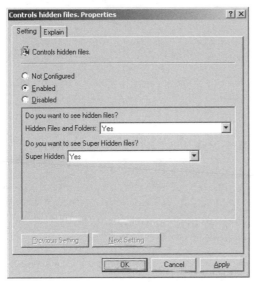

Figure 11-3 Shown is an example of the GPME configuration that results from having multiple registry values in the same .adm template.

PART

Use the PART syntax to specify options such as drop-down lists, text boxes, and text in the lower pane of a policy in the GPME. The previous example shows the PART syntax used in the .adm template and the resulting GPME interface from Figure 11-3.

You can also use the PART syntax to create an introduction or information about the policy in the lower pane of the policy. This PART syntax would simply introduce a clarifying sentence, without associating it with a registry value.

```
PART "Do you want to see Super Hidden files?" TEXT
END PART
```

Associating a PART within a "policy" to a registry value would look like this:

```
PART "Super Hidden" DROPDOWNLIST
VALUENAME Showsuperhidden
   ITEMLIST
   NAME "Yes" VALUE Numeric 1
   NAME "No" VALUE Numeric 0
   END ITEMLIST
END PART
```

The PART syntax can handle the various types of registry values that you include in your custom .adm templates. Each type of registry value requires the use of additional syntax to handle the input for the registry value. The previous example uses ITEMLIST, but other syntax options are available that you will need to use. We will cover ITEMLIST and other syntax options later in this chapter.

> **Note**   The PART syntax requires an END PART to tell the GPME when to stop the configuration of the registry value within the interface. Additional syntax that you can use in conjunction with PART includes CHECKBOX, CLIENTTEXT, COMBOBOX, DROPDOWNLIST, EDITTEXT, LISTBOX, NUMERIC, END, PART, and TEXT.

To create the environment that allows the user to modify the registry values, you must include additional syntax after the PART syntax. Table 11-1 lists the valid syntax options that are used in conjunction with the PART syntax.

Table 11-1   Syntax Options for the PART Syntax

Type	Description
CHECKBOX	Displays a check box. The value is set in the registry with the REG_DWORD type. The value is other than zero if the check box is selected and zero if it is not selected.
CLIENTTEXT	Specifies which client-side extension to use for the specific policy setting.
COMBOBOX	Displays a combo box.
DROPDOWNLIST	Displays a combo box with a drop-down list style. The user can choose only one of the entries supplied.
EDITTEXT	Displays a text box that accepts alphanumeric text. The text is set in the registry with the REG_SZ or the REG_EXPAND_SZ type.
LISTBOX	Displays a list box with Add and Remove buttons. This is the only PART type that can be used to manage multiple values under one key.
NUMERIC	Displays a text box with an optional spin box control that accepts a numeric value. The value is set in the registry with the REG_DWORD type.
TEXT	Displays a line of static text. No registry value is associated with this PART type.

CHECKBOX   When you are combining multiple registry values under one policy, you use the CHECKBOX syntax to function like the VALUEON/VALUEOFF syntax. If the check box is selected (VALUEON), the registry value associated with the CHECKBOX syntax has a value of 1 written to the registry. A value of 0 is written to the registry if the check box is not selected (VALUEOFF).

You can also combine the CHECKBOX syntax with the VALUEON/VALUEOFF syntax to clearly specify what the registry values should be when the check box is selected and not selected. Here is a snippet of the System.adm template, which uses the CHECKBOX syntax:

```
PART !!StdCheckT CHECKBOX
VALUENAME "DisableRollback"
VALUEON NUMERIC 1
VALUEOFF NUMERIC 0
END PART
```

> **Note**   Additional syntax that you can use in conjunction with CHECKBOX includes
> KEYNAME, VALUENAME, ACTIONLISTON, ACTIONLISTOFF, VALUEON, VALUEOFF,
> DEFCHECKED, CLIENTTEXT, and END.

CLIENTTEXT   The CLIENTTEXT keyword is used to specify which client-side extension
(CSE) to the GPME needs to process the particular settings on the client computer. By default,
the registry extension processes all settings configured under the Administrative Templates
node. The CLIENTTEXT keyword changes the default behavior and causes the specified
extension to process these settings after the registry extension has placed them in the registry.

The CLIENTTEXT syntax is the keyword followed by the GUID, representing the CSE. This
implies that the registry key and value information will be stored in the registry.pol file when
the policy setting is configured to either an enabled state or a disabled state. Instead of the
registry CSE acting on this registry information, a different CSE represented by the GUID
value will be called to process the registry information during Group Policy processing on the
client computer. For example, the disk quota CSE uses the GUID value of {3610eda5-77ef-
11d2-8dc5-00c04fa31a66} in the following example. GUID values are used to represent CSEs
to employ a unique designation for each CSE.

The CLIENTTEXT syntax must be used within the POLICY scope or the PART scope and
should follow the VALUENAME statement.

CLIENTTEXT alters the default behavior of typical GPOs. Typical GPOs process all settings
under the Administrative Templates node. The CLIENTTEXT syntax specifies the specific
extension to process a GPO setting, after it has been placed in the registry.

The following is an example from the System.adm template. It configures the disk quotas
within the GPO. As you can see, Disk Quotas has a separate CSE, which is referenced within
the example code:

```
POLICY !!DQ_Enforce
KEYNAME "Software\Policies\Microsoft\Windows NT\DiskQuota"
   VALUENAME "Enforce"
   VALUEON NUMERIC 1
   VALUEOFF NUMERIC 0
   CLIENTTEXT {3610eda5-77ef-11d2-8dc5-00c04fa31a66}
END POLICY
```

> **Note**   The CLIENTTEXT syntax shown in this example assumes that a corresponding CSE has
> been written and is resident on each client machine that needs to process this registry
> information.

COMBOBOX   This PART type displays a combo box. It accepts the same options as
EDITTEXT, as well as the SUGGESTIONS option, which begins a list of suggestions to be
placed in the drop-down list. The suggestions are separated by spaces and must be enclosed

in quotation marks (") when a value includes spaces. If a suggestion name includes white space, it must be enclosed in quotation marks. The list ends with END SUGGESTIONS.

For example, you can establish a list of screen saver names so that the administrator does not have to know the names of the screen savers. Here is a snippet of the original .adm template code for the screen saver file name and the modified syntax using the COMBOBOX syntax:

```
POLICY !!ScreenSaverFilename
KEYNAME "Software\Policies\Microsoft\Windows\Control Panel\Desktop"
   PART !!ScreenSaverFilename EDITTEXT
   VALUENAME "SCRNSAVE.EXE"
   END PART
END POLICY
```

Here's an updated version of the screen saver option with a COMBOBOX.

```
POLICY !!ScreenSaverFilename
KEYNAME "Software\Policies\Microsoft\Windows\Control Panel\Desktop"
   PART !!Screensaverpicker COMBOBOX
   VALUENAME "SCRNSAVE.EXE"
      SUGGESTIONS
        C:\WINNT\System32\ssstars.scr
        C:\WINNT\System32\ssbezier.scr
        C:\WINNT\System32\ssflwbox.scr
      END SUGGESTIONS
   END PART
END POLICY
```

The resulting GPME text for this new syntax appears as shown Figure 11-4.

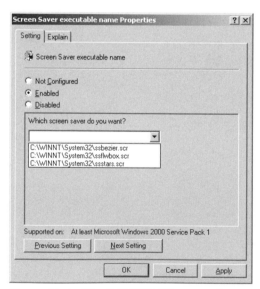

Figure 11-4   The COMBOBOX syntax allows you to provide a set list of options instead of forcing administrators to remember the file names for certain registry value data.

Tip If you use the STRINGS syntax for the name of the COMBOBOX, the entry can be just a single word, where the variable is an entire sentence. This approach is useful, because if you have more than one word within the quotation marks, you will receive an error when you attempt to import the administrative template into the GPO. Additional syntax that you can use in conjunction with COMBOBOX includes KEYNAME, VALUENAME, DEFAULT, SUGGESTIONS, REQUIRED, MAXLENTGH, OEMCONVERT, END, EXPANDABLETEXT, NOSORT, and CLIENTEXT.

DROPDOWNLIST The DROPDOWNLIST syntax provides a combo box with a drop-down list style. It is similar to the COMBOBOX syntax, except that the actual registry value is converted to simple language text. The user can choose only one of the entries from the drop-down list. The DROPDOWNLIST syntax is preferable to the COMBOBOX syntax when the registry value does not indicate clearly what setting the policy will accomplish. To better illustrate this, let's take a look at the COMBOBOX example with a DROPDOWNLIST solution:

```
POLICY !!ScreenSaverFilename
KEYNAME "Software\Policies\Microsoft\Windows\Control Panel\Desktop"
    PART "What screen saver do you want?" DROPDOWNLIST
    VALUENAME "SCRNSAVE.EXE"
        ITEMLIST
        NAME "Starfield"
        VALUE C:\WINNT\System32\ssstars.scr
        NAME "Bezier"
        VALUE C:\WINNT\System32\ssbezier.scr
        NAME "Flowerbox"
        VALUE C:\WINNT\System32\ssflwbox.scr
        END ITEMLIST
    END PART
END POLICY
```

The resulting GPME text for this syntax and administrative template is shown in Figure 11-5.

Tip If any item in the drop-down list requires more than one word, you must use the STRINGS syntax for the entries; otherwise, the .adm template will generate an error during importing. The STRINGS syntax allows you to use a single word for each entry, but the GPME converts the string variable to the actual string for the list.

Note Additional syntax that you can use in conjunction with DROPDOWNLIST includes KEYNAME, VALUENAME, DEFAULT, REQUIRED, ITEMLIST, END, NOSORT, and CLIENTEXT.

EDITTEXT The EDITTEXT syntax allows the user to enter alphanumeric text into an edit field or text box. Here again is the example of editing text in the screen saver file name.

```
POLICY !!ScreenSaverFilename
KEYNAME "Software\Policies\Microsoft\Windows\Control Panel\Desktop"
  PART !!ScreenSaverFilename EDITTEXT
  VALUENAME "SCRNSAVE.EXE"
  END PART
END POLICY
```

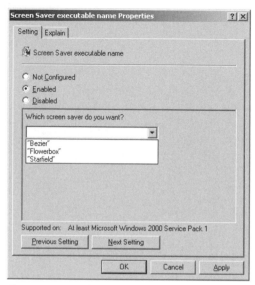

Figure 11-5   The DROPDOWNLIST syntax allows you to supply a friendly list of names instead of the complex registry value name.

By default, the EDITTEXT syntax provides an empty text box for editing the policy. If you want to display an initial value in the text box, you can use the DEFAULT syntax along with the EDITTEXT syntax. The options you can use with EDITTEXT syntax include:

- **DEFAULT value**   Specifies the initial string to place in the edit field. If this option is not specified, the field is initially empty.

- **EXPANDABLETEXT**   Specifies that the text is set in the registry with the REG_EXPAND_SZ type. By default, the text is set in the registry with the REG_SZ type.

- **MAXLEN value**   Specifies the maximum length of a string. The string in the edit field is limited to this length.

- **REQUIRED**   Specifies that the GPME does not allow a policy containing this PART to be enabled unless a value has been entered for it.

- **OEMCONVERT**   Sets the ES_OEMCONVERT style in the edit field so that typed text is mapped from ASCII to OEM and back. ES_OEMCONVERT converts text entered in the edit control. The text is converted from the Windows character set (ASCII) to the OEM character set and then back to the Windows set. This ensures proper character conversion when the application calls the *CharToOem* <*JavaScript:hhobj_1.Click()*> function to convert an ASCII string in the edit control to OEM characters. This style is most useful for edit controls that contain file names.

> **Note**   Additional syntax that you can use in conjunction with EDITTEXT includes KEYNAME, VALUENAME, DEFAULT, REQUIRED, MAXLENGTH, OEMCONVERT, END, EXPANDABLETEXT, and CLIENTTEXT.

LISTBOX   The LISTBOX PART component specifies various options such as drop-down list boxes, text boxes, and text in the lower pane of the GPME. The LISTBOX is a simple syntax, as you can see from this snippet from the System.adm template:

```
PART !!RestrictAppsList LISTBOX
   KEYNAME "Software\Microsoft\Windows\CurrentVersion\Policies\Explorer\RestrictRun"
   VALUEPREFIX ""
END PART
```

The resulting GPME interface is shown in Figure 11-6.

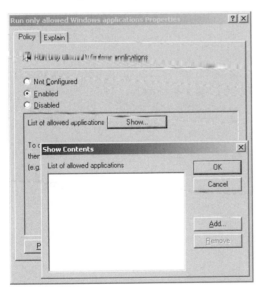

Figure 11-6   The LISTBOX syntax provides an interface in which multiple values can be entered for a single registry value.

In addition to the standard LISTBOX syntax, you can also add more options to the administrative template, including the following:

- **ADDITIVE**   By default, the content of list boxes overrides any values set in the target registry. This means that a control value is inserted in the policy file that causes existing values to be deleted before the values set in the policy file are merged. If this option is specified, existing values are not deleted and the values set in the list box are in addition to whatever values exist in the target registry. If a GPO that uses this syntax is disabled, the disabled settings are not applied and are thus removed from the registry.

> **Caution**   The ability to disable a GPO using the LISTBOX ADDITIVE syntax was introduced with Windows XP Professional SP2. If you attempt to administer a GPO that uses the new LISTBOX ADDITIVE syntax on a computer that does not run Windows XP Professional SP2 or Windows Server 2003 SP1, you will receive an error: "The following entry in the [strings] section is too long and has been truncated." To obtain hotfixes to correct this problem on different platforms, see article 842933 in the Microsoft Knowledge Base at *http://support.microsoft.com/kb/842933*.

- **EXPLICITVALUE**   This option requires the user to specify the value data and the value name. The list box shows two columns, one for the name and one for the data. This option cannot be used with the VALUEPREFIX option.

- **VALUEPREFIX prefix**   The prefix you specify is used in determining value names. If you specify a prefix, the prefix and an incremented integer are used instead of the default value naming scheme described previously. For example, a prefix of *SampleName* generates the value names *SampleName1*, *SampleName2*, and so on. The prefix can be empty (""), which causes the value names to be *1*, *2*, and so on.

> **Note**   Additional syntax that you can use in conjunction with LISTBOX includes KEYNAME, VALUEPREFIX, END, ADDITIVE, EXPLICITVALUE, EXPANDABLETEXT, NOSORT, and CLIENTEXT.

NUMERIC   Displays an edit field with an optional spin box control (an up-down control) that accepts a numeric value. It is best to use the MIN and MAX syntax in conjunction with the NUMERIC syntax to ensure that the registry does not become corrupted with invalid data. The following is a snippet from the System.adm template using the NUMERIC syntax:

```
PART !!ProfileSize
   NUMERIC REQUIRED SPIN 100
   VALUENAME "MaxProfileSize"
   DEFAULT 30000
   MAX 30000
   MIN 300
END PART
```

The SPIN syntax allows for a spin box control to set the range of values that can be set. This adds to the MIN and MAX controls to provide a boundary for the data of the registry value. Other syntax that you can use along with the NUMERIC syntax includes:

- **DEFAULT value**   Specifies the initial numeric value for the edit field. If this option is not specified, the field is initially empty.

- **MAX value**   Specifies the maximum value for the number. The default value is 9999.

- **MIN value**   Specifies the minimum value for the number. The default value is 0.

- **REQUIRED**   Specifies that the GPME does not allow a policy containing this PART to be enabled unless a value has been entered for this PART.

- **SPIN value**   Specifies increments to use for the spin box control. The default is SPIN 1.

- **SPIN 0**   Removes the SPIN control from the "policy" settings.

- **TXTCONVERT**   Writes values as REG_SZ strings ("1", "2", or "128") rather than as binary values.

> **Note**   Additional syntax that you can use in conjunction with NUMERIC includes KEYNAME, VALUENAME, END, MIN, MAX, SPIN, TXTCONVERT, REQUIRED, DEFAULT, and CLIENTEXT.

TEXT   The TEXT syntax can be used to display text on the property page of a policy setting. The following is a snippet from the System.adm template that uses the TEXT syntax:

```
PART !!GPRefreshRate_C_Desc1 TEXT
END PART
PART !!GPRefreshRate_C_Desc2 TEXT
END PART
```

This creates two lines of static text in the dialog box when you edit the policy setting.

ACTIONLIST

You can use the ACTIONLIST syntax to specify a set of arbitrary registry changes to make in response to a control being set to a particular state. Here is a snippet of code for the ACTIONLIST syntax:

```
POLICY "Deny connections requests"
    EXPLAIN "If enabled, TS will stop accepting connections"
    ACTIONLISTON
    VALUENAME "fDenyTSConnections" VALUE NUMERIC 1
    END ACTIONLISTON
    ACTIONLISTOFF
    VALUENAME "fDenyTSConnections" VALUE NUMERIC 0
    END ACTIONLISTOFF
END POLICY
```

ACTIONLIST has two variants that you can use with the POLICY and CHECKBOX syntax. Table 11-2 describes these variants.

Table 11-2   CHECKBOX Syntax Variants

Variant	Description
ACTIONLISTON	Specifies an optional action list to be used if the check box is selected.
ACTIONLISTOFF	Specifies an optional action list to be used if the check box is not selected.

Additional Statements in the .adm Template

You have now seen all of the essential syntax to add to your .adm templates to handle the array of registry values you need to offer. However, other syntax is important for development and troubleshooting purposes. These statements are not required in the .adm template, but they provide additional control over the registry values that you insert into the .adm template.

Comments

Although comments are not often used in standard .adm templates, using them in your custom .adm templates can benefit you and everyone else who needs to reference them. Comments do not alter the registry or the GPME interface—they are there to help you understand the syntax and code in the .adm template.

You can use two methods to add comments to an .adm template. You can precede the comment with a semicolon or two forward slashes, or you can add comments at the end of any valid line or on a line by themselves. Here is a short example that uses the comments syntax:

```
PART !!ProfileSize //This is the user profile
   NUMERIC REQUIRED SPIN 100
      ; The spin control will increment by 100s,
      ; starting at 300, then 400, 500, 600, etc.
   VALUENAME "MaxProfileSize"
   DEFAULT 30000
   MAX 30000
   MIN 300
END PART
```

REQUIRED

The REQUIRED syntax, when used in conjunction with another statement in the .adm template, requires the administrator to enter a value for the policy setting when it is set to the enabled state. The GPME will not allow a change to the policy setting state to be enabled without the value being entered, if it is marked REQUIRED.

MAXLEN

This syntax controls the maximum length of the text within a "policy" entry. This is useful when a single-digit value must be maintained for a "policy" entry.

EXPLAIN

The EXPLAIN syntax is used to provide online Help text for a specific GPO setting. Starting with Windows 2000, the Properties page for each policy setting includes an Explain tab, which provides the details about the policy settings.

Each custom GPO setting that you create should include one EXPLAIN keyword, followed by at least one space, and then the EXPLAIN string in quotation marks (") or a reference to the Help string. Here is an example snippet from the System.adm template that uses the EXPLAIN syntax. The resulting interface is shown in Figure 11-7.

```
POLICY !!Run_Startup_Script_Sync
EXPLAIN !!Run_Startup_Script_Sync_Help
   KEYNAME "Software\Microsoft\Windows\CurrentVersion\Policies\System"
   VALUENAME "RunStartupScriptSync"
   VALUEON NUMERIC 0
   VALUEOFF NUMERIC 1
END POLICY
```

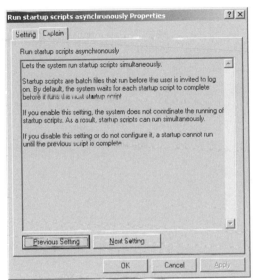

Figure 11-7 The EXPLAIN syntax appears on the Explain tab in the GPME.

If you want to create a hard return within the Help text, just use the /n syntax. If you want to create a line break, you can use the /n/n syntax. You can use up to 4,096 characters in any single EXPLAIN syntax entry—more than enough for a good description of the policy.

SUPPORTED

The GPME uses the SUPPORTED tag to populate the REQUIREMENT field. This tag informs the Group Policy administrator about the platforms or applications for which the policy setting is supported. For example, many of the policy settings included in the System.adm template use a SUPPORTED tag that identifies a specific service pack release. The string used for the SUPPORTED tag often refers to multiple operating systems or service packs.

Operating system components generally use an operating system or service pack reference in this field, whereas applications (which can be updated outside the release of a service pack) can refer to a specific version of an application. The SUPPORTED tag is essential for ensuring that Group Policy administrators have the information to make informed decisions about the use of the policy setting.

Your .adm template might also be localized, and you should use the *!!Stringname* construct in the SUPPORTED tag because it allows the referenced string to be localized easily. In addition, the SUPPORTED tag is supported only in Windows XP and later, so it should be enclosed within the *#if version* construct, as follows. (This ensures that the Windows 2000 version of the GPME does not attempt to interpret the SUPPORTED tag.)

```
POLICY !!ScreenSaverFilename
   #if version >= 4
   SUPPORTED !!SUPPORTED_Windows2003
   #endif
KEYNAME "Software\Policies\Microsoft\Windows\Control Panel\Desktop"
   PART !!ScreenSaverFilename EXPANDABLETEXT
   VALUENAME "SCRNSAVE.EXE"
   END PART
END POLICY
```

The SUPPORTED syntax and the operating system description accomplish two things in the GPME. First, they list the operating system version under the requirements label in the Extended view of the GPME, as shown in Figure 11-8. Second, it provides a way for the Filtering option to select the correct operating system versions to be displayed.

Figure 11-8   The GPME uses the SUPPORTED syntax to filter and indicate to the administrator which operating system the policy is designed for.

String and Tab Limits for .adm Templates

The .adm templates cannot contain unlimited amounts of information. Restrictions are bound to each .adm template (although the chances of reaching these limits for custom .adm entries are small). Table 11-3 lists these restrictions.

Table 11-3   String and Tab Limits for .adm Templates

File String	Tag Limit
Maximum string length for Explain text	4,096 characters
Maximum string length for Category Explain text	256 characters
Maximum string length for EDITTEXT string	1,023 characters

Best Practices for .adm Templates

In general, if a policy setting can be configured using a simple user interface and almost any configuration input can be stored in the registry as plain text, consider using an .adm template to configure the setting. Specifically, .adm templates are an appropriate solution for the following scenarios:

- Creating on/off or yes/no functionality. You can use .adm template settings to act as a switch, to turn functionality on or off. It is common for desktop features and functions to be controlled in this manner.

- Defining a set of static modes. For example, you can set the language used on a computer. You can set up a static list of language selections, and when the policy setting is enabled, the administrator can select a language from that list. This action is typically shown in the user interface as a drop-down list.

- Creating a policy setting that requires simple input that can be stored in the registry as plain text. For example, you can create a policy setting to define the screen saver or bitmap that is displayed on the user's desktop. With this policy setting enabled, Group Policy administrators see a text box into which they can type the name and path of the bitmap file to be used. This information is then stored in the registry as plain text.

 Note Binary values that are stored in the registry cannot be placed in an .adm file, because they are not in ASCII format. You can place binary registry values in Group Policy Preferences, under the Registry policy. For more information about the Registry policy, refer to Chapter 12, "Group Policy Preferences," which covers the Registry policy and all other new Group Policy Preference settings.

Consider using an administrative template to distribute registry-based policy settings for the following purposes:

- To help manage and increase security of desktop computers.

- To hide or disable a user interface option that can lead users into a situation that requires Help desk support.

- To hide or disable new behavior that might confuse users. This allows the Help desk to gradually introduce these new features until all users can be trained properly.

- To hide settings and options that tend to distract users or are too complex for them to configure without assistance from the Help desk.

There are also times when you should consider *not* using .adm templates to configure settings on all computers through GPOs. Here are some instances in which you should avoid using .adm templates:

- Implementing the entire list of settings and options for a large application. Large applications can contain hundreds or thousands of settings, which can slow down GPO processing and restrict users' ability to configure the application to their own needs. Be selective about the features you enable or disable. You should implement only a subset of the available options, based on whether an administrator would want this kind of management over the application.

■ Implementing unsupported policy settings. You should only implement .adm template settings that will be fully tested, validated, and supported.

As you design your custom .adm template settings, consider the end state, administration of the settings, support for distribution of the setting, and troubleshooting when settings fail to take effect as expected. You should consider the following guidelines when you design your policy settings:

■ Do not alter the standard .adm templates. This includes removing settings within the standard .adm templates or adding new settings to them. Subsequent versions of the .adm templates (released through updates or service packs) will add the settings back and overwrite any new custom settings.

■ Remember that computer policy settings always override user policy settings when they conflict.

■ When you create new policy settings, avoid using "enable" or "disable" in the title of your policy setting. This will prevent confusion when explaining the actions of the policy setting for the enabled, disable, and not configured states.

■ Consider making the enabled behavior of all .adm template settings the opposite of what the default behavior exhibits. This will keep the configurations within the policy setting consistent with the default behavior of Windows.

Note   This design might make some settings work as a "double negative," but it keeps the consistency of the default behavior and Enabled state intact. The Explain text that you include with your setting will help clarify what the Enabled and Disabled configurations produce.

■ Provide a thorough and detailed Explain tab. Well-written Explain text can help reduce support calls and troubleshooting for custom .adm template settings.

How It Works: Registry-Based GPO Policies

The overall structure of both the .adm template and ADMX file are the same in theory and implementation. These files have two major tasks in GPO management. First, they create entries in the GPME. This allows the administrator to "see" the policy setting so that he or she can "enable" it. After the policy setting is configured, it is stored in the registry.pol file, located in the Group Policy template (GPT).

Second, these files are responsible for mapping out the exact path to the registry value that is being modified. This includes the path to the registry value, as well as the data that will be stored for that value.

> After the exact path, value, and data are stored in the GPT, Group Policy processing and the CSE complete the rest of the work. When policy processing occurs, the data in the GPT is delivered to the target computer, where the registry CSE takes the raw information and converts it into a registry entry.
>
> For more information about the GPT, refer to Chapter 4, "Architecture of Group Policy," where the GPT and Group Policy container (GPC) for a GPO are discussed.

Creating Custom ADMX and ADML Files

The creation of ADMX and ADML files for custom entries requires the knowledge of how XML files are created and referenced. Both ADMX and ADML files use XML formatting and structural components. You can create additional ADMX files to accommodate custom registry-based entries in the GPME, so that these policy settings can be controlled centrally.

The ADMX file structure and components provide for a language-neutral environment that can be tailored to all of the supported languages discussed in Chapter 10, "ADM Templates, ADMX Files, and the ADMX Central Store," which discusses the core components of ADMX files. Two files must be created to customize ADMX files:

- .admx files describe the structure of the categories and Administrative template policy settings that are displayed in the GPME during editing of a GPO.
- .adml files allow for language-specific syntax to be displayed in the GPME. There must be a single .adml file per supported language for your custom entries.

ADMX Schema

The rules of ADMX and ADML file creation and syntax usage are defined in the ADMX schema. The schema is a set of three files that define the elements and attributes, how the syntax is constructed, and how the ADMX and ADML files are used in conjunction.

You can download the ADMX schema files from *http://go.microsoft.com/fwlink/ ?LinkId=86094*. After downloading and installing the admxSchema.msi file, you will have three additional files that you can use to help design new ADMX and ADML files. These files, located at C:\Program Files\Microsoft Group Policy\admxschema by default, include:

- BaseTypes.xsd
- PolicyDefinitionFiles.xsd
- PolicyDefinitions.xsd

These files can be used in conjunction with tools such as Microsoft Visual Studio to help create custom ADMX and ADML files. The rest of this chapter will discuss how you can leverage the information in these files, as well as additional reference documents, to create your own custom ADMX files, without the need for Visual Studio.

Direct from the Source: A New Class Option for ADMX Files

With .adm templates, you have only two CLASS options: MACHINE and USER. If you were to create a registry-based policy setting that could apply to both the computer and user portions of the registry, you would have to include two POLICY descriptions that were exactly the same, but locate one in the CLASS MACHINE and one in the CLASS USER portions.

For ADMX files, a third option was added to the attribute for a policy setting. You can now write the policy setting once in the ADMX file and define the *class* attribute to have a value of *Both*, such as *Class=Both*. This causes the GPME to display the policy setting in the exact same location, placed under the Computer Configuration and User Configuration sections.

The rest of the operations will apply. If the administrator configures the setting under Computer Configuration through the GPME, the policy setting will be saved as configuring the HKLM portion of the registry; for User Configuration, the configuration operation will cause the policy setting to configure the HKCU portion of the registry.

Judith Herman, Programming Writer, Microsoft

ADMX File Structure

ADMX files create the category structure and policy settings within the GPME. The overall structure of an ADMX file is shown in Figure 11-9.

Table 11-4 explains the use of each section in the ADMX file.

Table 11-4 ADMX File Section Descriptions

Section	Description
XML Declaration	Required to validate as an XML-based file.
policyDefinitions Element	Contains all other elements for the ADMX file.
policyNamespaces Element	Defines the unique namespace for this ADMX file. The *policyNamespaces* element also provides a mapping to external file namespaces if a reference to the *category* element is defined in a different ADMX file.
resources Element	Specifies the requirements for the language-specific resources; the minimum required version of the associated ADML file.
supportedOn Element	Specifies references to localized text strings defining the operating systems or applications affected by a specific policy setting.
categories Element	Specifies categories under which the policy setting in this ADMX file will be displayed in the GPME.
policies Element	Defines the individual policy settings in the GPME.

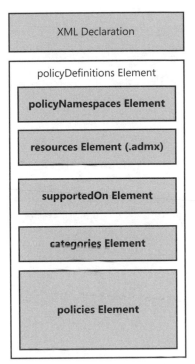

Figure 11-9   The ADMX file structure is divided into seven main sections.

ADML File Structure

The ADML files are responsible for defining the language-specific text that is shown in the GPME. These files are produced for each language that will be supported within your company (one file per language). The overall structure of the ADML file is shown in Figure 11-10.

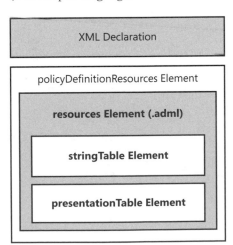

Figure 11-10   The ADML file structure is based on XML.

Table 11-5 explains the use of each section in the ADML file.

Table 11-5   ADML File Section Descriptions

Section	Description
XML declaration	Required to validate as an XML-based file.
policyDefinitionResources Element	Contains all other elements for the ADML file.
resources Element (.adml)	Contains a *stringTable* Element and a *presentationTable* Element for a specified language.

> **Warning**   A *stringTable* element and a *presentationTable* element must be defined in the ADML file in order, as required by the ADMX schema: *stringTable element* followed by *presentationTable element*. The parser for the Group Policy tools will present an error if the order of these two elements is reversed.

Core ADMX File Concepts

The creation of custom ADMX files can be made more efficient when you understand some of the key concepts. Here, you will see how the default ADMX files can be leveraged with your new ADMX files to ensure consistency and reduce errors within the GPME. This section also describes some of the core communication between the ADMX and ADML file syntax.

One of the default ADMX files is the Windows.admx file. This file provides baseline settings that define categories and text that defines the "supported on" text for the Windows products with which each policy setting can be used. You will want to reference this file for the defined categories and "supported on" definitions within it.

Referencing the Windows Base ADMX File

The Windows base ADMX file must be referenced by the unique namespace that is contained with the file, which is Microsoft.Policies.Windows, noting that the string is case sensitive. To reference this aspect of the file from your ADMX file, use the *using* element within your *policyNamespaces* element, as shown here:

```
<policyNamespaces>
    <target prefix="example" namespace="Microsoft.Policies.Example"/>
    <using prefix="windows" namespace="Microsoft.Policies.Windows"/>
</policyNamespaces>
```

The *namespace* attribute must match the defined namespace entry from the Windows base file. The *prefix* attribute can be any unique entry that you want; however, as a best practice, it should match the prefix of Windows.

Referencing Category Elements from the Windows Base ADMX File

Default categories are defined within the GPME that organize the policy settings into logical nodes or areas. Figure 11-11 shows some of the categories that are configured in a default GPO.

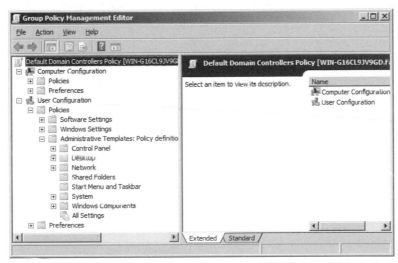

Figure 11-11 Some of the default categories defined in a GPO include Control Panel, Desktop, Network, and Shared Folders.

These categories are defined in the Windows.admx base file. If you want your setting to appear under one of these nodes, you must reference the *category* elements defined in the Windows base file.

For your custom ADMX file, you can use the *category* element from the Windows base file as the *parentCategory* element or a *policy* element within your ADMX file. As a best practice, you should place your categories under the existing Windows base file categories. You can do this by adding the "windows:" prefix to the *ref* attribute of the *parentCategory* element. Here is an example that illustrates how you would reference the Windows base file for the *category* element to place a Sample category node under the Windows component node:

```
<category name="SAMPLE" displayName="$(string.SAMPLE)" explainText="$(string.SAMPLEHELP)">
  <parentCategory ref="windows:WindowsComponents"/>
</category>
```

Warning If you define the *category* element name within your custom ADMX file, the GPME will display a duplicate node. This is because there is a different namespace defined beyond the default namespace mentioned earlier, and it is evaluated as a unique element by the GPME. This should be avoided, because it will cause confusion for those administering the GPO.

You can also just add more policies to the existing categories defined in the Windows base file. This will eliminate the additional node example from the preceding example. To add a custom policy entry to an existing category from the Windows base file, you would use coding similar to the following:

```
<policy name="Sample_NoParamPolicy" class="Both" displayName="$(string.Sample_NoParamPolicy)"
explainText="$(string.Sample_NoParamPolicy_Help)" key="Software\Policies\Examples"
valueName="Example1NoParam">
  <parentCategory ref="windows:WindowsComponents"/>
  <supportedOn ref="SUPPORTED_ProductOnly"/>
  <enabledValue>
    <decimal value="1"/>
  </enabledValue>
  <disabledValue>
    <decimal value="0"/>
  </disabledValue>
</policy>
```

Referencing Category Elements from the Windows Base ADMX File

Because many changes have been made to Group Policy over the years, every administrator needs to know the policy settings that correspond to specific operating system versions. The *supportedOn* elements help handle this declaration within the GPME.

The Windows base file dictates the default declarations that the specific policy settings affect in the operating system. Those default *supportedOn* values are listed in Table 11-6.

Table 11-6 Windows Base File supportedOn Values and Descriptions

supportOn Value	Description of supportOn Value
SUPPORTED_AllowWebPrinting	Windows 2000 or later, running Internet Information Services; not supported on Windows Server 2003
SUPPORTED_IE6SP1	At least Microsoft Internet Explorer 6 SP1
SUPPORTED_Win2k	At least Windows 2000
SUPPORTED_Win2kOnly	Windows 2000 only
SUPPORTED_Win2kSP1	At least Windows 2000 SP1
SUPPORTED_Win2kSP3	At least Windows 2000 SP3
SUPPORTED_Win2kSP3_Or_XPSP1	At least Windows 2000 SP3 or Windows XP Professional SP1
SUPPORTED_WindowsNET	At least Windows Server 2003
SUPPORTED_WindowsNETOnly	Windows Server 2003 only
SUPPORTED_WindowsNET_XP	Windows Server 2003 and Windows XP only
SUPPORTED_WindowsPreVista	Windows Server 2003, Windows XP, and Windows 2000 only
SUPPORTED_WindowsUpdate	At least Windows 2000 SP3, Windows XP Professional SP1, or Windows Server 2003 family
SUPPORTED_WindowsVista	At least Windows Vista

Table 11-6   Windows Base File supportedOn Values and Descriptions

supportOn Value	Description of supportOn Value
SUPPORTED_WindowsXP	At least Windows XP Professional or Windows Server 2003 family
SUPPORTED_WindowsXP_Or_Vista	At least Windows XP or Windows Vista
SUPPORTED_WindowsXP_SP1_W2K_SP4_NETSERVER	At least Windows 2000 SP4, Windows XP Professional SP1, or Windows Server 2003 family
SUPPORTED_WindowsXP_SP2_W2K_SP5_NETSERVER_SP1	At least Windows 2000 SP5, Windows XP Professional SP2, or Windows Server 2003 family SP1
SUPPORTED_WindowsXPOnly	Windows XP Professional only
SUPPORTED_WindowsXPSP1	At least Windows XP Professional SP1 or Windows Server 2003 family
SUPPORTED_WindowsXPSP2	At least Windows XP Professional SP2
SUPPORTED_WindowsXPSP2_Or_WindowsNET	At least Windows XP Professional SP2 or Windows Server 2003 family
SUPPORTED_WindowsXPSP2_Or_WindowsNETSP1	At least Windows XP Professional SP2 or Windows Server 2003 family SP1
SUPPORTED_WindowsXPOrServerOnly	Windows Server 2003 and Windows XP only

To reference the *supportOn* element from the Windows base file, you simply add the "windows:" prefix to the *ref* attribute, referencing a predefined *supportedOn* element within the Windows.admx file.

> **Warning**   If you use an invalid *supportedOn* element name, the GPME will not display any information regarding the operating systems that the policy setting supports. Also, no error message will be displayed, because the system will ignore the *supportedOn* element altogether.

An example of a reference to the *supportedOn* element from the Windows base file is as follows:

```
<policy name="Sample_NoParamPolicy" class="Both" displayName="$(string.Sample_NoParamPolicy)"
explainText="$(string.Sample_NoParamPolicy_Help)" key="Software\Policies\Examples"
valueName="Example1NoParam">
  <parentCategory ref="SAMPLE"/>
  <supportedOn ref="windows:SUPPORTED_WindowsXP"/>
  <enabledValue>
    <decimal value="1"/>
  </enabledValue>
  <disabledValue>
    <decimal value="0"/>
  </disabledValue>
</policy>
```

Tying the ADMX and ADML Files Together

The ADMX file is responsible for creating the category and policy structure within the GPME, whereas the ADML file is responsible for the text for the category, policy, and any other elements used. Any number of ADML files can be used with a single ADMX file to create language-specific interfaces.

The policy section in the ADMX file creates each individual policy within the GPME. Because the policy must have associated text , the ADMX file must reference the ADML file to supply the correct text for the policy wording. To do this, use the *presentation* element in the policy statement, as shown in the following snippet from an ADMX file:

```
<policy name="Sample_Checkbox" class="Machine"
            displayName="$(string.Sample_Checkbox)"
            explainText="$(string.Sample_Checkbox_Help)"
            presentation="$(presentation.Sample_Checkbox)"
            key="Software\Policies\Examples">
    <parentCategory ref="CHECKBOX_CATEGORY"/>
    <supportedOn ref="windows:SUPPORTED_ProductOnly"/>
    <elements>
        <boolean id="Checkbox" valueName="ExampleCheckbox">
          <trueValue>
            <decimal value="1"/>
          </trueValue>
          <falseValue>
            <decimal value="0"/>
          </falseValue>
        </boolean>
    </elements>
```

...

Note that the *presentation* element references the *presentation.Sample_Checkbox* variable. This variable is defined in the ADML file, shown here:

```
<presentation id="Sample_Checkbox">
   <checkBox refId="Checkbox">Check box text</checkBox>
</presentation>
```

Because these two entries for presentation match and there are the same number of entries in both the ADMX and ADML file, the display should correctly show the check box with the "Check box text."

> **Warning**   If the ADML file does not have the exact same name as the ADMX file, the GPME will display an error, indicating that the ADML file is not available. Also, the ADMX file and the ADML file must contain the same number of elements for the text to appear in the GPME—if they do not, an error will appear, indicating a mismatch.

You should also be aware of the data type that is used in the ADMX file and how it matches with the parameter definition in the ADML file. The ADMX file uses the boolean data type, which matches the *checkBox* parameter definition in the ADML file. Table 11-7 shows how to match the data types from the ADMX file to the associated parameter definitions in the ADML file.

Table 11-7   ADMX Data Type to ADML Parameter Definition Matrix

ADMX File Data Type	ADML File Parameter Definition
boolean Element	checkBox Element
text Element	textBox Element
decimal Element (elements)	decimalTextBox Element
text Element	comboBox Element
enum Element	dropdownList Element
item Element	dropdownList Element
list Element	listBox Element

Using ADMX File Language

The ADMX file language is similar to that of the .adm template, with just a few oddities. Table 10-1 in Chapter 10 provides a conversion of .adm template syntax to that of ADMX and ADML file syntax. Together, Table 10-4, the .adm template syntax in Table 11-7, Table 11-8, and the file on the resource CD named "Group Policy ADMX Syntax Reference Guide" provide an excellent breakdown of how to use the ADMX file syntax to create any type of policy setting that you desire within the GPME for a GPO.

Table 11-8 provides a summary of all of the elements available for use in both the ADMX and ADML files. For a more in-depth view of the ADMX and ADML file syntax, refer to the syntax reference guide on the resource CD, which describes in detail each element that can be used in these files.

Table 11-8   ADMX and ADML File Element Syntax

ADMX File Data Type	ADML File Parameter Definition
additive Attribute	A Boolean value. If true, the existing subkeys are not deleted, and the values set in the list box are appended to the existing subkeys. If false, the existing subkeys are deleted and the values in the list box replace the existing subkeys.
annotation Element	Adds a localized comment at the beginning of the .adml file.
boolean Element	Sets a value based on the true and false cases in a policy setting. It is generally associated with *checkBox* parameters in the GPME.
category Element	Specifies the name of a unique category to be displayed in the GPME.
categories Element	A table of *category* elements.
checkBox Element	Represents a check box parameter. It must be associated with a *boolean* element defined in the *elements* element.
class Attribute	Identifies whether the policy setting will be located under a single node of the GPME (computer or user) or both nodes. This is defined in the .admx file.
clientExtension Attribute	Defines the client-side extension that will process, on the client computer, the particular settings represented by the *boolean*, *decimal*, text, *enum*, or *list* element.

Table 11-8   ADMX and ADML File Element Syntax

ADMX File Data Type	ADML File Parameter Definition
comboBox Element	Represents a combo box parameter. It must be associated with a *text* element defined in the *elements* element.
decimal Element (elements)	Sets the registry value to the specified numeric value when a policy setting is enabled through the GPME. It determines whether the registry key will be created as a REG_DWORD or REG_SZ when storing the numeric value.
decimal Element (value)	Sets a value to an unsigned integer decimal value.
decimal TextBox Element	Represents a text box with or without a spin box control for entering decimal numbers as a policy setting parameter. It must be associated with a *decimal* element defined in the *elements* element.
default Element	A localized default displayed when the combo box parameter is active.
defaultChecked Element	A Boolean value. If true, the check box parameter is displayed as selected; otherwise, the check box parameter is displayed as cleared.
defaultItem Element	The numerical value that identifies the default choice from the items in the drop-down list. The item list is numbered starting from 0.
defaultKey Attribute	Specifies a default registry subkey for all items in the *enabledList* element, *disabledList* element, or *valueList* element.
defaultValue Attribute	Specifies the default numerical value of the parameter. If not specified, the *defaultValue* attribute is set to 1.
defaultValue Element	A localized string that is initially displayed in the text box parameter when the policy setting is enabled.
definition Element	Creates the mapping between the logical name to an existing reference supported on string text in the .adml file.
definitions Element	A table of *definition* elements for the *supportedOn* text.
delete Element	Represents a deleted registry value or key.
description Element	The localized description of policy settings contained in the .adml file.
disabledList Element	Sets the multiple registry values when a policy setting is disabled through the GPME.
disabledValue Element	Sets the registry value when a policy setting is disabled through the GPME.
displayName Attribute	A string value referenced in the .adml file. This attribute can be used in the *category*, *definition*, *enum*, or *policy* element. This is defined in the .admx file.
displayName Element	The localized friendly name of the .adml file.
dropdownList Element	Represents a drop-down list parameter. It must be associated with an *enum* element defined in the *elements* element.
elements Element	Represents the types of optional parameters defined in a policy setting. The child elements for the *elements* element represent these optional parameters available for a policy setting.
enabledList Element	Sets the multiple registry values when a policy setting is enabled through the GPME.

Table 11-8   ADMX and ADML File Element Syntax

ADMX File Data Type	ADML File Parameter Definition
enabledValue Element	Sets the registry value when a policy setting is enabled through the GPME.
enum Element	Sets the specified registry subkey to a specified value or a list of registry subkeys to values chosen from a drop-down list when a policy setting is enabled through the GPME.
expandable Attribute	A Boolean value. If true, the registry subkey value will be created as an expandable string type (REG_EXPAND_SZ); otherwise, the registry subkey value will be created as a string type (REG_SZ).
explainText Attribute	A string value referenced in the .adml file representing Help or Explain text for either a category or policy setting. This is defined in the .admx file.
explicitValue Attribute	A Boolean value. If true, the user must specify the registry subkey name and the registry subkey value. The list box shows two columns, one for the name and one for the data. If false, the user specifies only the registry subkey value. The registry subkey name is created automatically.
fallbackCulture Attribute	Specifies the default language to use when the .adml file does not exist on the machine or ADMX central store for the required language.
falseList Element	Sets the multiple registry values when a *boolean* element is set to the false state.
falseValue Element	Sets the registry value for the false condition of a *boolean* element.
fileName Attribute	Specifies a valid file name.
id Attribute	Specifies a string used as a logical name for an element.
item Element	Represents a singe registry entry and its value.
item Element (enum)	A child element of the *enum* element, representing a display name associated with a single value or a single value with a set of registry subkey values.
key Attribute	Specifies a string that represents the name of the registry subkey.
keywords Element	A list of searchable keywords associated with categories and policy settings.
label Element	A localized string label for the text box parameter.
list Element	Sets a list of registry subkeys when a policy setting is enabled through the GPME. It is generally associated with a show box parameter in the GPME.
listBox Element	Represents a list parameter. It must be associated with a *list* element defined in the *elements* element.
maxLength Attribute	Specifies the maximum number of text characters for a *text* element. The default value is 1023.
maxValue Attribute	Specifies the maximum value for a *decimal* element. The default value is 9999.
minRequiredRevision Attribute	Determines the minimum version of the .adml file that will interoperate with the .admx file. It is an attribute of the .admx *resources* element.

Table 11-8   ADMX and ADML File Element Syntax

ADMX File Data Type	ADML File Parameter Definition
minValue Attribute	Specifies the minimum value for a *decimal* element. The default value is 0.
name Attribute	A logical or friendly name used as a mapping to a string value referenced in the .adml file. This attribute can be used in the *category*, *definition*, or *policy* element.
nameSpace Attribute	Specifies the URI used to identify the elements within an ADMX file.
noSort Attribute	A Boolean value. If true, display the suggested values in the defined order of the *suggestion* elements; otherwise, sort the suggested values in alphabetical or numerical order.
parentCategory Element	Specifies the location of the category in relationship to its parent category in the GPME tree structure.
policy Element	Corresponds to a single Group Policy setting displayed in the GPME. It describes all of the information about the policy setting but includes a reference to the parameter definition.
policyDefinitionResources Element	The *document* element for an .adml file that defines all the localized resource information with a single language or culture per file for each supported language or culture setting. It also declares a default namespace for all of the elements in the .adml file.
policyDefinitions Element	The *document* element for an .admx file that defines a set of registry-policy settings. It also declares a default namespace for all of the elements in the .admx file.
policyNamespaces Element	Defines the unique name for the policy namespace in an ADMX file as well as any namespaces it references in other ADMX files.
policies Element	A table of *policy* elements.
prefix Attribute	Specifies the logical name that refers to the namespace within the current or referenced ADMX file.
presentation Attribute	A presentation value referenced in the .adml file representing the localized portions of a policy setting parameter. This is defined in the .admx file.
presentation Element	Corresponds to the parameters for a single Group Policy setting displayed in the GPME.
presentationTable Element	A table of *presentation* elements representing the layout of parameter controls for individual Group Policy settings. The layout of parameter controls includes: type of parameter entry mechanism (edit box, spin box, drop-down list, list box, show box, and combo box), labels and prompt text for the parameter entry, and the default and range values for each parameter entry.
ref Attribute	References a logical name for the parent category.
refId Attribute	Specifies a string used as a logical name. This attribute allows an element from the .admx file to refer to an element in the .adml file.
required Attribute	Specifies a Boolean value that represents whether a value must be specified for the parameter.
resources Element (.adml)	Contains the *stringTable* and *presentationTable* elements for specific MUI languages. This is located in the .adml file.

Table 11-8   ADMX and ADML File Element Syntax

ADMX File Data Type	ADML File Parameter Definition
resources Element (.admx)	Specifies the minimum revision level of the matching .adml file and, optionally, the fallback language to use. This is located in the .admx file.
revision Attribute	Provides a method of tracking changes made to the .admx or .adml file.
schemaVersion Attribute	Specifies the ADMX schema version that the .admx and .adml files conform to.
seeAlso Element	A descriptive phrase that can be used to reference related categories or policy settings.
soft Attribute	A Boolean value. If true, a registry value will not overwrite a previously set value; otherwise, registry values will always be saved.
spin Attribute	A Boolean value. If true, a spin box control is created in addition to the numeric text box; otherwise, a numeric text box is created.
spinStep Attribute	Specifies the increment of change for the spin box control. If not specified, it is set to 1.
storeAsText Attribute	A Boolean value. If true, the *decimal* element will store the decimal value as a REG_SZ registry value; otherwise, as a REG_DWORD.
string Element (.adml)	Represents a localized display string.
string Element (.admx)	Sets a value to string text.
stringTable Element	Contains the display strings for the following types of information: Group Policy setting title Explain text *SupportedOn* text Category names and Explain text Parameter labels
suggestion Element	A localized string displayed as a drop-down choice of the combo box parameter.
supersededAdm Element	References an .adm template to be replaced by an ADMX file. GPME will not read any .adm template designated as superseded.
supportedOn Element	Provides a mapping of products to definitions.
supportedOn Element (policy)	Provides a mapping of products to policy setting definitions.
target Element	Provides the mapping of a logical or friendly name to a unique URI name representing a policy namespace.
text Element	Sets the specified registry value to a specified text input value when a policy setting is enabled through the GPME.
text Element (presentation)	A localized string displayed within the parameter box by the GPME, used within the *presentation* element.
textbox Element	Represents a text box parameter. It must be associated with a *text* element defined in the *elements* element.
trueList Element	Sets the multiple registry values when a *boolean* element is set to the true state.

Table 11-8   ADMX and ADML File Element Syntax

ADMX File Data Type	ADML File Parameter Definition
trueValue Element	Sets the registry value for the true condition of a *boolean* element.
using Element	Provides the mapping of the logical name to a unique URI name of a previously defined policy namespace located in a different ADMX file. This is an optional element with no limit to the maximum number of *using* elements that can be declared in a *policyNamespaces* element.
value Attribute	Specifies the numerical value for the *decimal* element.
value Element	Represents the actions to delete a registry subkey or set the value of the registry subkey to a decimal or string value.
valueList Element	Sets the multiple registry values within the *item* element when defined as a child of the *enum* element.
valueName Attribute	Specifies a string that contains the name for a registry entry.
valuePrefix Attribute	Specifies the text string that will be prepended to an incremented integer. The combined text string and integer will create the registry subkey used in setting policy values.
XML declaration	Specify that this is an XML document. All ADMX files may start with the XML declaration. The XML declaration is not considered to be part of the ADMX document. However, it is good practice to start the ADMX file with the XML declaration to specify that this is an XML document.
xmlns Attribute	Specifies the default namespace for all elements in either the .admx or .adml file.

For more information on how to splice together ADMX files, refer to Appendix A, "Third-Party Group Policy Tools," which discusses some of the tools that exist today for working with ADMX files in a friendly environment.

Registry-Based Policy Settings: Three Options

You have three options for creating custom registry-based entries through Group Policy. Each option has advantages, but some advantages might be more helpful than others. Of course, there are disadvantages too.

The first option is to use the legacy .adm template. The technology and syntax within the .adm template is known and familiar, and the template is easy to import. However, files can get quite large, and they are stored in the GPT of the GPO. This causes a size increase in the GPT, and therefore in the SYSVOL.

The second option is to use ADMX files. These files and their structure are not readily familiar, but because they are based on XML, that should not be an issue. Creation of ADMX files involves some extra work because there are two files: ADMX and ADML. However, this is actually a benefit, because it provides the language neutrality that the .adm templates do not possess. Because ADMX files can take advantage of the central store, there is no SYSVOL bloat, no need to manage the versioning, and no thread of using errant versions of the files.

A final option for customizing registry-based entries in a GPO is to use the Registry policy under the Preferences node. This option has a few major benefits. First, there is absolutely no scripting or coding required. Also, the registry path is easy to find and document—you simply browse for it in the interface through the GPME. Another benefit is that these settings can be flagged to behave more like a policy than a preference, with the option to remove the policy when it no longer applies. Finally, with the targeting capabilities of the preferences, the registry-based entry can be dynamic, based on any of the available criteria.

For more information about registry-based settings using Group Policy Preferences, refer to Chapter 12, which covers all settings, configurations, and options related to preferences.

Summary

Customizing the .adm templates and ADMX files can add value to the control that Group Policy provides over registry settings on any computer. With the flexibility of both file types, nearly any registry value can be controlled using Group Policy.

Although .adm templates are legacy files, they are widely used today and can still be used in the future with Windows Server 2008 and Windows Vista. There are drawbacks to using these files, but if there is an established structure with them, it might be easier to keep them rather than migrate them to ADMX files.

ADMX files provide a cleaner, language-neutral, centralized management environment. They are a bit more complex than .adm templates, but they provide more control and are more efficient. ADMX files must be accompanied by ADML files, which provide the language-specific text for the GPME interface.

Additional Resources

- The ADMX Technology Review page, at *http://www.microsoft.com/technet/windowsvista/library/ef346453-eee8-4abe-ba6c-2160fee3be46.mspx*, includes more information about ADMX files.

- The Managing Group Policy ADMX Files Step-by-Step Guide, at *http://technet2.microsoft.com/WindowsVista/en/library/02633470-396c-4e34-971a-0c5b090dc4fd1033.mspx?mfr=true*, includes more information about managing ADMX files.

- The Microsoft Help and Support article titled "How to create a Central Store for Group Policy Administrative Templates in Window Vista," at *http://support.microsoft.com/kb/929841*, includes more information about creating the central store.

- Chapter 4, "Architecture of Group Policy," includes information about the storage of .adm templates in the GPT of a GPO.

- Chapter 10, "ADM Templates, ADMX Files, and the ADMX Central Store," includes information about the use of .adm templates, ADMX files, and the central store.

- Chapter 12, "Group Policy Preferences," includes information about the settings contained under the Preferences nodes within the GPME.

- Appendix A, "Third-Party Group Policy Tools," includes information about the array of Group Policy tools that are available for managing ADMX files.

Part VI
Group Policy Settings

Chapter 12
Group Policy Preferences

One of the most exciting changes to Group Policy with the release of Windows Server 2008 is the addition of Group Policy Preferences. Group Policy Preferences is sure to change the way in which most companies manage computers running Windows.

Group Policy Preferences are designed to supplement the Group Policy Policies that have been in GPOs since Windows 2000. Group Policy Preferences are designed to configure settings on computers running Windows without enforcing the settings. This provides a centralized methodology with which administrators can create a standardized user environment, while still allowing users to customize settings.

Group Policy Preferences are backward compatible, allowing companies to take advantage of these powerful and flexible settings without the need to upgrade all servers and desktops. Windows XP Service Pack 2 (SP2), Microsoft Windows Server 2003 Service Pack 1 (SP1), Windows Vista, and Windows Server 2008 can all consume Group Policy Preferences.

Over 20 client-side extensions (CSEs) are associated with Group Policy Preferences. The settings associated with these CSEs allow administrators to control aspects of a computer that they cannot with other GPO settings. Some of the settings related to Group Policy Preferences include drive mappings, printer mappings, custom registry modifications, local user password control, and environment variable management.

By using Group Policy Preferences, many companies will be able to eliminate log-on scripts, increase security, and reduce desktop image management.

> **Note**   Group Policy Preferences are the result of the acquisition of PolicyMaker from DesktopStandard Corporation. The options and settings that were available in PolicyMaker are nearly the same in Group Policy Preferences, with changes only to some of the interfaces, terms, and a few features.

Benefits of Group Policy Preferences

The benefits of Group Policy Preferences are numerous. The combination of its additional settings and targeting capabilities makes Group Policy Preferences influential and efficient. The benefits of using Group Policy Preferences span across the entire spectrum of the company, from financial savings to ultimate control over any desktop in the environment.

User-Friendly Interface

Group Policy Preferences are designed with administration in mind—they are not the typical Group Policy setting. Group Policy Preferences are designed with a friendly graphical user interface (GUI) that not only makes the implementation easier, but clearly identifies the purpose of each setting. All Group Policy Preferences include a dialog box with at least two tabs, and in some cases up to eight. Figure 12-1 shows the interface for configuring Microsoft Internet Explorer settings, which falls under the Group Policy Preferences node in the User Configuration section of the GPO.

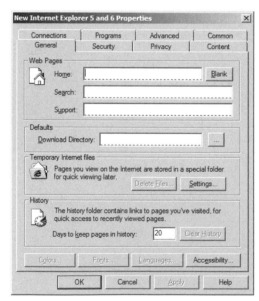

Figure 12-1   The Internet Settings suite of settings provides a friendly and robust interface for controlling Internet Explorer settings.

This easy-to-use interface will reduce errors in applying settings and testing for results of vague setting descriptions, and it will also decrease the overall time required to configure GPO settings.

Thousands More Settings

Group Policy Preferences have over 20 new areas of configuration within a GPO. Within these areas of configuration are thousands of new settings. Figure 12-2 shows the Group Policy Preferences nodes for the Computer Configuration section.

Figure 12-2   The Computer Configuration section has settings for Group Policy Preferences under both the Windows Settings and the Control Panel Settings nodes.

Figure 12-3 shows the Group Policy Preferences nodes under the User Configuration section in a GPO.

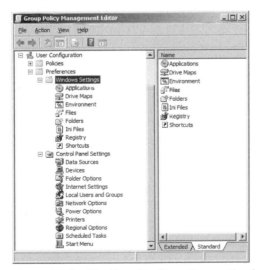

Figure 12-3   The User Configuration section has settings for Group Policy Preferences under both the Windows Settings and the Control Panel Settings nodes.

Practical and Valuable Settings

Group Policy Preferences offer control over a computer that was only possible using scripts or third-party tools in the past. Even custom .adm templates could not accommodate some of the valuable settings that Group Policy Preferences provide. Some of the most useful settings include:

- Drive mappings
- Printer mappings
- File and folder creation, deletion, and management
- Local user account password modification
- Service account password management
- Browser-based registry management
- Power scheme management

As companies try to meet security compliance regulations, make password management more efficient, and gain a higher return on IT investments, Group Policy Preferences and these valuable settings will be used frequently.

For more information about all of these settings, refer to the "Group Policy Preferences Settings" section, later in this chapter.

Reduced Desktop Images

Most companies have to create, maintain, and support multiple desktop images to meet the needs of unique departmental, application, and user environment configurations. In some cases companies must maintain images on 50 or more desktops.

Group Policy Preferences offer configuration management over many areas of the desktop that can dramatically reduce the need to have so many desktop images. By implementing Group Policy Preferences for applications, environment variables, files, folders, registry changes, mail profiles, and data sources, the total number of desktop images can be reduced by distributing these settings via Group Policy.

For more information about all of the settings that can help reduce desktop image management, refer to the "Group Policy Preferences Settings" section, later in this chapter.

Reduced Need for Log-on Scripts

Most companies use log-on scripts to configure user settings and preferences related to network resources, including network drives and printers. Log-on scripts are also used to modify registry values, copy files, and manage folders. Log-on scripts are not reliable mechanisms for delivering these settings because they run only when a user is logging on. Users who keep their computers on for nightly maintenance often simply lock their computers, instead of logging off, before leaving work. In this scenario, changes to the log-on script are not applied.

A second issue with log-on scripts is the management of the scripts themselves. Most log-on scripts are batch files that have limited capabilities. Third-party tools are available to help you expand script capabilities, but their inconvenience may outweigh their benefits.

Group Policy Preferences provide an easy-to-configure interface, granular targeting, and detailed management of the common log-on script contents. Many companies have eliminated the log-on script completely and instead use Group Policy Preferences to perform these configurations.

For more information about how these settings can help reduce the need for log-on scripts, refer to the "Group Policy Preferences Settings" section, later in this chapter.

Working with Any Organizational Unit Design

All Group Policy Preferences provide the advanced targeting feature called item-level targeting. This feature allows administrators to target any Group Policy Preferences setting, on a per-setting basis, using one or more targeting criteria. These criteria are shown in Figure 12-4.

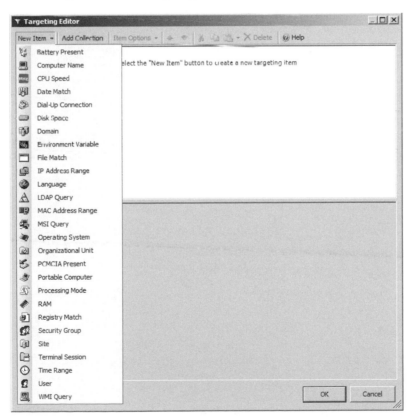

Figure 12-4   Item-level targeting provides a granular method for ensuring that the correct users and computers receive the Group Policy Preferences setting.

For more information about item-level targeting, refer to the "Item-Level Targeting" section, later in this chapter.

Preferences vs. Policies

The term *preferences* has been used in relation to Group Policy to help define another Group Policy term, which is *policies*. These two terms are now exposed and used in the Group Policy Management Editor (GPME) interface to distinguish the two types of settings available in a GPO.

The most significant difference between the two terms is that preferences are not enforced. This means that when Group Policy applies a preference setting, the user of the computer can alter that setting. Policy settings are not alterable. This is because the location of the policy in the registry is secured. Another difference is that policy settings typically dim the setting in the user interface, preventing the user from making any modification to the setting.

Other areas where preferences and policies differ include:

- **Flexibility**   Preferences are very flexible, allowing for custom entries through the use of .adm templates, ADMX files, or Group Policy Registry settings. Policies are not easily created, because they require application support to function.

- **Local Group Policy**   Preferences are not included in local Group Policy settings. Policies are available in both local Group Policy and GPOs in Active Directory directory service.

- **Awareness**   Preferences are used for applications that are not Group Policy aware, whereas policies are used to support applications that are Group Policy aware.

- **Registry location and behavior**   Preferences are used to overwrite the original settings in the registry and are not removed when the GPO is deleted or when the object falls out of scope of management. Policies do not modify the original registry setting, but instead update values under one of the four Policies subkeys. When the object falls out of scope of management, the original setting is still intact and again controls the registry setting.

- **Targeting and filtering**   Preferences support item-level targeting. Policies support GPO-level Windows Management Instrumentation (WMI) filtering.

- **User interface**   Preferences are GUI based and user friendly; they usually duplicate the original interface for the application or feature being controlled. Policies are mostly text based, and in some cases you must test them to determine the outcome of the setting.

Table 12-1 summarizes the differences between preferences and policies within a GPO.

Table 12-1   Differences between Preferences and Policies

	Group Policy Preferences Settings	Group Policy Policies Settings
Enforcement	Preferences are not enforced.	Settings are enforced.
	The user interface is not disabled.	The user interface is disabled.
	Settings can be refreshed or applied once.	Settings are refreshed.

Table 12-1   Differences between Preferences and Policies

	Group Policy Preferences Settings	Group Policy Policies Settings
Flexibility	You can easily create preference items for registry settings, files, and so on.	You cannot create policy settings to manage files, folders, and so on.
	You can import individual registry settings or entire registry branches from a local or remote computer.	Adding policy settings requires application support and creation of administrative templates.
Local Group Policy	Not available in local Group Policy.	Available in local Group Policy.
Awareness	Applications that are not Group Policy–aware are supported.	Group Policy–aware applications are required.
Registry location and behavior	Original settings are overwritten.	Original settings are not changed.
	Removing the preference item does not restore the original setting.	Settings are stored in registry Policy branches.
		Removing the policy setting restores the original settings
Targeting and filtering	Targeting is granular, with a user interface for each type of targeting item.	Filtering is based on Windows WMI and requires writing WMI queries.
	Supports targeting at the individual preference item level.	Supports filtering at a GPO level.
User interface	Provides a familiar, easy-to-use interface for configuring most settings.	Provides an alternative user interface for most policy settings.

Direct from the Source: Policies vs. Preferences Processing

By default, most native Group Policy Policies are processed once, and then they are not processed again until a change is made. Because policies are enforced, the setting that is configured will remain the same on the end user's computer until the policy is changed in the GPO.

Most Group Policy Preferences, however, are processed during every Group Policy refresh (every 90 minutes, by default). Because users can change preference settings deployed through Group Policy, this gives the administrator the flexibility to reset the setting as defined in Group Policy during each Group Policy refresh.

Mark Gray, Program Manager, Microsoft

Management and Support of Group Policy Preferences

Because Group Policy Preferences is a new technology released in the Windows Server 2008 time frame, you will find that there are limitations on which legacy operating systems can manage them. Group Policy Preferences are available for management only on computers that can run the new Group Policy Management Console (GPMC). These operating systems include Windows Server 2008 and Windows Vista SP1.

You should also know which operating systems can consume the settings that are configured in the Group Policy Preferences settings. Table 12-2 illustrates which operating systems can manage and which operating systems can support the application of Group Policy Preferences.

Table 12-2   Group Policy Preferences Platform Support

Operating System	Can Apply Group Policy Preferences	Can Manage Group Policy Preferences through GPME
Windows 2000	Not supported	Not supported
Windows XP (32-bit and 64-bit)	Supported with SP2 (after CSE installation)	Not supported
Windows Vista (32-bit and 64-bit)	Supported (after CSE installation)	Supported (after installation of SP1)
Windows Server 2003 (32-bit and 64-bit)	Supported with SP1 (after CSE installation)	Not supported
Windows Server 2008 (32-bit and 64-bit)	Integrated	Integrated

Managing Group Policy Preferences Using the GPME

The new Group Policy Management Editor (GPME) is the only version of the Group Policy management tools that supports the configuration of Group Policy Preferences. In turn, the GPME runs only through the new version of the GPMC. For computers that can manage the new Group Policy Preferences to be able to perform that duty, both the new GPMC (and thus the GPME) must be supported and installed.

Windows Server 2008

Windows Server 2008 comes with full support for Group Policy Preferences. The technology for this support is integrated directly with the product. There is nothing that must be done with Windows Server 2008 to manage Group Policy Preferences.

Windows Vista

To configure Group Policy Preferences for use with Windows Vista, you must perform additional installations. First you must install SP1, which provides additional support for running the GPMC that supports Group Policy Preferences. You must also install the Remote Server Administration Tools (RSAT), which provides an interface for the Group Policy Preferences in the GPME. RSAT can be downloaded and installed from the Microsoft Download Center.

Deploying the Group Policy Preferences CSEs

To receive and apply settings that are configured in the Group Policy Preferences settings area, a computer must have the Group Policy Preferences CSEs installed. Because Group Policy

Preferences are new technology released after Windows Vista, you must take additional measures to ensure that operating systems that support the application of Group Policy Preferences can apply them.

For more information about CSEs, refer to Chapter 4, "Architecture of Group Policy," which explains CSEs.

Windows Server 2008

There is no need to deploy the CSEs to Windows Server 2008 computers, because the CSEs for Group Policy Preferences are already installed and ready to consume settings. For more information about the CSEs, their location, and their registry settings, refer to Chapter 4, which covers the CSEs for Group Policy Preferences.

Windows Vista, Windows Server 2003 SP1, and Windows XP SP2

As you saw in Chapter 4, which covered the architecture of Group Policy, there is a new service that controls Group Policy. This service is fully capable of handling all of the settings that can be deployed using a GPO. The service itself does not apply the settings, rather, the CSE does this. However, the only operating system that comes with the CSEs installed to apply Group Policy Preferences is Windows Server 2008.

For Windows Vista, Windows Server 2003 SP1, and Windows XP SP2, the CSEs for Group Policy Preferences must be installed. The CSEs can be downloaded from the Microsoft Download Center.

Group Policy Preferences Settings

The Group Policy Preferences are divided into four areas within the GPME. There are two nodes for the Computer Configuration section and two nodes for the User Configuration section. Each of these sections has the same structure for the Group Policy Preferences, which are subnodes under the Preferences node: Windows Settings and Control Panel Settings.

Within each of these subnodes are the Group Policy Preferences nodes from which you can create settings. Some nodes appear under both the Computer Configuration and User Configuration sections, and some nodes are unique to just one section. The following sections describe each of the Group Policy Preferences settings and specify whether they appear under just one section. If nothing is mentioned, the setting appears under both sections.

Group Policy Preferences: Windows Settings

Nine nodes appear under the Windows Settings node within the Group Policy Preferences. These settings help eliminate log-on scripts and help control the files and folders on any computer that can receive Group Policy Preferences.

Applications

The Applications preference can be used to modify many of the Microsoft products, such as Office Word, Office PowerPoint, and Office Outlook. By default, the settings that can be configured under this node are not available. To make settings to configure applications, the following criteria must be met:

1. You must download and install the administration part of the Group Policy Preferences. The Applications preferences settings for Microsoft Office can be downloaded at *http://www.microsoft.com/downloads/details.aspx?FamilyID=92D8519A-E143-4AEE-8F7A-E4BBAEBA13E7&displaylang=en.*

> **Note**   The Microsoft Office download includes .adm template files, ADMX/ADML files, and files related to the Office Customization Tool (OCT). For information about using the .adm template files, see the sections called "2007 Office System Administrative Template Files" and "Using Group Policy Management Console and Group Policy Object Editor" in the article titled "Enforce Settings by Using Group Policy in the 2007 Office System," available at, *http:// technet2.microsoft.com/Office/en-us/library/873a5392-1b1a-47a1-a863-1f29ef116d0e1033.mspx?mfr=true*. For information about using ADMX files for Windows Vista, see the "Managing Group Policy ADMX Files Step-by-Step Guide," available at, *http:// technet2.microsoft.com/WindowsVista/en/library/02633470-396c-4e34-971a-0c5b090dc4fd1033.mspx?mfr=true*. For information about using the OCT, see the article titled "Office Customization Tool in the 2007 Office System," available at, *Office Customization Tool in the 2007 Office system," available at http://technet2.microsoft.com/Office/en-us/library/8faae8a0-a12c-4f7b-839c-24a66a531bb51033.mspx?mfr=true.*

2. RSAT must be installed on the computer performing the administration.

Group Policy Preferences are extensible, and the Applications preference settings are no different. Software developers can create plug-ins for other applications by using the Group Policy Software Development Kit.

> **Note**   The Applications preference is available only in the User Configuration section.

Drive Maps

The Drive Maps preference can control nearly any drive mapping on the target computer. The drive mappings can be created, replaced, updated, or deleted by using this preference setting. The setting is commonly used instead of a log-on script for mapping drives. The main benefit of using the Drive Maps preference instead of the log-on script is the capability of the item-level targeting that can be used in conjunction with this preference. Figure 12-5 illustrates the interface for the Drive Maps preference and the options that can be configured.

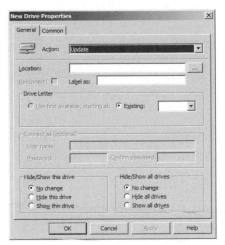

Figure 12-5 The Drive Maps preference can replace the need to script drive mappings in log-on scripts.

Note The Drive Maps preference is available only in the User Configuration section.

Environment

The Environment preference provides control over user and system environment variables on the target computer. This setting allows you to create, update, or delete environment variables. When used in conjunction with the item-level targeting, these variables can be used with other Group Policy Preferences settings to gain more control over computers and settings within the environment. Figure 12-6 illustrates the interface for the Environment preference and the options that can be configured.

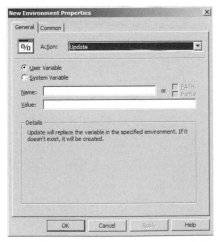

Figure 12-6 The Environment preference can create new variables or use existing variables to target settings more precisely.

Files

The Files preference allows centralized creation, replacement, updating, and deletion of files that reside on the computer that consumes the Group Policy Preferences setting. Because this setting supports wildcards and environment variables, almost any file can be targeted for control. Figure 12-7 illustrates the interface for the Files preference and the options that can be configured.

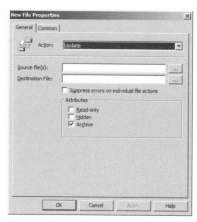

Figure 12-7   The Files preference can control nearly any file on the target computer, especially with the use of wildcards and environment variables.

Folders

The Folders preference gives the administrator control over folders that reside on the target computer. The ability to create, replace, update, and delete with custom settings makes this preference very powerful. You can leverage this preference with environment variables to target specific computers and folders. Figure 12-8 illustrates the interface for the Folders preference and the options that can be configured.

Figure 12-8   The Folders preference can control folders and the content of the folders on the target computer.

Ini Files

The Ini Files preference controls the creation and contents of .ini files on the target computer. The preference allows you to create, update, replace, and delete entire files or the properties within a file. Figure 12-9 illustrates the interface for the Ini Files preference and the options that can be configured.

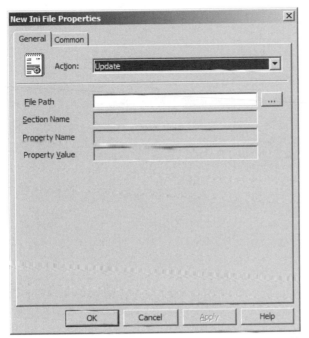

Figure 12-9   The Ini Files preference can control .ini files and the content of the files on the target computer.

Network Shares

The Network Shares preference allows you to control shares, hidden shares, and administrative shares on target computers. The shares can be created, deleted, updated, or replaced by the settings you configure in the dialog box for the preference. The dialog box also allows you to control whether the share will support Access-based Enumeration, as shown in Figure 12-10.

Note   The Network Shares preference is available only in the Computer Configuration section. This setting is valid only when applied to computers that are running Windows Server 2003 R2, Windows Server 2003 SP1, or Windows Server 2008.

Registry

The Registry preference is highly useful for modifying nearly any setting in the registry. This preference is wizard based, allowing you to find and configure the registry value and data

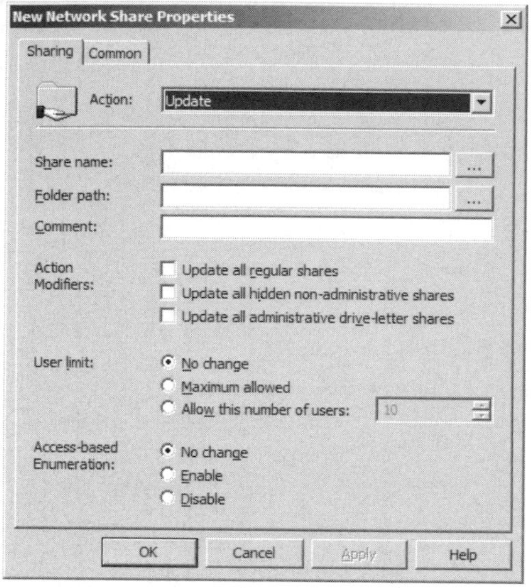

Figure 12-10   The Network Shares preference can control shares, hidden shares, and administrative shares on computers that apply Group Policy Preferences settings.

without having to code anything into a file, like you must do with .adm templates or ADMX files. This preference also allows for collections, which provide a mechanism for you to place numerous registry entries into a single location without having to keep the hierarchy needed by the registry. Finally, a remote connection wizard allows you to browse for registry values on other machines, again making it unnecessary for you to know the exact path. Figure 12-11 illustrates the interface for the Registry preference and the options that can be configured.

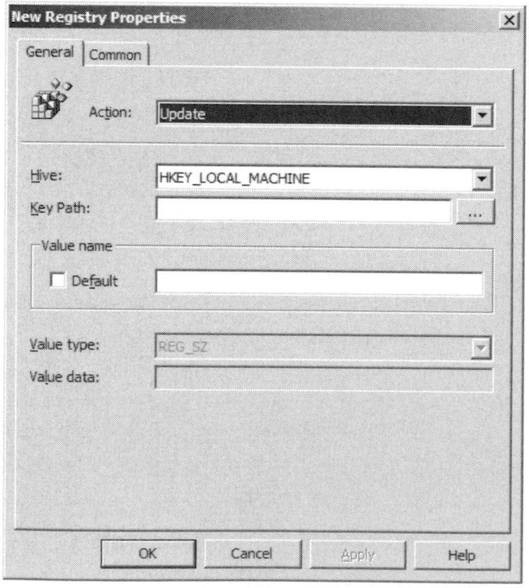

Figure 12-11   The Registry preference is GUI based and can control nearly any registry value on the target computer.

Shortcuts

The Shortcuts preference allows you to create, replace, update, and delete shortcuts from nearly anywhere on the computer. Shortcuts can include file system objects, URLs, or shell objects. The shortcuts can be placed in almost any location, including the desktop, Start menu, Favorites folder, Quick Launch toolbar, and more. Figure 12-12 illustrates the interface for the Shortcuts preference and the options that can be configured.

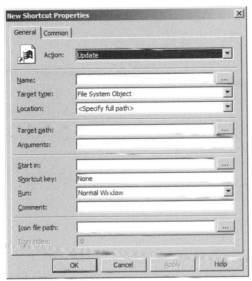

Figure 12-12   The Shortcuts preference allows you to create any type of shortcut, in nearly any location on the target computer.

Group Policy Preferences: Control Panel Settings

The following sections describe each of the Group Policy Preferences settings that fall under the Computer Configuration and User Configuration sections. If the setting falls under only one section, that is specified. If nothing is mentioned, the setting appears under both sections.

Data Sources

The Data Sources preference provides a way to centralize the configuration of Open Database Connectivity (ODBC) data sources. The data sources can be created, replaced, updated, and deleted for both users and computers. Figure 12-13 illustrates the interface for the Data Sources preference and the options that can be configured.

Devices

The Devices preference allows you to centrally control one or more devices that connect to the computer. You can enable or disable devices, including USB ports, floppy drives, removable media, and more, by using this preference. For this policy setting to function properly, the device must be active on the computer. This policy setting does not control devices or prevent

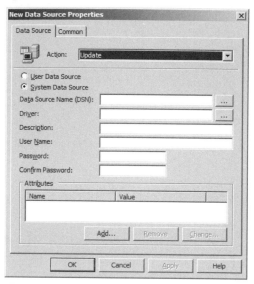

Figure 12-13   The Data Sources preference allows you to modify data source connections on any target computer.

devices from being installed. Figure 12-14 illustrates the interface for the Devices preference and the options that can be configured.

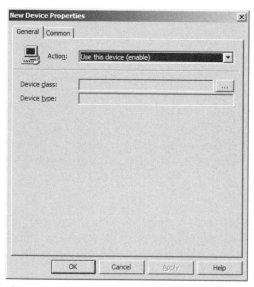

Figure 12-14   The Devices preference allows you to enable or disable devices on a target computer.

Folder Options

The Folder Options preference is divided into two parts to control two types of items. The first part includes the folder options themselves, which is further split to control settings separately for Windows XP and Windows Vista. The other part is the Open With configurations, which control file extensions and the applications that open them. Figure 12-15 illustrates the interface for the Folder Options preference and the options that can be configured.

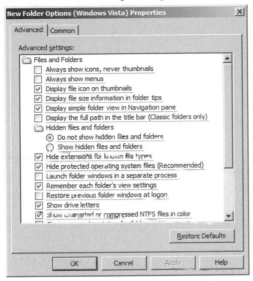

Figure 12-15   The Folder Options preference allows you to centralize the configuration of the folder options on a target computer.

Internet Settings

The Internet Settings preference provides control over Internet Explorer 5, Internet Explorer 6, and Internet Explorer 7. Some settings overlap with the Internet Explorer Maintenance settings, but these preference settings are not enforced. Figure 12-16 illustrates the interface for the Internet Settings preference and the options that can be configured.

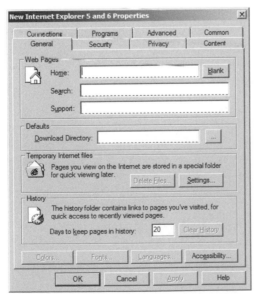

Figure 12-16   The Internet Settings preference allows you to configure security, connection, and other important settings for Internet Explorer on a target computer.

> **Note**   The Internet Settings preference is available only in the User Configuration section.

Local Users and Groups

The Local Users and Groups preference is one of the most powerful and useful of all of the Group Policy Preferences settings. This preference can control local accounts on desktops and servers that have joined a domain. It covers the creation and modification of existing accounts, including resetting the password for local accounts. This preference also controls local group accounts, including the membership of the account. Although seemingly similar to the standard Restricted Groups policy setting, the Local Users and Groups preference does not "delete and replace" the group membership. Figure 12-17 illustrates the interface for the Local Users preference and the options that can be configured.

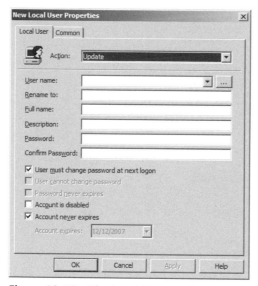

Figure 12-17   The Local Users and Groups preference allows control over local user accounts on a target computer.

Network Options

The Network Options preference provides two options for you to configure. The first is VPN connections, including settings for security and connection type. The second is Dial-Up Networking (DUN) connections, including settings for the scope of users who can make a DUN connection. Figure 12-18 illustrates the interface for the Network Options preference and the options that can be configured.

Power Options

The Power Options preference can configure power options and power schemes to control the power consumption on both desktops and mobile computers. You can control the settings as

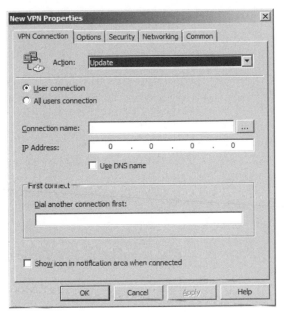

Figure 12-18   The Network Options preference allows you to control local user accounts, as well as groups and their memberships, on a target computer.

if you were controlling the computer itself. Settings include hibernation, sleep, and behavior of the computer when the power button is pressed, when the lid is closed on a laptop, and so on. Using these settings in conjunction with item-level targeting can provide a powerful way to decrease power consumption on every desktop in the organization. Windows XP and Windows Vista have different settings for Power Options because of the existing settings that are provided for Windows Vista in a GPO. Figure 12-19 illustrates the interface for the Power Options preference and the options that can be configured.

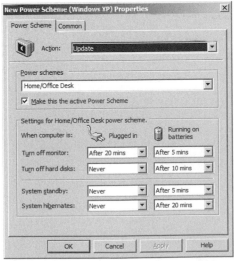

Figure 12-19   The Power Options preference allows you to control how the computer consumes power on a target computer.

Printers

The Printers preference allows you to map and configure printers. It includes options for configuring local printers, as well as for mapping TCP/IP printers or shared printers from the network. When you use this preference in conjunction with item-level targeting, you can manage printers centrally so that mobile users receive the proper printer as they go from branch office to branch office. Windows Vista Group Policy provides native support for deploying printers. However, it supports shared printers only and requires Active Directory schema extensions. In contrast, the Printers extension supports shared, local, and TCP/IP printers on Windows XP SP2 and Windows Vista, and it also allows you to configure the default printer. Figure 12-20 illustrates the interface for the Printers preference and the options that can be configured.

Figure 12-20   The Printers preference allows you to map printers (local, TCP/IP, and shared) on a target computer.

Regional Options

The Regional Options preference is simple, allowing configuration of the user locale settings, which include number, currency, time, and date formats. Figure 12-21 illustrates the interface for the Regional Options preference and the options that can be configured.

Note   The Regional Options preference is available only in the User Configuration section.

Scheduled Tasks

The Scheduled Tasks preference provides full control over existing and new scheduled tasks that will run on the targeted computer. Executables, scripts, and other command-line tools can

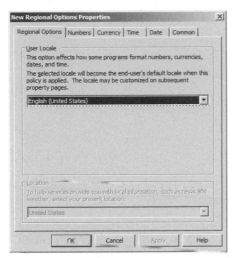

Figure 12-21   The Regional Options preference allows you to control how the computer will structure numbers, currency, time, and date formats.

be configured to run on a schedule with nearly any credential within the configured preference. Using this preference with the new Task Scheduler in Windows Vista can provide a powerful control mechanism over computers running Windows Vista. Figure 12-22 illustrates the interface for the Scheduled Tasks preference and the options that can be configured.

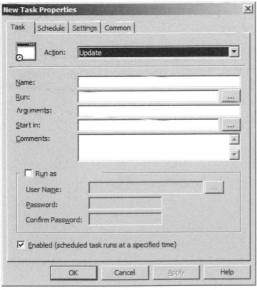

Figure 12-22   The Scheduled Tasks preference allows you to configure scheduled tasks that are created and controlled for a target computer.

Services

The Services preference gives you control over services that are running locally on each target computer. Providing the ability to control the start-up type, service account, and recovery options, the preference setting for services resolves many issues that were previously difficult to manage because of decentralized management of the services. Figure 12-23 il lustrates the interface for the Services preference and the options that can be configured.

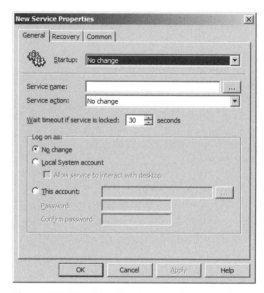

Figure 12-23 The Services preference allows you to control most options for services running on a target computer.

 Note The Services preference is available only in the Computer Configuration section.

Start Menu

The Start Menu preference provides settings to control the Start menus on both Windows XP and Windows Vista. This includes nearly every facet of the Start menu, including tools listed, formatting of the menu, and customization of the shortcuts that are displayed on the menu. Figure 12-24 illustrates the interface for the Start Menu preference and the options that can be configured.

 Note The Start Menu preference is available only in the User Configuration section.

Figure 12-24 The Start Menu preference provides centralized control over the settings related to the Start menu on a target computer.

Advanced Group Policy Preferences Settings

Group Policy Preferences come with more than just the standard settings that can be configured in the GPME. Group Policy Preferences provide advanced settings that give the settings under Preferences more control and power compared to all other Group Policy settings.

Action Modes

Group Policy Preferences settings come with a suite of action modes that control the preference being configured. The action modes perform a general set of actions, but each preference might have a slightly unique way of dealing with the action specified—it is important that you review the online Help for Windows Server 2008 for further clarification. The action modes and behavior are defined as follows:

- **Create** Create the object only if it does not already exist.

- **Replace** Delete the object first, then create it.

- **Update** Create the object if it does not exist; otherwise modify it.

- **Delete** Delete the object.

- **Migrate** Modify an item if it exists; otherwise do nothing.

Common Tab

The advanced features and settings for Group Policy Preferences are available on the Common tab when you are configuring any of the Group Policy Preferences within the GPME, as shown in Figure 12-25.

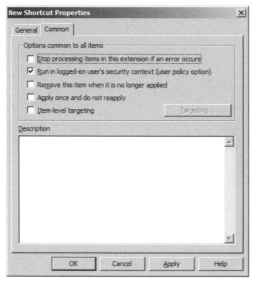

Figure 12-25   Every Group Policy Preferences setting comes with advanced settings available on the Common tab when you edit the GPO in the GPME.

The settings on the Common tab include four check boxes, an option to configure targeting, and a text box for entering a description of the GPO setting for documentation and troubleshooting purposes. The settings include the following:

- **Stop processing items in this extension if an error occurs**   The default behavior of Group Policy processing is that all settings will be processed, even if there are multiple settings with the same CSE and one of those settings fails. If you want the processing of the settings to take place within a single CSE stop after one of the settings within that CSE fails, enable this option. This setting has only the scope of the current GPO.

- **Run in logged-on user's security context (user policy option)**   When Group Policy settings (both policies and preferences) apply, they apply using the local System account. Because the local System account has access only to the system environment variables and local resources, the user context is not available. To allow access to the user environment variables and network resources, you can enable this option to process Group Policy Preferences using the logged-on user's account.

■ **Remove this item when it is no longer applied**   Group Policy Preferences settings are not removed from the registry when the GPO is removed from the user or computer, nor when the user or computer falls out of scope of management of the GPO. To have preferences settings removed when the GPO no longer applies to the user or computer object, you can enable this option.

> **Warning**   Enabling the option to remove the item when it is no longer applied will not replace the Group Policy Preferences setting with the original value. Instead, it will remove the registry value. If the operating system relies on the value that has associated data, the system could receive a stop error, causing a blue screen on the computer. Before configuring any setting with this option, you should fully test the option and understand how the registry value associated with the particular Group Policy Preferences setting is used by the operating system.

■ **Apply once and do not reapply**   Group Policy has a default refresh interval of approximately 90 minutes. This refresh interval allows new settings to be applied, and old settings to be reapplied, without requiring the computer to restart or the user to log off and log back on. If the Group Policy Preferences setting that you are configuring should apply to the computer one time only and never update on a refresh interval, you can enable this setting. This is an excellent setting for establishing an initial array of configurations that Group Policy Preferences can affect, while still allowing users to create customized environments by changing the settings after logging on and not having their settings overwritten. If the setting appears under User Configuration, Group Policy Preferences will apply these settings once on each computer the user logs on to. If the setting appears under Computer Configuration, Group Policy Preferences will apply the setting once per computer affected.

■ **Item-Level Targeting**   By default, all users and computers under the scope of management of the GPO will receive the settings within the GPO. If you want the Group Policy Preferences settings configured in a GPO to apply only to a subset of the default users and computers, you can use targeting. Over 25 targeting items are available that can be used alone or in conjunction with other items. Refer to the "Item-Level Targeting" section, later in this chapter, for more information about the targeting options and configurations.

■ **Description**   Because every Group Policy Preferences setting allows for these advanced features and settings, it is important to document the configurations of each setting. You can use the Description text box to describe the settings, options, and targeting items for each Group Policy Preferences setting. The text that you enter into this text box will appear when the Group Policy Preferences setting is selected within the GPME (without requiring you to edit the Group Policy Preferences setting itself), as shown in Figure 12-26.

Figure 12-26   The description of the Group Policy Preferences settings appears in the summary pane next to the Group Policy Preferences configured setting.

Item-Level Targeting

By default, every user and computer in the scope of management of a GPO will receive the settings contained in the GPO. Before the availability of item-level targeting, there were a few options available to alter this default application of GPO settings. These options include:

- WMI Filtering

- Block Policy Inheritance

- Enforce (per GPO, which applies to all settings in the GPO)

- Security Filtering

For more information about how GPO settings are processed for users and computers, refer to Chapter 5, "Group Policy Processing," which describes the default behavior for GPO application, as well as all options for altering default policy processing.

All of these options for altering the default processing and inheritance of GPO settings affect, at a minimum, all of the settings in a GPO. This global control of the settings within a GPO is hard to work with, hard to manage, and very difficult to troubleshoot.

Group Policy Preferences offers item-level targeting, which provides a highly granular filtering capability that is nothing like the other options that alter the default processing of GPO settings. Item-level targeting provides many benefits over the other options, including:

- Item-level targeting for each setting

- Combining of Boolean item filters, to ensure that Group Policy Preferences settings target the correct user or computer

- Over 25 targeting items to choose from

- API-based foundation, which provides fast and efficient application of the Group Policy Preferences settings

Every Group Policy Preferences setting can be configured with item-level targeting. To configure the item-level targeting for a Group Policy Preferences setting, you must access the Common tab for the setting by following these steps:

1. From the GPMC, edit a GPO that contains a Group Policy Preferences setting.

2. Right-click any configured Group Policy Preferences setting, and then click Properties.

3. In the Properties dialog box, select the Common tab.

4. Select the Item-Level Targeting check box, and then click Targeting.

5. The Targeting Editor appears, as shown in Figure 12-27.

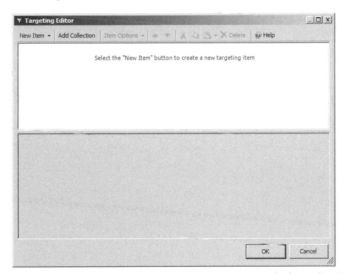

Figure 12-27   The Targeting Editor can be viewed after selecting the Item-Level Targeting check box and then clicking Targeting.

Item-Level Targeting Items

Every Group Policy Preferences setting has the full range of item-level targeting capabilities. Each item within the target provides the ability to allow or deny the application of the associated setting to the user or computer being controlled. The items within the Targeting Editor can all be referenced by clicking the New Item menu, which exposes the full list of items, as shown in Figure 12-28.

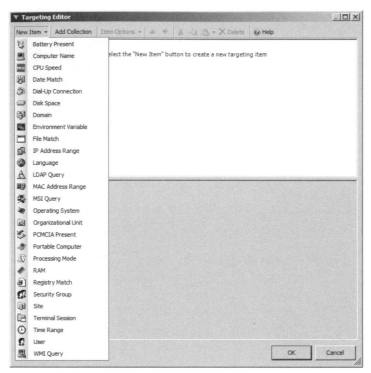

Figure 12-28   The New Item menu exposes the full list of items that can be included in the Targeting Editor.

Battery Present   A Battery Present targeting item allows a preference item to be applied to computers or users only if one or more batteries are present in the processing computer.

> **Note**   If an uninterruptible power supply (UPS) is connected to the processing computer, a Battery Present targeting item may detect the UPS and identify it as a battery.

Computer Name   A Computer Name targeting item, shown in Figure 12-29, allows a preference item to be applied to computers or users only if the computer's name matches the specified computer name in the targeting item. The Computer Name text box accepts preference processing variables. Press F3 to display the Select a Variable dialog box, which lists the system-defined variables from which you can select.

CPU Speed   A CPU Speed targeting item allows a preference item to be applied to computers or users only if the processing computer's CPU speed is greater than or equal to the value specified in the targeting item. The MHz box accepts preference processing variables. Press F3 to display the Select a Variable dialog box, which lists the system-defined variables from which you can select.

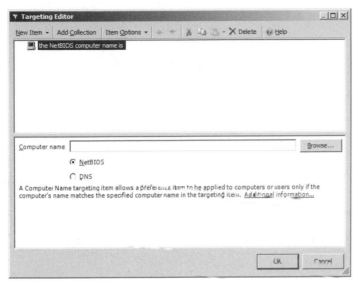

Figure 12-29 You can configure a Computer Name item in item-level targeting for Group Policy Preferences.

Date Match   A Date Match targeting item, shown in Figure 12-30, allows a preference item to be applied to computers or users only if the day or date matches that specified in the targeting item. The configuration can be for one or more days of the week (weekly), on a set date or dates each month (monthly), or on a specific date of the year (which can also be set to recur yearly).

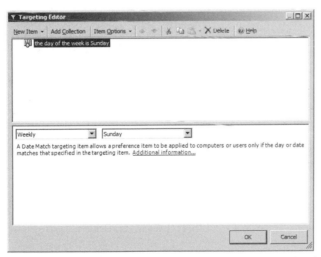

Figure 12-30 You can use a Date Match item in item-level targeting for Group Policy Preferences.

Dial-Up Connection   A Dial-Up Connection targeting item, shown in Figure 12-31, allows a preference item to be applied to users only if a network connection of the type specified in the targeting item is connected. This targeting item is available only for Group Policy Preferences settings that appear in the User Configuration section of the GPO.

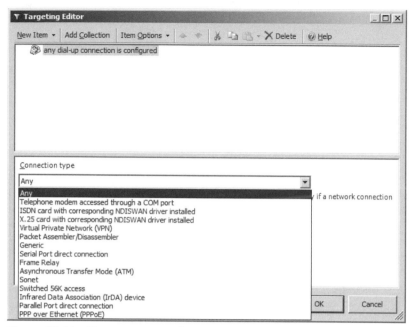

Figure 12-31   You can use a Dial-Up Connection item in item-level targeting for Group Policy Preferences.

 Note   Dial-Up Connection targeting items detect whether a type of network connection exists, not whether the user is logged on through a connection of that type.

Disk Space   A Disk Space targeting item, shown in Figure 12-32, allows a preference item to be applied to computers or users only if the processing computer's available disk spa ce is greater than or equal to the amount specified in the targeting item. The Free Disk Space list accepts preference processing variables. Press F3 to display the Select a Variable dialog box, which lists the system-defined variables from which you can select.

Domain   A Domain targeting item, shown in Figure 12-33, allows a preference item to be applied to computers or users only if the user is logged on to, or the computer is a member of, the domain or workgroup specified in the targeting item. The NetBIOS Domain Name text box accepts preference processing variables. Press F3 to display the Select a Variable dialog box, which lists the system-defined variables from which you can select.

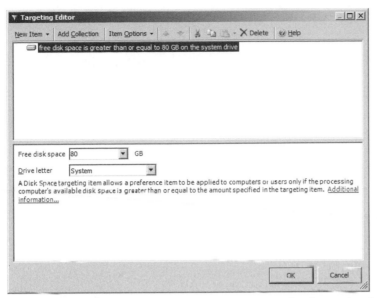

Figure 12-32   You can use a Disk Space item in item-level targeting for Group Policy Preferences.

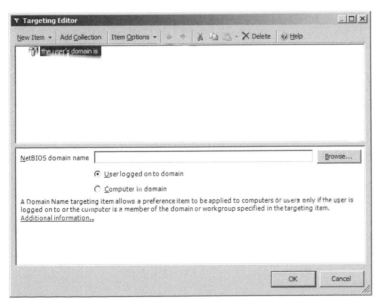

Figure 12-33   You can use a Domain item in item-level targeting for Group Policy Preferences.

Environment Variable   An Environment Variable targeting item, shown in Figure 12-34, allows a preference item to be applied to computers or users only if the Environment Variable and value specified in the targeting item are equal. The Value text box accepts preference processing variables. Press F3 to display the Select a Variable dialog box, which lists the system-defined variables from which you can select.

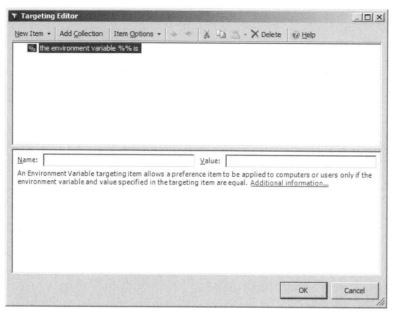

Figure 12-34   You can use an Environment Variable item in item-level targeting for Group Policy Preferences.

> **Best Practices**   If you need to use a set of item-level targeting items for many Group Policy Preferences settings, you can replace the complex array of items with a single custom environment variable. To do so, create a custom Environment Variable preference item with a value of 1 on each computer where the complex array of item-level targeting items are all true. This allows you to use the new environment variable for the other Group Policy Preferences settings on which you want to use the complex array of targeting criteria. You can now use the single variable =, instead of configuring the array of multiple item-level targeting items for each Group Policy Preferences setting.

File Match   A File Match targeting item, shown in Figure 12-35, allows a preference item to be applied to computers or users only if the file or folder specified in the targeting item exists, or only if the file exists and is a version within the range specified in the targeting item. You can select the match to be a file, folder, or file version. If you select the Match File Version option, an additional set of text boxes will appear, allowing you to enter the version range.

IP Address Range   An IP Address Range targeting item allows a preference item to be applied to computers or users only if the processing computer's IP address is within the range specified in the targeting item. Range starting points and ending points are inclusive. You can specify a single address by typing the same value in both boxes.

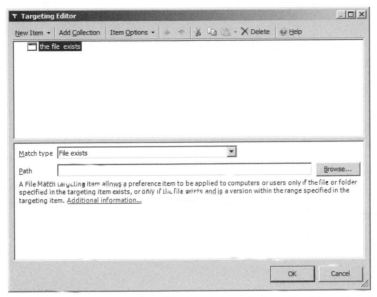

Figure 12-35   You can use a File Match item in item-level targeting for Group Policy Preferences.

Language   A Language targeting item, shown in Figure 12-36, allows a preference item to be applied to computers or users only if the locale specified in the targeting item is installed on the processing computer. Additional options allow you to restrict the targeting to the user's or computer's locale. Selecting the User check box will restrict the targeting of the item to include the user's locale. (This option is available only for Group Policy Preferences settings that appear in the User Configuration section of the GPO.) Selecting the System check box will restrict the targeting of the item to include the locale of the operating system.

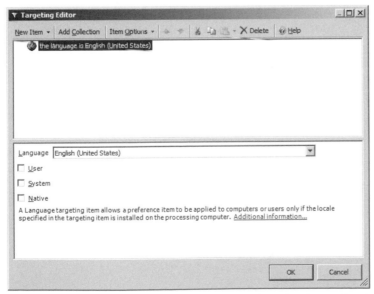

Figure 12-36   You can use a Language item in item-level targeting for Group Policy Preferences.

Selecting the Native check box will restrict the targeting of the item to include the specified locale of the NTDLL.DLL file. Selecting multiple check boxes will automatically select the OR logical operation to combine the targeted preference items together, allowing one of the languages to match that which is specified in the Language list.

LDAP Query   An LDAP Query targeting item, shown in Figure 12-37, allows a preference item to be applied to computers or users only if the LDAP query returns a value for the attribute specified in the targeting item. If the query returns any value, the LDAP Query item will process as true. The Binding configuration, such as LDAP:// CN=Employees,OU=HR,DC=contoso,DC=com, specifies where the search is performed. The Filter and Attribute configurations are optional, allowing you to narrow your criteria. The Environment Variable Name is optional and is the name of the environment variable to which the targeting item sets the value of the Attribute, if one is found.

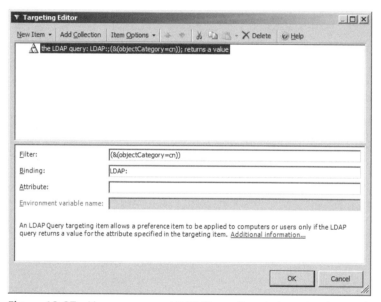

Figure 12-37   You can use an LDAP Query item in item-level targeting for Group Policy Preferences.

MAC Address Range   A MAC Address Range targeting item allows a preference item to be applied to computers or users only if any of the processing computer's MAC addresses are within the range specified in the targeting item.

MSI Query   An MSI Query targeting item, shown in Figure 12-38, allows a preference item to be applied to computers or users only if certain aspects of an MSI installed product, update, or component on the processing computer match the specified criteria in the targeting item. The item will process based on which Query Type and Target Types are selected. Table 12-3 helps clarify what the item will process based on the criteria selected.

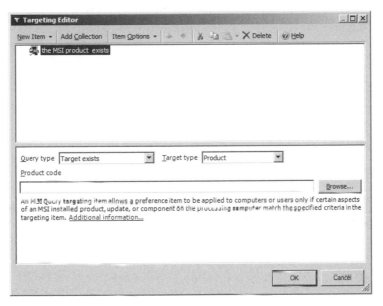

Figure 12-38 You can use an MSI Query item in item-level targeting for Group Policy Preferences.

Table 12-3 MSI Query Item-Level Targeting Criteria

Query Type	Target Type	Will Process If...
Target exists	Product	The product with the specified Product code is installed.
	Patch	The update with the specified Patch code is installed.
	Component	The keyfile of a component with the specified Component code is installed.
Version match	Product	The product with the specified Product code is within the specified version range.
	Component	The keyfile of a component with the specified Component code is within the specified version range.
Get property or Get information	Product	The product with the specified Product code is installed.
	Component	The keyfile of a component with the specified Component code is installed.
Match property or Match information	Product	The product with the specified Product code is installed.
	Component	The keyfile of a component with the specified Component code is installed.

> **Note**   The targeting item does not allow the preference item to process if the property or information item has no value.

Operating System   An Operating System targeting item, shown in Figure 12-39, allows a preference item to be applied to computers or users only if the processing computer's operating system's product name, release, edition, or computer role matches those specified in the targeting item.

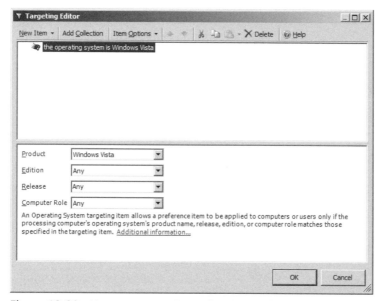

Figure 12-39   You can use an Operating System item in item-level targeting for Group Policy Preferences.

Organizational Unit   An Organizational Unit targeting item, shown in Figure 12-40, allows a preference item to be applied to computers or users only if the user or computer is a member of the organizational unit specified in the targeting item. The Organizational Unit box accepts preference processing variables. Press F3 to display the Select a Variable dialog box, which lists the system-defined variables from which you can select.

> **Note**   Having membership in a security group that is located in the configured organizational unit does not make the user or computer a member of the organizational unit.

PCMCIA Present   A PCMCIA Present targeting item allows a preference item to be applied to computers or users only if the processing computer has at least one PCMCIA (Personal Computer Memory Card International Association) slot present. A PCMCIA slot is considered present when the drivers for the slot are installed and the slot is functioning correctly.

Portable Computer   A Portable Computer targeting item, shown in Figure 12-41, allows a preference item to be applied to computers or users only if the processing computer is

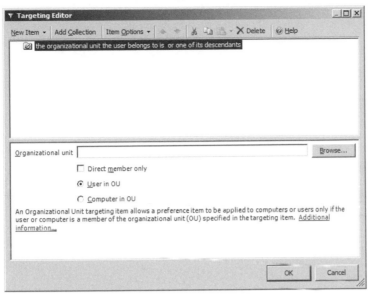

Figure 12-40   You can use an Organizational Unit item in item-level targeting for Group Policy Preferences.

identified as a portable computer in the current hardware profile on the processing computer, or if the processing computer is identified as a portable computer with the docking state specified in the targeting item. Selecting a docking state in the targeting item is optional. If no states or all states are selected, the targeting item detects only whether the processing computer is a portable computer.

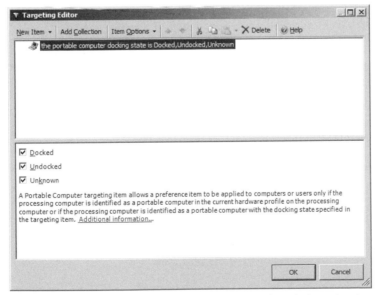

Figure 12-41   You can use a Portable Computer item in item-level targeting for Group Policy Preferences.

> **Best Practices**   Using the Battery Present item and PCMCIA Present item in conjunction with the Portable Computer Query item can also be useful for targeting portable computers.

Processing Mode   A Processing Mode targeting item, shown in Figure 12-42, allows a preference item to be applied to computers or users only if the Group Policy processing mode or conditions on the processing computer match at least one of those specified in the targeting item. Table 12-4 defines each option for the Processing Mode item.

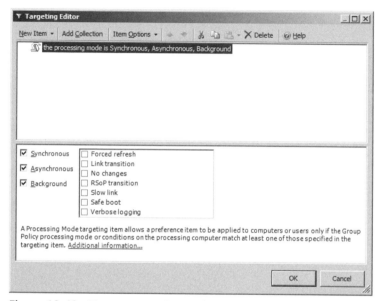

Figure 12-42   You can use a Processing Mode item in item-level targeting for Group Policy Preferences.

Table 12-4   Processing Mode Configuration Options

Processing Mode or Condition	Description
Synchronous	GPO processing is set to synchronous.
Asynchronous	GPO processing is set to asynchronous.
Background	GPO processing is performed in the background, not foreground.
Forced refresh	The background refresh was forced.
Link transition	A change in link speed occurred between the current application and an earlier application of Group Policy.
No changes	No new Group Policy settings are applied to the computer or user.
RSoP transition	A change in Resultant Set of Policy (RSoP) logging occurred between the current application and an earlier application of Group Policy.
Slow link	Group Policy is applying over a slow network connection.
Safe boot	Windows is operating in safe mode.
Verbose logging	Verbose logging is enabled.

RAM   A RAM targeting item allows a preference item to be applied to computers or users only if the total amount of physical memory in the processing computer is greater than or equal to the amount specified in the targeting item. The MB list accepts preference processing variables. Press F3 to display the Select a Variable dialog box, which lists the system-defined variables from which you can select.

Registry Match   A Registry Match targeting item, shown in Figure 12-43, allows a preference item to be applied to computers or users only if the registry key or value specified in the targeting item exists, if the registry value contains the data specified in the targeting item, or if the version number in the registry value is within the range specified in the targeting item. If the targeting item allows the preference item and if Get Value Data is selected in the targeting item, the targeting item saves the value data of the specified registry value to the environment variable specified in the targeting item. The Key Path text box and Value Name text box accept preference processing variables. Press F3 to display the Select a Variable dialog box, which lists the system-defined variables from which you can select.

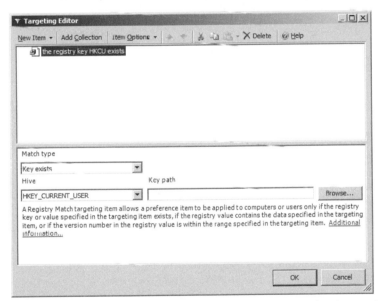

Figure 12-43   You can use a Registry Match item in item-level targeting for Group Policy Preferences.

Security Group   A Security Group targeting item, shown in Figure 12-44, allows a preference item to be applied to computers or users only if the processing computer or user is a member of the group specified in the targeting item and, optionally, only if the specified group is the primary group for the processing computer or user. The group's security identifier is used to determine group membership, not the display name of the group. The types of groups that are supported include:

- Domain groups
    - Global groups
    - Universal groups

- Local groups

    □ Local groups (including built-in groups)

    □ Domain local groups

    □ Well-known groups

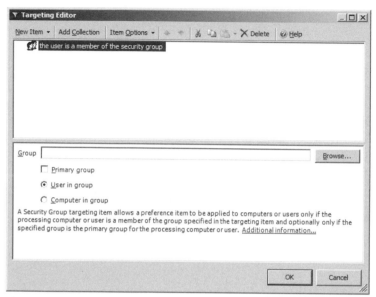

Figure 12-44 You can use a Security Group item in item-level targeting for Group Policy Preferences.

Site A Site targeting item allows a preference item to be applied to computers or users only if the processing computer is in the site in Active Directory specified in the targeting item. The Site box accepts preference processing variables. Press F3 to display the Select a Variable dialog box, which lists the system-defined variables from which you can select.

Terminal Session A Terminal Session targeting item allows a preference item to be applied to users only if the processing user is logged on to a terminal services session with the settings specified in the targeting item.

Time Range A Time Range targeting item allows a preference item to be applied to computers or users only if the current time on the end user's computer is within the time range specified in the targeting item.

User A User targeting item, shown in Figure 12-45, allows a preference item to be applied to users only if the processing user is the user specified in the targeting item. When the Match by SID option is enabled, you must browse to select the user. If you do not select Match by SID, a string match is performed. Although the domain and user name of that user at the time of selection are displayed, the targeting item saves the user's SID for comparison to that of the processing user. The User text box accepts preference processing variables. Press F3 to display the Select a Variable dialog box, which lists the system-defined variables from which you can select.

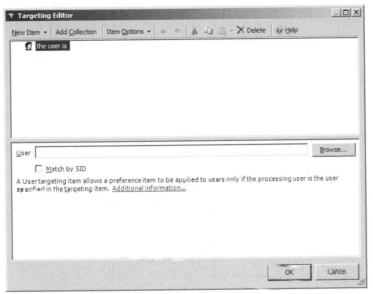

Figure 12-45   You can use a User item in item-level targeting for Group Policy Preferences.

Note   User targeting is available only for preference items under User Configuration.

WMI Query   A WMI Query targeting item, shown in Figure 12-46, allows a preference item to be applied to computers or users only if the processing computer evaluates the WMI query as true. If any of the value is returned from the query, the filter will return true.

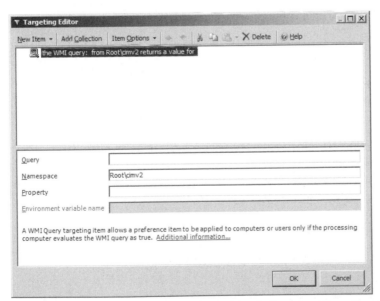

Figure 12-46   You can use a WMI Query item in item-level targeting for Group Policy Preferences.

> **Note**   For more information about processing variables described in any of these item-level targeting items, see the "Process Variables" section, later in this chapter.

> **Note**   For all of the item-level targeting items, text boxes for Computer Name (NetBIOS only), Domain, Site, Terminal Session, and User (if not matched by SID) accept single-character (?) and multiple-character (*) wildcards.

Item-Level Targeting Controls

For each target item or group of items that you create, the result will be a returned value of true or false. If you choose to include multiple targeting items in one decision, you must use the logical operators, AND or OR, to combine the items so that a final decision can be made from the target item suite. All of the items will be considered with the logical operators that you configure. The final result of all items and logical operations together will be a single true or false.

To change whether an item uses an AND or an OR, follow these steps from within the Targeting Editor:

1.   Select the item from the list of selected items.

2.   Right-click the item, and then click Item Options.

3.   Click either AND or OR.

You can also include or exclude the item decision that you have configured. This is controlled by the IS or IS NOT configuration, which is per item listed in the Targeting Editor. To configure this setting for an existing item listed in the Targeting Editor, follow these steps:

1.   Select the item from the list of selected items.

2.   Right-click the item, and then click Item Options.

3.   Click either IS or IS NOT.

If the list of targeting items that you need to use become too numerous with too many logical operators, it is a best practice to use the targeting collection item. This item allows you to create parenthetical expressions. Like an algebra equation, the targeting collection allows you to make decisions on items within the overall expression. Figure 12-47 illustrates a complex expression within the Targeting Editor.

Common Item-Level Targeting Scenarios

Item-level targeting has been used in many scenarios to provide extra value to the Group Policy Preferences settings, as well as for unique environments. Common scenarios include the following.

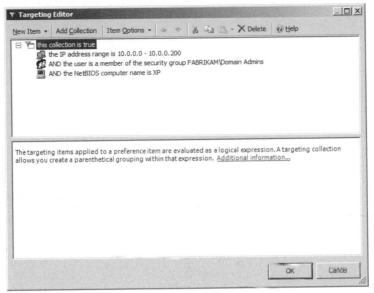

Figure 12-47 The Targeting Collection item allows you to create complex targeting queries, which function similar to parenthetical expressions.

Desktop vs. Laptop There may be times when you want to delineate your laptops from your desktops. You may want to do this for many reasons, such as to configure VPN connections for mobile users, configure printers differently between the two types of computers, and many more possibilities. You can accomplish this easily by using the Portable Computer targeting item. If you were to create an environment variable using the Environment Variable item, you could affix to each an easy way of querying the computer type, which could be used by any of the targeting items.

Computer Performance Depending on the setting that you are delivering or making on the target computer, faster computers might need one setting level and slower computers a different setting level. Another factor might be disk space—some settings could be applied to only computers that meet certain disk space criteria. By using the CPU Speed item and Disk Space item, you can target each preference as required.

Operating System Targeting With the targeting item that allows for separation of all operating system versions that support Group Policy Preferences, you can now use the Operating System item to target any Group Policy Preferences setting to the operating system that you want. This is especially useful for settings and features that are valid only on certain operating systems.

Drive Mapping Security Many companies have financial or human resources applications that access private data. The data is usually located on the network, but some users have access to the drive mapping even though they do not have the application installed. Instead of allowing all users in a department to have a mapped drive to a private data share, you can use the File Match item or the Registry Match item to narrow the scope of users who receive the drive mapping to the private data. The File Match item and the Registry Match item can target the installation files and registry values to ensure that the application is installed.

Process Variables

Group Policy Preferences also provide a seamless integration with environment variables. The environment variables that Group Policy Preferences support include those that the system generates, as well as numerous additional environment variables to the process environment.

The environment variables are available for use in many of the text boxes associated with Group Policy Preferences. Some of the settings allow for environment variables, as do some of the item-level targeting entries. As a general rule, if the environment variable contains text properties that are associated with the text box you are filling out, the environment variable will function properly.

To access the environment variables via a shortcut, press the F3 key from within the text box where you want to use the environment variable. The Select a Variable dialog box appears, as shown in Figure 12-48.

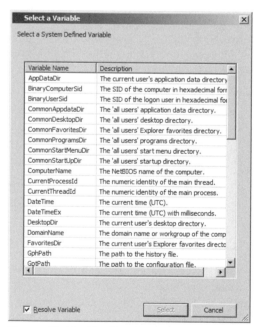

Figure 12-48 The list of supported environment variables appears when you press F3 from within the GPME; this can help you configure Group Policy Preferences settings and targeting items.

The environment variables that are supported in Group Policy Preferences settings include those listed in Table 12-5.

Table 12-5   Environment Variables Supported in Group Policy Preferences

Environment Variable	Variable Use
%AppDataDir%	The current user's Application Data directory
%BinaryComputerSid%	The SID of the computer in hexadecimal format
%BinaryUserSid%	The SID of the log-on user in hexadecimal format
%CommonAppdataDir%	The "all users" Application Data directory
%CommonDesktopDir%	The "all users" Desktop directory
%CommonFavoritesDir%	The "all users" Explorer Favorites directory
%CommonProgramsDir%	The "all users" Programs directory
%CommonStartMenuDir%	The "all users" Start Menu directory
%CommonStartUpDir%	The "all users" Startup directory
%ComputerName%	The NetBIOS name of the computer
%CurrentProcessId%	The numeric identity of the main client process
%CurrentThreadId%	The numeric identity of the main client thread
%DateTime%	The current time (UTC)
%DateTimeEx%	The current time (UTC) with milliseconds
%DesktopDir%	The current user's Desktop directory
%DomainName%	The domain name or workgroup of the computer
%FavoritesDir%	The current user's Explorer Favorites directory
GphPath	The path to the Group Policy history file
GptPath	The path to the Group Policy configuration file
GroupPolicyVersion	The version of the running Group Policy CSE
LastDriveMapped	The drive letter of the last successful network drive mapping
%LastError%	The last error code encountered during configuration
%LastErrorText%	The last error code text description
%LdapComputerSid%	The SID of the computer in LDAP escaped binary format
%LdapUserSid%	The SID of the current user in LDAP escaped binary format
%LocalTime%	The current local time
%LocalTimeEx%	The current local time with milliseconds
%LogonDomain%	The domain of the current user
%LogonServer%	The domain controller that authenticated the current user
%LogonUser%	The user name of the current user
%LogonUserSid%	The SID of the current user
%MacAddress%	The first detected MAC address on the computer
%NetPlacesDir%	The current user's My Network Places directory
%OsVersion%	The operating system: Windows Server 2008, Windows Vista, Windows Server 2003 R2, Windows Server 2003, Windows XP, or Unknown
%ProgramFilesDir%	The Windows Program Files directory
%ProgramsDir%	The current user's Programs directory

Table 12-5   Environment Variables Supported in Group Policy Preferences

Environment Variable	Variable Use
%RecentDocumentsDir%	The current user's Recent Documents directory
%ResultCode%	The client's exit code
%ResultText%	The client's exit code text description
%ReversedComputerSid%	The SID of the computer in reversed byte order hexadecimal format
%ReversedUserSid%	The SID of the current user in reversed byte order hexadecimal format
%SendToDir%	The current user's Send To directory
%StartMenuDir%	The current user's Start Menu directory
%StartUpDir%	The current user's Startup directory
%SystemDir%	The Windows System directory
%SystemDrive%	The name of the drive from which the operation system is running
%TempDir%	The current user's Temp directory as determined by Windows API, which is Local System when running in the computer context.
%TimeStamp%	The time stamp of the configurations being executed
%TraceFile%	The path/name of the trace file
%WindowsDir%	The Windows directory

Group Policy Preferences in Settings Reports

Another great feature of Group Policy Preferences is their inclusion in the reports that are generated using the GPMC. Group Policy Preferences will be included on the GPMC Settings tab for the GPO, as well as when a GPO is saved to a file.

To see the Group Policy Preferences settings and filters within a GPO on the Settings tab, follow these steps:

1. In the GPMC, expand the forest node, and then expand the domain node.

2. Expand the Group Policy Objects node.

3. Select the GPO for which you want to see a report.

4. In the details pane, click the Settings tab.

5. Select Close or Add in the Internet Explorer warning dialog box. (This step might be optional, depending on your Internet Explorer security settings.)

You will see the full list of settings within the GPO, for both computer configuration and user configuration, as shown in Figure 12-49.

When you save the report for a GPO in HTML format using the GPMC, the Group Policy Preferences settings and targeting items that are configured in the GPO are also included. To save a report of a GPO in HTML format from within the GPMC, follow these steps:

1. In the GPMC, expand the forest node, and then expand the domain node.

2. Expand the Group Policy Objects node.

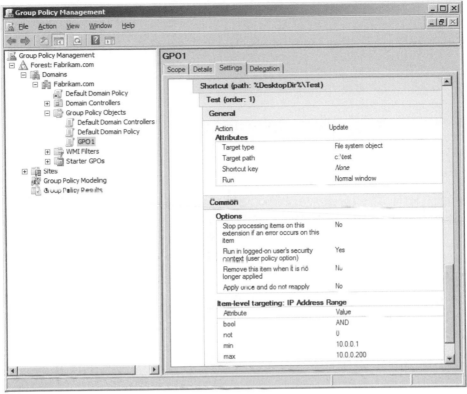

Figure 12-49 Group Policy Preferences settings and targeting items are reported on the Settings tab within the GPMC for each GPO with a configured preference.

3. Right-click the GPO for which you want to save a report, and then click Save Report. The Save GPO Report dialog box appears.

4. Click Browse Folders (this option may already be active), select the location where the report will be saved, type a name for the report in the File Name text box, and then select a file type (HTML or XML) from the Save As Type drop-down list.

5. Click Save.

For more information about the GPMC and generating reports, refer to Chapter 6, "GPMC Basics," and Chapter 7, "Advanced GPMC Management."

Software Development Kit for Group Policy Preferences

The settings associated with the Group Policy Preferences Applications and Mail Services are extendable. Any vendor or customer can extend these areas to make custom entries for personal use. This could include line-of-business applications with settings that snap in directly to the Group Policy Preferences Applications node within the GPME.

Summary

Group Policy Preferences are one of the most important and powerful additions to Group Policy for Windows Server 2008 and Windows Vista. With over 20 client-side extensions, Group Policy Preferences more than double the previous number of CSEs, as well as the number of overall settings available in a GPO.

Management of Group Policy Preferences is provided through integrated solutions for Windows Server 2008 and through the RSAT on Windows Vista. Operating systems as early as Windows XP SP2 can support the application of Group Policy Preferences.

The overall settings, control features, and item-level targeting options give Group Policy Preferences power and precision during application. Group Policy Preferences give administrations an advantage when deploying the settings, because they remove many of the Active Directory design and targeting limitations that were prevalent before Group Policy Preferences were available.

Additional Resources

- The Microsoft download page at *http://www.microsoft.com/downloads/ details.aspx?FamilyID=92D8519A-E143-4AEE-8F7A-E4BBAEBA13E7&displaylang=en* allows you to download the applications preferences settings for Microsoft Office.

- The 2007 Office Resource Kit page titled "Enforce Settings by Using Group Policy in the 2007 Office System," at *http://technet2.microsoft.com/Office/en-us/library/873a5392-1b1a-47a1-a863-1f29ef116d0e1033.mspx?mfr=true*, provides information about using the .adm template files for the Microsoft Office suite.

- The TechNet article titled "Managing Group Policy ADMX Files Step-by-Step Guide," at *http://technet2.microsoft.com/WindowsVista/en/library/02633470-396c-4e34-971a-0c5b090dc4fd1033.mspx?mfr=true*, provides information about using ADMX files for Windows Vista.

- The 2007 Office Resource Kit page titled "Office Customization Tool in the 2007 Office System," at *http://technet2.microsoft.com/Office/en-us/library/8faae8a0-a12c-4f7b-839c-24a66a531bb51033.mspx?mfr=true*, provides information about using the Office Customization Tool in the 2007 Office system.

- Chapter 4, "Architecture of Group Policy," includes information about the storage of .adm templates in the Group Policy template (GPT) of a GPO.

- Chapter 5, "Group Policy Processing," includes information about how Group Policy processes settings using CSEs.

- Chapter 6, "GPMC Basics," includes information about the GPMC.

- Chapter 7, "Advanced GPMC Management," includes information about backing up and reporting on GPO settings using the GPMC.

- Chapter 10, "ADM Templates, ADMX Files, and the ADMX Central Store," includes information about the use of .adm templates, ADMX files, and the central store.

Chapter 13

Settings Breakdown for Windows Server 2008 and Windows Vista

With over 5,000 settings in a single GPO, there are plenty of options that you can configure. This chapter is designed to help you understand the structure of a GPO, as well as the areas of configuration that are available. This chapter is not designed to examine every setting and option—that would be an entire book by itself. Understanding how the GPO is structured, the settings that are available under the various nodes, and the overall reasoning behind the organization of settings is important for any administrator of Group Policy to understand.

Throughout this chapter, you will find references to documents and Web sites that provide further information on the definitions and configurations for the GPO settings under specified nodes. As with any complex and powerful technology, you should test all GPO settings in a test environment before implementing them in a production environment.

This chapter ends with a summary of settings for each topic that you might want to configure. The goal of these summaries is to help you optimize your efforts and research when you need to configure computers for specific technologies or areas of configuration. These summaries do not include every possible setting for each topic; they are merely guides to help you find settings more quickly and hopefully encompass a larger array of settings as you consider each topic for your network.

Overall GPO Structure

A new structure within a GPO highlights the areas that can be configured. Within the two main sections of a GPO, Computer Configuration and User Configuration (described in

Chapter 3, "Group Policy Basics"), you will see two new nodes: Policies and Preferences. This structure is shown in Figure 13-1.

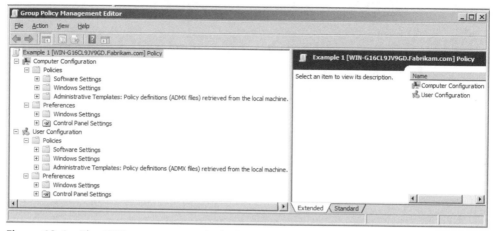

Figure 13-1   The GPO structure now includes two top-level nodes: Policies and Preferences.

The settings included under the Policies node are designed to be enforced. This means that when a setting is made under this node, the user will not be able to modify that setting through the user interface. Instead, the interface will deny access to that user, or the option will be dimmed.

The settings included under the Preferences node are designed to be less rigid than the settings under the Policies node. These settings will modify the setting that exists on the computer, but they will not prohibit the user from changing the setting in the interface.

> **Note**   For more information about the differences between policies and preferences, refer to Chapter 12, "Group Policy Preferences," which includes detailed information about how these two technologies differ.

Policies

Experienced users of Group Policy are familiar with the Policies node and subnodes. There are new settings within the nodes, but the node structure should be very familiar, including the standard Software Settings, Windows Settings, and Administrative Templates nodes that have been included since Windows 2000. The following is a brief summary of each of the sections, with overviews of the subnodes of settings in each.

Software Settings

The Software Settings node is where you can configure the deployment of software to both computer and user accounts. There are slight differences between deploying software to computers and users, but they are minimal. Here are some things you should be aware of when deploying software using Group Policy (Figure 13-2 illustrates the interface for the Software Settings):

■ You should ensure that the installation package is located in a shared folder that can be referenced using a Universal Naming Convention (UNC) path, such as \\Server1\Apps\app1.msi.

■ You should ensure that the permissions to the shared folder where the installation package resides are sufficient to access the software to be installed.

■ You should ensure that the permissions to the installation package are sufficient to install the software.

■ Software can be assigned to both computer and user accounts. Assignment will place an icon for the application on the Start menu, as if the application is installed.

■ Software can be published to user accounts. Publishing software will add the application to the Add/Remove Programs list. Users must install the application from the Add/Remove Programs applet in Control Panel manually.

■ Generally, installation packages that have an .msi extension will be deployed using Group Policy.

■ Applications that have only an .exe installation can be used in conjunction with a .zap package for deployment using Group Policy. For more information about .zap packages, refer to the Microsoft TechNet article "File Types That You Use with Group Policy Software Installation," at *http://technet2.microsoft.com/windowsserver/en/library/3512b600-5bb4-4dae-8b2c-7b71ef9951a01033.mspx?mfr=true*, which provides information about the syntax of the .zap package.

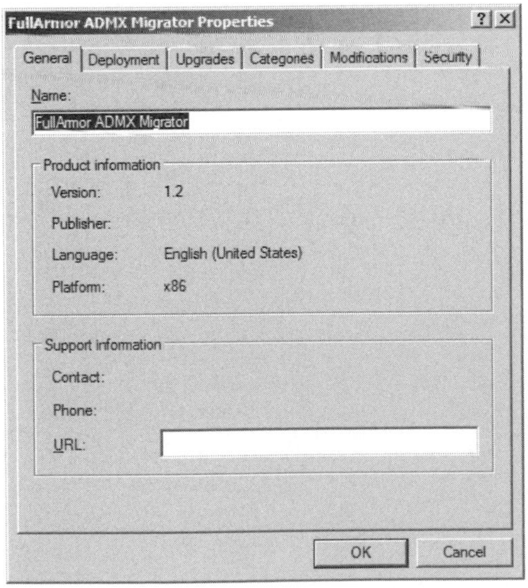

Figure 13-2   The Software Settings policy allows you to configure the software deployment.

- Software deployed using Group Policy can be updated using .msp packages, which can also deploy bug fixes and service packs.

- Specific software applications can be installed from a suite of applications by using an .mst (transform) package.

- Software deployed using Group Policy can also remove the application if the computer or user falls out of the scope of management (SOM). For more information about SOM, refer to Chapter 5, "Group Policy Processing."

> **Note** For more details about deploying software using Group Policy, refer to the Microsoft TechNet article "Group Policy Software Installation Overview," at *http://technet2.microsoft.com/ WindowsServer/en/library/b7c2efc1-207e-4089-8490-0d002daf8b6c1033.mspx?mfr=true*, where you will find detailed steps for using this setting.

Windows Settings

The Windows Settings node is a large, high-level Group Policy node that contains settings ranging from log-on scripts to IPsec policies. The majority of the settings that fall under this node are security related. The Security Settings node and its subnodes contain essential settings that help secure domain controllers, servers, and desktops. You will want to spend time with these settings to ensure that you have covered all of the possible options that you want for protecting your network, communication on the network, and data that resides on the computers.

Remote Installation Services (User Configuration Only)

This policy is designed to control the options that users have when they initiate Remote Installation Services (RIS). The four areas of configuration, shown in Figure 13-3, include:

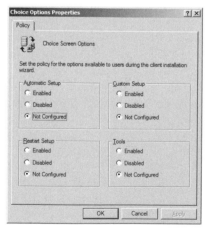

Figure 13-3   The RIS policy allows you to configure user options at the beginning of a RIS installation.

- Automatic Setup

- Custom Setup

- Restart Setup

- Tools

Scripts

You can configure four types of scripts using Group Policy. Two reside under the Computer Configuration section, and two reside under the User Configuration section. With scripts, you can make configurations when the "object" being targeted starts and then ends.

For example, the scripts that coincide with a computer starting and shutting down are Startup scripts and Shutdown scripts. Similarly, user accounts can have Logon scripts and Logoff scripts.

Note   For more information about the four types of scripts available using Group Policy, including examples, refer to the TechNet article (in two parts) at *http://www.microsoft.com/ technet/scriptcenter/topics/gp/extension1.mspx* and *http://www.microsoft.com/technet/ scriptcenter/topics/gp/extension2.mspx*, which provides an in-depth explanation of the scripting extension, examples, and information about how to troubleshoot issues related to scripts.

Security Settings

The Security Settings node contains many subnodes that are essential to your Active Directory domain, as well as the overall security of your network. Settings under this node and its subnodes are included in both the Default Domain Policy and the Default Domain Controllers Policy, which can be referenced in Chapter 3. The important subnodes that you will find under the Security Settings node include Account Policies, User Rights Assignment, Restricted Groups, and Software Restriction Policies. You will notice that under the Computer Configuration section, the Security Settings node has many more settings than it does under the User Configuration section.

Best Practices   For best practice guidelines on establishing security settings for domain controllers, servers, desktops, and more, refer to the Windows Server 2003 Security Guide at *http://www.microsoft.com/technet/security/prodtech/windowsserver2003/w2003hg/ sgch00.mspx*.

Account Policies (Computer Configuration Only)   This node and its subnodes contain some of the most important security settings for your Active Directory domain and for the computers that are joined to the domain. Within this node, you will find the three important security nodes that control user account passwords, lockout policy, and Kerberos policy settings.

- **Password Policy**   This node and its settings control the passwords for user accounts. The Default Domain Policy uses these settings to establish the default password policy for all domain user accounts, as well as for local user accounts on domain member computers.

> **Note**   Refer to Chapter 3 for more information about the default settings configured in the Default Domain Policy.

- **Account Lockout Policy**   This node and its settings control how the system reacts when users forget their passwords. You can control how many log-on attempts users have and how long they are locked out of the system if they fail to remember their passwords.

- **Kerberos Policy**   Although it is not a standard practice to alter the settings under this node, you can modify nearly every aspect of the Kerberos ticket-granting process with these settings.

Local Policies (Computer Configuration Only)   The settings under the Local Policies node in a GPO are designed to target the settings that reside on every computer. They are called "local" policies because these settings reside locally on each and every computer on the network. In some situations, a grouping of computers (for example, all computers in the HR department) must have the exact same settings that fall under these nodes. In other cases, different groupings of computers (for example, Web servers versus Microsoft Exchange servers) must have different settings. Group Policy in conjunction with Active Directory structuring can make the implementation of these scenarios easy to deploy. For more information about how Group Policy works with Active Directory structuring, refer to Chapter 4, "Architecture of Group Policy," and Chapter 5.

- **Audit Policy**   These settings allow you to track activity to Event Viewer. The available options are numerous, including tracking account management, computer tasks (such as logon using Terminal Services or performance of a backup), file access, and user logon. The list of audit policy settings includes:

  - ❑ Audit account log-on events
  - ❑ Audit account management
  - ❑ Audit directory service access
  - ❑ Audit log-on events
  - ❑ Audit object access
  - ❑ Audit policy change
  - ❑ Audit privilege use
  - ❑ Audit process tracking
  - ❑ Audit system events

- **User Rights Assignment**   Management of a computer occurs at the computer and is controlled by user rights. The ability to log on locally, log on over the network, back up files, generate security audits, and much more is controlled by user rights. The full list of user rights includes the following:

  - ❏ Access this computer from the network
  - ❏ Act as part of the operating system
  - ❏ Add workstations to domain
  - ❏ Adjust memory quotas for a process
  - ❏ Allow logon through Terminal Services
  - ❏ Back up files and directories
  - ❏ Bypass traverse checking
  - ❏ Change the system time
  - ❏ Create a pagefile
  - ❏ Create a token object
  - ❏ Create global objects
  - ❏ Create permanent shared objects
  - ❏ Debug programs
  - ❏ Deny access to this computer from the network
  - ❏ Deny logon as a batch job
  - ❏ Deny logon as a service
  - ❏ Deny logon locally
  - ❏ Deny logon through Terminal Services
  - ❏ Enable computer and user accounts to be trusted for delegation
  - ❏ Force shutdown from a remote system
  - ❏ Generate security audits
  - ❏ Impersonate a client after authentication
  - ❏ Increase scheduling priority
  - ❏ Load and unload device drivers
  - ❏ Lock pages in memory
  - ❏ Log on as a batch job
  - ❏ Log on as a service
  - ❏ Log on locally

- ❏   Manage auditing and security log
- ❏   Modify firmware environment values
- ❏   Perform volume maintenance tasks
- ❏   Profile single process
- ❏   Profile system performance
- ❏   Remove computer from docking station
- ❏   Replace a process level token
- ❏   Restore files and directories
- ❏   Shut down the system
- ❏   Synchronize directory service data
- ❏   Take ownership of files and other objects

- ■ **Security Options**   With nearly 80 settings under this node, you have many options to choose from to help secure your domain controllers, servers, and desktops. The settings under this node are primarily for prohibiting access to the computer, as well as for communicating with other computers over the network. The settings are divided into subcategories, which include the following:

  - ❏   Accounts
  - ❏   Audit
  - ❏   DCOM
  - ❏   Devices
  - ❏   Domain controller
  - ❏   Domain member
  - ❏   Interactive logon
  - ❏   Microsoft network client
  - ❏   Microsoft network server
  - ❏   Network access
  - ❏   Network security
  - ❏   Recovery console
  - ❏   Shutdown
  - ❏   System cryptography
  - ❏   System objects
  - ❏   System settings
  - ❏   User Account Control

- **Event Log** These settings allow you to control the three primary logs in Event Viewer: Application, Security, and System. These three logs can be managed in the following ways:

    - By size of log
    - By retention method
    - By days to retain log
    - By access to log

Restricted Groups (Computer Configuration Only) This setting allows you to centralize the group membership of both groups that reside in Active Directory and those that live locally in the Security Accounts Manager (SAM) on each computer, referred to as local groups. The setting allows you to control group membership, which includes both user accounts and group accounts. You can also control the groups in which a specified group has membership. Both options are shown in Figure 13-4.

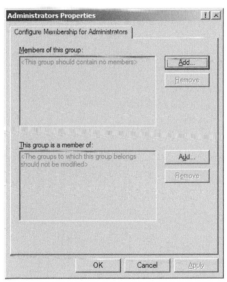

Figure 13-4 The Restricted Groups policy allows you to control group membership.

Warning Restricted Groups is a delete-and-replace policy. This means that if you define a list of user and group accounts to have membership in a specified group, the existing group members will first be deleted and replaced with the user and group accounts that you define in the policy.

Note If you want to control the membership of local groups without having the delete-and-replace behavior of Restricted Groups, consider using Group Policy Local Users and Groups, which are described in Chapter 12.

System Services (Computer Configuration Only)   This policy allows you to control certain aspects of services that reside on the target computer. The settings available in this policy include the ability to control the following aspects of services (also shown in Figure 13-5):

■ Start-up mode

■ Security permissions to control service

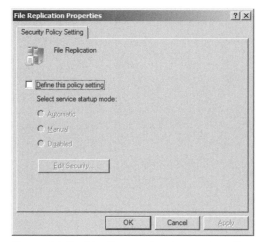

Figure 13-5   The System Services policy allows you to control the start-up mode and permissions of the service.

Note   To control more details of services that are running on target computers, you can use Group Policy Services, described in Chapter 12.

Registry (Computer Configuration Only)   This policy is designed to control permissions on registry keys. You can control the full array of NTFS permissions, including advanced permissions, auditing, and ownership of the objects configured in the policy. After the policy is configured, you have the option of controlling whether the permissions will propagate down through the subkeys in the registry or only apply to the registry key defined, as shown in Figure 13-6.

Warning   Application of permissions to registry keys can be resource intensive and cause delayed computer start-up. You should use this policy only when absolutely necessary and only after testing to ensure that the performance of the start-up is satisfactory for your production environment.

File System (Computer Configuration Only)   Like the Registry policy, this policy allows you to configure NTFS permissions for files and folders on a target computer. You can configure advanced permissions, auditing, and ownership, as well as propagation of the permissions to subfolders.

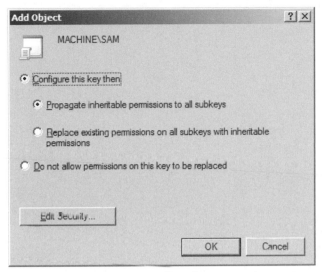

Figure 13-6   The Registry policy allows you to control security permissions and other NTFS aspects of registry keys.

Warning   Application of permissions to files and folders can be resource intensive and cause delayed computer start-up. You should use this policy only when absolutely necessary and only after testing to ensure that the performance of the start-up is satisfactory for your production environment.

Wired Network (IEEE 802.3) Policies (Computer Configuration Only)   This policy is designed to control wired network security for computers running Windows Vista. The settings in this policy allow you to control many areas of network security. Some of the settings that you can control include the following, which can also be seen in Figures 13-7 and 13-8:

- Authentication protocols
- Authentication modes
- Single sign on controls

Windows Firewall with Advanced Security (Computer Configuration Only)   The updated firewall that comes with Windows Vista and Windows Server 2008 provides additional configurations that enable granular security control over inbound and outbound communications and connection-specific security. You can configure these policies through a set of wizards.

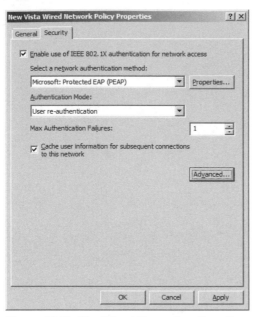

Figure 13-7   The Wired Network policy allows control over the authentication protocol and modes.

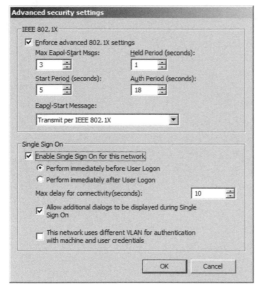

Figure 13-8   Advanced settings in the Wired Network policy allow control over single sign on and advanced IEEE 802.1x settings.

■ **Inbound Rule**   This policy allows you to configure the security of all inbound communications to the target computer. It allows you to configure the type of rule that will be configured (program, ports, services, or customized configuration), action for the rule (allow or block communications), and scope of the rule (domain, private, or public). The interface for the inbound rule is shown in Figure 13-9.

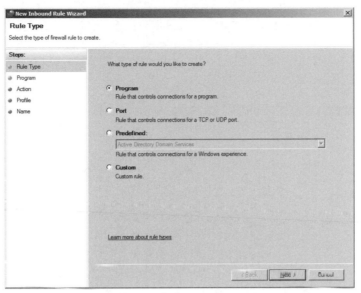

Figure 13-9   This figure shows the Inbound Rule Wizard for the Windows Firewall and Advanced Security policy.

- **Outbound Rule**   This policy allows you to configure the security of all outbound communications to the target computer. It allows you to configure the type of rule that will be configured (program, ports, services, or customized configuration), action for the rule (allow or block communications), and scope of the rule (domain, private, or public). The interface for the outbound rule is shown in Figure 13-10.

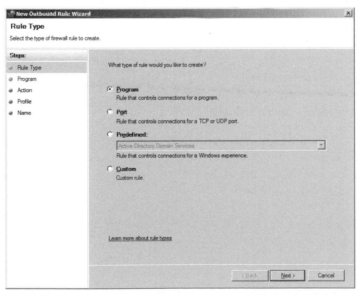

Figure 13-10   This figure shows the Outbound Rule Wizard for the Windows Firewall and Advanced Security policy.

■ **Connection Security Rule**   This policy allows you to configure connection-specific security for the target computer. It allows you to configure the type of rule that will be configured (isolation, authentication controls, server-to-server, tunnel, or custom communication), authentication for the rule, and scope of the rule (domain, private, or public). The interface for the connection security rule is shown in Figure 13-11.

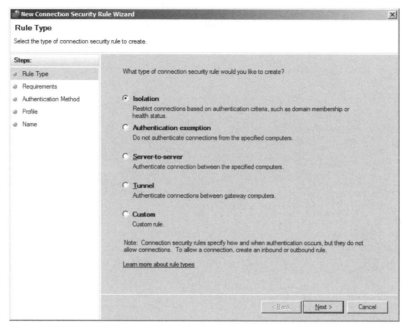

Figure 13-11   This figure shows the Connection Security Rule Wizard for the Windows Firewall and Advanced Security policy.

Wireless Network (IEEE 802.11) Policies (Computer Configuration Only)   This node provides the ability to configure wireless networks for desktops running Windows XP or Windows Vista that are joined to the domain. The options for configuring the wireless network for Windows XP is somewhat limited compared to those for Windows Vista. The policy for Windows XP is shown in Figure 13-12.

The policy available to configure desktops running Windows Vista provides additional setting and configuration options beyond those for desktops running Windows XP. The policy for Windows Vista is shown in Figure 13-13. Some of the additional configurations available for Windows Vista include:

■ Prevent connections to certain types of networks, such as ad-hoc and infrastructure

■ View denied wireless networks

■ Create all user profiles

■ Permissions for wireless networks (allow or deny)

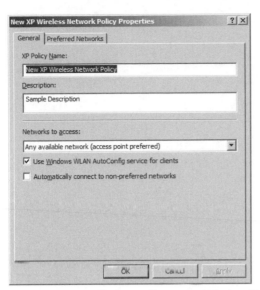

Figure 13-12   This figure shows the Wireless Network policy for a desktop running Windows XP.

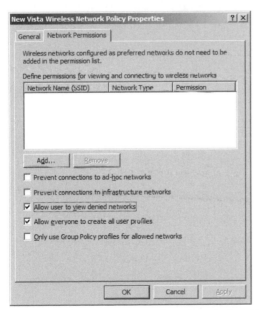

Figure 13-13   This figure shows the Wireless Network policy for a desktop running Windows Vista.

Public Key Policies   The policies included under this node are designed to configure, control, and manage the public key infrastructure for your company. The settings include control over EFS, certificate requests, certificate trust lists, and certificate authorities. Two of the policies are located under the root node, and the rest are located under one of the following subnodes:

- Encrypting File System
- Automatic Certificate Request Settings
- Trusted Root Certification Authorities
- Enterprise Trust
- Intermediate Certification Authorities
- Trusted Publishers
- Untrusted Certificates
- Trusted People

Software Restriction Policies This node provides you with the ability to control which applications can run on a desktop that is affected by the GPO where the policies are configured. These policies do not allow or prevent the software from existing on the desktop; rather, if the software is present, the policies determine whether it is allowed to run. This node and its subnodes contain numerous options for configuration that allow you to control the software that runs on any desktop in the domain. The majority of the settings fall under the following two subnodes, although a few policies are located under the main node:

- **Security Levels** The security levels control what level of privilege and which permissions will be adhered to within the software restriction policy. The following three levels can be configured:
  - ❏ Disallowed: software will not run, regardless of the user permissions and privilege.
  - ❏ Basic User: allows applications to execute for users who do not have Administrative privileges, but the application will still access resources as a normal user.
  - ❏ Unrestricted: the permissions to run the software are determined by the access rights of the user account.
- **Additional Rules** The additional rules control whether the software is allowed to run. These rules allow you to be very specific to an application, such as the hash rule, whereas other rules are more generic, such as the path rule. Figure 13-14 illustrates a path rule policy. Four rules can be configured:
  - ❏ Certificate rule
  - ❏ Hash rule
  - ❏ Network zone rule
  - ❏ Path rule

> **Note** For more information about configuring and using the Software Restriction policy in a GPO, refer to *http://support.microsoft.com/kb/324036*.

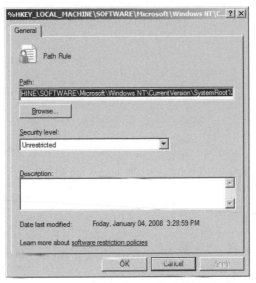

Figure 13-14   The Software Restriction policy provides the ability to control applications through Path rules.

Network Access Protection (Computer Configuration Only)   These policy settings control the environment of Network Access Protection (NAP) for target computers. The settings that fall under this node in a GPO control which service will quarantine the clients, the NAP interface details, and which servers will be used for obtaining health certificates.

- **Enforcement Clients**   These policies determine which service or technology will enforce NAP and quarantining of the client. The options include:

    ❏ DHCP Quarantine Enforcement Client

    ❏ Remote Access Quarantine Enforcement Client

    ❏ IPsec Relying Party

    ❏ TS Gateway Quarantine Enforcement Client

    ❏ EAP Quarantine Enforcement Client

- **User Interface Settings**   This policy simply configures the details that the client will see in the NAP interface.

- **Health Registration Settings**   These settings control the hash algorithms and health registration authority servers that clients will use to obtain their health certificates. Two subnodes contain policy settings, which must be configured to complete the health registration settings:

    ❏ Request Policy

    ❏ Trusted Server Groups

Note   For more information about using and configuring NAP, refer to *http:// www.microsoft.com/downloads/details.aspx?FamilyID=8e47649e-962c-42f8-9e6f- 21c5ccdcf490&displaylang=en.*

IP Security Policies on Active Directory (Computer Configuration Only)   IPsec is a protocol that can help increase security of data that is communicated from computer to computer. In most cases, IPsec is used to protect data communicated over a network that is not secure. IPsec has many configurations, all of which can be customized. Three policies are preconfigured and ready to use, if you do not want to customize your own IPsec policy:

- **Client (Respond Only)**   This policy is intended to be used for computers that will respond to computers requesting the use of IPsec for data communication. This is ideal for environments in which IPsec is not used on all servers; but when it is used on some servers, this policy allows the client to respond appropriately to the IPsec request.

- **Secure Server (Require Security)**   This policy is designed to force a server to use IPsec for all communication.

- **Server (Request Security)**   This policy is designed to be flexible with the use of IPsec. In essence, the policy will try to use IPsec with all communications, but when communicating with a downlevel client that does not support IPsec, it will not cause the communication to fail.

Note   For more information about IPsec, configuring IPsec policies, and when to use IPsec, refer to the documents at *http://technet.microsoft.com/en-us/network/bb531150.aspx.*

Folder Redirection (User Configuration Only)   When a computer and user are working within the context of a domain instead of a workgroup, it is ideal to centralize the data that users utilize for security, roaming users, and disaster recovery reasons. To accommodate this environment, the folder redirection policies allow you to control which user folders store data locally on the user's hard drive and which user folders are redirected to a network share, so that the data can be controlled by the IT staff. The folders that can be redirected using this policy include:

- AppData (Roaming)
- Desktop
- Start Menu
- Documents
- Pictures
- Music
- Videos

- Favorites

- Contacts

- Downloads

- Links

- Searches

- Saved Games

> **Note**   For more information about configuring and managing folder redirection policies, refer to *http://www.microsoft.com/technet/windowsvista/library/fb3681b2-da39-4944-93ad-dd3b6e8ca4dc.mspx.*

Policy-Based QoS   Quality of Service (QoS) is a suite of technologies that manage network traffic to optimize the bandwidth, cost, and overall network constraints. With QoS policies, you can manage and optimize network traffic when network conditions change and become congested to ensure that applications function optimally.

> **Note**   For more information about designing, configuring, and managing Policy-based QoS, refer to the documents available at *http://technet.microsoft.com/en-us/network/bb530836.aspx.*

Internet Explorer Maintenance (User Configuration Only)   The policies located under this node and its subnodes are designed to configure, control, and secure many aspects of Microsoft Internet Explorer. In some cases, you will use the settings that are set on the computer that is performing the editing of the GPO to configure the policies; in other cases, you can make manual entries to the policy settings. The result is a suite of Internet Explorer settings stored in the GPO that is deployed to all users who fall under SOM of the GPO. The subnodes of policy settings that fall under this node include the following:

- **Browser User Interface**   This node of policies is designed to configure the interface to Internet Explorer. Three policies fall under this subnode:

  - ❏ Browser Title

  - ❏ Custom Logo and Animated Bitmaps

  - ❏ Browser Toolbar Customizations

- **Connection**   Many settings are associated with Internet Explorer when a unique or specific connection must be made to access the Internet. The settings in this node can help you make the appropriate configurations to ensure connectivity. Four policies fall under this node:

  - ❏ Connection Settings

  - ❏ Automatic Browser Configuration

- ❑ Proxy Settings

- ❑ User Agent String

- **URLs**   You can help users in your environment to be more productive and efficient by providing them with URLs to locations that are important to them. Two types of URLs can be configured under this policy node:

  - ❑ Favorites and Links

  - ❑ Important URLs

- **Security**   You can use this policy to establish the security zones, content ratings, and Authenticode settings for Internet Explorer. These settings can be ignored by the GPO processing or imported from the computer performing the editing of the GPO.

- **Programs**   You can configure Internet Explorer to use specific programs to control the HTML editor, E-mail, Newsgroups, Internet calls, Calendar, and Contact list. This policy can be configured by importing the local Internet Explorer settings from the editing computer.

Administrative Templates

The Administrative Templates node and subnodes in a GPO update the registry on the target computer, either under the HKEY_LOCAL_MACHINE or HKEY_CURRENT_USER portion of the registry. Thousands of settings can be configured under these nodes. The settings are categorized and logically organized so that it is easier to find them. The following is a summary of the categorized nodes of settings available under the Administrative Templates nodes that fall under both the Computer Configuration and User Configuration sections of a GPO:

Control Panel

- Add or Remove Programs (User Configuration only)
- Display (User Configuration only)
- Printers (User Configuration only)
- Programs (User Configuration only)
- Regional and Language Options
- User Accounts (Computer Configuration only)

Desktop (User Configuration only)

- Active Directory
- Desktop

Network

- Background Intelligent Transfer Services (BITS) (Computer Configuration only)
- DNS Client (Computer Configuration only)

- Link-Layer Topology Discovery (Computer Configuration only)

- Microsoft Peer-to-Peer Networking Services (Computer Configuration only)

- Network Connections

- Offline Files

- QoS Packet Scheduler (Computer Configuration only)

- SNMP (Computer Configuration only)

- SSL Configuration Settings (Computer Configuration only)

- Windows Connect Now

Printers (Computer Configuration only)
Shared Folders (User Configuration only)
Start Menu and Taskbar (User Configuration only)
System

- Credentials Delegation (Computer Configuration only)

- Ctrl+Alt+Del Options (User Configuration only)

- Disk NV Cache (Computer Configuration only)

- Disk Quotas (Computer Configuration only)

- Distributed COM (Computer Configuration only)

- Driver Installation

- Folder Redirection

- Group Policy

- Internet Communication Management

- iSCSI (Computer Configuration only)

- KDC (Computer Configuration only)

- Kerberos (Computer Configuration only)

- Locale Services

- Logon

- Net Logon (Computer Configuration only)

- NTFS Filesystem (Computer Configuration only)

- Performance Control Panel

- Power Management

- Remote Assistance (Computer Configuration only)

- Remote Procedure Call (Computer Configuration only)

- Removable Storage Access

- Scripts

- Server Manager (Computer Configuration only)

- Shutdown Options (Computer Configuration only)

- System Restore (Computer Configuration only)

- Troubleshooting and Diagnostics (Computer Configuration only)

- Trusted Platform Module Services (Computer Configuration only)

- User Profiles

- Windows File Protection (Computer Configuration only)

- Windows HotStart

- Windows Time Service (Computer Configuration only)

Windows Components

- Active Directory Federation Services (Computer Configuration only)

- ActiveX Installer Service (Computer Configuration only)

- Application Compatibility

- Attachment Manager (User Configuration only)

- AutoPlay Policies

- Backup

- BitLocker Drive Encryption (Computer Configuration only)

- Credential User Interface (Computer Configuration only)

- Desktop Window Manager

- Digital Locker

- Event Forwarding (Computer Configuration only)

- Event Log Service (Computer Configuration only)

- Event Viewer (Computer Configuration only)

- Game Explorer (Computer Configuration only)

- Import Video

- Instant Search (User Configuration only)

- Internet Explorer

- Internet Information Services (Computer Configuration only)

- Microsoft Management Console (User Configuration only)

- NetMeeting
- Network Access Protection (Computer Configuration only)
- Network Projector
- Network Sharing (User Configuration only)
- Online Assistance (Computer Configuration only)
- Parental Controls (Computer Configuration only)
- Password Synchronization (Computer Configuration only)
- Presentation Settings
- RSS Feeds
- Search (Computer Configuration only)
- Security Center (Computer Configuration only)
- Server for NIS (Computer Configuration only)
- Shutdown Options (Computer Configuration only)
- Smart Card (Computer Configuration only)
- Sound Recorder
- Tablet PC
- Task Scheduler
- Terminal Services
- Windows Calendar
- Windows Color System
- Windows Customer Experience Improvement Program (Computer Configuration only)
- Windows Defender (Computer Configuration only)
- Windows Error Reporting
- Windows Explorer
- Windows Installer
- Windows Logon Options
- Windows Mail
- Windows Media Center
- Windows Media Digital Rights Management (Computer Configuration only)
- Windows Media Player
- Windows Meeting Space

- Windows Messenger
- Windows Mobility Center
- Windows Movie Maker
- Windows PowerShell
- Windows Remote Management (WinRM) (Computer Configuration only)
- Windows Remote Shell (Computer Configuration only)
- Windows Sidebar
- Windows SideShow
- Windows System Resource Manager (Computer Configuration only)
- Windows Update

Preferences

Both the Computer Configuration and User Configuration sections of a GPO contain a suite of settings under a Preferences node. These settings are new additions to Group Policy for Windows Server 2008 and Windows Vista. They are intended to control areas of the computer that have not been available in past versions of Windows.

Chapter 12 provides full details on all of the settings available under the Preferences nodes, as well as the possible configurations for these settings. The following is a list of nodes that exist under the Preferences nodes:

- Applications
- Drive Maps
- Environment
- Files
- Folders
- Ini Files
- Registry
- Network shares
- Shortcuts
- Data Sources
- Devices
- Folder Options
- Internet Settings

- Local Users and Groups

- Network Options

- Power Options

- Printers

- Regional Options

- Scheduled Tasks

- Services

- Start Menu

Terminal Services

Many areas of Terminal Services can be configured using Group Policy. As Terminal Services has grown into a useful and powerful solution for many companies, so have the number of settings that are available in a GPO. Some settings target the computer, which affects all users who log on to that computer. Other settings target users, providing granular and flexible control over how each user connects to and uses Terminal Services. Table 13-1 summarizes the majority of the Terminal Services settings that you will find in a GPO.

> **More Info**   Table 13-1 summarizes the majority of the Terminal Services settings that can be configured in a GPO. The policy name is listed in the table. If you are having trouble finding the policy within the Group Policy Management Editor (GPME), you can download and refer to spreadsheet, WindowsServerGroupPolicySettings.xls, from the Microsoft Download Center at http://www.microsoft.com/Downloads/.

Table 13-1   Terminal Services Settings

Full Policy Name	Computer or User
Allow audio redirection	Computer
Allow remote start of unlisted programs	Computer
Redirect only the default client printer	Computer
Use Terminal Services Easy Print driver first	Computer
Use TS Session Broker Load Balancing	Computer
Allow .rdp files from unknown publishers	Computer
Allow .rdp files from valid publishers and user's default .rdp settings	Computer
Configure server authentication for client	Computer
Do not allow passwords to be saved	Computer
Prompt for credentials on the client computer	Computer
Specify SHA1 thumbprints of certificates representing trusted .rdp publishers	Computer
Allow users to connect remotely using Terminal Services	Computer

Table 13-1   Terminal Services Settings

Full Policy Name	Computer or User
Automatic reconnection	Computer
Configure keep-alive connection interval	Computer
Deny logoff of an administrator logged in to the console session	Computer
Limit number of connections	Computer
Restrict Terminal Services users to a single remote session	Computer
Set rules for remote control of Terminal Services user sessions	Computer
Allow time zone redirection	Computer
Do not allow clipboard redirection	Computer
Do not allow COM port redirection	Computer
Do not allow drive redirection	Computer
Do not allow LPT port redirection	Computer
Do not allow smart card device redirection	Computer
Do not allow supported Plug and Play device redirection	Computer
Hide notifications about TS Licensing problems that affect the terminal server	Computer
Set the Terminal Services licensing mode	Computer
Use the specified Terminal Services license servers	Computer
Do not allow client printer redirection	Computer
Do not set default client printer to be default printer in a session	Computer
Specify terminal server fallback printer driver behavior	Computer
Set path for TS Roaming Profiles	Computer
Set TS User Home Directory	Computer
Use mandatory profiles on the terminal server	Computer
Always show desktop on connection	Computer
Enforce Removal of Remote Desktop Wallpaper	Computer
Limit maximum color depth	Computer
Remove "Disconnect" option from Shut Down dialog	Computer
Remove Windows Security item from Start menu	Computer
Start a program on connection	Computer
Always prompt for password upon connection	Computer
Do not allow local administrators to customize permissions	Computer
Require secure RPC communication	Computer
Require use of specific security layer for remote (RDP) connections	Computer
Require user authentication for remote connections by using Network Level Authentication	Computer
Server Authentication Certificate Template	Computer
Set client connection encryption level	Computer
Set time limit for active but idle Terminal Services sessions	Computer

Table 13-1   Terminal Services Settings

Full Policy Name	Computer or User
Set time limit for active Terminal Services sessions	Computer
Set time limit for disconnected sessions	Computer
Set time limit for logoff of RemoteApp sessions	Computer
Terminate session when time limits are reached	Computer
Do not delete temp folder upon exit	Computer
Do not use temporary folders per session	Computer
Join TS Session Broker	Computer
Configure TS Session Broker farm name	Computer
Configure TS Session Broker server name	Computer
Use IP Address Redirection	Computer
License server security group	Computer
Prevent license upgrade	Computer
Allow admin to install from Terminal Services session	Computer
Allow log on through Terminal Services	Computer
Redirect only the default client printer	User
Use Terminal Services Easy Print driver first	User
Allow time zone redirection	User
Do not allow clipboard redirection	User
Always show desktop on connection	User
Start a program on connection	User
Remove remote desktop wallpaper	User
Allow .rdp files from unknown publishers	User
Allow .rdp files from valid publishers and user's default .rdp settings	User
Do not allow passwords to be saved	User
Specify SHA1 thumbprints of certificates representing trusted .rdp publishers	User
Set rules for remote control of Terminal Services user sessions	User
Start a program on connection	User
Set time limit for active but idle Terminal Services sessions	User
Set time limit for active Terminal Services sessions	User
Set time limit for disconnected sessions	User
Terminate session when time limits are reached	User
Enable connection through TS Gateway	User
Set TS Gateway authentication method	User
Set TS Gateway server address	User

User Account Control

User Account Control (UAC) is one of the most important security-related technologies in Windows Vista and Windows Server 2008. UAC provides control over the level of privilege that a user or administrator has when routinely using the computer. UAC forces the privilege level to be a standard user until elevated privileges (typically administrative) are required.

Two different scenarios are important to understand when using UAC. First, when a user is logged on with administrative privileges, the level of privilege is a standard user until a task needs to be run that requires elevation. When elevated privileges are required, a dialog box asks the user whether he or she wants to continue to run the application or task with elevated privileges, as shown in Figure 13-15.

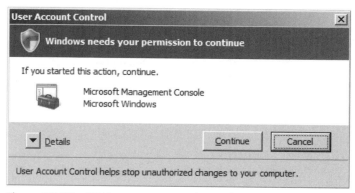

Figure 13-15   UAC prompts a user logged on with administrative privileges before running an application or task that requires administrative privileges.

This is an excellent security measure, because any application requiring elevated privileges will be denied processing until approved. This is important, because many viruses and malware require elevated privileges to run.

The second scenario is when a standard user is logged on and attempts to run an application that requires elevated privileges. In this case, the user is prompted, but not with the same prompt given to the user logged on with administrative privileges. Instead, the user is prompted with the dialog box shown in Figure 13-16.

UAC also has many control settings that allow you to alter how applications and tasks that require administrative privileges are handled. Table 13-2 summarizes the settings available for controlling UAC in a GPO.

> **More Info**   Table 13-2 summarizes the majority of the UAC settings that can be configured in a GPO. The policy name is listed in the table. If you are having trouble finding the policy within the GPME, you can download and refer to spreadsheet, WindowsServerGroupPolicy Settings.xls, from the Microsoft Download Center at http://www.microsoft.com/Downloads/.

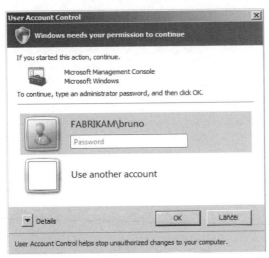

Figure 13-16 UAC prompts a user who is logged on with standard privileges with a dialog box asking for administrative credentials.

Table 13-2 UAC Settings

Full Policy Name	Computer or User
Enumerate administrator accounts on elevation	Computer
Require trusted path for credential entry	Computer
Detect application failures caused by deprecated Windows DLLs or COM objects	Computer
Detect application install failures	Computer
Detect application installers that need to be run as administrator	Computer
Detect applications unable to launch installers under UAC	Computer
Notify blocked drivers	Computer
User Account Control: Admin Approval Mode for the Built-in Administrator account	Computer
User Account Control: Allow UI Access applications to prompt for elevation without using the secure desktop.	Computer
User Account Control: Behavior of the elevation prompt for administrators in Admin Approval Mode	Computer
User Account Control: Behavior of the elevation prompt for standard users	Computer

Log-on Scripts

Most companies use log-on scripts to configure the user environment automatically for drive mappings, printer mappings, registry customization, file transfers, and so on. These log-on scripts can become very long and complex. In some cases, developers must spend countless hours developing and testing executable scripts to perform tasks that routine log-on scripts cannot handle.

By using the settings available in Group Policy, most companies can eliminate the need for log-on scripts altogether. Table 13-3 lists some of the most common settings that can be configured in a Group Policy that replace and expand on the settings that are typically in a log-on script.

> **More Info** Table 13-3 summarizes the majority of the log-on script settings that can be configured in a GPO. The policy name is listed in the table. If you are having trouble finding the policy within the GPME, you can download and refer to spreadsheet, WindowsServer GroupPolicySettings.xls, from the Microsoft Download Center at http://www.microsoft.com/Downloads/.

Table 13-3 Log-on Scripts Settings

Full Policy Name	Computer or User
Action on server disconnect	Computer
Administratively assigned offline files	Computer
Allow or Disallow use of the Offline Files feature	Computer
At logoff, delete local copy of user's offline files	Computer
Configure Slow link speed	Computer
Configure slow-link mode	Computer
Default cache size	Computer
Encrypt the Offline Files cache	Computer
Event logging level	Computer
Files not cached	Computer
Initial reminder balloon lifetime	Computer
Limit disk space used by offline files	Computer
Nondefault server disconnect actions	Computer
Prevent use of Offline Files folder	Computer
Prohibit 'Make Available Offline' for these files and folders	Computer
Prohibit user configuration of Offline Files	Computer
Reminder balloon frequency	Computer
Reminder balloon lifetime	Computer
Remove 'Make Available Offline'	Computer
Subfolders always available offline	Computer
Synchronize all offline files before logging off	Computer
Synchronize all offline files when logging on	Computer
Synchronize offline files before suspend	Computer
Turn off reminder balloons	Computer
Turn on economical application of administratively assigned Offline Files	Computer
Add Printer wizard - Network scan page (Managed network)	Computer
Add Printer wizard - Network scan page (Unmanaged network)	Computer
Allow Print Spooler to accept client connections	Computer

Table 13-3 Log-on Scripts Settings

Full Policy Name	Computer or User
Allow printers to be published	Computer
Allow pruning of published printers	Computer
Always render print jobs on the server	Computer
Automatically publish new printers in Active Directory	Computer
Check published state	Computer
Computer location	Computer
Custom support URL in the Printers folder's left pane	Computer
Directory pruning interval	Computer
Directory pruning priority	Computer
Directory pruning retry	Computer
Disallow installation of printers using kernel-mode drivers	Computer
Log directory pruning retry events	Computer
Prepopulate printer search location text	Computer
Printer browsing	Computer
Prune printers that are not automatically republished	Computer
Web-based printing	Computer
Remove Boot/Shutdown/Logon/Logoff status messages	Computer
Verbose vs. normal status messages	Computer
Use localized subfolder names when redirecting Start and My Documents	Computer
Always use classic logon	Computer
Always wait for the network at computer start-up and logon	Computer
Do not process the legacy run list	Computer
Do not process the run once list	Computer
Don't display the Getting Started welcome screen at logon	Computer
Hide entry points for Fast User Switching	Computer
Run these programs at user logon	Computer
Turn off Windows Startup Sound	Computer
Allow log-on scripts when NetBIOS or WINS is disabled	Computer
Maximum wait time for Group Policy scripts	Computer
Run log-on scripts synchronously	Computer
Run shutdown scripts visible	Computer
Run start-up scripts asynchronously	Computer
Run start-up scripts visible	Computer
Add the Administrators security group to roaming user profiles	Computer
Delete cached copies of roaming profiles	Computer
Delete user profiles older than a specified number of days on system restart	Computer
Do not check for user ownership of Roaming Profile Folders	Computer

Table 13-3   Log-on Scripts Settings

Full Policy Name	Computer or User
Do not detect slow network connections	Computer
Do not forcefully unload the users registry at user logoff	Computer
Do not log users on with temporary profiles	Computer
Leave Windows Installer and Group Policy Software Installation Data	Computer
Maximum retries to unload and update user profile	Computer
Only allow local user profiles	Computer
Prevent Roaming Profile changes from propagating to the server	Computer
Prompt user when a slow network connection is detected	Computer
Set maximum wait time for the network if a user has a roaming user profile or remote home directory	Computer
Set roaming profile path for all users logging on to this computer	Computer
Slow network connection timeout for user profiles	Computer
Timeout for dialog boxes	Computer
Wait for remote user profile	Computer
Environment	Computer
Files	Computer
Folders	Computer
Ini Files	Computer
Registry	Computer
Shortcuts	Computer
Power Options	Computer
Printers	Computer
Scheduled Tasks	Computer
Browse a common Web site to find printers	User
Browse the network to find printers	User
Default Active Directory path when searching for printers	User
Only use Package Point and print	User
Package Point and print - Approved servers	User
Point and Print Restrictions	User
Prevent addition of printers	User
Prevent deletion of printers	User
Action on server disconnect	User
Administratively assigned offline files	User
Event logging level	User
Initial reminder balloon lifetime	User
Nondefault server disconnect actions	User
Prevent use of Offline Files folder	User

Table 13-3   Log-on Scripts Settings

Full Policy Name	Computer or User
Prohibit 'Make Available Offline' for these file and folders	User
Prohibit user configuration of Offline Files	User
Reminder balloon frequency	User
Reminder balloon lifetime	User
Remove 'Make Available Offline'	User
Synchronize all offline files before logging off	User
Synchronize all offline files when logging on	User
Synchronize offline files before suspend	User
Turn off reminder balloons	User
Allow DFS roots to be published	User
Allow shared folders to be published	User
Don't display the Getting Started welcome screen at logon	User
Don't run specified Windows applications	User
Prevent access to registry editing tools	User
Prevent access to the command prompt	User
Run only specified Windows applications	User
Do not automatically make redirected folders available offline	User
Use localized subfolder names when redirecting Start and My Documents	User
Do not process the legacy run list	User
Do not process the run once list	User
Run these programs at user logon	User
Run legacy log-on scripts hidden	User
Run log-off scripts visible	User
Run log-on scripts synchronously	User
Run log-on scripts visible	User
Connect home directory to root of the share	User
Exclude directories in roaming profile	User
Limit profile size	User
Network directories to sync at Logon/Logoff time only	User
Prevent users from sharing files within their profile	User
Do not display the Welcome Center at user logon	User
Applications	User
Drive Maps	User
Environment	User
Files	User
Folders	User
Ini Files	User

Table 13-3   Log-on Scripts Settings

Full Policy Name	Computer or User
Registry	User
Shortcuts	User
Internet Settings	User
Power Options	User
Printers	User
Scheduled Tasks	User
Start Menu	User

Servers

Plenty of Group Policy settings are intended for configuring servers, not just desktops. It is common for desktops to be centrally managed and configured using tools and technologies. With Group Policy, servers can also be centrally managed. This will improve efficiency of server management, as well as security of servers. Grouping servers that can have the same configurations will not only make the overall management of them more efficient and stable, it will also reduce the time needed to configure the GPOs to make the settings. Table 13-4 lists many of the Group Policy settings that are available to target servers in your environment.

> **More Info**   Table 13-4 summarizes the majority of the server-related settings that can be configured in a GPO. The policy name is listed in the table. If you are having trouble finding the policy within the GPME, you can download and refer to spreadsheet, WindowsServer GroupPolicySettings.xls, from the Microsoft Download Center at http://www.microsoft.com/Downloads/.

Table 13-4   Servers Settings

Full Policy Name	Computer or User
Turn off Federation Service	Computer
Allow Print Spooler to accept client connections	Computer
Web-based printing	Computer
Activate Shutdown Event Tracker System State Data feature	Computer
Do not display Manage Your Server page at logon	Computer
Enable Persistent Time Stamp	Computer
Allow Cross-Forest User Policy and Roaming User Profiles	Computer
Always use local ADM files for Group Policy Object Editor	Computer
Do not allow additional session logins	Computer
Do not allow changes to initiator iqn name	Computer
Do not allow changes to initiator CHAP secret	Computer

Table 13-4   Servers Settings

Full Policy Name	Computer or User
Do not allow connections without IPsec	Computer
Do not allow sessions without mutual CHAP	Computer
Do not allow sessions without one-way CHAP	Computer
Do not allow adding new targets via manual configuration	Computer
Do not allow manual configuration of discovered targets	Computer
Do not allow manual configuration of iSNS servers	Computer
Do not allow manual configuration of target portals	Computer
Netlogon share compatibility	Computer
Sysvol share compatiblllty	Computer
Ignore Delegation Failure	Computer
Do not display Initial Configuration Tasks window automatically at logon	Computer
Do not display Server Manager automatically at logon	Computer
Global Configuration Settings	Computer
Configure Windows NTP Client	Computer
Enable Windows NTP Client	Computer
Enable Windows NTP Server	Computer
Allow remote start of unlisted programs	Computer
Redirect only the default client printer	Computer
Use Terminal Services Easy Print driver first	Computer
Use TS Session Broker load balancing	Computer
Disk Diagnostic: Configure custom alert text	Computer
Disk Diagnostic: Configure execution level	Computer
Report unplanned shutdown events	Computer
Prevent access to 16-bit applications	Computer
Remove Program Compatibility Property Page	Computer
Turn Off Application Compatibility Engine	Computer
Turn Off Program Compatibility Wizard	Computer
Prevent IIS installation	Computer
Set the number of retries for Password sync Servers	Computer
Set the retry interval for Password sync Servers	Computer
Turn On Extensive logging for Password sync Servers	Computer
Turn on the Windows to NIS password sync for migrated users for Password sync Servers	Computer
Set Update Interval to NIS subordinate servers	Computer
Turn on extensive logging for domain controllers running Server for NIS	Computer
Allow .rdp files from unknown publishers	Computer
Allow .rdp files from valid publishers and user's default .rdp settings	Computer

Table 13-4   Servers Settings

Full Policy Name	Computer or User
Configure server authentication for client	Computer
Do not allow passwords to be saved	Computer
Prompt for credentials on the client computer	Computer
Specify SHA1 thumbprints of certificates representing trusted .rdp publishers	Computer
Allow reconnection from original client only	Computer
Allow users to connect remotely using Terminal Services	Computer
Automatic reconnection	Computer
Configure keep-alive connection interval	Computer
Deny logoff of an administrator logged in to the console session	Computer
Limit number of connections	Computer
Restrict Terminal Services users to a single remote session	Computer
Set rules for remote control of Terminal Services user sessions	Computer
Allow audio redirection	Computer
Allow time zone redirection	Computer
Do not allow clipboard redirection	Computer
Do not allow COM port redirection	Computer
Do not allow drive redirection	Computer
Do not allow LPT port redirection	Computer
Do not allow smart card device redirection	Computer
Do not allow supported Plug and Play device redirection	Computer
Hide notifications about TS Licensing problems that affect the terminal server	Computer
Set the Terminal Services licensing mode	Computer
Use the specified Terminal Services license servers	Computer
Do not allow client printer redirection	Computer
Do not set default client printer to be default printer in a session	Computer
Specify terminal server fallback printer driver behavior	Computer
Set path for TS Roaming Profiles	Computer
Set TS User Home Directory	Computer
Use mandatory profiles on the terminal server	Computer
Always show desktop on connection	Computer
Enforce Removal of Remote Desktop Wallpaper	Computer
Limit maximum color depth	Computer
Remove "Disconnect" option from Shut Down dialog	Computer
Remove Windows Security item from Start menu	Computer
Start a program on connection	Computer
Always prompt for password upon connection	Computer
Do not allow local administrators to customize permissions	Computer

Table 13-4   Servers Settings

Full Policy Name	Computer or User
Require secure RPC communication	Computer
Require use of specific security layer for remote (RDP) connections	Computer
Require user authentication for remote connections by using Network Level Authentication	Computer
Server Authentication Certificate Template	Computer
Set client connection encryption level	Computer
Set time limit for active but idle Terminal Services sessions	Computer
Set time limit for active Terminal Services sessions	Computer
Set time limit for disconnected sessions	Computer
Terminate session when time limits are reached	Computer
Do not delete temp folder upon exit	Computer
Do not use temporary folders per session	Computer
Join TS Session Broker	Computer
Configure TS Session Broker farm name	Computer
Configure TS Session Broker server name	Computer
Use IP Address Redirection	Computer
License server security group	Computer
Prevent license upgrade	Computer
Prevent Windows Media DRM Internet Access	Computer
Set the Email IDs to which notifications are to be sent	Computer
Set the SMTP Server used to send notifications	Computer
Set the Time interval in minutes for logging accounting data	Computer
Turn on Accounting for WSRM	Computer
Microsoft network server: Amount of idle time required before suspending session	Computer
Microsoft network server: Digitally sign communications (always)	Computer
Microsoft network server: Digitally sign communications (if client agrees)	Computer
Microsoft network server: Disconnect clients when log-on hours expire	Computer
Environment	Computer
Registry	Computer
Network Shares	Computer
Data Sources	Computer
Local Users and Groups	Computer
Services	Computer

Hardware Components

With so many desktops and servers in a typical Windows environment, it is hard to manage all of the hardware that is connected to each computer. Because security and control over desktops is so important, it is also important to control the hardware that can be used and accessed on desktops. Numerous Group Policy settings can be configured to control all aspects of hardware that run on servers and desktops. Table 13-5 summarizes many of the settings that can help you gain better control over hardware in your environment.

> **More Info**   Table 13-5 summarizes the majority of the hardware component settings that can be configured in a GPO. The policy name is listed in the table. If you are having trouble finding the policy within the GPME, you can download and refer to spreadsheet, WindowsServerGroupPolicySettings.xls, from the Microsoft Download Center at http://www.microsoft.com/Downloads/.

Table 13-5   Hardware Components Settings

Full Policy Name	Computer or User
Default behavior for AutoRun	Computer
Do not turn off system power after a Windows system shutdown has occurred.	Computer
Allow remote access to the PnP interface	Computer
Configure device installation timeout	Computer
Do not create a system restore point when a new device driver is installed	Computer
Do not send a Windows Error Report when a generic driver is installed on a device	Computer
Treat all digitally signed drivers equally in the driver ranking and selection process	Computer
Turn off "Found New Hardware" balloons during device installation	Computer
Allow administrators to override Device Installation Restriction policies	Computer
Allow installation of devices that match any of these device IDs	Computer
Allow installation of devices using drivers that match these device setup classes	Computer
Display a custom message when installation is prevented by policy (balloon text)	Computer
Display a custom message when installation is prevented by policy (balloon title)	Computer
Prevent installation of devices not described by other policy settings	Computer
Prevent installation of devices that match any of these device IDs	Computer
Prevent installation of devices using drivers that match these device setup classes	Computer
Prevent installation of removable devices	Computer
Allow non-administrators to install drivers for these device setup classes	Computer
Turn off Windows Update device driver search prompt	Computer
Do not allow additional session logins	Computer
Do not allow changes to initiator iqn name	Computer
Do not allow changes to initiator CHAP secret	Computer
Do not allow connections without IPsec	Computer
Do not allow sessions without mutual CHAP	Computer
Do not allow sessions without one way CHAP	Computer
Do not allow adding new targets via manual configuration	Computer
Do not allow manual configuration of discovered targets	Computer

Table 13-5   Hardware Components Settings

Full Policy Name	Computer or User
Do not allow manual configuration of iSNS servers	Computer
Do not allow manual configuration of target portals	Computer
Select an Active Power Plan	Computer
Specify a Custom Active Power Plan	Computer
Select the Lid Switch Action (On Battery)	Computer
Select the Lid Switch Action (Plugged In)	Computer
Select the Power Button Action (On Battery)	Computer
Select the Power Button Action (Plugged In)	Computer
Select the Sleep Button Action (On Battery)	Computer
Select the Sleep Button Action (Plugged In)	Computer
Select the Start Menu Power Button Action (On Battery)	Computer
Select the Start Menu Power Button Action (Plugged In)	Computer
Turn Off the Hard Disk (On Battery)	Computer
Turn Off the Hard Disk (Plugged In)	Computer
Critical Battery Notification Action	Computer
Critical Battery Notification Level	Computer
Low Battery Notification Action	Computer
Low Battery Notification Level	Computer
Turn Off Low Battery User Notification	Computer
Allow Standby States (S1-S3) When Sleeping (On Battery)	Computer
Allow Standby States (S1-S3) When Sleeping (Plugged In)	Computer
Require a Password When a Computer Wakes (On Battery)	Computer
Require a Password When a Computer Wakes (Plugged In)	Computer
Specify the System Hibernate Timeout (On Battery)	Computer
Specify the System Hibernate Timeout (Plugged In)	Computer
Specify the System Sleep Timeout (On Battery)	Computer
Specify the System Sleep Timeout (Plugged In)	Computer
Turn Off Hybrid Sleep (On Battery)	Computer
Turn Off Hybrid Sleep (Plugged In)	Computer
Turn on Applications to Prevent Sleep Transitions (On Battery)	Computer
Turn on Applications to Prevent Sleep Transitions (Plugged In)	Computer
Turn Off Adaptive Display Timeout (On Battery)	Computer
Turn Off Adaptive Display Timeout (Plugged In)	Computer
Turn Off the Display (On Battery)	Computer
Turn Off the Display (Plugged In)	Computer
All Removable Storage classes: Deny all access	Computer
All Removable Storage: Allow direct access in remote sessions	Computer

Table 13-5   Hardware Components Settings

Full Policy Name	Computer or User
CD and DVD: Deny read access	Computer
CD and DVD: Deny write access	Computer
Custom Classes: Deny read access	Computer
Custom Classes: Deny write access	Computer
Floppy Drives: Deny read access	Computer
Floppy Drives: Deny write access	Computer
Removable Disks: Deny read access	Computer
Removable Disks: Deny write access	Computer
Tape Drives: Deny read access	Computer
Tape Drives: Deny write access	Computer
Time (in seconds) to force reboot	Computer
WPD Devices: Deny read access	Computer
WPD Devices: Deny write access	Computer
Configure the list of blocked TPM commands	Computer
Ignore the default list of blocked TPM commands	Computer
Ignore the local list of blocked TPM commands	Computer
Turn on TPM backup to Active Directory Domain Services	Computer
Do not allow Inkball to run	Computer
Do not allow printing to Journal Note Writer	Computer
Do not allow Snipping Tool to run	Computer
Do not allow Sticky Notes to be run	Computer
Do not allow Windows Journal to be run	Computer
Turn off pen feedback	Computer
Turn off automatic learning	Computer
Turn off handwriting personalization	Computer
Prevent Back-ESC mapping	Computer
Prevent launch an application	Computer
Prevent press and hold	Computer
Turn off hardware buttons	Computer
For tablet pen input, don't show the Input Panel icon	Computer
For touch input, don't show the Input Panel icon	Computer
Include rarely used Chinese, Kanji, or Hanja characters	Computer
Prevent Input Panel tab from appearing	Computer
Switch to the Simplified Chinese (PRC) gestures	Computer
Turn off AutoComplete integration with Input Panel	Computer
Turn off password security in Input Panel	Computer
Turn off tolerant and Z-shaped scratch-out gestures	Computer

Table 13-5   **Hardware Components Settings**

Full Policy Name	Computer or User
Prevent Flicks Learning Mode	Computer
Prevent flicks	Computer
Turn off Tablet PC Pen Training	Computer
Turn off Tablet PC touch input	Computer
Don't set the always do this checkbox	Computer
Turn off Autoplay	Computer
Allow active content from CDs to run on user machines	Computer
Turn off Connect to a Network Projector	Computer
Do not allow Sound Recorder to run	Computer
Devices: Allow undock without having to log on	Computer
Devices: Allowed to format and eject removable media	Computer
Devices: Prevent users from installing printer drivers	Computer
Devices: Restrict CD-ROM access to locally logged-on user only	Computer
Devices: Restrict floppy access to locally logged-on user only	Computer
Devices: Unsigned driver installation behavior	Computer
Registry	Computer
Devices	Computer
Power Options	Computer
Turn off Autoplay	User
Code signing for device drivers	User
Configure driver search locations	User
Turn off Windows Update device driver search prompt	User
Prompt for password on resume from hibernate / suspend	User
All Removable Storage classes: Deny all access	User
CD and DVD: Deny read access	User
CD and DVD: Deny write access	User
Custom Classes: Deny read access	User
Custom Classes: Deny write access	User
Floppy Drives: Deny read access	User
Floppy Drives: Deny write access	User
Removable Disks: Deny read access	User
Removable Disks: Deny write access	User
Tape Drives: Deny read access	User
Tape Drives: Deny write access	User
Time (in seconds) to force reboot	User
WPD Devices: Deny read access	User
WPD Devices: Deny write access	User

Table 13-5   Hardware Components Settings

Full Policy Name	Computer or User
Do not allow Inkball to run	User
Do not allow printing to Journal Note Writer	User
Do not allow Snipping Tool to run	User
Do not allow Sticky Notes to be run	User
Do not allow Windows Journal to be run	User
Turn off pen feedback	User
Turn off automatic learning	User
Turn off handwriting personalization	User
Prevent Back-ESC mapping	User
Prevent launch an application	User
Prevent press and hold	User
Turn off hardware buttons	User
For tablet pen input, don't show the Input Panel icon	User
For touch input, don't show the Input Panel icon	User
Include rarely used Chinese, Kanji, or Hanja characters	User
Prevent Input Panel tab from appearing	User
Switch to the Simplified Chinese (PRC) gestures	User
Turn off AutoComplete integration with Input Panel	User
Turn off password security in Input Panel	User
Turn off tolerant and Z-shaped scratch-out gestures	User
Prevent Flicks Learning Mode	User
Prevent flicks	User
Turn off Tablet PC Pen Training	User
Turn off Tablet PC touch input	User
Default behavior for AutoRun	User
Don't set the always do this checkbox	User
Allow active content from CDs to run on user machines	User
Turn off Connect to a Network Projector	User
Do not allow Sound Recorder to run	User
Registry	User
Devices	User

Network Security

Security is important at the computer level, as well as on the network as a whole. Security can be set to protect data that resides on servers and desktops, as well as data that is sent over the network. Numerous Group Policy settings are intended for protection of data, network communications, authentication, and more. Table 13-6 summarizes many of the settings that can help you make your network more secure using Group Policy.

> **More Info**   Table 13-6 summarizes the majority of the network security settings that can be configured in a GPO. The policy name is listed in the table. If you are having trouble finding the policy within the GPME, you can download and refer to spreadsheet, WindowsServer GroupPolicySettings.xls, from the Microsoft Download Center at http://www.microsoft.com/ Downloads/.

Table 13-6   Network Security Settings

Full Policy Name	Computer or User
SSL Cipher Suite Order	Computer
Windows Firewall: Allow authenticated IPsec bypass	Computer
Windows Firewall. Allow ICMP exceptions	Computer
Windows Firewall: Allow inbound file and printer sharing exception	Computer
Windows Firewall: Allow inbound remote administration exception	Computer
Windows Firewall: Allow inbound Remote Desktop exceptions	Computer
Windows Firewall: Allow inbound UPnP framework exceptions	Computer
Windows Firewall: Allow local port exceptions	Computer
Windows Firewall: Allow local program exceptions	Computer
Windows Firewall: Allow logging	Computer
Windows Firewall: Define inbound port exceptions	Computer
Windows Firewall: Define inbound program exceptions	Computer
Windows Firewall: Do not allow exceptions	Computer
Windows Firewall: Prohibit notifications	Computer
Windows Firewall: Prohibit unicast response to multicast or broadcast requests	Computer
Windows Firewall: Protect all network connections	Computer
Windows Firewall: Allow ICMP exceptions	Computer
Windows Firewall: Allow inbound file and printer sharing exception	Computer
Windows Firewall: Allow inbound remote administration exception	Computer
Windows Firewall: Allow inbound Remote Desktop exceptions	Computer
Windows Firewall: Allow inbound UPnP framework exceptions	Computer
Windows Firewall: Allow local port exceptions	Computer
Windows Firewall: Allow local program exceptions	Computer
Windows Firewall: Allow logging	Computer
Windows Firewall: Define inbound port exceptions	Computer
Windows Firewall: Define inbound program exceptions	Computer
Windows Firewall: Do not allow exceptions	Computer
Windows Firewall: Prohibit notifications	Computer
Windows Firewall: Prohibit unicast response to multicast or broadcast requests	Computer
Windows Firewall: Protect all network connections	Computer
Update Security Level	Computer
Update Top Level Domain Zones	Computer

Table 13-6   **Network Security Settings**

Full Policy Name	Computer or User
Disable password strength validation for Peer Grouping	Computer
Communities	Computer
Permitted Managers	Computer
Traps for public community	Computer
Allow local activation security check exemptions	Computer
Define Activation Security Check exemptions	Computer
IP Security policy processing	Computer
Wired policy processing	Computer
Wireless policy processing	Computer
Define host name-to-Kerberos realm mappings	Computer
Define interoperable Kerberos V5 realm settings	Computer
Require strict KDC validation	Computer
Allow cryptography algorithms compatible with Windows NT 4.0	Computer
Contact PDC on log-on failure	Computer
Expected dial-up delay on logon	Computer
Final DC Discovery Retry Setting for Background Callers	Computer
Initial DC Discovery Retry Setting for Background Callers	Computer
Log File Debug Output Level	Computer
Maximum DC Discovery Retry Interval Setting for Background Callers	Computer
Maximum Log File Size	Computer
Negative DC Discovery Cache Setting	Computer
Netlogon share compatibility	Computer
Positive Periodic DC Cache Refresh for Background Callers	Computer
Positive Periodic DC Cache Refresh for Non-Background Callers	Computer
Scavenge Interval	Computer
Site Name	Computer
Sysvol share compatibility	Computer
Automated Site Coverage by the DC Locator DNS SRV Records	Computer
DC Locator DNS records not registered by the DCs	Computer
Domain Controller Address Type Returned	Computer
Dynamic Registration of the DC Locator DNS Records	Computer
Force Rediscovery Interval	Computer
Location of the DCs hosting a domain with single label DNS name	Computer
Priority Set in the DC Locator DNS SRV Records	Computer
Refresh Interval of the DC Locator DNS Records	Computer
Sites Covered by the Application Directory Partition Locator DNS SRV Records	Computer
Sites Covered by the DC Locator DNS SRV Records	Computer
Sites Covered by the GC Locator DNS SRV Records	Computer

Table 13-6   Network Security Settings

Full Policy Name	Computer or User
Try Next Closest Site	Computer
TTL Set in the DC Locator DNS Records	Computer
Weight Set in the DC Locator DNS SRV Records	Computer
Restrictions for Unauthenticated RPC clients	Computer
RPC Endpoint Mapper Client Authentication	Computer
RPC Troubleshooting State Information	Computer
Network Access Protection: Support XP 802.1x QEC	Computer
Always prompt for password upon connection	Computer
Do not allow local administrators to customize permissions	Computer
Require secure RPC communication	Computer
Require use of specific security layer for remote (RDP) connections	Computer
Require user authentication using RDP 6.0 for remote connections	Computer
Server Authentication Certificate Template	Computer
Set client connection encryption level	Computer
Allow Basic authentication	Computer
Allow unencrypted traffic	Computer
Disallow Digest authentication	Computer
Disallow Kerberos authentication	Computer
Disallow Negotiate authentication	Computer
Trusted Hosts	Computer
Allow automatic configuration of listeners	Computer
Allow Basic authentication	Computer
Allow unencrypted traffic	Computer
Disallow Kerberos authentication	Computer
Disallow Negotiate authentication	Computer
Allow Remote Shell Access	Computer
MaxConcurrentUsers	Computer
Specify idle Timeout	Computer
Specify maximum amount of memory in MB per Shell	Computer
Specify maximum number of processes per Shell	Computer
Specify maximum number of remote shells per user	Computer
Specify Shell Timeout	Computer
Maximum lifetime for service ticket	Computer
Maximum lifetime for user ticket	Computer
Maximum lifetime for user ticket renewal	Computer
Maximum tolerance for computer clock synchronization	Computer
DCOM: Machine Access Restrictions in Security Descriptor Definition Language (SDDL) syntax	Computer

Table 13-6   **Network Security Settings**

Full Policy Name	Computer or User
DCOM: Machine Launch Restrictions in Security Descriptor Definition Language (SDDL) syntax	Computer
Domain controller: LDAP server signing requirements	Computer
Domain member: Digitally encrypt or sign secure channel data (always)	Computer
Domain member: Digitally encrypt secure channel data (when possible)	Computer
Domain member: Digitally sign secure channel data (when possible)	Computer
Domain member: Disable machine account password changes	Computer
Domain member: Require strong (Windows 2000 or later) session key	Computer
Microsoft network client: Digitally sign communications (always)	Computer
Microsoft network client: Digitally sign communications (if server agrees)	Computer
Microsoft network client: Send unencrypted password to third-party SMB servers	Computer
Microsoft network server: Amount of idle time required before suspending session	Computer
Microsoft network server: Digitally sign communications (always)	Computer
Microsoft network server: Digitally sign communications (if client agrees)	Computer
Microsoft network server: Disconnect clients when log-on hours expire	Computer
Network access: Allow anonymous SID/Name translation	Computer
Network access: Do not allow anonymous enumeration of SAM accounts	Computer
Network access: Do not allow anonymous enumeration of SAM accounts and shares	Computer
Network access: Do not allow storage of credentials or .NET Passports for network authentication	Computer
Network access: Let Everyone permissions apply to anonymous users	Computer
Network access: Named Pipes that can be accessed anonymously	Computer
Network access: Remotely accessible registry paths	Computer
Network access: Remotely accessible registry paths	Computer
Network access: Remotely accessible registry paths and subpaths	Computer
Network access: Restrict anonymous access to Named Pipes and Shares	Computer
Network access: Shares that can be accessed anonymously	Computer
Network access: Sharing and security model for local accounts	Computer
Network security: Do not store LAN Manager hash value on next password change	Computer
Network security: Force logoff when log-on hours expire	Computer
Network security: LAN Manager authentication level	Computer
Network security: LDAP client signing requirements	Computer
Network security: Minimum session security for NTLM SSP based (including secure RPC) clients	Computer
Network security: Minimum session security for NTLM SSP based (including secure RPC) servers	Computer
Registry	Computer
Data Sources	Computer
Services	Computer

Summary

Group Policy has expanded to include over 5,000 settings in a single GPO. With this many settings available to you, it is important that you understand how a GPO is structured, as well as how the settings are organized into categories within the GPO.

A GPO is first divided into two main sections: Computer Configuration and User Configuration. From there, two top-level nodes organize the remaining settings: Policies and Preferences. Policies are meant to enforce settings, whereas Preferences are intended for making settings for the computer and user, although they can be altered after they are configured by the user.

Having an understanding of all of the different parts and categories of a GPO is important when you start to organize your GPO structure and the settings that you want to deploy. This chapter has summarized all of the settings in a GPO, as well as some of the settings for each topic, such as Terminal Services, UAC, and more.

Additional Resources

- The Microsoft Help and Support article at *http://support.microsoft.com/kb/823659* describes many security settings, their uses, and incompatibilities.

- The Microsoft TechNet article at *http://technet2.microsoft.com/windowsserver/en/library/3512b600-5bb4-4dae-8b2c-7b71ef9951a01033.mspx?mfr=true* provides information about the syntax of the .zap package.

- The Windows Server 2003 Security Guide, at *http://www.microsoft.com/technet/security/prodtech/windowsserver2003/w2003hg/sgch00.mspx*, provides detailed information about securing all types of computers on the network by using Group Policy.

- The TechNet articles at *http://www.microsoft.com/technet/scriptcenter/topics/gp/extension1.mspx* and *http://www.microsoft.com/technet/scriptcenter/topics/gp/extension2.mspx* provide in-depth explanation of the scripting extension, examples, and information about how to troubleshoot issues related to scripts.

- The Microsoft Help and Support article at *http://support.microsoft.com/kb/324036* provides information about configuring and using the Software Restriction policy in a GPO.

- The article titled "Network Access Protection Policies in Windows Server 2008," at *http://www.microsoft.com/downloads/details.aspx?FamilyID=8e47649e-962c-42f8-9e6f-21c5ccdcf490&displaylang=en*, provides information about using and configuring NAP.

- The TechNet article at *http://technet.microsoft.com/en-us/network/bb531150.aspx* provides more information about IPsec, configuring IPsec policies, and when to use IPsec.

- The article titled "Managing Roaming User Data Deployment Guide," at *http://www.microsoft.com/technet/windowsvista/library/fb3681b2-da39-4944-93ad-dd3b6e8ca4dc.mspx*, offers more information about configuring and managing folder redirection policies.

- Quality of Service, at *http://technet.microsoft.com/en-us/network/bb530836.aspx*, provides information about designing, configuring, and managing Policy-based QoS.

- Chapter 3, "Group Policy Basics," covers the default GPOs that contain numerous settings.

- Chapter 4, "Architecture of Group Policy," provides information about how GPOs are structured and stored.

- Chapter 5, "Group Policy Processing," covers the concepts of scope of management (SOM).

- Chapter 12, "Group Policy Preferences," covers the settings that are available under the Preferences nodes in a GPO.

Part VII
Advanced Topics

Chapter 14
Advanced Group Policy Management

Microsoft made great strides with the release of the Group Policy Management Console (GPMC). The capabilities and overall management resources that the GPMC provided, and continues to provide, are extremely beneficial for all Active Directory directory service customers and administrators. Chapter 6, "GPMC Basics," provides full details about the GPMC and all its features.

However, the GPMC is not the ultimate in Group Policy management—it has some limitations that can hamper the overall goals of Group Policy management, even for smaller companies. The counterpart to the GPMC is Microsoft Advanced Group Policy Management (AGPM).

AGPM provides some highly sought-after—almost vital—features not available in the GPMC. This chapter covers all of the great features available in AGPM, with details on how it works and how to use it. The significant features include:

- Offline editing of GPOs
- Change management
- Workflow for creation and deployment of GPOs
- Roll back and roll forward of archived GPOs
- Reporting

- Use of templates for new GPO creation
- Recycle Bin for deleted GPOs
- Restoration of GPOs and GPO links

As you can see from this list, these features are very important to any company that uses Group Policy extensively. The GPMC provides some of these features, but with AGPM, these features are all built in, automated, and seamless.

History of AGPM

DesktopStandard Corporation owned AGPM before Microsoft acquired it in 2006. DesktopStandard produced and sold software that took Group Policy management and settings to a new level; these improvements are almost all included in Windows Server 2008 and Windows Vista in some fashion. When AGPM was owned by DesktopStandard, AGPM was called GPOVault. GPOVault and AGPM were almost identical products at this time, but AGPM was tailored to be a Microsoft product and included the Microsoft Desktop Optimization Pack (MDOP) offering for software assurance customers. To read more about MDOP, visit the MDOP Web site at *http://www.microsoft.com/windows/ products/windowsvista/enterprise/mdop/overview.mspx.*

The only way to get AGPM now is through the MDOP. However, the MDOP is one of the most impressive offerings that Microsoft has ever provided. It includes five software tools, all for a very inexpensive price of $10 per desktop (the price may vary depending on the number of desktops).

Architecture of AGPM

AGPM is a straightforward implementation of a Group Policy management product. The product installs seamlessly into your existing Active Directory installation, without even a hint that it is there. Of course, you have an administrative interface from which you can manage the GPOs, but Active Directory and the infrastructure are not altered in any other way.

AGPM is a simple installation that does not require any back-office products such as a SQL database or Microsoft System Center for management. AGPM has some requirements that coincide with the operating systems required to support the features and the GPMC, used as the host for administering GPOs.

Operating System Support

AGPM was released in a final version in the summer of 2007, falling directly in the Windows Vista and Windows Server 2008 release time frame—these are the operating systems from which you can manage Group Policy by using the AGPM interface. You can also manage an Active Directory enterprise of GPOs running Windows 2000 or Microsoft Windows Server 2003 from AGPM, but you must do so from Windows Vista, Windows Server 2003, or Windows Server 2008.

GPMC Requirements

The GPMC has been the primary tool for administration of Group Policy for years. The GPMC is a centralized view of all GPOs, from a single forest with just one domain, to multiple forests with multiple domains. AGPM utilizes this view of Group Policy within the GPMC by adding a simple snap-in that allows control over the GPOs per domain, just like the GPMC originally intended.

AGPM adds a new node in the GPMC called Change Control, which is where all AGPM features are controlled. This node is shown in Figure 14-1.

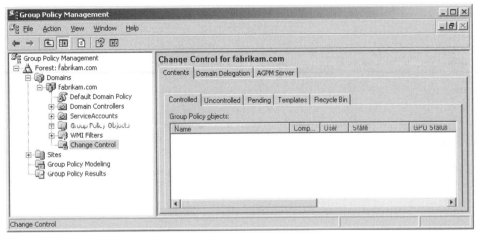

Figure 14-1   AGPM includes a Change Control node in the GPMC interface for managing your GPOs offline.

With Windows Vista, the GPMC comes installed and ready to use by default. However, if you have installed Windows Vista Service Pack 1, you will need to install the updated GPMC, which provides support for the new Windows Server 2008 features, such as searching and filtering.

Server Installation

AGPM does require a server installation portion. This installs the AGPM Service on the selected server that communicates with the production version of the GPOs. Because AGPM provides offline editing of the GPOs, it must be able to get a copy of the GPO from the production domain controllers and then put the updated GPOs into production. The service provides this functionality.

In addition to the service, installation of AGPM on the server creates the archive for the GPOs. The default location should meet the following criteria:

- It should have enough space to archive all of the GPOs that you create and manage through AGPM.

- It should allow the AGPM service account access only.

The archive does not require, nor does it support, any SQL or database. However, there must be enough room on your AGPM server to support the historical archive. The sizing of AGPM is rather easy to determine, as long as you know how many GPOs you have (available through the GPMC) and how often you modify GPOs. Because AGPM only duplicates the Group Policy template (GPT), you can find the size of each GPO's GPT to calculate the overall size needed.

Table 14-1 offers a sample calculation for sizing the archive on the AGPM server. This example focuses on a domain environment running Windows Server 2008, which does not store the .adm templates in the GPT.

Table 14-1   Windows Server 2008 Domain AGPM Server Sizing Example

Number of GPOs in Production	Average Size of GPOs	Average Number of Changes to GPOs in One Year	Size for Storing One Year of Changes	Size for Storing Five Years of Changes
500	5 KB	5	12.5 MB	62.5 MB

If you have a legacy Active Directory installation and are still using domain controllers running Windows 2000 or Windows Server 2003, you will still have your .adm files stored in the GPT. The calculation for the AGPM server in this case is quite different, because the size of the archive must include a copy of the .adm files for each archive point. Table 14-2 illustrates a sample calculation for this environment.

Table 14-2   Windows 2000 or Windows Server 2003 Domain AGPM Server Sizing Example

Number of GPOs in Production	Average Size of GPOs	Average Number of Changes to GPOs in One Year	Size for Storing One Year of Changes	Size for Storing Five Years of Changes
500	4 MB	5	10 GB	50 GB

These calculations are for storing only the archived GPOs. The server must also have enough disk space for the operating system and anything else that will run on it.

After sizing the server, you must consider the installation of AGPM. This involves the simple installation of a single .msi file called AGPMServer.msi. The following steps and choices must be made by a member of the Domain Admins group to install AGPM on a server:

1. Start the installation by double-clicking the AGPMServer.msi file.

2. The Welcome to the Setup Wizard for Microsoft Advanced Group Policy Management – Server page indicates that AGPM Server will be installed. This page clearly states that Domain Admins membership is required to install the product, as shown in Figure 14-2. Click Next.

> **Note**   If a previous version of GPOVault is found, it will be uninstalled before AGPM Server is installed. The GPOVault data will be migrated to the AGPM archive. This deletion and migration is not reversible!

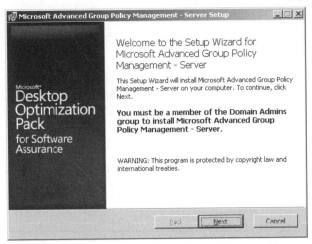

Figure 14-2   AGPM Server installation is clean and easy, driven by a standard Windows wizard.

3. Accept the license terms, and then click Next.

4. On the Application Path page, select the path to install AGPM Server. The default path is C:\Program Files\Microsoft\AGPM\Server, which should work in most cases. The Application Path page, shown in Figure 14-3, indicates that you can select your install path or keep the default.

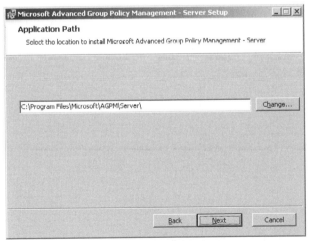

Figure 14-3   For product installation, you can select the default path or specify where you want the AGPM Server files to reside and install.

5. On the Archive Path page, select the path to the AGPM Server archive. This is the location where the GPOs will be stored for offline editing and recovery from the archived GPOs. The default location for the archive is C:\Documents and Settings\All Users\Application Data\Microsoft\AGPM, as shown in Figure 14-4.

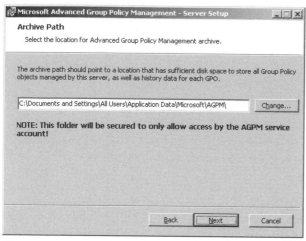

Figure 14-4   The path for the AGPM Server archive defaults to the All Users profile, which can be changed if you want to alter where you keep the GPO archives.

> **Note**   The archive folder is accessible only to the AGPM Server account, for security reasons. This can be changed after the installation, but it is not recommended because it will defeat the delegation benefits that AGPM provides for the management and tracking of GPO updates.

6. On the AGPM Service Account page, in the User Account box, select the AGPM service account that will be used to run the service. This user account should be a domain user account, not the Administrator account. It is always ideal to name the service account according to the service, as shown in Figure 14-5.

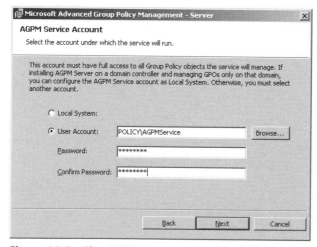

Figure 14-5   The AGPM Server service account should be a domain account that is named appropriately for the service it is servicing.

Note If you install AGPM Server on a domain controller, you can use the Local System account for the service account.

Best Practices AGPM Server should be installed on a domain member server, not a domain controller. This is for no other reason than to keep the management of offline GPOs using AGPM separate from a domain controller. It is always a best practice to install services on a domain member server, rather than a domain controller, when possible.

7. In the Archive Owner page, select the AGPM archive owner in the User Account box. This user account will be used to set up the AGPM delegation, and it will have full control over all functionality within AGPM. This should not be an existing user account; it should be a special account designed to control the setup of AGPM, as shown in Figure 14-6.

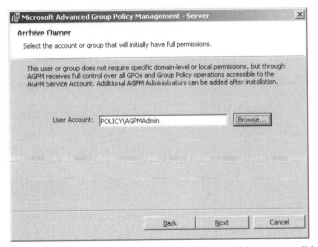

Figure 14-6 The AGPM owner account will be responsible for all initial configurations of the archive and AGPM.

8. Approve your input, and then install AGPM Server.

After you have installed AGPM Server, the foundation of AGPM is ready to go. You can verify that you have AGPM installed correctly on your server (this is always a good idea) in a couple of ways. First, you will want to ensure that the service installed, is running properly, and has the appropriate service account configured. To do this, follow these steps:

1. On the AGPM Server, start Computer Management Console.

2. Expand the Services and Applications node.

3. Select the Services node.

4. In the details pane, view the AGPM Service account, as shown in Figure 14-7.

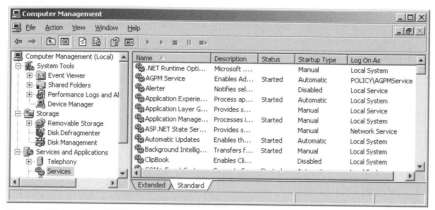

Figure 14-7 The AGPM service should be started and have the service account you selected in the installation configured to run the service.

After you confirm that the service is running and configured properly, ensure that the archive location is established. Remember that the default location of the archive is C:\Documents and Settings\All Users\Application Data\Microsoft\AGPM, as shown in Figure 14-8.

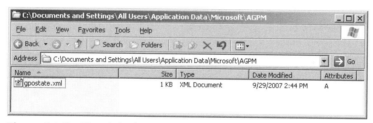

Figure 14-8 The default AGPM archive location will work in most cases, but you should confirm that the folder was created after you install AGPM Server.

Client Installation

After AGPM Server is installed, you must install the AGPM Client so that you can administer the GPOs from within the AGPM environment. The AGPM Client is not a client in the sense that it receives any information from the server. Rather, the AGPM Client is the administrative interface for the AGPM management environment.

The AGPM Client adds a new node within the GPMC, which is why the GPMC was mentioned earlier as a requirement for AGPM. The result of the AGPM Client installation is the same as what you looked at earlier, but the Change Control node is added to the GPMC.

The AGPM Client must be installed on a computer running Windows Server 2003, Windows Server 2008, or Windows Vista. To install the AGPM Client, double-click the AGPMClient.msi file, which launches the AGPM Client Setup Wizard. To install the full product, follow these steps:

1. Double-click the AGPMClient.msi file.

2. On the Welcome to the Microsoft Advanced Group Policy Management – Client Setup Wizard page, read and agree to the terms, and then click Next.

3. Read and agree to the licensing terms.

4. On the Application Path page, select the path to install the AGPM Client. The default path is C:\Program Files\Microsoft\AGPM\Client, which should work in most cases. During the installation, you can select your installation path or keep the default.

5. On the AGPM Server page, enter the fully qualified DNS name for the AGPM Server in the Name box. This should be in the form: <*servername*>.*domainname*.com (for example, Server1.fabrikam.com).

6. Enter the port number on which the AGPM Server service is running in the Port box. The default is 4600, but you can change it if you are already using this port for a different service or application.

7. Agree to the configurations that you made, and then install the AGPM Client.

> **Best Practices**   It is always a best practice to administer services running on Windows servers from an administrative desktop. This is ideal so that the server remains locked and the possibility of causing other errant configurations or issues on the server is reduced. With the AGPM Client, it is ideal to install it on a computer running Windows Vista, but it can also be run from Windows Server 2003 or Windows Server 2008.

After the AGPM Client is installed, you will be able to launch the GPMC and start to administer GPOs from within the AGPM tool. To verify that the AGPM Client is installed properly and functioning, follow these steps:

1. Start the GPMC management tool.

2. Click the Change Control node under the domain where you installed the AGPM Server.

3. You should see a list of the GPOs that are already controlled, or a list of uncontrolled GPOs, in the details pane.

Offline Editing of GPOs

AGPM provides many benefits. The benefit that most administrators claim to be most important to them is the ability to edit GPOs offline. This is in contrast to the GPMC management of GPOs, which modifies only the GPOs in production. The negative aspect of administering the GPOs via the GPMC method is that any change that is made to a GPO affects the production GPO immediately. Thus, if you make the change errantly, the target computers or users could be affected by the background refresh within minutes of the GPO being modified.

> ## How It Works: GPO Changes Using the GPMC and the GPME
> When a GPO is edited directly by using the GPMC, the changes made are immediate. This is an important issue, because changes can be made errantly or with malicious intent, with immediate results. To see this, edit a GPO from within the GPMC, under the Group Policy Objects node. The Group Policy Management Editor will show the

contents of the GPO settings. As an example, you can modify any setting and see that the GPT will immediately show that change after you confirm the setting. To see this, expand the Computer Configuration container to where you can alter a security setting, such as Enabling or Disabling the Administrator account. This path is Computer Configuration\Windows Settings\Security Settings\Local Policies\Security Options. If you were to open the to where a setting from this location in the GPO is stored, you could see the setting take effect immediately. To do this, on the domain controller running the PDC Emulator role, go to C:\Windows\Sysvol\sysvol\<domainname>\Policies\<GUID of GPO>\Machine\Microsoft\Windows NT\SecEdit. Here you will find the GPTTmpl.inf file (if you have not made the setting yet, this path and file will not exist). Now, go back to the GPME and set the Administrator account status to Enabled, and then click OK. If you open the GPTTmpl.inf file, you will see an entry that says EnableAdminAccount = 1. Notice that you are still in the GPME, but the setting has been already written to the GPT. At this point, the contents of the GPT are already being replicated to all other domain controllers, as well as the contents of the GPC. If the target computers happen to refresh Group Policy at this point, they will receive this setting, even though you are still in the GPME.

Change Management

It is the desire of everyone involved with IT administration that a record be kept of things that happen on the network. With regard to Group Policy, this includes tracking any changes that occur within any GPO. AGPM tracks all of these changes and more, giving you a clear view into all of the change management events that you will want to know about.

Some of the important aspects of Group Policy change management that you will want to track include the following:

- When the changes were made to the GPO
- Who made the changes to the GPO
- What changes were made to the GPO

These are all very important aspects of Group Policy change management; both IT administrators and security auditors want this information. However, the GPMC does not track changes that occur to GPOs that are updated. If you were to compare change management in the GPMC and AGPM, you would find that the GPMC provides none of the features that AGPM provides.

The GPMC does provide a mechanism to back up and restore GPOs, but the entire process is manual. AGPM is automated and provides all of the change management capabilities listed earlier.

When the Changes Were Made

The first requirement of Group Policy change management is the tracking of when a GPO was changed. Troubleshooting issues with Group Policy can be difficult, but if isolating a specific change to a GPO can help narrow the overall issue, a list of when GPOs were altered is very useful.

AGPM tracks the day and time when a GPO was altered. This is done per GPO, as it should be. An archive point is established for every time a GPO in AGPM is edited. Tracking the day and time of every edit establishes a timeline for the GPO. Figure 14-9 shows a GPO that has been altered many times. Note that each time the GPO is edited, an entry is made for the day and time.

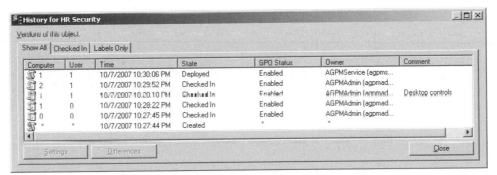

Figure 14-9   Every time a GPO is edited within AGPM, an entry is made to the archive, establishing the day and time of the change.

Who Made the Changes

Tracking the user who made the changes can be helpful for several reasons. First, the user might have had a specific reason for making the change but did not document it. Contacting the user who made the change is an easy way to determine why settings were updated in a GPO.

Second, it is always important to know who is making changes to critical areas of the network. Group Policy is extremely powerful and can do damage if left in the wrong hands. The fact that each user's changes are tracked helps monitor who has the ability to make the changes.

Finally, malicious activity does occur on a network. Knowing which users made specific settings in a GPO is very useful if you are trying to track down a rogue administrator. It is never pleasant to consider someone doing something negative to the network, but it does happen.

What Changes Were Made

The ability to track when changes were made to the GPO and who made them is nice for auditing and identifying the guilty individual in case of an errant setting. However, the real benefit of change management is the ability to track what settings were modified, added, or deleted in the GPO. This objective is very difficult to achieve, because the changes that occur in the GPO must be compared to the previous version of the GPO, or an even older version.

AGPM allows you to look at the settings that are in the GPO and also compare the GPO to any historical GPO in the archive. This provides a clear view of the GPO changes in comparison to any version of the GPO. A deeper look into these reports is offered later in this chapter. Figure 14-10 illustrates how the change management aspect of AGPM tracks changes that were made in the GPO.

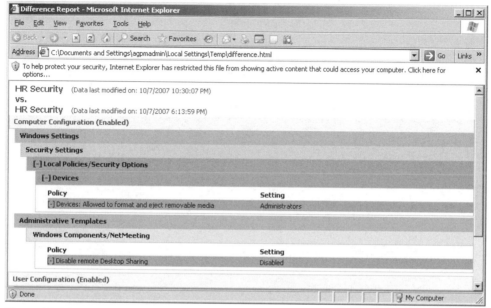

Figure 14-10   Every change made in a GPO is recorded and can then be compared to a different version of the GPO in the archive, providing a difference report.

Workflow

Although workflow is not used very much in Microsoft products or technologies, it is used within AGPM. The workflow mechanism within AGPM is designed to work with the delegation that is also built into AGPM. Workflow can be defined as activity that is systematic and follows a set pattern. The activity can be control of resources, roles, or information flow.

AGPM provides this and more; it also provides change management and many other amenities that make managing Group Policy simple. Workflow is important for even the smallest of companies that delegate Group Policy management. Workflow allows all administrators of Group Policy to do their jobs without having to spend time communicating with other Group Policy administrators. AGPM uses workflow to allow a Group Policy administrator to trigger a task to be performed, without actually performing the task. This is a very efficient model that eliminates the need for communication outside of AGPM.

The workflow built in to AGPM provides a few options for communication within the tool, as well as options for controlling a few aspects of Group Policy management. All of the workflow is related to the capabilities of the administrator performing the task and the administrators who are set up to receive correspondence that a task has been performed. There are two methods for workflow communication and two tasks that fall under workflow procedures within AGPM:

Workflow communication methods

- E-mail
- Pending tab in AGPM

Workflow tasks

- Creation of a live GPO
- Deployment of a GPO
- Deletion of a GPO from Production
- Interaction with the live environment

E-Mail Configuration

It is no surprise that e-mail is an option for communication within AGPM for workflow. However, e-mail is not a *required* form of communication within AGPM. E-mail messages that indicate that a task has been performed include all of the pertinent information related to the task. They include information regarding the action, the GPO being modified, the user requesting the task, and a comment if necessary.

Initially, e-mail is not used or configured for use with the workflow in AGPM. To configure the e-mail option within AGPM, follow these steps:

1. Open the GPMC as a user with full control over AGPM.
2. Click the Change Control node in the domain or forest in which you want to manage GPOs.
3. Click the Domain Delegation tab in the details pane.
4. Enter the information related to e-mail in the top portion of the tab. You will need to include the following information, which is also shown in Figure 14-11:
   - From: The e-mail address that you will use, which will appear to AGPM administrators who have approval capability in the workflow process.
   - To: The e-mail addresses of AGPM administrators who should always be notified of workflow tasks. This is a comma-delimited list.

> **Note** Additional e-mail addresses can be entered when the e-mail message is sent from the GPO administrator. The To: line is just for administrators who should receive every workflow e-mail message.

   - SMTP server: A valid SMTP server.

❑   User name: A valid user name, with access to the SMTP server.

❑   Password and Confirm password: A valid password for the user name you entered.

5.   Enter the e-mail address of the user who should receive all workflow e-mail messages related to AGPM in the To box, as shown in Figure 14-11.

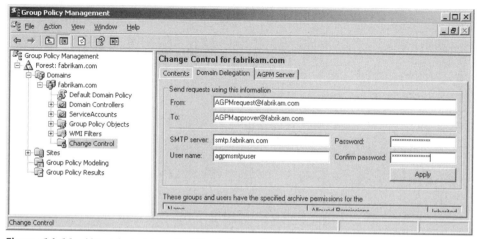

Figure 14-11   You must enter all of the information related to e-mail addresses and SMTP server to ensure that the e-mail portion of workflow functions for AGPM.

When a user performs a task that he or she does not have permission to perform, the user is not denied that action explicitly. Instead, the workflow-related tasks offer that an e-mail message could be sent to the AGPM administrator responsible for that level of task. The e-mail message sent to the approving administrator contains all of the significant information.

Pending Tab

If the e-mail portion of workflow is not configured, workflow still functions. E-mail is just an option, whereas the Pending tab communication method works with no configuration. The Pending tab alerts the AGPM administrator when an administrator performs a task that is not completed because of the limited permissions of the administrator who attempted the task.

When a task has been performed that requires approval, it appears on the Pending tab, as shown in Figure 14-12.

All pending requests include the information that the approving administrator needs to know to make a decision. Pending requests include the following:

■   GPO name

■   Computer part version number

■   User part version number

■   Pending state of the GPO

■   GPO status

■ Windows Management Instrumentation (WMI) filters associated with the GPO

■ Date GPO was modified and put in pending state

■ Owner of the modified GPO

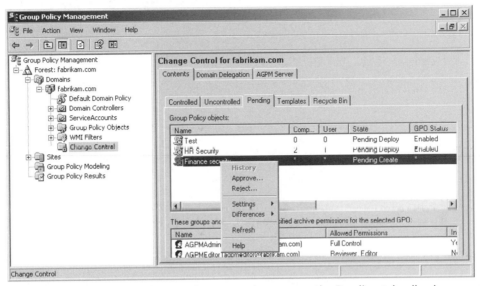

Figure 14-12   All actions that require approval appear on the Pending tab, allowing approving administrators to view and update pending requests at their leisure.

GPOs that appear on the Pending tab will remain there until approved or rejected.

Creating GPOs

Creation of a GPO in AGPM is possible only if the administrator performing the creation has the appropriate permissions. The reasons for limiting the creation of GPOs are obvious. First, if everyone could create GPOs, the domain would be flooded with GPOs that didn't do anything or were configured incorrectly. Second, an errant GPO could cause limited connectivity on the network, or with no connectivity at all.

Therefore, the creation of GPOs is limited to only a few administrators who can be trusted with such an awesome task. After an administrator has been granted the correct delegated permissions (in both the GPMC and AGPM), the ability to create a GPO within AGPM is granted.

For more information on controlling delegation for creating GPOs in the GPMC and AGPM, refer to Chapter 9, "Security Delegation for Administration of GPOs."

Best Practices   It is a best practice to grant administrators the ability to create GPOs from within AGPM only. If an administrator creates or controls GPOs from the native GPMC console (without AGPM), the GPO is not controlled, managed offline, backed up automatically, and so on.

Creating a GPO (with Create Permissions)

During the creation process of a GPO from within AGPM, you have the choice to create the GPO live or offline. In both cases, the GPO will be created and placed on the Controlled tab in AGPM. If you create the GPO offline, it will appear on the Controlled tab, but it will not be deployed to a domain controller into production. If the GPO is created live, it will be deployed and put into the production environment.

To create a GPO from AGPM, follow these steps:

1. In the GPMC, right-click the Change Control node, and then click New Controlled GPO.

2. In the New Controlled GPO dialog box, enter the name of your GPO in the GPO Name box.

3. (Optional) Type a comment for the GPO in the Comment box.

4. Select either Create Live or Create Offline.

5. From the GPO Template list, select the GPO template on which you will base the new GPO. You use this GPO template as a starting point for the new GPO.

> **Note**   The first time a GPO is created, a dialog box appears indicating that a GPO template has not yet been created and that one will be created for you. This GPO template will be created with no settings and will be marked as default. For future GPOs created in AGPM, this dialog box will not appear.

Creating a GPO (without Create Permissions)

If the administrator does not have permission to create a GPO from within AGPM, but does have other permissions, the option to create a new GPO will still be available. This is because the workflow process that is built in to AGPM can send a request to create a new GPO. In this instance, the GPO will not be created—it will be placed in a pending state for the approving AGPM administrator to approve.

To create a GPO without create permissions using the workflow mechanism, follow these steps:

1. In the GPMC, right-click the Change Control node, and then click New Controlled GPO.

2. In the Submit New Controlled GPO Request dialog box, type the e-mail address of additional administrators that should receive the request.

3. Type the name of the GPO in the GPO Name box.

4. (Optional) Type a comment for the GPO in the Comment box.

5. Select either Create Live or Create Offline.

6. From the GPO Template list, select the GPO template on which you will base the new GPO. You use this GPO template as a starting point for the new GPO.

> **Note**   If the SMTP portion of AGPM is not configured, the request is not e-mailed and will appear in the GPO creation confirmation as failing. The GPO is created on the Pending tab, but no administrator is notified of the pending request.

Withdrawing a GPO That Is Pending Creation

If a request to create a GPO is sent errantly or should be withdrawn, the administrator who sent the request can withdraw it. To do this, the GPO that was placed under the Pending tab will be right-clicked, and then the withdraw menu option will be selected. An e-mail message will be sent to the administrators who are configured within the SMTP area, as well as those in the CC box of the New Request dialog box. This message simply informs the recipients of the original request that it no longer requires any action.

Approving or Rejecting a Pending GPO

If the request to create a new GPO was not in error and the administrator with approval permissions is notified of the pending GPO creation, he or she can either approve or reject the GPO as shown previously in Figure 14-12.

Approving the GPO will create it, either live or offline depending on the initial creation settings. Rejecting the GPO will delete it, and nothing will be created in production or AGPM.

Deploying GPOs

Deploying GPOs from AGPM can be done in many different ways and for many different reasons. For the purposes of this discussion, the term *deploy* is defined as taking a GPO from AGPM and putting it into production on a domain controller.

Deploying a GPO That Was Created Offline (with Deploy Permissions)

GPOs created offline, meaning in AGPM only, must be deployed before they can affect a computer or user with their settings. Follow these steps to deploy a GPO that was created in AGPM:

1.   In the GPMC, click the Controlled tab in the details pane.

2.   Right-click the GPO that you want to deploy, and then click Deploy.

3.   In the Deploy GPO dialog box, click Yes, as shown in Figure 14-13.

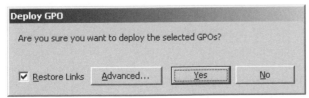

Figure 14-13   The Deploy GPO dialog box asks you to confirm deployment of your GPO.

Deploying a GPO That Was Created Offline (without Deploy Permissions)

GPOs created by administrators who do not have the deploy permission will follow a similar deployment process, with a different final step. In this scenario, the GPO deployment will move to a pending state. Follow these steps to deploy a GPO without deploy permissions:

1. In the GPMC, click the Controlled tab in the details pane.

2. Right-click the GPO you want to deploy, and then click Deploy.

3. In the Submit Deploy Request dialog box, click Submit, as shown in Figure 14-14.

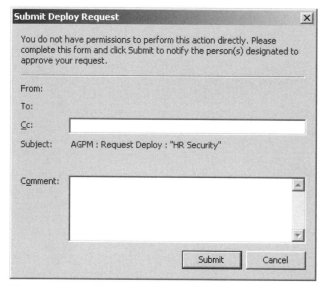

Figure 14-14 If an administrator without deploy permissions wants to deploy a GPO, a request for this action must be sent to an administrator with the appropriate permissions.

After the GPO request is sent, the GPO will appear on the Pending tab, as shown in Figure 14-15.

> **Note** A GPO that is pending deployment has the same control options as a GPO that is pending creation. This includes the option for the requestor to withdraw and the option for the approver to approve or reject. See the section "Creating GPOs," earlier in this chapter, for more information on these options.

Deploying a GPO from the Archive (with Deploy Permissions)

A GPO that already exists in production and AGPM will include archived versions of the GPO. In the event that an older or newer GPO must be deployed from AGPM to production, an administrator can perform the task by following these steps:

1. In the GPMC, click the Controlled tab in the details pane.

2. Double-click the GPO that you want to deploy.

3. Right-click an archived version of the GPO, and then click Deploy.

4. In the Deploy GPO dialog box, click Yes.

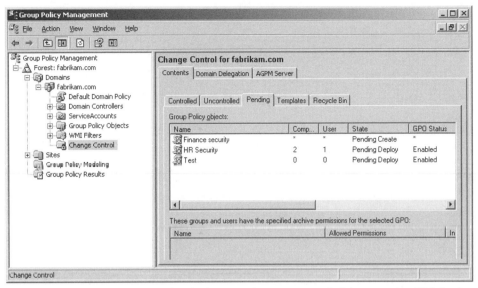

Figure 14-15 After a request for deployment is sent to an administrator, the GPO is placed on the Pending tab for approval.

Deploying a GPO from the Archive (without Deploy Permissions)

An administrator who has limited control over GPOs in AGPM but does not have deploy permissions can still trigger a deploy request from the archived list of GPOs. The steps are similar to those for an administrator who does have deploy permissions, with the inclusion of a request for deployment:

1. In the GPMC, click the Controlled tab in the details pane.

2. Double-click the GPO that you want to deploy.

3. Right-click an archived version of the GPO, and then click Deploy.

4. In the Submit Deploy Request dialog box, click Submit.

Rolling Back and Rolling Forward

When a GPO within AGPM is edited, a copy is placed in the archive. This feature allows for an excellent backup and restore process—all GPOs are backed up automatically and can be easily accessed at any time for restoration.

Whenever you edit a GPO, a copy is automatically saved; this process cannot be altered. To see how the automatic backup process works, follow these steps:

1. In the GPMC, click the Controlled tab in the details pane.

2. Right-click the GPO in the list that you want to edit, and then click Check Out.

3. (Optional) Type a comment in the Comment box, and then click OK.

4. After the GPO is checked out, click Close.

5. On the Controlled tab, right-click the GPO in the list again, and then click Edit.

6. Make any modifications to the GPO that you want, and then exit the GPME.

7. On the Controlled tab, double-click the GPO.

8. View the new archived copy of the GPO, listed in the History for *<GPO name>* dialog box, as shown in Figure 14-16.

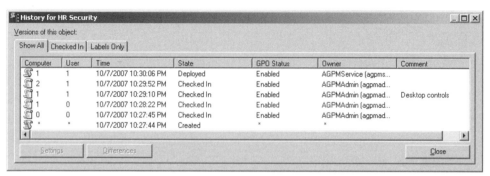

Figure 14-16   Every time a GPO within AGPM is edited, a copy is placed in the archive, providing an automated mechanism for restoration of any GPO.

This historical archive gives you control over every GPO that is included in AGPM. You can choose to keep the current version or "roll back" to an older version. If you deploy a GPO that causes a problem, breaks an application, or behaves badly in some other way, you can easily roll back to an older version. To roll a GPO back to an older version (or even roll it forward to a newer version in time), follow these steps:

1. In the GPMC, click the Controlled tab in the details pane.

2. Double-click the GPO that you want to deploy.

3. Right-click the archived version of the GPO, and then click Deploy.

4. In the Deploy GPO dialog box, click Yes.

Reporting

Although the GPMC provides some limited reporting for Group Policy management, this feature is significantly lacking. AGPM provides advanced reporting capabilities, including both settings reports and difference reports, described in detail in this section.

Settings Reports

AGPM provides settings reports on every single GPO that is located in the archive. This includes not only the currently deployed GPO, but also any GPO that was added to the archive because it was edited.

The settings report in AGPM provides details on the actual GPO settings only, not miscellaneous settings such as security, WMI filters, and so on. This is because AGPM controls GPO settings only, not the links, filters, and other features that the GPMC provides. You must still rely on the GPMC to work with these other tangible and important settings related to the GPO.

To view the settings report of any GPO that is located in the AGPM archive, follow these steps:

1. In the GPMC, click the Controlled tab in the details pane.

2. Double-click the GPO for which you want a settings report.

3. Right-click the archived version of the GPO, click Settings, and then click HTML Report.

    The result is a Web-based report in Microsoft Internet Explorer, as shown in Figure 14-17.

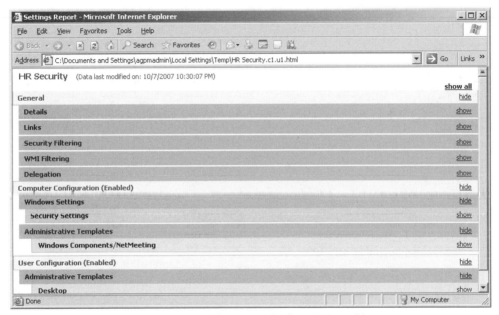

Figure 14-17   You can view a report of any GPO in the AGPM archive.

> **Note**   You can also just right-click any GPO listed on the Controlled tab, which selects the deployed GPO (or the latest version of a GPO that has not been deployed).

Reports can be reviewed in HTML or XML.

Difference Reports

The AGPM settings report is certainly valuable. However, experienced administrators of AGPM often state that difference reports are one of the most useful and powerful features of AGPM. Difference reports compare the contents of two different GPOs. They are HTML or XML based, and they clearly indicate where settings have been changed, added, or deleted.

The GPMC does not provide anything comparable to difference reports. If you do not have AGPM, you must devise an elaborate system to compare the two GPOs, or manually compare them. The manual method takes a very long time with complicated GPOs that contain a multitude of settings.

Difference Report between Two Versions of the Same GPO

To obtain a difference report between two different versions of the same GPO, follow these steps:

1. In the GPMC, click the Controlled tab in the details pane.

2. Double-click the GPO for which you want a difference report.

3. Press the SHIFT key and right-click the two archived versions of the GPO, and then click Differences – HTML Report.

    The result is a Web-based report in Internet Explorer, as shown in Figure 14-18.

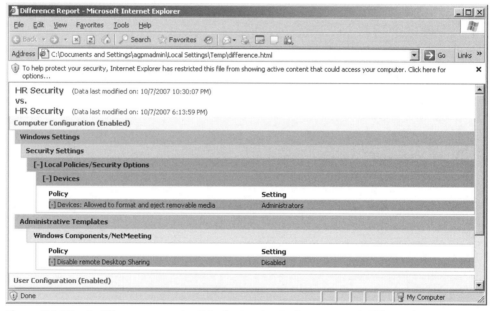

Figure 14-18   A difference report will indicate what is the same and different between two versions of the same GPO.

Difference Report between Two GPOs

To obtain a difference report between two different GPOs, follow the steps in the preceding section, but select the GPOs from the main Controlled tab, instead of the GPO History window. The steps and result will be very similar to those for a difference report of two versions of the same GPO.

Difference Report between a GPO and an AGPM Template

You can also compare any GPO to a template by following these steps:

1. In the GPMC, click the Controlled tab in the details pane.

2. Double-click the GPO for which you want a report.

3. Right-click the archived version of the GPO for which you want to compare to a GPO template, and then click Differences – Template.

4. Select the GPO template that you want to use from the Template list.

5. Select HTML Report or XML Report for the report format.

   The result is a Web-based report in Internet Explorer.

Using Templates

AGPM GPO templates are nothing more than predefined GPOs. The ability to define a GPO full of settings—that can then be used to create new GPOs—is very useful in simple to complex environments. You can create multiple GPO templates, each containing a preset suite of GPO settings. In most cases, these preset GPO settings create a "baseline" of settings that all similar GPOs will contain.

After a GPO template is created, anyone within the AGPM environment that has been granted the ability to create GPOs can use them. Any new GPO within AGPM can be modeled after a GPO template, avoiding the need to create an empty GPO that then must be configured.

> **Note**   After a template is created, it cannot be modified. It is a best practice to take existing GPOs and make templates out of them, to create a baseline of settings.

To create a GPO template from scratch, follow these steps:

1. In the GPMC, select the Change Control panel.

2. Click the Controlled tab in the details pane.

3. Right-click the GPO on which you want to create a GPO template, and then click Save As Template.

4. Type a name for the new template in the Name box, add an optional comment, and then click OK.

5. When the progress indicator window shows that the progress is complete, click Close. Look for the new template on the Templates tab.

In some cases, you may want to create a GPO template originating your process from an existing GPO. This will allow you to take an existing GPO (and its settings), and then reuse it as the model for additional GPOs. To create a GPO template using an existing GPO, follow these steps:

1. In the GPMC, click the Controlled tab in the details pane.

2. Right-click the GPO on which you want to create a GPO template, and then click Save As Template.

3. Type a name for the new template in the Name box, and add an optional comment.

A GPO within AGPM includes all of the settings that can be contained in a GPO, including software deployment, security settings, user rights, audit policy settings, IP security settings, and Administrative Template settings (registry settings).

> **Best Practices**   It is a best practice to create GPO templates based on departments, types of computers, types of users, and so on. Then, establish the delegation on the GPO template, which will then be carried over to the newly created GPO. This copying of the delegated permissions is an ideal way to ensure that only those administrators who should have control over the GPO and the settings can alter the settings in the template and new GPO residing in AGPM.

Recycle Bin

Every administrator who has made a mistake that cost his or her company hundreds or thousands of dollars has wished to go back in time and undo the mistake. Such an error might include a misconfiguration, an errant deployment, inadequate testing of a technology, or a deleted file. When GPOs are deleted from AGPM, they are not deleted immediately. Instead, they are placed in a Recycle Bin, just in case the administrator has doubts or made a mistake.

> **Note**   The history of a GPO will be restored during the restoration process of a GPO in AGPM. However, if the GPO is destroyed from AGPM, the history is also destroyed.

The Recycle Bin is a default feature of AGPM and cannot be eliminated. It retains all GPOs that are deleted from within AGPM. When a GPO is deleted from anywhere in the AGPM tool, it is placed in the Recycle Bin, as shown in Figure 14-19.

To access the Recycle Bin and either restore or destroy a GPO, follow these steps:

1. In the GPMC, click the Recycle Bin tab in the details pane.

2. Right-click the GPO that you want to control, and then click either Destroy, to permanently delete the GPO from AGPM and GPMC, or Restore, to place the GPO back on the Controlled tab within AGPM.

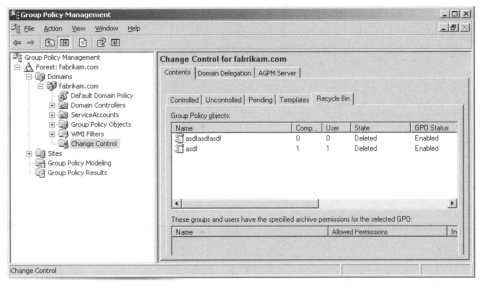

Figure 14-19   All GPOs that are deleted from within AGPM are placed in the Recycle Bin, in case the administrator wants to put them back into production.

Note   Restoring a GPO from the Recycle Bin will not put the GPO back into production. It will only place the GPO back on the Controlled tab in AGPM.

Restoring GPOs and GPO Links

GPOs that are stored in AGPM are not completely controlled by AGPM. Some configurations are not manageable or even tracked within the tool. One such configuration is GPO links, which are completely controlled by the GPMC.

There is one exception: When an administrator deletes or otherwise manipulates a GPO, AGPM tracks the GPO links. If the GPO is restored, deployed, or in any way put back into production, you may choose which GPO links to restore. To view and select the links that are associated with a GPO that an administrator is putting back into production, follow these steps:

1.   In the GPMC, click the Controlled tab in the details pane.

2.   Right-click the GPO for which you want to view links, and then click Deploy.

3.   Ensure that the Restore Links check box is selected, and then click Advanced.

4.   In the GPO Links for Selected GPO dialog box, select the Active Directory nodes that you want to have the GPO linked to so that you can view the links, as shown in Figure 14-20.

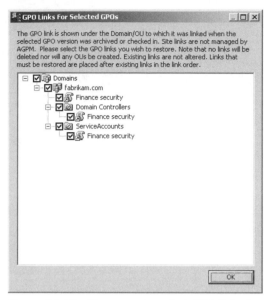

Figure 14-20   You cannot control GPO links from within AGPM, but you can restore the links when you deploy a GPO into production.

If you want to see where a GPO is linked before deployment, you can view a report of GPO links by following these steps:

1. In the GPMC, click the Controlled tab in the details pane.

2. Double-click the GPO for which you want to view a report.

3. Right-click the archived version of the GPO, and then click Settings – GPO Links.

    The results appear in the GPO Links for Selected GPOs dialog box.

Summary

This chapter provided an in-depth overview of the Advanced Group Policy Management tool included in the Microsoft Desktop Optimization Pack. AGPM is a straightforward tool that provides many of the features that the GPMC omits. The architecture of AGPM simple, yet it provides very robust features. There is no need to install AGPM on a domain controller—in fact, you should *not* do so as a best practice. AGPM can be administered from almost any administrative desktop using the GPMC and AGPM client.

AGPM provides an array of functionality, including offline editing, roll back, roll forward, change management, workflow, and robust reporting of GPO settings. All of these features are needed in any organization that uses Group Policy. Without these features, administrators are limited to what the GPMC can provide.

The reporting and template feature within AGPM is truly magnificent. The ability to compare any two GPOs to one another can save days of time for a Group Policy administrator.

Templates can also save time: One GPO template can include the majority of the settings that every GPO created needs to have, which might include hundreds of settings. This efficient method of creating GPOs from a template can save time.

Finally, AGPM provides disaster recovery through use of the Recycle Bin and restoration of GPOs and their links; disaster recovery is not even addressed in the GPMC natively. These features make AGPM an essential tool for any enterprise that uses Active Directory.

Additional Resources

- The Microsoft Advanced Group Policy Management Web site, at *http://www.microsoft.com/windows/products/windowsvista/enterprise/agpm.mspx,* includes more information about Advanced Group Policy Management.

- The Microsoft Desktop Optimization Pack Web site, at *http://www.microsoft.com/ windows/products/windowsvista/enterprise/mdopoverview.mspx,* provides more information about the Microsoft Desktop Optimization Pack.

- Chapter 3, "Group Policy Basics," includes information on GPO links.

- Chapter 4, "Architecture of Group Policy," includes information on GPO links.

- Chapter 6, "GPMC Basics," includes information about the functionality and features of the GPMC.

- Chapter 9, "Security Delegation for Administration of GPOs," includes information on how to delegate administration of Group Policy management.

Troubleshooting GPOs

Because Group Policy is so complex, errors in configuration can cause problems with Group Policy application. Problems can arise with any of the numerous Group Policy elements, and related technologies can also cause Group Policy application to fail.

Fortunately, common problems that arise with the technologies that are directly related to Group Policy are generally easy to locate and fix. All of these technologies have been discussed within this book, and references to the corresponding sections are included in this chapter. Common problems might involve Active Directory replication, Domain Name System (DNS), or authentication. An entire section of this chapter is dedicated to these issues.

Tools are also available to help you troubleshoot Group Policy. For example, built-in tools such as GPUpdate, GPOTool, and GPResult provide the ability to control and review the state of Group Policy. Other tools, such as event logging, allow you to track issues related to Group Policy to help you solve both simple and complex problems.

Group Policy Troubleshooting Essentials

When you discover a problem with Group Policy processing, you have several options for locating the source of the problem. Because Group Policy processing has many elements with many interdependent pieces of infrastructure, it is important that you take a methodical approach to troubleshooting. By using the information that has been presented throughout this book, we can list some common areas in which Group Policy might fail, or appear to be failing. Here are some common problem areas to check, along with references to chapters for you to review.

- Check the required infrastructure. Make sure that required services and components are running and configured as expected. Refer to Chapter 4, "Architecture of Group Policy," for more information about how Active Directory, DNS, File Replication Service (FRS), Distributed File System (DFS), Distributed File System Replication (DFSR), and Network Location Awareness (NLA) dependencies relate to Group Policy.

- Check computer core configuration. Verify that the computer is connected to the network, is joined to the domain, is authenticated to a domain controller, and has the correct system time.

- Check the scope of management (SOM). Ensure that the user or computer object is located under the correct organizational unit. Ensure that the GPO is linked to the correct Active Directory node. Refer to Chapter 5, "Group Policy Processing," which covers SOM concepts and details.

- Verify that default GPO processing has not been altered. Blocking policy inheritance, enforcing a GPO, security filtering, WMI filtering, and Group Policy Preferences item-level targeting alter default policy processing. Refer to Chapter 5 and Chapter 12, "Group Policy Preferences," for more information about these configurations.

- Ensure that the GPO and the Group Policy Preferences are not disabled. If a GPO or a portion of a GPO is disabled, this can prevent the application of the settings contained within the GPO from applying. Also, if individual settings are disabled (allowed by Group Policy Preferences), the policy might not process the settings. Refer to Chapter 6, "GPMC Basics," which describes how to enable and disable portions of a GPO. Also refer to Chapter 12, which explains how to disable or enable individual preference settings.

Common Problems with GPOs

Although the failure of all or part of Group Policy to process can be caused by many misconfigurations, some problems are common and can easily be identified and fixed. This section describes a variety of scenarios, problems, and solutions for situations in which Group Policy fails or provides undesired results.

DNS-Related Problems

Many companies, including Microsoft, have reported that over 70 percent of all GPO problems are associated with DNS. So when a Group Policy problem arises, you should always think DNS first! There can be many hidden issues with DNS; here are the steps you should take to check DNS settings:

1. Ensure that the client has the correct IP address configurations. If the client cannot contact DNS, GPOs will not apply. You can run the Ipconfig command from the command prompt to verify the IP address.

2. Make sure that the Dynamic Host Configuration Protocol (DHCP) server has all of the IP configurations correct. These include DNS server, default gateway, domain name, and subnet mask. The DHCP administration tool is available in the Administrative Tools menu.

3.   Make sure that the client is receiving IP information, if it is DHCP enabled. You can run the Ipconfig command with the /all switch to see all related IP information for that computer.

4.   Make sure that the correct records are listed in DNS, for both client and server (including domain controllers). There must be a CNAME entry for all computers on the network (domain controllers, servers, and desktops), and the correct SRV records for the domain controllers must be running the domain. Refer to the article titled "How DNS Support for Active Directory Works," at *http://technet2.microsoft.com/windowsserver/en/library/ 9d62e91d-75c3-4a77-ae93-a8804e9ff2a11033.mspx?mfr=true*, for information about how DNS and Active Directory work together.

5.   Make sure that the correct DNS server is listed in the primary and secondary settings on all computers (domain controllers, servers, and desktops). Without the correct DNS server configured, the domain controller SRV record will not be found and Group Policy will not apply. You can view the current DNS server configured on the computer by running the Ipconfig command with the /all switch.

How It Works: Internal and ISP DNS Servers

If the DHCP service is controlled by the outward-facing router that is receiving the IP address from the ISP, it is likely that this router is receiving the DNS server information from the Internet service provider (ISP). In this case, the DHCP server might be configuring clients with the ISP-delivered DNS server, rather than the internal Active Directory–based DNS server. If so, all computers running Windows that are located on the local LAN must be configured with a manual DNS server, which must be the internal DNS server. The internal DNS server will be configured to forward all requests that are not for the internal domain to the DNS servers at the ISP.

Asynchronous Group Policy Processing

When Group Policy is configured to process GPO settings asynchronously, it might take one, two, or even three reboots or logons to get all of the settings to apply. For your review, asynchronous and synchronous processing are defined as follows:

■   **Asynchronous**   Windows does not wait for the network stack to initialize before starting and allowing the user receive the desktop.

■   **Synchronous**   Windows waits for the network stack to initialize, and all Group Policy foreground processing occurs before the user receives the desktop.

If you want all settings to apply on a foreground refresh, you must configure Group Policy to apply synchronously. For more information regarding policy processing settings and an explanation of which client-side extensions (CSEs) react to asynchronous processing the most, refer to Chapter 5.

Foreground-Only GPO Settings

Some GPO settings do not process in the background. For example, you might see that a GPO setting is updated, and then run GPUpdate to apply the setting. You run Resultant Set of Policy (RSoP) to determine whether the policy has applied, and you notice that it has. However, the setting that you configured in the GPO is still not appearing on the computer.

If the setting is under a CSE such as software installation, folder redirection, Group Policy drive maps, scripts, deployed printer connections, Microsoft Internet Explorer branding, Group Policy printers, or offline files, you will notice this behavior. All of the settings that fall under these CSEs update only on a foreground refresh. For more information regarding foreground and background refreshes, refer to Chapter 5.

Network Connection

In any case in which you are not connected to the network, you will not get Group Policy updates. When a background or foreground refresh occurs, Group Policy updates occur only if the entire authentication and discovery process occurs. This includes much of what we have discussed in this troubleshooting section, including accessing DNS, authenticating to a domain controller, and providing the correct log-on credentials.

To verify that you have network connectivity, you can use the Ping command. When using the Ping command, you should always Ping many computers and interfaces. At a minimum, you should Ping your own IP address, the IP address of a computer on your subnet, the default gateway, and a domain controller.

To determine which domain controller authenticated your computer at logon, you can run the Set command from a command prompt. This command displays many variables, but the Logonserver variable indicates which domain controller authenticated you. You can also Ping this domain controller name to determine whether you have connectivity.

If you do not have network connectivity, you should answer the following questions:

- Is the network adapter enabled?
- Is the network cable plugged in?
- Did the DHCP server configure IP information?
- Is the computer set up for DHCP or static IP information?
- Is the DNS server configured properly?
- Are the IP address and subnet mask correct if configured statically?

GPO Function after WMI Filter Deletion

WMI filters can target specific computers based on the current state, environment, and setup of the computer. However, if you have linked a WMI filter to a GPO, but you no longer want the WMI filter to apply to the GPO, you should not just delete the WMI filter file.

The reason for this is that the WMI filter file is not a part of the GPO—it is linked to a GPO. When you delete the WMI filter file without removing the link to the GPO, the GPO still thinks the WMI filter should be used. When the GPO refers to the WMI filter to return the list of objects to apply the GPO to, it returns a null set, and the GPO will not apply to any object. For more information about WMI filters, refer to Chapter 5.

Time Synchronization

Kerberos validation and authentication will fail if the time difference between a client computer and its log-on domain controller is greater than five minutes. This failure can in turn cause problems with DNS registration, Group Policy processing, and other essential computer processes. To check a computer's current system time and date, type the following command exactly as shown at a command prompt.

```
net time \\%ComputerName%
```

The output is the current time and date on the local computer:

```
Current time at \\CLIENT1 is 12/7/2007 2:02 PM
```

To check the system time on the log-on domain controller, type the following command at a command prompt:

```
net time
```

The output is the current time and date on the log-on domain controller:

```
Current time at \\SERVER1 is 12/7/2007 2:02 PM
```

> **Note**   You can type **net time /set** to synchronize the local computer time with the time on the log-on domain controller. To automatically synchronize time for all computers in a domain, you can use the Windows Time Synchronization service (W32Time). For more information about W32Time, refer to the article titled "Basic Operation of the Windows Time Service" at *http://support.microsoft.com/kb/224799*.

Unavailable PDC Emulator

When the domain controller that controls the PDC emulator role is not available, editing of GPOs will fail. This is because the system relies on the PDC emulator to make changes to all GPOs by default. This is not a hard-coded feature, and in some cases it can be beneficial to not use the PDC emulator. For example, if you want to target a domain controller in a remote site for updating a GPO that will affect users in the site more quickly, you will want to use the domain controller in that site, which might not be the PDC emulator.

If the PDC emulator is not available, you will be prompted to select another domain controller, as shown in Figure 15-1. In this dialog box, you can select a different domain controller to make the changes to the GPO. The replication of both the Group Policy template (GPT) and Group

Policy container (GPC) will still function as normal, and the changes will be sent to all domain controllers as usual.

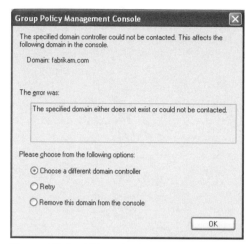

Figure 15-1   When the PDC emulator is not available for GPO editing, a dialog box prompts you to select a different domain controller.

For more information about selecting a domain controller or choosing a different domain controller for optimizing GPO processing performance, refer to Chapters 4 and 6.

Using Event Logging for Troubleshooting

An important new addition in Windows Vista and Windows Server 2008 is the updated Event Viewer features and logs. One of the most significant additions is a log dedicated to Group Policy. In addition to this log, you will find features such as a centralized event-logging system, cross-log querying capabilities, scheduled task integration, and filtered views that make using Event Viewer easier and more efficient than ever before.

For more information about working with the new Event Viewer in Windows, refer to *http://www.microsoft.com/technet/technetmag/issues/2006/11/EventManagement/*, an article that discusses some of the finer points of Event Viewer.

> **Note**   The Userenv logs are no longer available with Windows Vista and Windows Server 2008. These logs, and all other granular logs for CSEs, are captured in Event Viewer and use a source name of Group Policy.

Compared with the myriad logs and triggers needed in earlier versions of the Windows operating system to get advanced log information related to Group Policy, the new Event Viewer features make troubleshooting Group Policy much easier. All Group Policy–related events are now stored in Event Viewer logs with the source name of GroupPolicy, so it is easy to quickly see these events and even make custom views with just Group Policy events in them. Group Policy events will appear under both System event logs and the Group Policy operational event logs. In addition to these benefits, you will also notice improvements made to descriptions of the events and their possible causes, as well as the follow-up actions suggested.

Group Policy Operational Log

The primary location for storage of Group Policy events is in the Group Policy operational log. As stated earlier, this is where the past Userenv text file event logging is stored. To access the Group Policy operational log, follow these steps:

1. Start Event Viewer.

2. Expand Applications And Services Logs.

3. Expand Microsoft, then Windows, and finally Group Policy.

4. Click Operational.

All of the Event Viewer views have been updated with new interfaces, options, and information. It is important that you understand how these new views and information correspond to information being displayed within the Event Viewer. Figure 15-2 shows the General tab, and Figure 15-3 shows the Details tab.

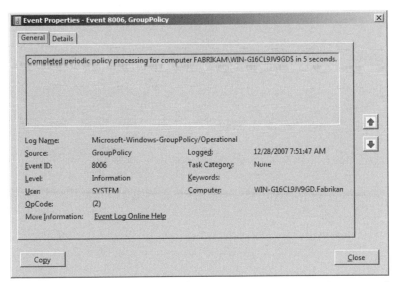

Figure 15-2   This figure shows the General tab of a standard Group Policy event in Event Viewer.

Each section on the General tab provides important information to help you resolve the issue:

- **Description box**   Contains text that describes the logged event. Group Policy events usually contain information describing the events, possible reasons why the event occurred, and suggested follow-up actions.

- **Source**   The name of the software that logs the event. Group Policy events always use the source name Group Policy.

- **Event ID**   A numerical ID representing the type of event logged. Administrative events in the System event log and the Group Policy operation event log use event IDs. You can find more information about specific Group Policy events and event IDs in the appendices of this book.

- **Level**   Classifies the severity of an event. Group Policy events use Error, Informational, and Warning event levels.

- **User**   The name of the user account that triggered the logged event. The Group Policy service uses the name SYSTEM for recording events related to computer policy processing. User policy processing events use the name of the user who is processing policy.

- **Logged**   The date and local time when the event logging system logged the event. Group Policy in Windows Vista has the opportunity to refresh more often. When troubleshooting Group Policy, make sure that the events you are viewing match the time of the reported problem.

- **Computer**   The name of the computer on which the event occurred.

- **More Information**   A hyperlink to the Microsoft TechNet Web site. Clicking this link provides you with information about the event, possible causes for the event, and suggestions that may resolve the issue, if the event is a warning or an error.

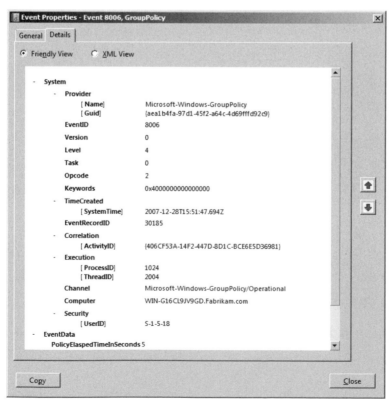

Figure 15-3   This figure shows the Details tab of a standard Group Policy event in Event Viewer.

Like the General tab, the Details tab provides important information that can help you troubleshoot Group Policy problems, including the following:

- **System\Correlation:ActivityID**   The ActivityID represents one instance of Group Policy processing. The Group Policy service creates a unique ActivityID each time Group Policy refreshes. For example, consider a computer that processes Group Policy during start-up. At that time, the Group Policy service assigns that instance of processing an ActivityID. Further events logged during that instance use the same ActivityID until that instance of Group Policy processing completes (Group Policy processing completes when the process ends either successfully or with errors). Users process Group Policy during the log-on process. Again, the Group Policy service assigns a unique ActivityID to that instance of Group Policy processing and uses it until processing completes. This behavior repeats for each new instance of Group Policy processing, which includes automatic and forced Group Policy refreshes. You can view this value on all Group Policy events.

- **EventData\PolicyActivityID**   This is the same value as the System\Correlation:ActivityID. The Group Policy service uses this value to identify an instance of Group Policy processing. You can view this value in policy start events (4000–4007).

- **EventData\PrincipalSamName**   This value contains the name of the security principal to which the Group Policy service applies, the name of the computer during computer policy processing, and the name of the user during user policy processing. The event displays the format as domainname\computer or domainname\user. This information appears in policy start events (4000–4007), next policy application events (5315), policy end events (8000–8007), and scripts processing start and end events (4018, 5018).

- **EventData\IsDomainJoined**   This value is True when the computer is a member of a domain and False when it is not. You can view this value on policy start events (4000–4007).

- **EventData\IsBackgoundProcessing**   This value is True when the Group Policy service applies policy settings in the background. Otherwise, this value is False. When this value and the IsAsyncProcessing value are False, the Group Policy service applies policy settings synchronously in the foreground. You can view this value on policy start events (4000–4007).

- **EventData\IsAsyncProcessing**   This value is True when the Group Policy service applies policy setting asynchronously in the foreground. Otherwise, this value is False. When this value and the IsBackgroundProcessing value are False, the Group Policy service applies policy settings synchronously in the foreground. You can view this value on policy start events (4000–4007).

- **EventData\PolicyApplicationMode**   The Group Policy service records the type of Group Policy processing in the PolicyApplicationMode field. The PolicyApplicationMode field is one of three values. Those values are described in Table 15-1.

Table 15-1   PolicyApplicationMode Values

Value	Explanation
0	Background processing: The instance of Group Policy processing occurring after the initial instance of Group Policy processing. Background processing occurs when the Group Policy service refreshes. For example, the Group Policy service periodically refreshes Group Policy every 90 minutes.
1	Synchronous foreground processing: Foreground processing is the instance of policy processing that occurs at computer start-up and user logon. Synchronous foreground processing is when the processing of computer Group Policy must complete before Windows displays the log-on dialog box, and user Group Policy processing, which happens during user logon, must complete before Windows displays the user's desktop.
2	Asynchronous foreground processing: Asynchronous foreground processing is the instance of Group Policy processing that occurs at computer start-up and user logon. However, Windows does not wait for computer Group Policy processing to complete before displaying the log-on dialog box. Additionally, Windows does not wait for user Group Policy processing to complete before displaying the user's desktop.

- **EventData\PolicyProcessingMode**   You use the PolicyProcessingMode field to determine the presence of loopback processing and whether loopback processing is in Merge or Replace mode. The three possible values are described in Table 15-2.

Table 15-2   PolicyProcessingMode Values

Value	Explanation
0	Normal Processing mode: Loopback is not enabled.
1	Loopback Merge mode: Loopback processing is enabled. The Group Policy service merges user settings within the scope of the computer with user settings within the scope of the user.
2	Loopback Replace mode: Loopback processing is enabled. The Group Policy service replaces user settings within the scope of the user with user settings within the scope of the computer.

- **EventData\ProcessingTimeInMilliseconds**   You use the ProcessingTimeInMilliseconds field to determine the amount of time, in milliseconds, that the described event used to complete the operation.

> **Note**   Remember that one millisecond is 0.1 seconds. To determine the number of elapsed seconds, divide the value in ProcessingTimeInMilliseconds by 1,000.

- **EventData\DCName**   The Group Policy service records the name of a domain controller in the DCName field. The name found in this field is the domain controller that the Group Policy service uses when communicating with Active Directory.

- **EventData\ErrorCode and EventData\ErrorDescription**   These two fields appear only on error events. The ErrorCode field provides a value, represented as a decimal, that the described event encountered. The ErrorDescription field provides a short description of the ErrorCode value.

Event Viewer Troubleshooting Procedure

To take full advantage of the new Event Viewer features and capabilities, it is a best practice to follow a set procedure to ensure that you are viewing the most relevant information for the problem that you are having. To do this, you should follow these steps:

1. Evaluate the System event log for Group Policy events.

2. Evaluate the Group Policy operational log:

    A.   Determine the ActivityID of Group Policy processing.

    B.   Create a custom view of a Group Policy instance.

3. Divide the custom view of the log into three phases.

    A.   Preprocessing

    B.   Processing

    C.   Postprocessing

4. Associate all Starting events with the correct Ending event.

5. Investigate all Errors, Warnings, and Failures.

6. Isolate the event that is causing the problem, and address the problem.

7. Run GPUpdate on the computer with the Group Policy problem to determine whether the problem persists. If so, repeat these steps to find other issues.

Evaluate the System Event Log

The Group Policy service writes events to the System event log indicating an administrative alert, representing the latest status of the Group Policy service. Here you can quickly determine whether the Group Policy service is the source of the problem. You might see any of the following three events in the System event log for Group Policy:

- **Informational event**   Indicates that the Group Policy service is functioning properly.

- **Warning event**   Indicates that the Group Policy service is functioning properly, but other dependencies may have failed.

- **Error event**   Indicates that the Group Policy service has failed.

Evaluate the Group Policy Operational Log: Determine the ActivityID of Group Policy Processing

Every time Group Policy background or foreground processing occurs, an ActivityID is generated that groups all of the specific actions that occurred during that Group Policy processing. It is important that you determine the ActivityID of the process so that you can isolate all events related to that process. To determine the ActivityID for an event, follow these steps:

1. Start Event Viewer.

2. Under Event Viewer, click to expand Applications And Services Logs, and then expand Microsoft, expand Windows, expand GroupPolicy, and click Operational.

3. In the details pane, click the GroupPolicy warning or error event that you want to troubleshoot.

4. In the details pane, click the Details tab the lower pane for the event, and then click Friendly view.

5. On the event's Details tab, click System to expand the System node.

6. Scroll until you find the ActivityID in the System node details. This value (without the opening and closing braces) is the ActivityID.

Evaluate the Group Policy Operational Log: Create a Custom View of a Group Policy Instance

After the ActivityID is determined, all events related to that ID must be isolated for easier and more efficient evaluation. To isolate all of the events that are associated with the ActivityID that you found, follow these steps:

1. Start Event Viewer.

2. Right-click Custom Views, and then click Create Custom View. The Create Custom View dialog box appears.

3. Click the XML tab, and then select the Edit Query Manually check box. Event Viewer displays a dialog box, which explains that editing a query manually prevents you from modifying the query using the Filter tab. Click Yes.

4. Copy the Event Viewer query (provided at the end of this step) to the clipboard. Paste the query into the Query box. Your query should look something like the following:

    <QueryList><Query Id="0" Path="Application"><Select Path="Microsoft-Windows-GroupPolicy/ Operational">*[System/Correlation/@ActivityID='{INSERT ACTIVITY ID HERE}']</Select> </Query></QueryList>

5. Enter the ActivityID that you determined in the preceding procedure in place of the "INSERT ACTIVITY ID HERE" text from step 4. Click OK.

 Note   The leading and trailing {} characters are essential for the query to work.

6. In the Save Filter to Custom View dialog box, type a name and description meaningful to the view you created, and then click OK.

7. The name of the saved view appears under Custom Views in the console tree. Click the name of the saved view to display its events in Event Viewer, as shown in Figure 15-4.

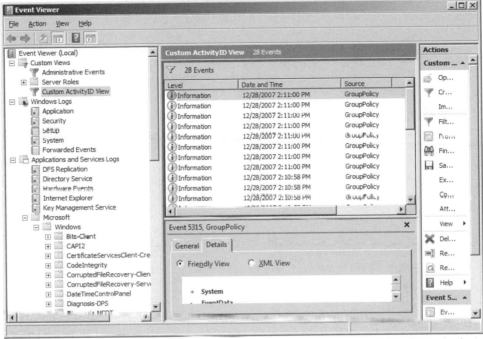

Figure 15-4   The custom view in Event Viewer isolates all of the events related to a single ActivityID.

Divide the Custom View of the Log into Three Phases: Preprocessing

This phase begins the Group Policy processing and gathers information that is required to process Group Policy. The information gathered in this phase is used to cycle through each Group Policy extension. During this phase, the Group Policy service collects information that will be used to process each CSE. This information can be divided into small subsets, which include the following:

- Start policy processing
- Retrieve account information
- Domain controller discovery
- Computer role discovery
- Security principal discovery
- Loopback processing mode discovery
- GPO discovery
- Slow link detection
- Nonsystem GP extension discovery

For each subset in the preprocessing phase, specific event IDs are generated. The ability to track an event ID to a specific portion of the preprocessing phase can help significantly in identifying the root problem with Group Policy. Each subset is defined in the following sections.

Start Policy Processing   When the computer starts, a user logs on, a refresh occurs, or there is a change to a network interface, an instance of Group Policy is recorded in Event Viewer. This instance is tracked via the ActivityID, and one of the start events is recorded with it. The start events range from 4000 to 4007 and are described in Table 15-3.

Table 15-3   Group Policy Start Events

Event ID	Start Event Type
4000	Computer start-up
4001	User logon
4002	Computer network change
4003	User network change
4004	Computer manual refresh
4005	User manual refresh
4006	Computer periodic refresh
4007	User periodic refresh

Retrieve Account Information   For processing to occur, the Group Policy service must acquire the location of the user and computer object in Active Directory. This determines the SOM for the objects. Two sets of event IDs are recorded for this portion of the preprocessing phase. They include the following:

Informational/success interaction event

- This event records information about interaction with dependent components with one of three event IDs:

  - 5320 - Success interaction event: The interaction described in the event completed successfully.

  - 6320 - Warning interaction event: The interaction described in the event completed with one or more errors.

  - 7320 - Error interaction event: The interaction described in the event failed to complete.

Trace component event

- During the information gathering phase, the Group Policy service calls other functions in Windows, referred to as system calls. These events are recorded in Event Viewer and report one or more event IDs:

  - 4017 - Start-trace event: The beginning of a system call described in the event.

  - 5017 - Success end-trace event: The system call described in the event completed successfully.

❑ 6017 - Warning end-trace event: The system call described in the event completed with one or more errors.

❑ 7017 - Error end-trace event: The system call described in the event failed to complete.

> **Tip** All end-trace events contain the elapsed time used by the system call. A call that takes too much time could indicate that there is a problem. The Details tab (explained earlier) indicates the status of the end-trace event and the elapsed time.

Domain Controller Discovery   For Group Policy to process successfully, a domain controller must be discovered. During the discovery procedure, the system binds to Active Directory, discovers a domain controller to connect to, and makes a connection to the domain controller. The event IDs associated with each step in the process include the following:

Domain controller discovery start event

- This event occurs when the computer starts to find the domain controller.
- The following event IDs are associated with this event:
    - ❑ 5017 - Success end-trace event: The system call described in the event completed successfully.
    - ❑ 6017 - Warning end-trace event: The system call described in the event completed with one or more errors.
    - ❑ 7017 - Error end-trace event: The system call described in the event failed to complete.

DC discovery interaction event

- This event occurs when the computer begins to communicate with the domain controller.
- The following event IDs are associated with this event:
    - ❑ 5308 - Success DC interaction event: The interaction described in the paragraph before this table completed successfully.
    - ❑ 6308 - Warning DC interaction event: The interaction described in the paragraph before this table completed with one or more errors.
    - ❑ 7308 - Error DC interaction event: The interaction described in the paragraph before this table did not complete.

Domain controller discovery end event

- This event occurs when the computer ends communications with the domain controller.
- The following event IDs are associated with this event:
    - ❑ 5326 - Success DC discovery end event: The process of discovering a domain controller completed successfully.

❑ 6326 - Warning DC discovery end event: The process of discovering a domain controller completed with one or more errors.

❑ 7326 - Error DC discovery end event: The process of discovering a domain controller did not complete.

Computer Role Discovery   Group Policy is applied based on the computer role and membership in a domain. Group Policy applies differently based on the computer role. The roles that a computer can have include those listed in Table 15-4.

Table 15-4   Computer Roles and Values

Value	Computer role
0	The current computer is a stand-alone workstation or server.
1	The current computer is a member of a domain that does not support directory services.
2	The current computer is a member of a domain that supports directory services.
3	The current computer is a domain controller.

The events that will be written into the log, including these computer role values, will fall under the following category and event IDs:

Computer information event

■ The following event IDs are associated with this event:

❑ 5309 - Success computer information event: The discovery of computer information completed successfully.

❑ 6309 - Warning computer information event: The discovery of computer information completed with one or more errors.

❑ 7309 - Error computer information event: The discovery of computer information did not complete.

Security Principal Discovery   Because Group Policy applies only to computer and user objects, this portion of the process determines whether the current object focus is a user or computer so that the appropriate settings can be applied. This is written to the log with the following category and event IDs:

Security principal information event

■ The following event IDs are associated with this event:

❑ 5310 - Success security principal information event: Discovering information about the current security principal completed successfully.

❑ 6310 - Warning security principal information event: Discovering information about the current security principal completed with one or more errors.

❑ 7310 - Error security principal information event: Discovering information about the current security principal did not complete.

Loopback Processing Mode Discovery   Because loopback processing alters the default Group Policy processing behavior, the Group Policy service must be aware of any loopback settings. The following category and event IDs are registered after the loopback processing information is gathered:

Loopback processing mode event

- The following event IDs are associated with this event:
  - ❏ 5311 - Success loopback processing mode event: Determining the loopback processing mode completed.
  - ❏ 6311 - Warning loopback processing mode event: Determining the loopback processing mode completed with one or more errors.
  - ❏ 7311 - Error loopback processing mode event: Determining the loopback processing mode did not complete.

The event description will include one of three types of loopback processing that will occur:

- ❏ No loopback mode: Loopback processing is not enabled.
- ❏ Merge: Loopback processing is enabled. The Group Policy service merges user settings within the scope of the computer with user settings within the scope of the user.
- ❏ Replace: Loopback processing is enabled. The Group Policy service replaces user settings within the scope of the user with user setting from the scope of the computer.

GPO Discovery   After all of the initial information is gathered to create a list of applicable GPOs, the Group Policy service discovers the final list of GPOs that will apply to the computer or user object. After obtaining the list, the Group Policy service checks the accessibility of each GPO by reading the gpt.ini file. It uses the gpt.ini file location on the domain controller discovered in the domain discovery step. The events that could be recorded include the following:

- 5017 - Success end-trace event: The system call described in the event completed successfully.
- 6017 - Warning end-trace event: The system call described in the event completed with one or more errors.
- 7017 - Error end-trace event: The system call described in the event failed to complete.

After the gpt.ini files are checked, the system performs an additional check and records the following Applied GPO list event and event IDs:

Applied GPO list event

- This is where the Group Policy CSEs are listed based on the applicable settings in the GPO. The recorded events will include one of the following:
  - ❏ 5312 - Success applied GPO list event: The discovery of applicable Group Policy objects completed successfully.

❏ 6312 - Warning applied GPO list event: The discovery of applicable Group Policy objects completed with one or more errors.

❏ 7312 - Error applied GPO list event: The discovery of applicable Group Policy objects did not complete.

Finally, the system ends this portion of the phase by listing the filtered GPOs. The system processes the following Filtered GPO list event and event IDs:

Filtered GPO list event

■ The GPOs listed in these events will not be applied to the computer or user. The following event IDs are associated with this event:

❏ 5313 - Success filtered GPO list event: The discovery of filtered Group Policy objects completed successfully.

❏ 6313 - Warning filtered GPO list event: The discovery of filtered Group Policy objects completed with one or more errors.

❏ 7313 - Error filtered GPO list event: The discovery of filtered Group Policy objects did not complete.

Slow Link Detection   Multiple components rely on the speed of the network for the application of policy settings. For the Group Policy service to determine this criteria, it must perform two steps. First, it must determine the speed of the network. Second, it must determine whether the configured slow link setting in Group Policy classifies the determined speed as slow or fast. The following two events record this behavior, along with the associated event IDs:

Estimated bandwidth event

■ The results of the estimated bandwidth will be recorded in the event measured in kilobits per second (Kbps). The following event IDs are associated with this event:

❏ 5327 - Success estimated bandwidth event: Estimating the bandwidth for a network interface completed successfully.

❏ 6327 - Warning estimated bandwidth event: Estimating the bandwidth for a network interface completed with one or more errors.

❏ 7327 - Error estimated bandwidth event: Estimating the bandwidth for a network interface did not complete.

Network information event

■ After the estimated bandwidth speed is determined, the Group Policy service determines whether the speed is slow or fast. This event will classify the speed in one of the following three categories within the event recorded:

❏ The connection is a fast or slow link.

❑ The estimated bandwidth value, measured in Kbps.

❑ The slow link bandwidth threshold, also measured in Kbps.

> **Note**   You can find this information on TechNet at the following location: *http://technet2.microsoft.com/WindowsVista/en/library/7e940882-33b7-43db-b097-f3752c84f67f1033.mspx?mfr=true.*

This event will have the following event IDs associated with it:

❑ 5314 - Success network information event: The Group Policy service successfully determined a slow or fast link.

❑ 6314 - Warning network information event: The Group Policy service encountered one or more errors when determining a slow or fast link.

❑ 7314 - Error network information event: The Group Policy service encountered an error when attempting to determine a slow or fast link.

Nonsystem GP Extension Discovery   Any third-party Group Policy extensions that need to process are also tracked. The Group Policy service runs in a separate service host process from nonsystem extensions (third-party extensions) for stability reasons. This information is reported under the following event and event IDs:

Operational information event

■ The following event IDs are associated with this event:

❑ 5320 - Success operational information event: The event description provides information or describes a successful event.

❑ 6320 - Warning operational information event: The event description provides information about a recent warning event.

❑ 7320 - Error operational informational event: The event description provides information about a recent error event.

Divide the Custom View of the Log into Three Phases: Processing

This phase uses the information gathered in the preprocessing phase to cycle through each Group Policy extension. It is the extension that applies policy settings to the user or computer. The Group Policy service passes all of the information gathered in the preprocessing phase to each of the system and nonsystem CSEs. You can clearly see the beginning of this phase in the Event Viewer by noting that the Group Policy service records the CSE processing start event of 4016, including a list of all GPOs that have settings for the associated CSE. Afterward, with the successful completion of the CSE processing event, the service records a final event ID of 5016. Each CSE that is processed has a beginning event and an ending event.

Divide the Custom View of the Log into Three Phases: Postprocessing

The postprocessing phase reports the end of the policy processing instance and records whether the instance ended successfully, was processed with warnings, or failed. Table 15-5 describes the event IDs associated with the events and the levels of success or failure of the event recorded.

Table 15-5 Postprocessing Event IDs

Warning or Error Event ID	Failure Event ID	Successful Event ID	End Policy Processing Event
6000	7000	8000	Computer end event
6001	7001	8001	User end event
6002	7002	8002	Computer network change event
6003	7003	8003	User network change event
6004	7004	8004	Computer manual refresh event
6005	7005	8005	User manual refresh event
6006	7006	8006	Computer periodic refresh event
6007	7007	8007	User periodic refresh event

Associate All Starting Events with the Correct Ending Event

Each phase and each subset of the phases has a starting and ending event pair. This is extremely useful in troubleshooting, because it allows you to more narrowly identify where problems are occurring. If a pair of events or subevents has only success events, it is unlikely that the event pair is causing any problems with Group Policy processing.

Investigate All Errors, Warnings, and Failures

You should focus carefully on the errors, warnings, and failures that are logged in the events. These are the events most likely to cause the most problems with the application of Group Policy.

Isolate the Event Causing the Problem

After you determine the initial problem from the preceding steps, you should address it without concern for other errors that might be occurring. Group Policy application can often have a "trickling" affect on other areas of the processing. If too many problems are handled at one time, more problems can arise. Also, you should avoid spending time trying to fix a problem that may be a by-product of the original problem.

Run GPUpdate on the Computer with the Group Policy Problem

To determine whether Group Policy processing is fully functional after an error has been fixed, you can run GPUpdate to learn whether a new instance of the Group Policy processing causes any issues. If only successful events are logged and the behavior of the computer is as desired, the problem is fixed. If problems still exist, repeat the steps in this section until all errors and problems are resolved.

Summary of Group Policy Event IDs

Each event recorded with the GroupPolicy source name can be categorized into one of many ranges of related events. These ranges help you determine start, end, success, failure, and so on for each event. Table 15-6 summarizes each event ID range.

Table 15-6   Group Policy Event ID Ranges

Event ID Range	Description
4000–4007	Group Policy start events: These informational events appear in the event log when an instance of Group Policy processing begins.
4016–4299	Component start events: These informational events appear in the event log when a component of Group Policy processing begins the task described in the event.
5000–5299	Component success events: These informational events appear in the event log when a component of Group Policy processing successfully completes the task described in the event.
5300–5999	Informative events: These informational events appear in the event log during the entire instance of Group Policy processing and provide additional information about the current instance.
6000–6007	Group Policy warning events: These warning events appear in the event log when an instance of Group Policy processing completes with errors.
6017–6299	Component warning events: These warning events appear in the event log when a component of Group Policy processing completes the task described in the event with errors.
6300–6999	Informative warning events: These warning events appear in the event log to provide additional information about possible error conditions with the action described in the event.
7000–7007	Group Policy error events: These error events appear in the event log when the instance of Group Policy processing does not complete.
7017–7299	Component error events: These error events appear in the event log when a component of Group Policy processing does not complete the task described in the event.
7300–7999	Informative error events: These error events appear in the event log to provide additional information about the error condition with the action described in the event.
8000–8007	Group Policy success events: These informational events appear in the event log when the instance of Group Policy completes successfully.

Tip   Most of the events related to the GroupPolicy source appear in pairs. Group Policy processing includes a start event and an end event. The Event IDs within the 4000 range are all start events. These events are followed by events that fall in the other ranges, which are all ending events: error, fail, information, or success. Pairing the events will help you identify problems more quickly when using the Event Viewer and logs.

Table 15-7 summarizes all event IDs that occur in the System log for Group Policy.

Table 15-7   System Log Event IDs for Group Policy Events

Event ID	Event Type	Explanation
1002	Error	Failed Allocation: The Group Policy service logs this event when an attempt to allocate memory fails.
1006	Error	DS Bind Failure: The Group Policy service logs this event when an attempt to authenticate to Active Directory fails.
1007	Error	Site Query Failure: The Group Policy service logs this event when, using the credentials of the user or computer, an attempt to query the Active Directory Site fails.
1030	Error	GPO Query Failure: The Group Policy service logs this event when an attempt to query a Group Policy objects fails.
1052	Error	Computer Role Failure: The Group Policy service logs this event when an attempt to determine the role of the computer (workgroup, domain member, or domain controller) fails.
1053	Error	Username Resolution Failure: The Group Policy service logs this event when an attempt to resolve a user name fails.
1054	Error	DC Resolution Failure: The Group Policy service logs this event when an attempt to obtain the name of a domain controller fails.
1055	Error	Computer Name Resolution Failure: The Group Policy service logs this event when an attempt to resolve a computer name fails.
1058	Error	Policy Read Failure: The Group Policy service logs this event when an attempt to read the GPT.ini file of a Group Policy object fails.
1065	Error	WMI Evaluation Failure: The Group Policy service logs this event when an attempt to evaluate a WMI filter fails.
1079	Error	GPO Search Failure: The Group Policy service logs this event when an attempt to obtain a list of Group Policy objects fails.
1080	Error	OU Search Failure: The Group Policy service logs this event when an attempt to search the Active Directory Organizational Unit hierarchy fails.
1085	Warning	CSE Failure Warning: The Group Policy service logs this event when a Group Policy CSE fails.
1088	Error	Excessive GPO Failure: The Group Policy service logs this event when the scope of Group Policy objects for a computer or user exceeds 999.
1089	Warning	RSOP Session Failure: The Group Policy service logs this event when an RSoP session fails.
1090	Warning	WMI Failure: The Group Policy service logs this event when it encounters errors with the WMI service.
1091	Warning	RSOP CSE Failure: The Group Policy service logs this event when a Group Policy CSE fails to record RSoP information.
1095	Warning	RSOP Failure: The Group Policy service logs this event when an error occurs while recording RSoP information.

Table 15-7   System Log Event IDs for Group Policy Events

Event ID	Event Type	Explanation
1096	Error	Registry.pol Failure: The Group Policy service logs this event when an attempt to read the registry.pol file fails.
1097	Error	Computer Token Failure: The Group Policy service logs this event when an attempt to read the computer's authentication token fails.
1101	Error	Object Not Found Failure: The Group Policy service logs this event when an attempt to locate an Active Directory object fails.
1104	Warning	WMI Filter Not Found Warning: The Group Policy service logs this event when an attempt to locate an associated WMI filter fails.
1109	Warning	Cross Forest GP Disabled Warning: The Group Policy service logs this event when an attempt is disabled to process Group Policy across a forest.
1110	Error	Cross Forest Discovery Failure: The Group Policy service logs this event when an attempt fails to determine whether the user and computer belong to the same forest.
1112	Warning	CSE Synchronous Warning: The Group Policy service logs this event when a Group Policy CSE requires synchronous policy processing to apply one or more policy settings.
1126	Error	Time Skew Failure: The Group Policy service logs this event when the time on the local computer is not synchronized with the time on the domain controller.
1128	Warning	CSE Disabled Warning: The Group Policy service logs this event when it disables a Group Policy CSE to prevent unexpected termination of the Group Policy service.
1129	Error	DC Connectivity Failure: The Group Policy service logs this event when there is an absence of authenticated connectivity from the computer to the domain controller.
1130	Error	Script Failure: The Group Policy service logs this event when an attempt fails to run a script.
1500	Informational	Computer Policy Processing: The Group Policy service logs this event when an instance of computer Group Policy processing completes without encountering new policy settings.
1501	Informational	User Policy Processing: The Group Policy service logs this event when an instance of user Group Policy processing completes without encountering new policy settings.
1502	Informational	Computer Policy Processing: The Group Policy service logs this event when an instance of computer Group Policy processing completes with new or changed policy settings.
1503	Informational	User Policy Processing: The Group Policy service logs this event when an instance of user Group Policy processing completes with new or changed policy settings.

Table 15-8 summarizes all Event IDs that occur in the Group Policy operational log.

Table 15-8   Group Policy Operational Log Event IDs

Computer Start and End Events		
Event ID	Event Type	Explanation
4000	Informational	The Group Policy service logs this event when an instance of computer Group Policy processing begins.
6000	Warning	The Group Policy service logs this event when an instance of computer Group Policy processing completes with one or more errors.
7000	Error	The Group Policy service logs this event when an instance of computer Group Policy processing fails to complete.
8000	Success	The Group Policy service logs this event when an instance of computer Group Policy processing completes successfully.

User Log-on Start and End Events		
Event ID	Event Type	Explanation
4001	Informational	The Group Policy service logs this event when an instance of user Group Policy processing begins.
6001	Warning	The Group Policy service logs this event when an instance of user Group Policy processing completes with one or more errors.
7001	Error	The Group Policy service logs this event when an instance of user Group Policy processing fails to complete.
8001	Success	The Group Policy service logs this event when an instance of user Group Policy processing completes successfully.

Computer Network Change Start and End Events		
Event ID	Event Type	Explanation
4002	Informational	The Group Policy service logs this event when a network change triggers the start of an instance of computer Group Policy processing.
6002	Warning	The Group Policy service logs this event when an instance of computer Group Policy processing, triggered by a network change, completes with one or more errors.
7002	Error	The Group Policy service logs this event when an instance of computer Group Policy processing, triggered by a network change, fails to complete.
8002	Success	The Group Policy service logs this event when an instance of computer Group Policy processing, triggered by a network change, completes successfully.

User Network Change Start and End Events

Event ID	Event Type	Explanation
4003	Informational	The Group Policy service logs this event when a network change triggers the start of an instance of user Group Policy processing.
6003	Warning	The Group Policy service logs this event when an instance of user Group Policy processing, triggered by a network change, completes with one or more errors.
7003	Error	The Group Policy service logs this event when an instance of user Group Policy processing, triggered by a network change, fails to complete.
8003	Success	The Group Policy service logs this event when an instance of user Group Policy processing, triggered by a network change, completes successfully.

Computer Manual Refresh Start and End Events

Event ID	Event Type	Explanation
4004	Informational	The Group Policy service logs this event when a manual refresh triggers the start of an instance of computer Group Policy processing.
6004	Warning	The Group Policy service logs this event when an instance of computer Group Policy processing, triggered by a manual refresh, completes with one or more errors.
7004	Error	The Group Policy service logs this event when an instance of computer Group Policy processing, triggered by a manual refresh, fails to complete.
8004	Success	The Group Policy service logs this event when an instance of computer Group Policy processing, triggered by a manual refresh, completes successfully.

User Manual Refresh Start and End Events

Event ID	Event Type	Explanation
4005	Informational	The Group Policy service logs this event when a manual refresh triggers the start of an instance of user Group Policy processing.
6005	Warning	The Group Policy service logs this event when an instance of user Group Policy processing, triggered by a manual refresh, completes with one or more errors.
7005	Error	The Group Policy service logs this event when an instance of user Group Policy processing, triggered by a manual refresh, fails to complete.
8005	Success	The Group Policy service logs this event when an instance of user Group Policy processing, triggered by a manual refresh, completes successfully.

Computer Periodic Refresh Start and End Events

Event ID	Event Type	Explanation
4006	Informational	The Group Policy service logs this event when a periodic refresh triggers the start of an instance of computer Group Policy processing.
6006	Warning	The Group Policy service logs this event when an instance of computer Group Policy processing, triggered by a periodic refresh, completes with one or more errors.
7006	Error	The Group Policy service logs this event when an instance of computer Group Policy processing, triggered by a periodic refresh, fails to complete.
8006	Success	The Group Policy service logs this event when an instance of computer Group Policy processing, triggered by a periodic refresh, completes successfully.

User Periodic Refresh Start and End Events

Event ID	Event Type	Explanation
4007	Informational	The Group Policy service logs this event when a periodic refresh triggers the start of an instance of user Group Policy processing.
6007	Warning	The Group Policy service logs this event when an instance of user Group Policy processing, triggered by a periodic refresh, completes with one or more errors.
7007	Error	The Group Policy service logs this event when an instance of user Group Policy processing, triggered by a periodic refresh, fails to complete.
8007	Success	The Group Policy service logs this event when an instance of user Group Policy processing, triggered by a periodic refresh, completes successfully.

Client-Side Extension Processing

Event ID	Event Type	Explanation
4016	Informational	The Group Policy service logs this event each time a Group Policy CSE begins processing.
5016	Success	The Group Policy service logs this event when a Group Policy CSE completes its processing successfully.
6016	Warning	The Group Policy service logs this event when a Group Policy CSE completes its processing while encountering one or more errors.
7016	Error	The Group Policy service logs this event when a Group Policy CSE fails to complete its processing.

Trace Events		
Event ID	Event Type	Explanation
4017	Informational	The Group Policy service logs this event to mark the beginning of the service making a system call.
5017	Success	The Group Policy service logs this event when a system call completes successfully.
6017	Warning	The Group Policy service logs this event when a system call completes while encountering one or more errors.
7017	Error	The Group Policy service logs this event when a system call fails to complete.

Scripts Processing		
Event ID	Event Type	Explanation
4018	Informational	The Group Policy service logs this event when it begins to process Group Policy scripts.
5018	Success	The Group Policy service logs this event when Group Policy scripts processing completes successfully.
6018	Warning	The Group Policy service logs this event when Group Policy scripts processing completes while encountering one or more errors.
7018	Error	The Group Policy service logs this event when Group Policy scripts processing fails to complete.

Individual Script Processing		
Event ID	Event Type	Explanation
4019	Informational	The Group Policy service logs this event when it begins to process an individual script during the processing of Group Policy scripts.
5019	Success	The Group Policy service logs this event when an individual script, during Group Policy script processing, completes successfully.
6019	Warning	The Group Policy service logs this event when an individual script, during Group Policy script processing, completes while encountering one or more errors.
7019	Error	The Group Policy service logs this event when an individual script, during Group Policy script processing, fails to complete.

Domain Controller Discovery

Event ID	Event Type	Explanation
4326	Informational	The Group Policy service logs this event when it begins to discover an Active Directory domain controller.
5326	Success	The Group Policy service logs this event when the discovery of an Active Directory domain controller completes successfully.
6326	Warning	The Group Policy service logs this event when the discovery of an Active Directory domain controller completes while encountering one or more errors.
7326	Error	The Group Policy service logs this event when the discovery of an Active Directory domain controller fails to complete.

Domain Controller Information

Event ID	Event Type	Explanation
5308	Success	The Group Policy service logs this event when an attempt to display information about a discovered domain controller completes successfully.
6308	Warning	The Group Policy service logs this event when an attempt to display information about a discovered domain controller completes while encountering one or more errors.
7308	Error	The Group Policy service logs this event when an attempt to display information about a discovered domain controller fails to complete.

Computer Information

Event ID	Event Type	Explanation
5309	Success	The Group Policy service logs this event when an attempt to display information about a computer completes successfully.
6309	Warning	The Group Policy service logs this event when an attempt to display information about a computer completes while encountering one or more errors.
7309	Error	The Group Policy service logs this event when an attempt to display information about a computer fails to complete.

Security Principal Information

Event ID	Event Type	Explanation
5310	Success	The Group Policy service logs this event when an attempt to display security principal information about a user completes successfully.
6310	Warning	The Group Policy service logs this event when an attempt to display security principal information about a user completes while encountering one or more errors.
7310	Error	The Group Policy service logs this event when an attempt to display security principal information about a user fails to complete.

Loopback Processing Mode

Event ID	Event Type	Explanation
5311	Success	The Group Policy service logs this event when an attempt to display information about loopback processing mode completes successfully.
6311	Warning	The Group Policy service logs this event when an attempt to display information about loopback processing mode completes while encountering one or more errors.
7311	Error	The Group Policy service logs this event when an attempt to display information about loopback processing mode fails to complete.

Applied GPO List

Event ID	Event Type	Explanation
5312	Success	The Group Policy service logs this event when an attempt to display a list of applied Group Policy objects completes successfully.
6312	Warning	The Group Policy service logs this event when an attempt to display a list of applied Group Policy objects completes while encountering one or more errors.
7312	Error	The Group Policy service logs this event when an attempt to display a list of applied Group Policy objects fails to complete.

Filtered GPO List

Event ID	Event Type	Explanation
5313	Success	The Group Policy service logs this event when an attempt to display a list of filtered Group Policy objects completes successfully.
6313	Warning	The Group Policy service logs this event when an attempt to display a list of filtered Group Policy objects completes while encountering one or more errors.
7313	Error	The Group Policy service logs this event when an attempt to display a list of filtered Group Policy objects fails to complete.

Network Information

Event ID	Event Type	Explanation
5314	Success	The Group Policy service logs this event when an attempt to display network information completes successfully.
6314	Warning	The Group Policy service logs this event when an attempt to display network information completes while encountering one or more errors.
7314	Error	The Group Policy service logs this event when an attempt to display network information fails to complete.

Next Policy Processing Information		
Event ID	**Event Type**	**Explanation**
5315	Success	The Group Policy service logs this event when an attempt to display information about the next instance of Group Policy processing completes successfully.
6315	Warning	The Group Policy service logs this event when an attempt to display information about the next instance of Group Policy processing completes while encountering one or more errors.
7315	Error	The Group Policy service logs this event when an attempt to display information about the next instance of Group Policy processing fails to complete.

Successful or Informational Interaction		
Event ID	**Event Type**	**Explanation**
5320	Success	The Group Policy service logs this event to display successful information about the current instance of Group Policy processing.
6320	Warning	The Group Policy service logs this event to display warning information about the current instance of Group Policy processing.
7320	Error	The Group Policy service logs this event to display failure information about the current instance of Group Policy processing.
5321	Success	The Group Policy service logs this event to display successful information about the current instance of Group Policy processing.
6321	Warning	The Group Policy service logs this event to display warning information about the current instance of Group Policy processing.
7321	Error	The Group Policy service logs this event to display failure information about the current instance of Group Policy processing.

Note   The events that end in 1 in these criteria typically have more verbose information in the log, but the information is similar to those events that end in 0.

Computer Start-up Wait Information		
Event ID	**Event Type**	**Explanation**
5322	Success	The Group Policy service logs this event to display successful information about the service waiting for the network.
6322	Warning	The Group Policy service logs this event to display warning information about the service waiting for the network.
7322	Error	The Group Policy service logs this event to display failure information about the service waiting for the network.

Winlogon Notification Information		
Event ID	**Event Type**	**Explanation**
5324	Success	The Group Policy service logs this event to display successful information about a notification received from Winlogon.
6324	Warning	The Group Policy service logs this event to display warning information about a notification received from Winlogon.
7324	Error	The Group Policy service logs this event to display failure information about a notification received from Winlogon.

Service Control Manager Notification Information		
Event ID	**Event Type**	**Explanation**
5325	Success	The Group Policy service logs this event to display successful information about a notification received from the Service Control Manager.
6325	Warning	The Group Policy service logs this event to display warning information about a notification received from the Service Control Manager.
7325	Error	The Group Policy service logs this event to display failure information about a notification received from the Service Control Manager.

Network Bandwidth Information		
Event ID	**Event Type**	**Explanation**
5327	Success	The Group Policy service logs this event to display successful information about network bandwidth.
6327	Warning	The Group Policy service logs this event to display warning information about network bandwidth.
7327	Error	The Group Policy service logs this event to display failure information about network bandwidth.

Service Configuration Information		
Event ID	**Event Type**	**Explanation**
5331	Success	The Group Policy service logs this event to display successful information about the Group Policy service's configuration.
6331	Warning	The Group Policy service logs this event to display warning information about the Group Policy service's configuration.
7331	Error	The Group Policy service logs this event to display failure information about the Group Policy service's configuration.

Network Location Awareness Service Warning		
Event ID	Event Type	Explanation
6323	Warning	The Group Policy service logs this event to display warning information about the operability of the NLA service.
7323	Error	The Group Policy service logs this event to display failure information about the operability of the NLA service.

Client-Side Failure Information		
Event ID	Event Type	Explanation
6330	Warning	The Group Policy service logs this event to display warning information about a Group Policy CSE that failed in an earlier instance of Group Policy processing.

Common GPO Troubleshooting Tools

When you are troubleshooting a tough Group Policy processing problem, you have several tools to help you. The following tools are either built in to the operating system or can be quickly downloaded and installed from the Microsoft Web site.

GPLogView

If you need to archive Group Policy logs or troubleshoot a computer in a remote location, it might be easier to do so using a text output of the log, instead of trying to use Event Viewer. If you want to generate and view Group Policy logs in text, HTML, or XML format, you can use the GPLogView utility. You can use GPLogView to export Group Policy event data from the system and Group Policy operational log. You can download gpLogView.msi from the Microsoft Download Center (*http://go.microsoft.com/fwlink/?LinkId=75004*). The following sections show the syntax of commonly used options for GPLogView.

Export All Group Policy Events

You can use GPLogView to export all Group Policy–related events from the system log and the operational log. The –o switch is used to specify the output file name.

```
gplogview -o c:\gpevents.txt
```

Export Group Policy Events with a Specific ActivityID

GPLogView filters Group Policy–related events by ActivityID, which is useful for troubleshooting a specific instance of Group Policy processing. The –a switch is used in conjunction with the ActivityID.

```
gplogview -a 8A7C7CE5-F7D0-4d32-8700-57C650A53839 -o c:\gpevents.txt
```

> **Tip**   Events with the same ActivityID are all color-coded with the same color. This allows you to quickly see which events belong together, optimizing your troubleshooting effort and time.

Run in Monitor Mode

You can use GPLogView to capture Group Policy events in real time, by using the –m switch. GPLogView writes all Group Policy–related events to the command window, as they occur, as shown in Figure 15-5. Press Ctrl+C to exit monitor mode, or press Q and Enter simultaneously.

```
gplogview -m
```

```
C:\Program Files\GroupPolicy LogView\gplogview -m

Running in Monitor Mode.
SUCCESS: Subscribing to all Events from System Channel...
SUCCESS: Subscribing to all Events from Microsoft-Windows-GroupPolicy/Operationa
l Channel...
2007-12-28 14:23:43.830 4004 a8c2094b-a61f-45ac-ab99-775305401d69 Starting manua
l processing of policy for computer FABRIKAM\WIN-G16CL9JU9GD$.
                                                             Activity id: <
A8C2094B-A61F-45AC-AB99-775305401D69>
2007-12-28 14:23:43.840 4005 b90f90aa-765f-4381-8267-447c098d7515 Starting manua
l processing of policy for user FABRIKAM\Administrator.
                                                             Activity id: <
B90F90AA-765F-4381-8267-447C098D7515>
2007-12-28 14:23:43.880 5320 b90f90aa-765f-4381-8267-447c098d7515 Attempting to
retrieve the account information.
2007-12-28 14:23:43.880 4017 b90f90aa-765f-4381-8267-447c098d7515 Making system
call to get account information.

2007-12-28 14:23:44.091 5017 b90f90aa-765f-4381-8267-447c098d7515 The system cal
l to get account information completed.
                                                             CN=Administrat
or,CN=Users,DC=Fabrikam,DC=com
                                                             The call compl
eted in 211 milliseconds.
2007-12-28 14:23:44.091 5320 b90f90aa-765f-4381-8267-447c098d7515 Retrieved acco
unt information.
2007-12-28 14:23:44.101 4326 b90f90aa-765f-4381-8267-447c098d7515 Group Policy i
s trying to discover the Domain Controller information.
2007-12-28 14:23:44.101 5320 b90f90aa-765f-4381-8267-447c098d7515 Retrieving Dom
ain Controller details.
2007-12-28 14:23:44.151 5320 a8c2094b-a61f-45ac-ab99-775305401d69 Attempting to
retrieve the account information.
2007-12-28 14:23:44.151 4017 a8c2094b-a61f-45ac-ab99-775305401d69 Making system
call to get account information.

2007-12-28 14:23:44.151 5017 a8c2094b-a61f-45ac-ab99-775305401d69 The system cal
l to get account information completed.
                                                             CN=WIN-G16CL9J
U9GD,OU=Domain Controllers,DC=Fabrikam,DC=com
                                                             The call compl
eted in 0 milliseconds.
2007-12-28 14:23:44.151 5320 a8c2094b-a61f-45ac-ab99-775305401d69 Retrieved acco
unt information.
2007-12-28 14:23:44.151 4326 a8c2094b-a61f-45ac-ab99-775305401d69 Group Policy i
s trying to discover the Domain Controller information.
2007-12-28 14:23:44.151 5320 a8c2094b-a61f-45ac-ab99-775305401d69 Retrieving Dom
ain Controller details.
2007-12-28 14:23:47.095 4017 a8c2094b-a61f-45ac-ab99-775305401d69 Making LDAP ca
lls to connect and bind to Active Directory.
                                                             WIN-G16CL9JU9G
D.Fabrikam.com
```

Figure 15-5   GPLogView allows you to view events in real time for Group Policy processing.

Use an External Event Log for Input

By default, GPLogView reads the event logs on the current computer running Windows Vista. However, you can change the GPLogView input source to an exported event log from another computer running Windows Vista, by using the –i switch. This change gives you the ability to export multiple views of Group Policy processing that happened on another computer.

```
Gplogview -i savedevents.evtx -o gpevents.txt
```

> **Note**   The saved event log must come from a computer running Windows Vista. GPLogView does not work with saved event logs from earlier versions of Windows.

GPMC

The Group Policy Management Console (GPMC) provides numerous tools and features that help with the troubleshooting of Group Policy. Chapter 6 and Chapter 7, "Advanced GPMC Management," describe all of these features in detail; however, it is important to know which features will help for a specific issue. Table 15-9 lists many issues that arise with Group Policy, along with the feature in the GPMC that will help and the chapter in which you can find a description.

Table 15-9   GPMC Troubleshooting Features

Group Policy Issue	Feature	Chapter
You need to select a different domain controller for Group Policy management.	Change Domain Controller menu option	6
You need to restore a GPO from Backup.	Group Policy Backup menu option	6
A GPO from the domain or high-level organizational unit is not applying to computer or user objects located in a lower-level organizational unit.	Block Inheritance menu option	6
Settings in a GPO linked to a lower-level organizational unit are being overwritten by settings in a GPO linked to the domain or a higher-level organizational unit.	Enforce menu option	6
Settings in a GPO are not applying to all user and computer objects that fall under the scope of management of the GPO.	Security filtering and WMI filtering	6
You want to determine the current final GPO settings for a computer or user.	Group Policy Results	7
You want to determine the potential GPO settings for a computer or user if moved to different location in Active Directory.	Group Policy Modeling	7
You want to determine only the configured Administrative Template settings in a GPO.	Filtering Administrative Templates	7
A GPO from one domain must be used in a different domain, but user accounts, group accounts, and UNC paths are not working properly.	Migration tables	7

Dcgpofix.exe

If you are having problems with the default GPOs that are created on every new domain, this tool might be helpful. The two default GPOs, Default Domain Policy and Default Domain

Controller Policy, are essential for configuring account policies, security settings, and domain controller user rights in the enterprise. If these GPOs get corrupt or misconfigured, they can be set back to the default settings by using the Dcgpofix tool.

Dcgpofix is an easy-to-use default tool for Windows Server 2008 that reports the results of the GPOs that were recovered. You can restore the Default Domain Policy or the Default Domain Controller Policy individually, or you can restore both to the original settings.

> **Warning**   If you have made any changes to these two GPOs after the initial installation of the domain, the changes that you made will be lost.

One potential concern with running this tool is the version of the Active Directory schema. Microsoft Windows Server 2003 and Windows Server 2008 domains have a different schema, and these versions are meticulously watched by the Active Directory when anything that interfaces with Active Directory is not working with the correct schema version. By specifying the /ignoreschema parameter, you can enable Dcgpofix.exe to work with different versions of Active Directory. However, default policy objects might not be restored to their original state. To ensure compatibility, use the version of Dcgpofix.exe that is installed with the current operating system and service pack.

The tool syntax is very simple and straightforward:

```
dcgpofix [/ignoreschema][/target: {domain | dc | both}]
```

The parameters for the command are as follows:

```
/ignoreschema
```

This is an optional switch that ignores the Active Directory schema version number:

```
/target: {domain | dc | both}
```

This is an optional switch that specifies the target domain, domain controller, or both. If you do not specify /target, dcgpofix uses both by default.

You can find Dcgpofix.exe in the C:\Windows\System32 folder of a domain controller running Windows Server 2008. Before the tool runs, it checks the schema version to ensure compatibility of the operating system with the GPOs that you want to replace. You must be a domain administrator or an enterprise administrator to use this tool.

The following extension settings are maintained in a default Group Policy object: Remote Installation Services (RIS), security settings, and Encrypting File System (EFS).

The following extension settings are not maintained or restored in a default Group Policy object: software installation, Internet Explorer maintenance, scripts, folder redirection, and administrative templates.

The following changes are not maintained or restored in a default Group Policy object: Security settings made by Microsoft Exchange 2000 Setup, security settings migrated to default Group Policy during an upgrade from Microsoft Windows NT to Windows 2000, and policy object changes made through Systems Management Server (SMS).

GPMonitor.exe

By far one of the most complex and sophisticated mechanisms in Active Directory is a GPO. Possibly the only thing more complex than a GPO is the logging associated with the GPOs. GPMonitor is designed to help centralize reports created from the GPOs on a computer.

GPMonitor is part of the Microsoft Windows Server 2003 Resource Kit Tools and can be downloaded free from Microsoft at *http://www.microsoft.com/downloads/details.aspx? familyid=9d467a69-57ff-4ae7-96ee-b18c4790cffd&displaylang=en*.

GPMonitor sends information back to the centralized share when a refresh or a forced update to a GPO occurs on the target computer. When the information is sent back to the centralized share, it is stored in files that can then be queried. The querying occurs with the GPMonitor interface.

GPMonitor works by running on the computers that will store their information in the centralized share. The configuration of the GPMonitor service and settings is controlled by a GPO. When you install the GPMonitor service, you are provided with a GPMonitor.adm template. This template is imported into a GPO at the Active Directory level to target computers in the domain. The GPMonitor.adm template configures the following settings:

- **UNC path to centralized share**   This is the server and share where all of the GPO information is stored. You can have different paths for different types of computers on the network, or they can all share the same shared folder.

- **Refresh interval**   This indicates how often the GPMonitor service will update the information stored in the share. By default, this is set to every eight refreshes. You can adjust the frequency down to every refresh if the server holding the share can store all of the information from all members.

GPResult

This tool reports the final settings applied from the GPOs on the local computer and from Active Directory. The tool works in conjunction with the RSoP tool. If you are troubleshooting the actual settings, attempting to determine which GPOs applied, or seeking other details of GPO application on a computer, this is an essential tool.

GPResult is a built-in tool for Windows XP, Windows Vista, Windows Server 2003, and Windows Server 2008. If you are running Windows 2000, you must obtain the tool from the Microsoft Windows 2000 Resource Kit. The two versions are not compatible.

GPResult is a pure command-line tool, but it can provide invaluable information regarding the GPOs for a target system. The tool reports on both user and computer policies. If you run the GPResult tool with just the /R switch, it reports the important information regarding the GPOs in the command prompt window. If you want to save the report in HTML format, use the /H switch in combination with the path and file name, such as gpresult /h c:\gpresult.html. The resulting .html file is shown in Figure 15-6.

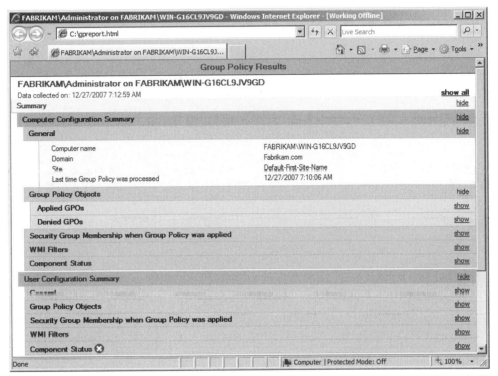

Figure 15-6   The GPResult command-line tool provides a report on the current Group Policy settings in HTML format.

If this is not enough information to help you identify your GPO problem, you can expand the output by using the /V switch, which is the verbose option. This will include more detailed information about the GPOs that were applied, including setting information.

If the verbose information is not enough, you can use the "super verbose" switch, /Z. This will give you all that the verbose option does, as well as binary information on some of the GPO settings, if you need to troubleshoot down to this level.

Note   As with any other command-line tool, typing **gpresult /?** will provide information on all switches and examples.

GPUpdate

GPUpdate will automatically cause a refresh of the GPOs from the local computer and all of the GPOs at the Active Directory level. If you do not want to log off and log back on, restart the computer, or wait for the periodic refresh interval, this is an ideal option for applying GPOs. Use of this tool is very common for testing or initially implementing GPO settings.

The tool allows you to update just the user GPO, just the computer GPO, or both user and computer GPOs. If you run the tool with no switches, it will refresh both user and computer GPO settings.

A valuable feature of this tool is the option to "force" the application of the GPOs from Active Directory, even if the GPO version number has not changed. This is ideal for ensuring that any local settings that have been altered manually are changed back to what the GPO indicates they should be.

> **Warning**   Using the /force switch with GPUpdate will not force a foreground refresh of Group Policy. The only way to force a foreground refresh of Group Policy is to restart the computer for computer settings and log off and log back on for user settings.

A drawback of the tool is that you cannot use it remotely; it works only for the computer where it is being run.

GPOTool

GPOTool helps locate inconsistencies with the GPO versions stored in Active Directory and in SYSVOL. Of course, we now know that an inconsistent GPO for these two storage locations can break them.

GPOTool is available in the resource kits for both Windows 2000 and Windows Server 2003. If you do not have one of these resource kits, you can download GPOTool from Microsoft at *http://www.microsoft.com/downloads/details.aspx?familyid=9d467a69-57ff-4ae7-96ee-b18c4790cffd&displaylang=en.*

GPOTool checks for inconsistency between Active Directory and SYSVOL versions of the same GPO across peer domain controllers. This information can help you determine whether replication latency is causing failure of computers or users to receive updates to new GPO settings that have not yet converged between domain controllers.

Some of the more interesting and useful switches included with GPOTool include /checkacl and /verbose. The /checkacl switch verifies the SYSVOL ACL, which is often changed by administrators trying to lock down and target GPOs.

Summary

Troubleshooting Group Policy takes time and patience. It also takes knowledge of how Group Policy is configured, its processes, and the dependencies that it relies on to perform actions. Certain basic configurations and dependencies should always be investigated first if something goes wrong with Group Policy application. These are simple settings that are hard to track, yet they can cause dramatic results.

Common problems should also always be evaluated when attempting to solve Group Policy issues. DNS-related issues should be at the forefront of all troubleshooting processes. Other common issues such as network connectivity, time synchronization, and policy processing toggles should also be reviewed initially.

There are plenty of tools available to help you with troubleshooting Group Policy. Event Viewer now has a dedicated GroupPolicy source for events related to Group Policy. Following the procedures discussed in this chapter will help you scan through the logs efficiently, looking for the root problem. Other tools, such as GPUpdate, GPResult, and GPOTool, are also useful when trying to solve difficult Group Policy problems.

Additional Resources

- The Microsoft TechNet article titled "Your Guide to Group Policy Troubleshooting," at *http://www.microsoft.com/technet/technetmag/issues/2007/02/Troubleshooting/default.aspx*, offers information about troubleshooting Group Policy.

- The Microsoft TechNet page at *http://www.microsoft.com/emea/spotlight/sessionh.aspx?videoid=221* provides a video of Derek Melber's Tech·Ed presentation on troubleshooting Group Policy.

- Chapter 4, "Architecture of Group Policy," provides information about how Active Directory, DNS, FRS, DFSR, DFS, and NLA dependencies interrelate with Group Policy.

- Chapter 5, "Group Policy Processing," covers the concepts and details of SOM, blocking policy inheritance, enforcement, security filtering, and WMI filtering.

- Chapter 6, "GPMC Basics," describes how to enable and disable portions of a Group Policy.

- Chapter 7, "Advanced GPMC Management," covers advanced management features of controlling GPOs and delegation of administration of GPOs.

- Chapter 12, "Group Policy Preferences," discusses item-level targeting and enabling and disabling preference settings.

Part VIII
Appendices

Appendix A
Third-Party Group Policy Tools

Group Policy has grown to be one of the most important technologies included in Active Directory. Group Policy settings have increased from 000 to well over 5,000 in just a few years. Microsoft has put time, effort, resources, and money into Group Policy to give it the potential it has today.

Third-party vendors have further improved upon the foundation provided by Microsoft and have made Group Policy what it is today. These vendors have produced amazing tools that help administrators and companies leverage all of the best features that Group Policy provides.

You will find vendors that help manage and control Group Policy in ways you never thought imaginable. Other companies extend Group Policy to provide even more settings. And still others take concepts of desktop management, centralized reporting, and security to new levels by leveraging Group Policy.

BeyondTrust: Privilege Manager

BeyondTrust Corporation is a newer company by name, but it is not without Group Policy expertise. BeyondTrust is a spin-off of DesktopStandard Corporation, which was acquired by Microsoft in 2006. The company now focuses almost solely on security, and the products it provides are superior when it comes to helping protect the desktop from the end user. With one of the only products on the market that addresses the least-privilege user access (LUA) bug, BeyondTrust is a fantastic company, and their products are easy to use.

Privilege Manager is the flagship product from BeyondTrust that addresses the issue of LUA by using Group Policy. The product allows standard users to run applications, processes, and Microsoft ActiveX controls without requiring the user to be an administrator. The technology works by altering the user process token, adding or removing individual user or group security identifiers (SIDs).

Privilege Manager is easy to implement—it plugs directly into the Windows Group Policy security infrastructure, and it supports Windows 2000, Window XP, Microsoft Windows Server 2003, and Windows Vista, including 64-bit versions.

Privilege Manager works seamlessly with Group Policy as an additional extension. It can be deployed to either user accounts or computer accounts, allowing very flexible control over its use. The per-setting filtering capability is similar to what you have with Group Policy Preferences, allowing for granular targeting of what you are controlling.

Privilege Manager is shown in Figure A-1. The main features of Privilege Manager include:

- The ability to enable standard users to run applications that require administrative privileges.

- The option to permit restricted users to change system-level configurations, defragmentation, the System Clock, and so on.

- The ability to allow users without administrative privileges to install approved applications and ActiveX controls.

- Transparent operation, so end users see no pop-ups or consent dialogues.

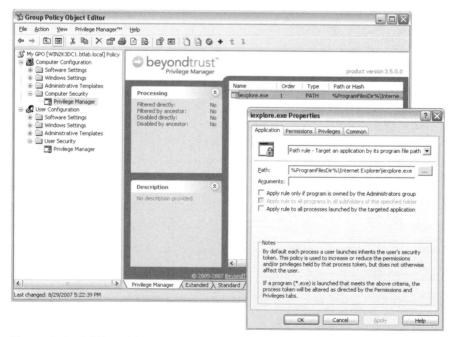

Figure A-1   Privilege Manager.

- Application of policy by creating rules in the Group Policy Management Editor (GPME).

- Support for Windows 2000, Windows XP, Windows Server 2003, and Windows Vista, including 64-bit platforms.

FullArmor: Workflow Studio

FullArmor Corporation is one of the oldest providers of Group Policy extensions and solutions. The company has worked both independently and with Microsoft to provide some of the enhancements to Group Policy that you see today. FullArmor is leading the way with some of the new technologies that can interface with Group Policy, such as workflow and Microsoft Windows PowerShell.

Workflow Studio takes advantage of Windows PowerShell to provide a centralized automation environment for Group Policy. The entire process falls into a workflow process that you can tailor to meet your own needs. You can control and manage the creation, maintenance, compliance, and security of Group Policy.

Workflow Studio is shown in Figure A-2. The benefits of Workflow Studio include the ability to:

- Provision new GPOs.

- Automate the backup of GPOs.

- Automate the restoration of GPOs.

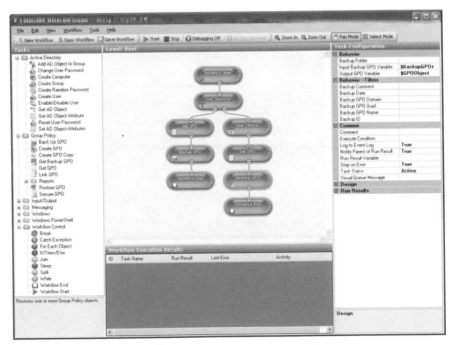

Figure A-2 Workflow Studio.

- Automate Resultant Set of Policy (RSoP) logging and planning reporting.
- Automate GPO settings reporting.

Moskowitz, Inc.

Moskowitz, Inc., is a small software development company that has provided years of support, education, and value to Group Policy. Now, Moskowitz, Inc., provides advanced additions to Group Policy with detailed configurations of some of your favorite applications.

PolicyPak for Applications

PolicyPak for Applications is a set of Group Policy snap-ins that allow you to control and manage applications that are running on the desktops throughout your environment. With control over applications such as Adobe Acrobat Reader, Adobe Acrobat Writer, and Windows Live Messenger, you can now utilize Microsoft technology to control these applications. The interface is the familiar GPME, and the integration is seamless for even the most novice of Group Policy administrators.

PolicyPak for Applications is shown in Figure A-3. The benefits of PolicyPak for Applications include the following:

- Preconfigured knowledge for applications you already have

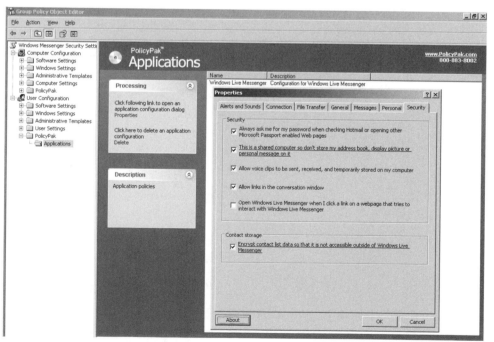

Figure A-3   PolicyPak for Applications.

- Never "tattoos" the registry
- Ready to use right away
- Looks almost exactly like the application you want to control

PolicyPak Group Policy Design Studio

The PolicyPak Group Policy Design Studio (GPDS) is a package that gives Group Policy administrators the power to create their own PolicyPak snap-ins. Nearly any application can be placed into a PolicyPak by using GPDS, so you can now manage all aspects of the application by using Group Policy. The resulting PolicyPak will mimic the application down to the last spin control, check box, and option button.

PolicyPak Group Policy Design Studio is shown in Figure A-4. PolicyPak Group Policy Design Studio offers the following benefits:

- It enables administrators to configure their own applications by using Group Policy.
- It offers an intuitive GUI environment.
- It allows you to drag and drop objects to replicate the GUI of the application you want to manage.
- It allows you to create portable files to be shared with other administrators.
- It automatically generates the snap-in for use within the GPME.

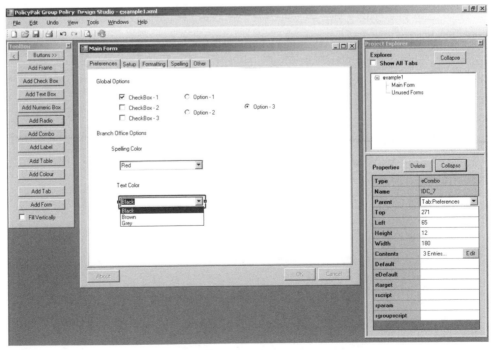

Figure A-4   Group Policy Design Studio.

NetIQ

NetIQ is known not only for its Active Directory and Microsoft management tools, but also for its excellent Group Policy management tools.

Group Policy Administrator

Group Policy Administrator (GPA) is a NetIQ tool that allows you to manage your Group Policy environment better than you can by simply working with the Group Policy Management Console (GPMC). GPA offers offline editing, change management, workflow procedures, reporting, and much more.

GPA, shown in Figure A-5, provides the following benefits:

- A secure offline repository to reduce the risk of making changes to GPOs in the production environment

- A workflow and delegation model

- Built-in tools to analyze, compare, troubleshoot, and test GPOs

- Comprehensive reporting to help document regulatory compliance

- Management of changes to GPOs in a safe, true offline environment (completely separate from Active Directory)

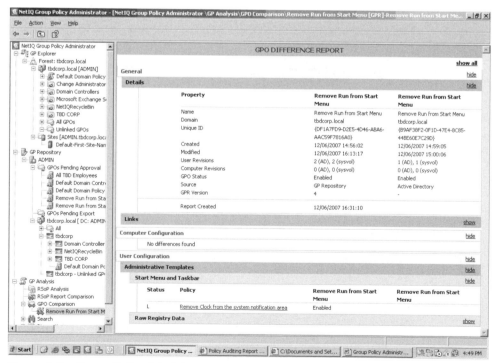

Figure A-5   Group Policy Administrator.

- Difference comparisons between GPOs

- Health checks to ensure that GPOs are not corrupted

- Option to roll back to a last-known good version of a GPO

- Storage of GPO backup copies, including Windows Management Instrumentation (WMI) filters and links

- Central management of Group Policy objects in domains that are not trusted

- Migration of GPOs from one domain to another

- Delegation of GPO changes to appropriate people, with limits on Active Directory permissions

Change Guardian

Change Guardian (CG) is a NetIQ monitoring tool that allows you to control when changes (either positive or negative) are made to Group Policy. CG works in real time and will notify specified administrators of any changes to the Group Policy environment.

CG not only notifies you of when a change was made, but it also helps track the changes that were made. It can track old settings, new settings, time of the change, and which administrator made the change. For auditing and compliance regulations, CG can help provide a solution.

Quest Software: Group Policy Manager

Quest Software is another large software vendor that provides solutions for many areas of the Microsoft environment. Group Policy Manager follows in the same tracks as other management tools by Quest, offering more control over all areas of Group Policy than the GPMC can provide.

Group Policy Manager is shown in Figure A-6. Some of the benefits of Group Policy Manager include the following:

- Management of scope of management (SOM)

- Control over WMI filters linked to GPOs

- Templates that help with deployment scenarios

- Cross-domain and cross-forest management capabilities

- A granular and comprehensive delegation model with a multi-level approval workflow

- A user-friendly (drag-and-drop) method of transitioning GPOs from one domain/forest to another

- Leveraging of Windows PowerShell to automate Group Policy Management tasks

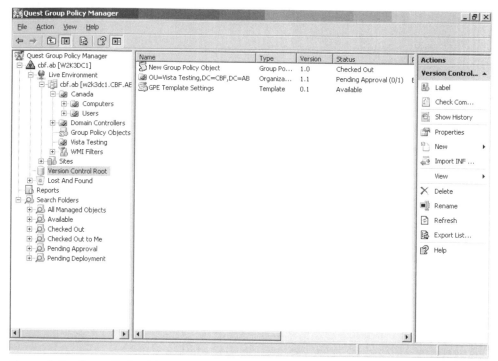

Figure A-6 Group Policy Manager.

SDM Software

SDM Software, Inc., has entered the Group Policy management area with some tools that take management, troubleshooting, and scripting to a new level. Although the company is newer, its knowledge and tools are not. While working in conjunction with popular Web sites such as GPOGUY.com and TeamGPExpert.com, SDM Software provides impressive tools and is making great strides daily.

GPExpert Troubleshooting Pak

The GPExpert Troubleshooting Pak provides four products for monitoring and troubleshooting the health of Group Policy processing on local or remote Windows systems:

- **GPExpert™ Health Reporter 1.6** This tool collects nearly every aspect of Group Policy and reports that information in an easy-to-read format for analysis and evaluation. The report comes with easily scannable red and green status updates for quick checks.

- **GPExpert™ Log Analyzer 1.1** This tool connects the issues that Group Policy is currently having with the logging files that are associated with them. The tool offers easy-to-read formatting, combined with tools that help you diagnose the health of the important aspects related to Group Policy. GPExpert Log Analyzer is shown in Figure A-7.

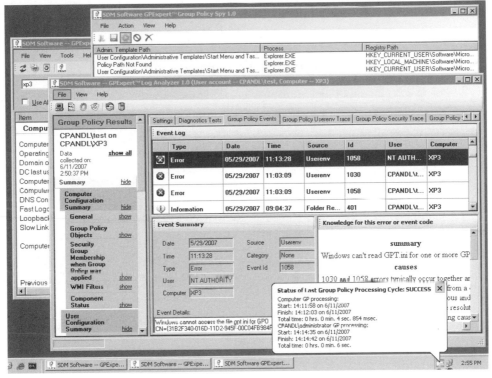

Figure A-7 GPExpert Log Analyzer.

- **GPExpert™ Group Policy Spy 1.1** This tool is a GUI-based utility that catches changes to the registry, which can help track where Group Policy, applications, and installations modify the registry. The tool is excellent for finding where conflicting settings are occurring in the registry. The tool also maps a registry entry back to the .adm template that could be causing the issue.

- **GPExpert™ Status Monitor 1.1** This tool is a system tray icon that, when clicked, displays the critical aspects of the current status of Group Policy for the desktop. Meant to be installed on all desktops, the tool can help report and track when Group Policy is processing properly and functioning the way it should.

GPExpert™ Scripting Toolkit for PowerShell

GPExpert Scripting Toolkit for PowerShell works in conjunction with Windows PowerShell, Microsoft Visual Basic Scripting Edition (VBScript), and .NET to interface with settings in both Active Directory and local GPOs. It offers support for scripting nearly every GPO extension area, including the following:

- Administrative Templates
- Software Installation
- Security

- Folder Redirection
- IE Maintenance

GPExpert™ Backup Manager for Group Policy

GPExpert Backup Manager for Group Policy provides a more in-depth solution for backing up and managing the archive of your Group Policy infrastructure. Instead of just backing up the GPO and the settings, the tool also backs up links to the GPO, tracking mechanisms for Group Policy versioning, and more. GPExpert Backup Manager for Group Policy is shown in Figure A-8.

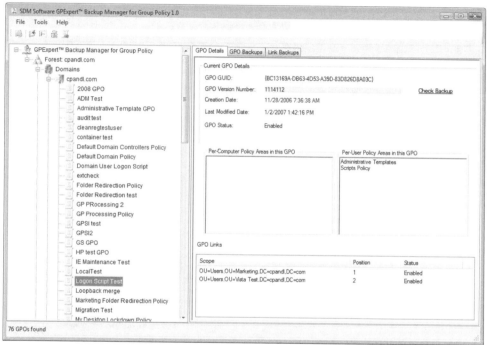

Figure A-8   GPExpert Backup Manager for Group Policy.

GPMC PowerShell Cmdlets

The PowerShell Cmdlets are free cmdlets that take the GPMC scripts and capabilities and put them into easy-to-use Windows PowerShell. It currently includes 12 cmdlets for performing routine GPMC tasks, such as creating GPOs, deleting GPOs, linking GPOs to Active Directory nodes, modifying security, and more. The cmdlets are available at *www.sdmsoftware.com/ freeware.php*.

Special Operations Software

With some of the most exciting and innovative Group Policy tools on the market, you will want to evaluate Special Operations Software. All of the tools produced by Special Operations Software work with Group Policy, and they take tasks that seem very difficult and complex and make them simple and easy.

Specops Deploy

Specops Deploy allows you to deploy nearly any software application by using Group Policy. Nothing like the Microsoft software deployment capabilities, Specops Deploy works with executables, .zip files, and MSI packages. The software also supports installation feedback, BITS control, background processing, scheduling for installations, and support for legacy applications.

Specops Deploy, shown in Figure A-9, includes the following features:

- Support for Windows installer packages or legacy setups such as setup.exe
- Live feedback when a software update, patch, or security fix is installed correctly, and alerts about those that did not install correctly
- Reporting that makes it possible to follow the entire software deployment process
- Support for installations in the background during run time or as usual during boot/login
- Advanced software targeting mechanism using optimal client-side evaluation
- Extended end user interaction features
- Scheduling of installations
- Ability to prioritize installations when software must be deployed quickly
- No need for reboots on target machines when deploying software

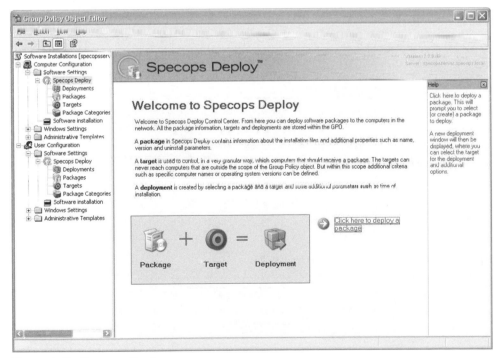

Figure A-9   Specops Deploy.

Specops Inventory

Specops Inventory can report on software and hardware that is installed on a target computer. The tool is designed to use Group Policy as the reporting mechanism. All information is sent back to a centralized database, allowing for easy reporting and management of the data. Because it uses Group Policy as the backbone for the inventory services, the configuration of what will be inventoried is easy to manage and deploy, using standard Group Policy deployment. The interface is easy to use and configure, and the client-side extensions (CSEs) are easy to deploy.

Specops Inventory, shown in Figure A-10, provides the following features and benefits:

- The ability to inventory 13 computer categories and 6 user categories

- The option to inventory categories as the computer (system) or as the user (logged-on user)

- HTML-based reporting, featuring drag and drop, grouping, sorting, filtering, and graphs

- License compliance console for administering software license compliance

- Scalable and suitable reporting for organizations of any size

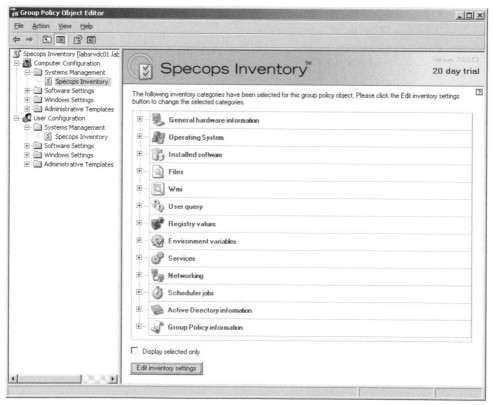

Figure A-10   Specops Inventory.

- Subscription functionality that notifies you when your licenses or maintenance contracts are about to expire

- Use of GPMC as the administration console

Specops Command

Specops Command takes advantage of Windows PowerShell. The tool allows you to deploy, schedule, and execute Windows PowerShell scripts and cmdlets for managing and controlling aspects of Group Policy. Specops Command combines the two technologies and adds new functionality to Windows PowerShell remoting, such as instant feedback, reporting, and scheduling.

Specops Command, shown in Figure A-11, provides the following features and benefits:

- Supports Windows PowerShell and VBScript

- Makes management of scripts more efficient

- Executes scripts at every Group Policy interval

- Uses scheduling to decide when and how often a script executes

- Targets controls where you want the script to execute

- Lets you undo scripts for when the GPO falls out of scope of management

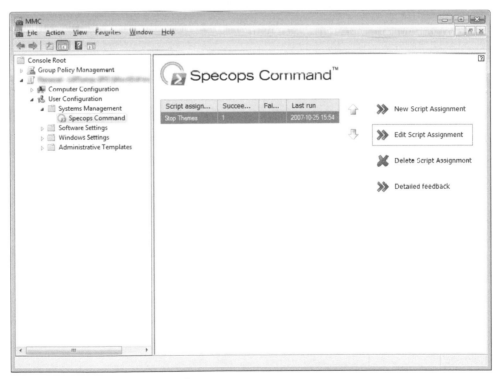

Figure A-11   Specops Command.

- Provides instant reporting and script execution feedback

- Runs scripts with user or computer credentials

Specops Password Policy

Specops Password Policy provides additional control over the password policy for an Active Directory domain. This Group Policy extension negates the limitations of Windows-based password policies by providing control over passwords at the user, computer, group, and organizational unit level. Specops Password Policy also provides granular control over password filtering, controlling nearly every aspect of the password characteristics. You can control password length, password complexity, combination of characters, types of characters, dictionary comparisons, and much more.

Specops Password Policy, shown in Figure A-12, provides the following features and benefits:

- Ability to set any combination of password restrictions

- Option to disallow user names in passwords and disallow words from word lists

- Minimum and maximum password length

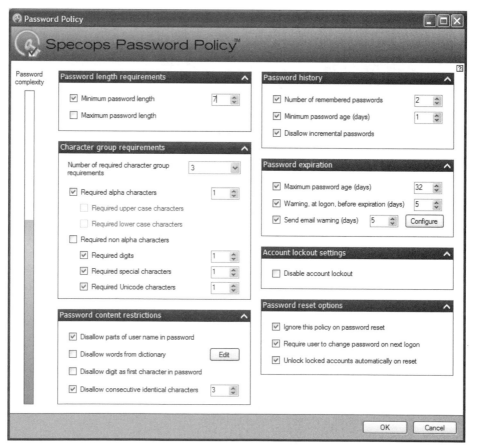

Figure A-12   Specops Password Policy.

- Extended password complexity

- Password reset rules

- Password expiration rules, commonly called *password age*

- Password history

- Option to disallow consecutive characters and incremental passwords

- Ability to disable account lockout

- Option to automatically send password expiration e-mail messages (very useful for Outlook Web Access users)

- Support for automation through Windows PowerShell or .NET

Specops Gpupdate

Specops Gpupdate allows you to refresh Group Policy from within the Active Directory Users and Computers console. Unlike any other solution for Group Policy, this tool allows you to push Group Policy refreshes (whereas the current solution requires you to be local to the desktop to refresh Group Policy). The tool requires a simple click within Active Directory Users and Computers to update a single object or an entire organizational unit full of objects.

Specops Gpupdate, shown in Figure A-13, allows you to:

- Refresh Group Policy

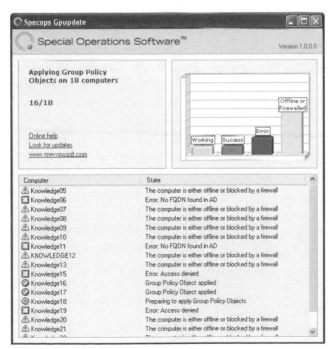

Figure A-13   Specops Gpupdate.

- Start computers using Wake-On-Lan

- Restart computers

- Shut down computers

- Access real-time graphical reporting

 Note   Specops Gpupdate is available for free to all organizations and can be downloaded from *http://www.specopssoft.com*.

Sysprosoft

Sysprosoft writes software for a niche market, namely large corporate networks. Their preferred method is to work with customers to develop their requirements; most of their work is specific to the client, not targeted to the general populace. However, they have three products that are sufficiently generic that they can be run by any Windows domain.

PolMan

PolMan provides a more centralized and in-depth view of Group Policy settings. The tool allows you to see settings for a single GPO, and it can also list all GPOs that include individual settings (if you select the option "Show all GPOs that modify this setting"). The tool provides a backup that allows you to compare changes made to GPOs, links, and much more.

PolMan is shown in Figure A-14. Some of the benefits of PolMan include the following:

- Identification of all GPOs with certain settings

- Identification of potential errors in the Group Policy structure

- Graphical display of links from sites and organizational units (OUs) to GPOs

- Tabular reports on Apply/No Apply security attributes of the GPOs

- Advanced RSoP reporting

- Monitoring of domain controllers with old versions of GPOs

- Monitoring of workstations to identify the policies and versions applied

- Multi-domain support

- Integrated Policy Reporter (UserEnv log display)

- Integrated ADM Template Editor

ADM Template Editor

ADM Template Editor is a GUI interface for creating and updating .adm templates. The tool decrypts much of the syntactical requirements used in .adm templates for an easy-to-use solution.

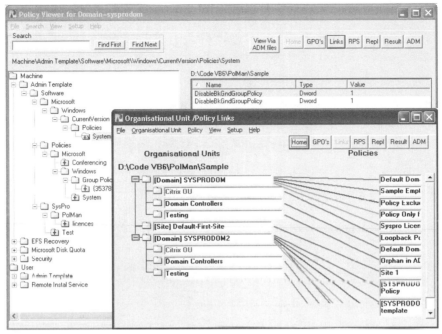

Figure A-14   PolMan.

The latest version provides support for ADMX files, including the creation of multi-language ADML files. ADM Template Editor, shown in Figure A-15, allows you to:

■ Create .adm templates without understanding the .adm template syntax.

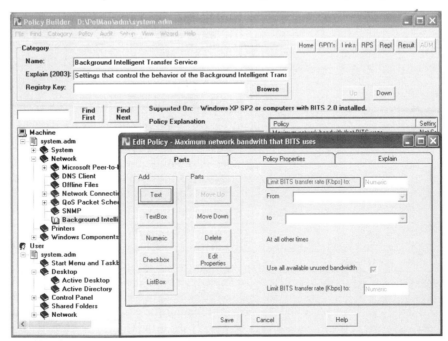

Figure A-15   ADM Template Editor.

- Ensure that .adm templates are syntactically correct.

- Avoid common errors when creating templates.

- Report on registry keys that are managed.

- Convert existing .adm files to ADMX files.

- Create and edit ADMX files.

- Create and edit ADML files for multiple languages.

Policy Reporter

Policy Reporter is a free tool that takes the complexity out of reading and analyzing the UserEnv logs. The tool identifies the main event that is occurring and associates the other aspects of the event in a tree view. The tool also helps you determine the time it took for Group Policy processing to occur, which can help you conclude how well Group Policy is functioning.

Figure A-16 illustrates Policy Reporter, which allows you to:

- Identify problems in Group Policy processing.

- Identify timing issues in Group Policy processing.

- View graphic depiction of the steps involved when processing a given set of policies.

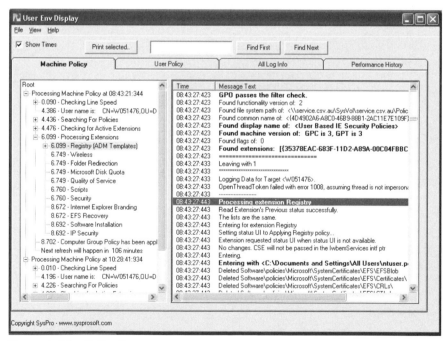

Figure A-16 Policy Reporter.

TeamGPExpert

TeamGPExpert is a resource site started by Group Policy experts Derek Melber and Darren Mar-Elia. The site is dedicated to providing free and inexpensive Group Policy resources, tools, and education. The site is run by both Derek and Darren, as well as the community as a whole.

You can access the site by visiting *http://www.teamgpexpert.com*. You can also send e-mail to Derek at *derekm@braincore.net* and Darren at *darren@sdmsoftware.com*.

Summary

Plenty of third-party Group Policy tools are available to help you with a variety of functions. Some tools provide advanced management of Group Policy, picking up where the built-in tools leave off. Other tools provide extensions to Group Policy. With such an emphasis on Group Policy from Microsoft, third-party vendors have provided some amazing tools to help manage and extend Group Policy. Other free and inexpensive resources such as those provided by TeamGPExpert.com provide excellent insight into Group Policy, as well as resources that can solve nearly any Group Policy problem.

Additional Resources

- The Windows Server Group Policy page, at *http://technet.microsoft.com/en-us/windowsserver/grouppolicy/default.aspx*, includes more information about all of the tools provided by Microsoft for Group Policy.

- The Microsoft article titled "Third-Party Tools and Extensions for Group Policy," at *http://www.microsoft.com/windowsserver2003/technologies/management/grouppolicy/gptools.mspx*, provides descriptions of many third-party Group Policy tools.

- The Group Policy wiki, located at *http://grouppolicy.editme.com/3rdParty*, provides a list of third-party tools.

Appendix B
Additional Resources

As interest in and reliance on Group Policy grows, so does the list of valuable resources.

Group Policy Wiki

The number of wiki sites on the Internet is growing at an impressive rate, so it is not surprising that Group Policy wiki sites are becoming popular. The Group Policy wiki is updated and controlled by the Microsoft Group Policy team, Group Policy Most Valuable Professionals (MVPs), and the community of Group Policy gurus. The site provides references, articles, documentation, and tools that can help you manage and control Group Policy better.

The Group Policy wiki can be found at *http://en.wikipedia.org/wiki/Group_policy*. You should pay close attention to the following:

- Definitions, identified by hyperlinks
- Article and documentation references
- "See also" document and page references
- External link references

Microsoft Group Policy Web Site

The Group Policy team at Microsoft has put significant emphasis on providing online help, direction, guidance, explanations, tools, and much more. You will find a tremendous amount of Group Policy information at *http://www.microsoft.com/grouppolicy*, including articles and tools that cover the following areas:

- Getting Started
- Planning and Architecture
- Deployment
- Security and Protection
- Operations
- Troubleshooting
- Technical Reference
- Development
- Windows Vista
- Microsoft Advanced Group Policy Management (AGPM)
- Downloads
- Community
- Resources

Figure B-1 illustrates the Microsoft Group Policy Web site and the resources that you can access from the main page.

Figure B-1 The Microsoft Group Policy Web site provides up-to-date information and tools for managing and controlling Group Policy.

Windows Server 2003 Web Site

Because Group Policy relies on Windows Server, it makes sense that the Microsoft Windows Server 2003 Web site has detailed information about Group Policy. You can find information about how Windows Server 2003 utilizes Group Policy, as well as links to other resources, at *http://www.microsoft.com/windowsserver2003/technologies/management/grouppolicy/default.mspx*.

Microsoft Group Policy Team Blog

The Group Policy blog is a great place to go for in-depth answers to obscure and detailed Group Policy questions. You can get the most up to-date information from the Group Policy team, as well as MVPs such as myself (Derek Melber), Darren Mar-Elia, and Jeremy Moskowitz. The site is completely dedicated to the most cutting-edge articles, technology, announcements, and white papers on Group Policy and related technologies.

The articles and posts on the site are archived, so you can always go back in time to get archived information. The site offers an RSS feed and a recent posts list, and it is fully tagged to help you find information quickly. You can find the Group Policy Team blog at *http://blogs.technet.com/grouppolicy/default.aspx*. Figure B-2 illustrates what you might see on the site.

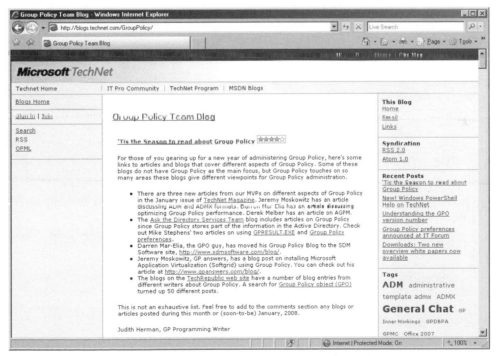

Figure B-2   The Microsoft Group Policy blog contains up-to-date information from the Group Policy team and many of the Group Policy MVPs.

Group Policy Webcast Web Site

If you want to view real-time webcasts, this site is here for you. New webcasts are frequently posted on the latest and greatest technologies that are related to or will help with Group Policy. You can get the current calendar for the webcasts at *http://technet2.microsoft.com/windowsserver/en/technologies/featured/gp/webcasts.mspx*.

Group Policy Script Repository

Microsoft has gone to great lengths to provide this site to the entire Group Policy, Active Directory, and development community. This site is dedicated to Group Policy scripts. Many of the scripts are included in Chapter 8, "Controlling Group Policy via Scripts and Automation."

This free site includes a list of the supported operating systems that can use scripts, as well as the script code itself. You can find the site at *http://www.microsoft.com/technet/scriptcenter/scripts/policy/default.mspx?mfr=true*. Figure B-3 shows a page that provides help and guidance with scripts.

Figure B-3   The Microsoft Web site on scripting for Group Policy provides many sample scripts, as well code that you can use to customize the scripts.

Microsoft TechNet

One of the most significant and up-to-date references regarding Microsoft technology is TechNet. This Web site is dedicated to Microsoft technology and includes white papers, articles, references, documentation, and tools. The information on the site can help you learn about Group Policy, as well as design, implement, manage, deploy, and troubleshoot Group Policy. You can find the TechNet Web site here: *http://technet.microsoft.com/en-us/default.aspx*.

To find Group Policy successfully on TechNet, pay special attention to the search string that you use. Here are some helpful hints for searching for Group Policy articles and references:

- Use the term *Group Policy* or *GPO*.

- Use specific wording from the term or phrase you are looking for. This might be a GPO setting, GPO explain text, or anything else that you need to get information about.

- Use specific wording or phrasing from errors or events that are generated with Group Policy.

- Always use the additional links and references, which might help you expand your search and deepen your knowledge on a topic.

- Use the enhanced search capabilities on the TechNet Web site when you need to conduct a very specific search. Figure B-4 illustrates some search tips

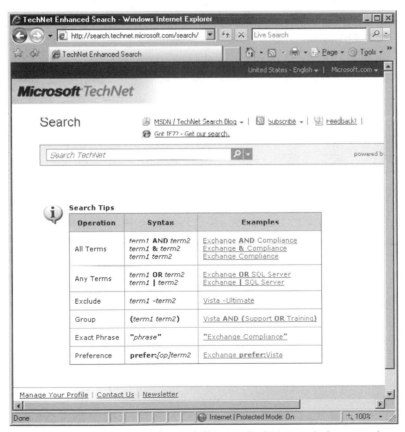

Figure B-4   Enhanced search capabilities on TechNet can help you reduce the number of sites that are returned to you.

TeamGPExpert.com

The GPExpert Web site is a resource site started by Group Policy experts Derek Melber and Darren Mar-Elia. The site is dedicated to providing free and inexpensive Group Policy resources, tools, and education. The site is run by both Derek and Darren, as well as the community as a whole.

You can access the site by visiting *www.teamgpexpert.com*. You can also send e-mail to Derek at *derekm@braincore.net* and Darren at *darren@sdmsoftware.com*.

BrainCore.net

This is a site run by Derek Melber. Derek has been an MVP for both Directory Services and Group Policy. Derek contributes to many conferences, publications, books, Web sites, and many more resources and references. He provides custom training and consulting for Active Directory, security, desktop management, and, of course, Group Policy.

On this site, you can find out where Derek will be in the near future and read about what he is writing for WindowsSecurity.com, *Redmond* magazine, and *TechNet Magazine*. Highlights of Derek's site include:

- Custom training and education on Microsoft technologies
- Consulting for all aspects of Microsoft technologies
- Public speaking engagements, even for your company or organization
- Windows security auditing education and consulting, including complete Windows audits

GPOGuy.com

This is a site run by Darren Mar-Elia. Darren has been providing the Group Policy community with free tools and advice for years. Darren is one of the few Group Policy MVPs in the world. This site is dedicated to providing free tools and information. Some highlights of the site include:

- FAQs on Group Policy
- White papers on Group Policy
- Free tools and scripts
- Group Policy blog

GPAnswers.com

This is a site run by Jeremy Moskowitz. Jeremy is a Group Policy MVP who provides education and tools for Group Policy. On his site, you will find one of the best Group Policy blogs and newsgroups online. Some of the highlights of GPAnswers.com include:

- White papers and guides
- Community room
- Newsletter
- FAQs on Group Policy
- Tips and tricks
- Links to other Group Policy resources

Summary

Plenty of Web sites, articles, white papers, documentation, videos, trainers, and consultants are available on the Web for Group Policy. Many of the sites and resources are run by people you know, such as myself. There is never a lack of information for Group Policy if you know where to find it. With blogs, videos, custom training, documentation on every aspect of Group Policy, and much more available at your fingertips, you will always have something new to learn and a place to go to get answers.

Index

About the Author

Derek Melber, MCSE, CISM, is one of just a few Microsoft Group Policy MVPs in the world. Derek is president of BrainCore.Net (*http://www.braincore.net*), a leading Windows technology education company. Derek specializes in Windows Active Directory directory services, Group Policy, security, auditing, and desktop management. Derek has written more than 15 books and continues to provide custom training and presentations to IT professionals. Some of Derek's accomplishments include the *Microsoft Windows Group Policy Guide* (*http://www.microsoft.com/mspress/books/8763.aspx*), a four-  book series on auditing Windows security (*http://www.theiia.org*), the position of chair at TechMentor conferences (*http://techmentorevents.com*), and the role of contributing editor for WindowsSecurity.com (*http://www.windowssecurity.com*). You can reach Derek at *derekm@braincore.net*.

System Requirements

To use this book's companion CD-ROM, you need a computer equipped with the following minimum configuration:

- Microsoft Windows Server 2008, Windows Vista, Windows Server 2003, or Windows XP
- 1 GHz 32-bit (x86) or 64-bit (x64) processor (depending on the minimum requirements of the operating system)
- 1 GB of system memory (depending on the minimum requirements of the operating system)
- A hard disk partition with at least 1 GB of available space
- Appropriate video output device
- Keyboard
- Mouse or other pointing device
- Optical drive capable of reading CD-ROMs

In addition, many of the tools have separate system requirements and may require one or more of the following:

- Microsoft Windows Server 2008 or Windows Vista
- Windows PowerShell 1.x
- A network connection

Please refer to the documentation for each tool to determine its system requirements.

Windows Server 2008—
Resources for Administrators

Windows Server® 2008 Administrator's Companion

Charlie Russel and Sharon Crawford
ISBN 9780735625051

Your comprehensive, one-volume guide to deployment, administration, and support. Delve into core system capabilities and administration topics, including Active Directory®, security issues, disaster planning/recovery, interoperability, IIS 7.0, virtualization, clustering, and performance tuning.

Windows Server 2008 Administrator's Pocket Consultant

William R. Stanek
ISBN 9780735624375

Portable and precise—with the focused information you need for administering server roles, Active Directory, user/group accounts, rights and permissions, file-system management, TCP/IP, DHCP, DNS, printers, network performance, backup, and restoration.

Windows Server 2008 Resource Kit

Microsoft MVPs with Windows Server Team
ISBN 9780735623613

Six volumes! Your definitive resource for deployment and operations—from the experts who know the technology best. Get in-depth technical information on Active Directory, Windows PowerShell™ scripting, advanced administration, networking and network access protection, security administration, IIS, and more—plus an essential toolkit of resources on CD.

Internet Information Services (IIS) 7.0 Administrator's Pocket Consultant

William R. Stanek
ISBN 9780735623644

This pocket-sized guide delivers immediate answers for administering IIS 7.0. Topics include customizing installation; configuration and XML schema; application management; user access and security; Web sites, directories, and content; and performance, backup, and recovery.

Windows PowerShell Step by Step

Ed Wilson
ISBN 9780735623958

Teach yourself the fundamentals of the Windows PowerShell command-line interface and scripting language—one step at a time. Learn to use *cmdlets* and write scripts to manage users, groups, and computers; configure network components; administer Microsoft® Exchange Server 2007; and more. Includes 100+ sample scripts.

Additional Resources for IT Professionals

Windows Server 2008 Virtualization Resource Kit
Robert Larson and Janique Carbone
ISBN 9780735625174

Internet Information Services (IIS) 7.0 Resource Kit
Mike Volodarsky et al. with Microsoft IIS Team
ISBN 9780735624412

Windows® Administration Resource Kit: Productivity Solutions for IT Professionals
Dan Holme
ISBN 9780735624313

Windows Server 2008 Security Resource Kit
Jesper M. Johansson, MVPs, Microsoft Security Team
ISBN 9780735625044

See our complete line of books at: **microsoft.com/mspress**

Microsoft Press® products are sold worldwide wherever quality computer books are sold. For more information, contact your bookseller, computer retailer, software reseller, or local Microsoft Sales Office, or visit our Web site at microsoft.com/mspress. To locate a source near you, or to order directly, call 1-800-MSPRESS in the United States. (In Canada call 1-800-268-2222).

Windows Server 2008 Resource Kit— Your Definitive Resource!

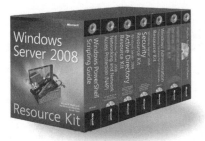

Windows Server® 2008 Resource Kit

Microsoft® MVPs with Microsoft Windows Server Team

ISBN 9780735623613

Your definitive reference for deployment and operations—from the experts who know the technology best. Get in-depth technical information on Active Directory®, Windows PowerShell™ scripting, advanced administration, networking and network access protection, security administration, IIS, and other critical topics—plus an essential toolkit of resources on CD.

Also available as single volumes

Windows Server 2008 Security Resource Kit

Jesper M. Johansson et al. with Microsoft Security Team

ISBN 9780735625044

Windows Server 2008 Networking and Network Access Protection (NAP)

Joseph Davies, Tony Northrup, Microsoft Networking Team

ISBN 9780735624221

Windows Server 2008 Active Directory Resource Kit

Stan Reimer et al. with Microsoft Active Directory Team

ISBN 9780735625150

Windows® Administration Resource Kit: Productivity Solutions for IT Professionals

Dan Holme

ISBN 9780735624313

Windows Powershell Scripting Guide

Ed Wilson

ISBN 9780735622791

Internet Information Services (IIS) 7.0 Resource Kit

Mike Volodarsky et al. with Microsoft IIS Team

ISBN 9780735624412

See our complete line of books at: **microsoft.com/mspress**

What do you think of this book?

We want to hear from you!

Do you have a few minutes to participate in a brief online survey?

Microsoft is interested in hearing your feedback so we can continually improve our books and learning resources for you.

To participate in our survey, please visit:

www.microsoft.com/learning/booksurvey/

...and enter this book's ISBN-10 or ISBN-13 number (located above barcode on back cover*). As a thank-you to survey participants in the United States and Canada, each month we'll randomly select five respondents to win one of five $100 gift certificates from a leading online merchant. At the conclusion of the survey, you can enter the drawing by providing your e-mail address, which will be used for prize notification only.

Thanks in advance for your input. Your opinion counts!

* Where to find the ISBN on back cover

ISBN-13: 000-0-0000-0000-0
ISBN-10: 0-0000-0000-0

Example only. Each book has unique ISBN.

Microsoft ®
Press